Volume 1

It is time for love.
Secret cell phone novelist vs. the most
popular boy in school.
A mission of love for absolute servitude.

Ema Toyama

**Translated and adapted by
Alethea Nibley and Athena Nibley**

Lettered by Paige Pumphrey

Missions of Love
Volume 1
Ema Toyama

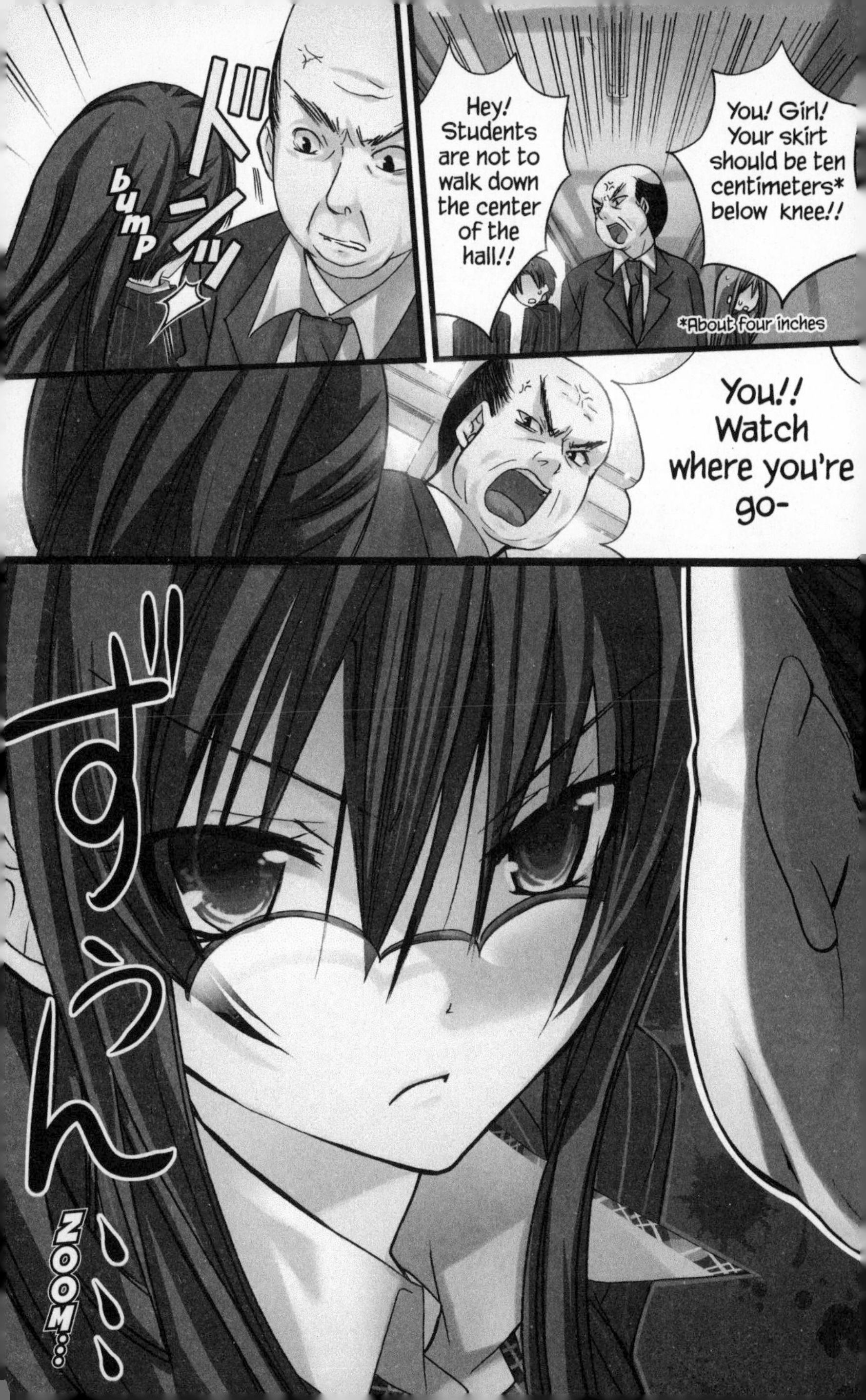
You! Girl! Your skirt should be ten centimeters* below knee!!
Hey! Students are not to walk down the center of the hall!!
*About four inches
bump
You!! Watch where you're go-
ずうん
ZOOM...

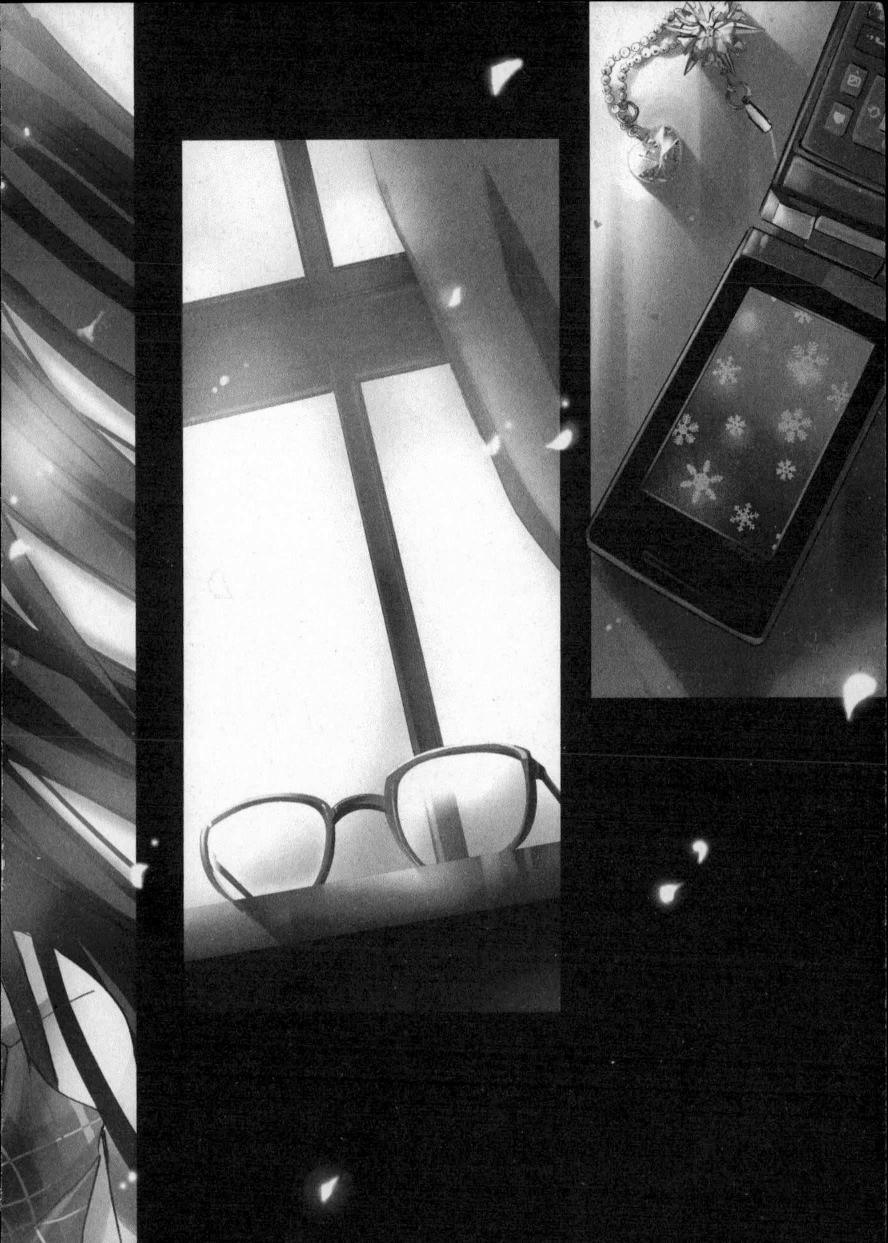

Mission 1

I Order You to Fall in Love with Me!

Missions of Love

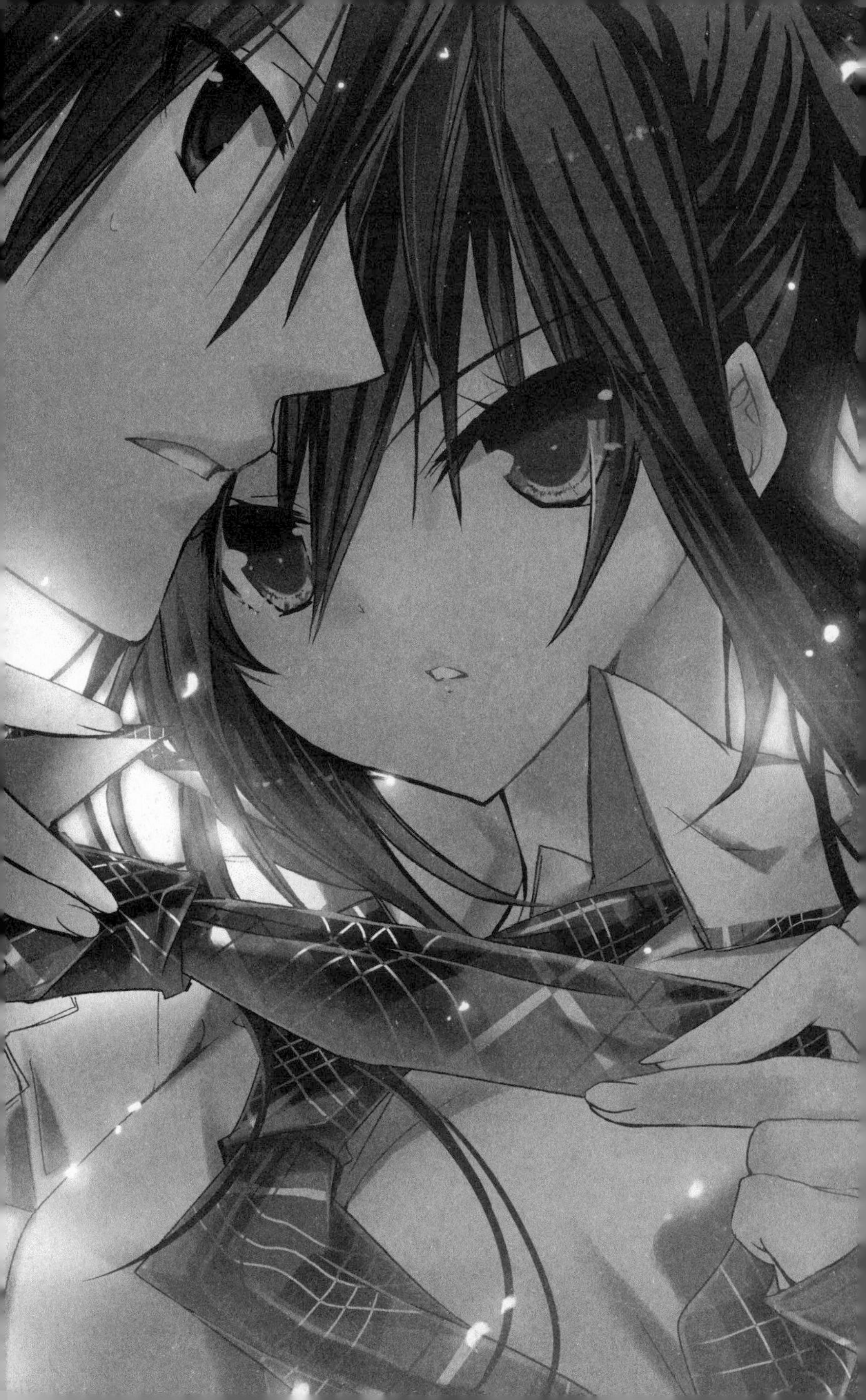

Missions of Love

It is time for love.
Secret cell phone
novelist vs. the most
popular boy in school.
A mission of love for
absolute servitude.

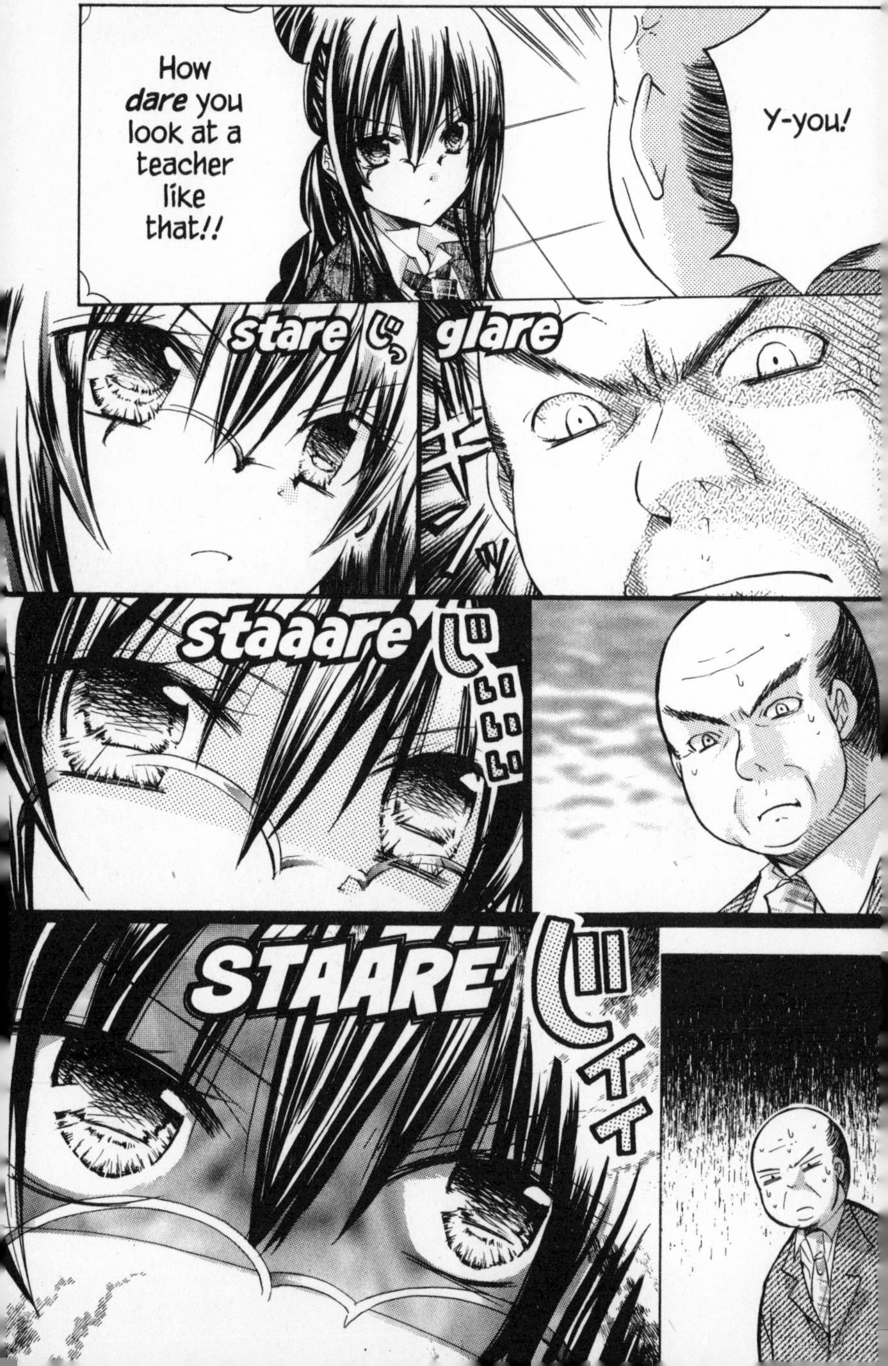
Y-you!
How *dare* you look at a teacher like that!!
glare
stare
staaare
STAARE

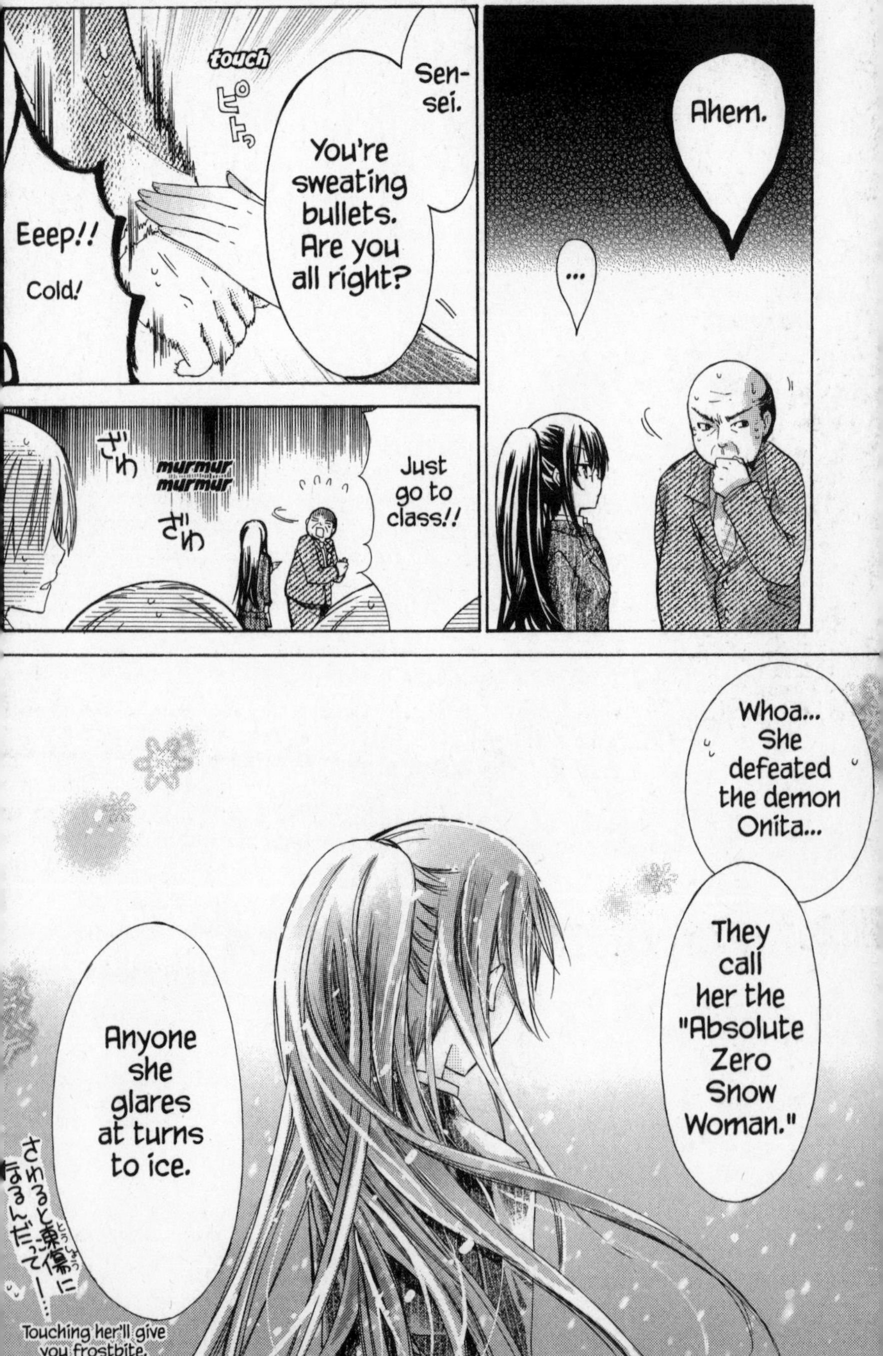
Ahem.
...
Sen-sei.
You're sweating bullets. Are you all right?
touch
ピトッ
Eeep!!
Cold!
Just go to class!!
ざわ
murmur murmur
ざわ
Whoa... She defeated the demon Onita...
They call her the "Absolute Zero Snow Woman."
Anyone she glares at turns to ice.
さわると凍傷になるんだって—…
Touching her'll give you frostbite.

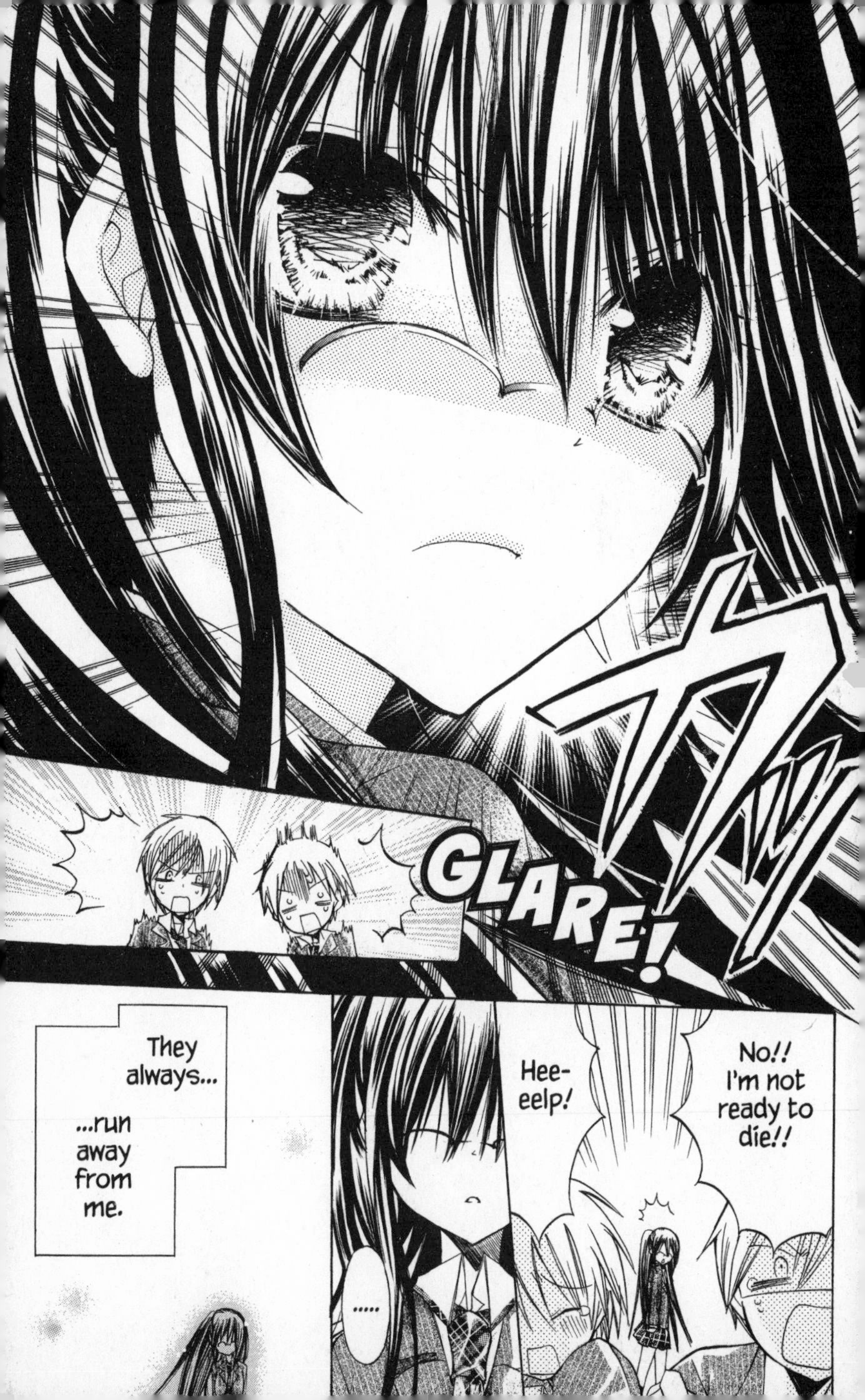
GLARE!
No!! I'm not ready to die!!
Hee-eelp!
.....
They always...
...run away from me.

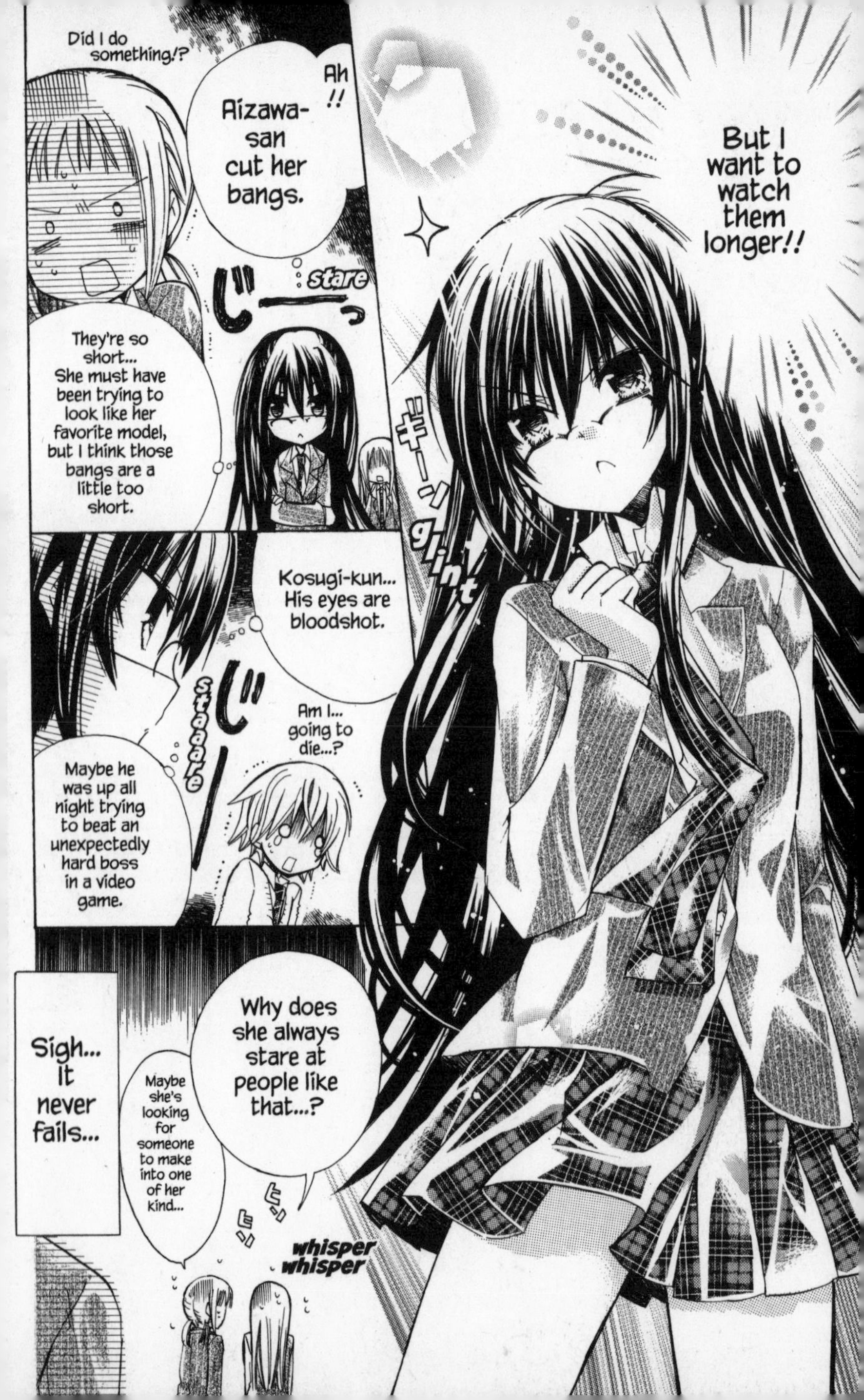
But I want to watch them longer!!
glint
Ah!! Aizawa-san cut her bangs.
Did I do something!?
stare
They're so short... She must have been trying to look like her favorite model, but I think those bangs are a little too short.
Kosugi-kun... His eyes are bloodshot.
staaare
Am I... going to die...?
Maybe he was up all night trying to beat an unexpectedly hard boss in a video game.
Why does she always stare at people like that...?
Maybe she's looking for someone to make into one of her kind...
whisper whisper
Sigh... It never fails...

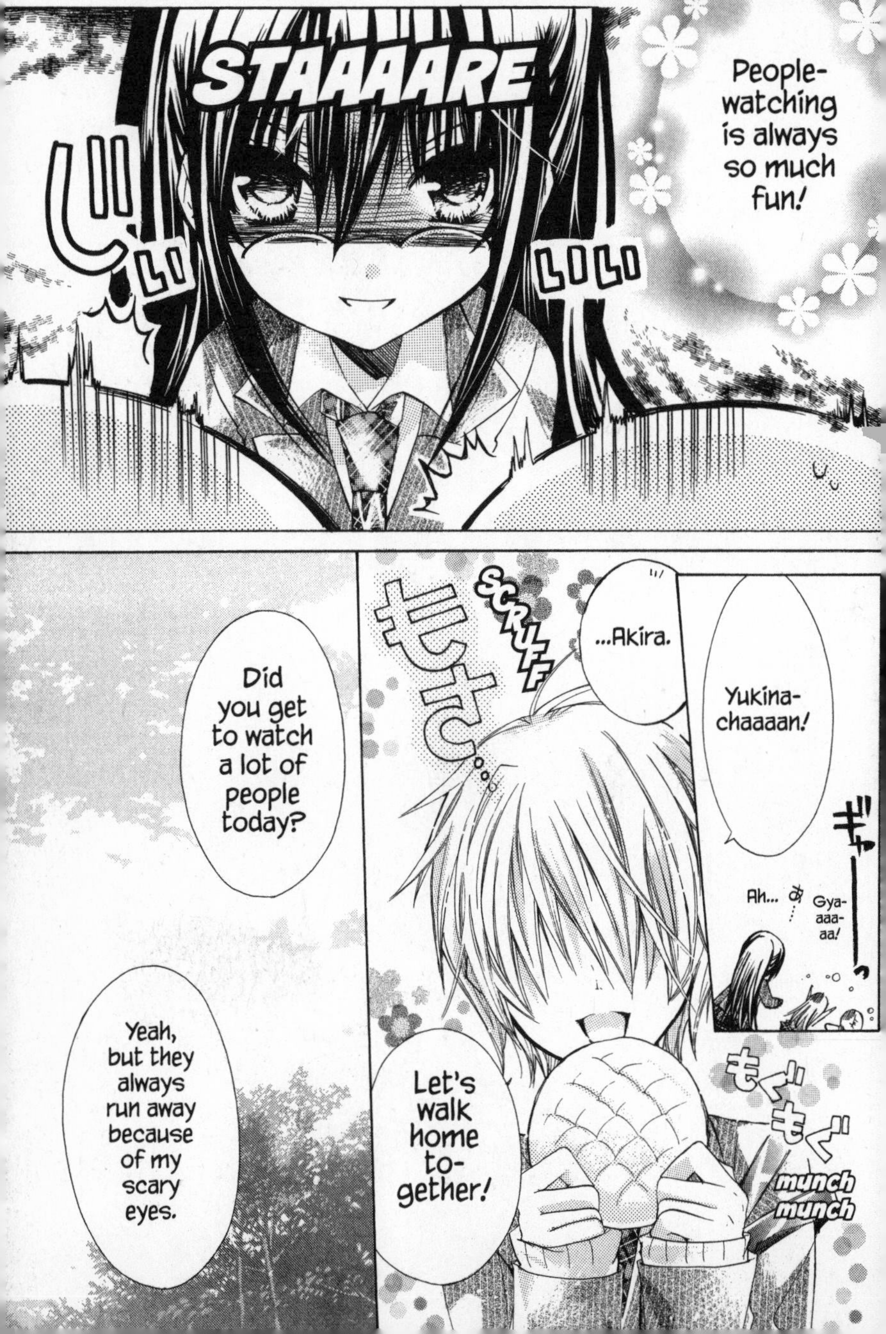

People-watching is always so much fun!
STAAAARE
LILI
LILI
Yukina-chaaaan!
Gya-aaa-aa!
Ah...
...Akira.
SCRUFF
Let's walk home to-gether!
munch munch
Did you get to watch a lot of people today?
Yeah, but they always run away because of my scary eyes.

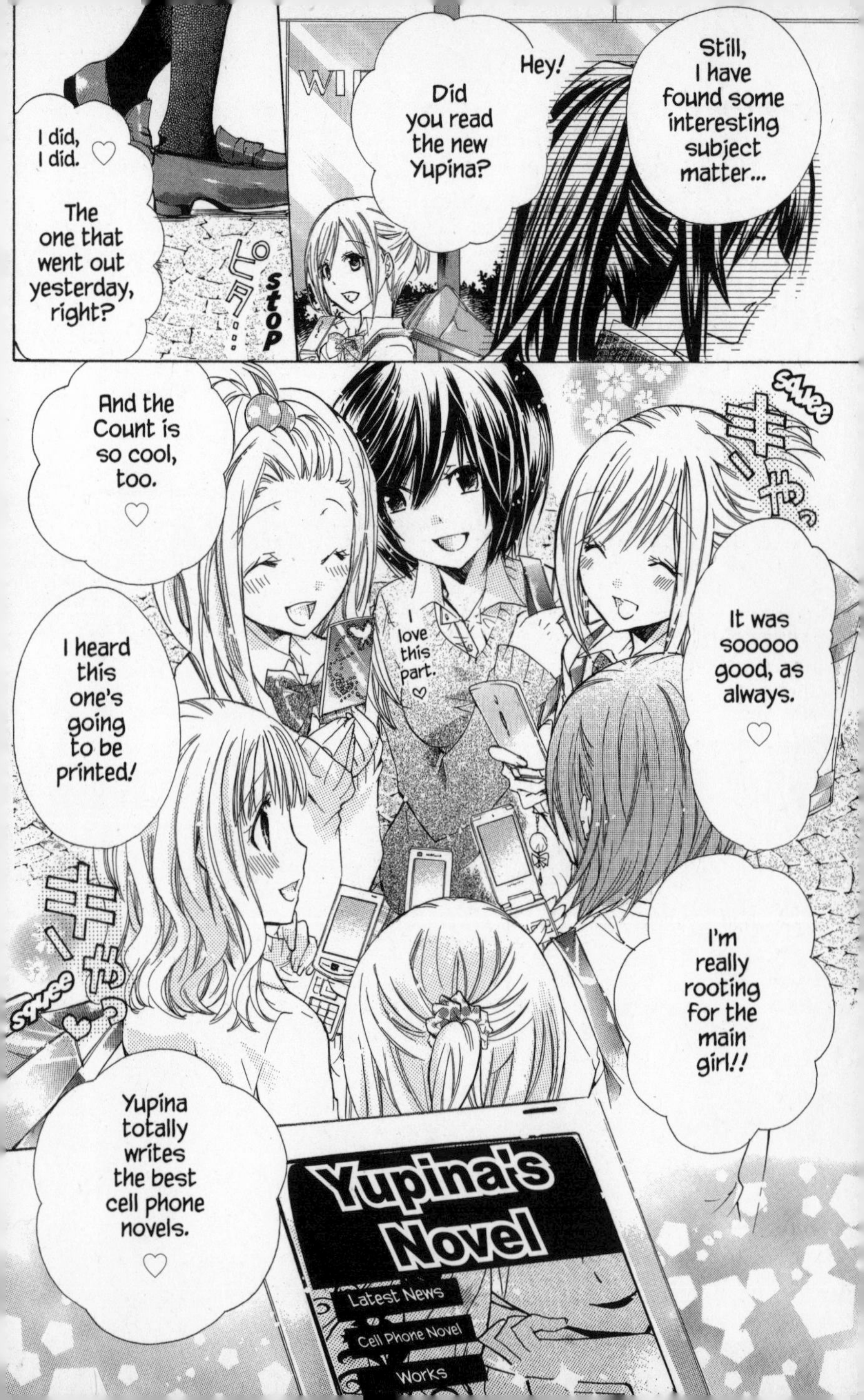
Still, I have found some interesting subject matter...
Hey!
Did you read the new Yupina?
I did, I did. ♡
The one that went out yesterday, right?
ピタ...
STOP
SQUEE
キャっ
It was sooooo good, as always. ♡
And the Count is so cool, too. ♡
I love this part. ♡
I heard this one's going to be printed!
I'm really rooting for the main girl!!
キャっ
SQUEE
Yupina totally writes the best cell phone novels. ♡
Yupina's Novel
Latest News
Cell Phone Novel
Works

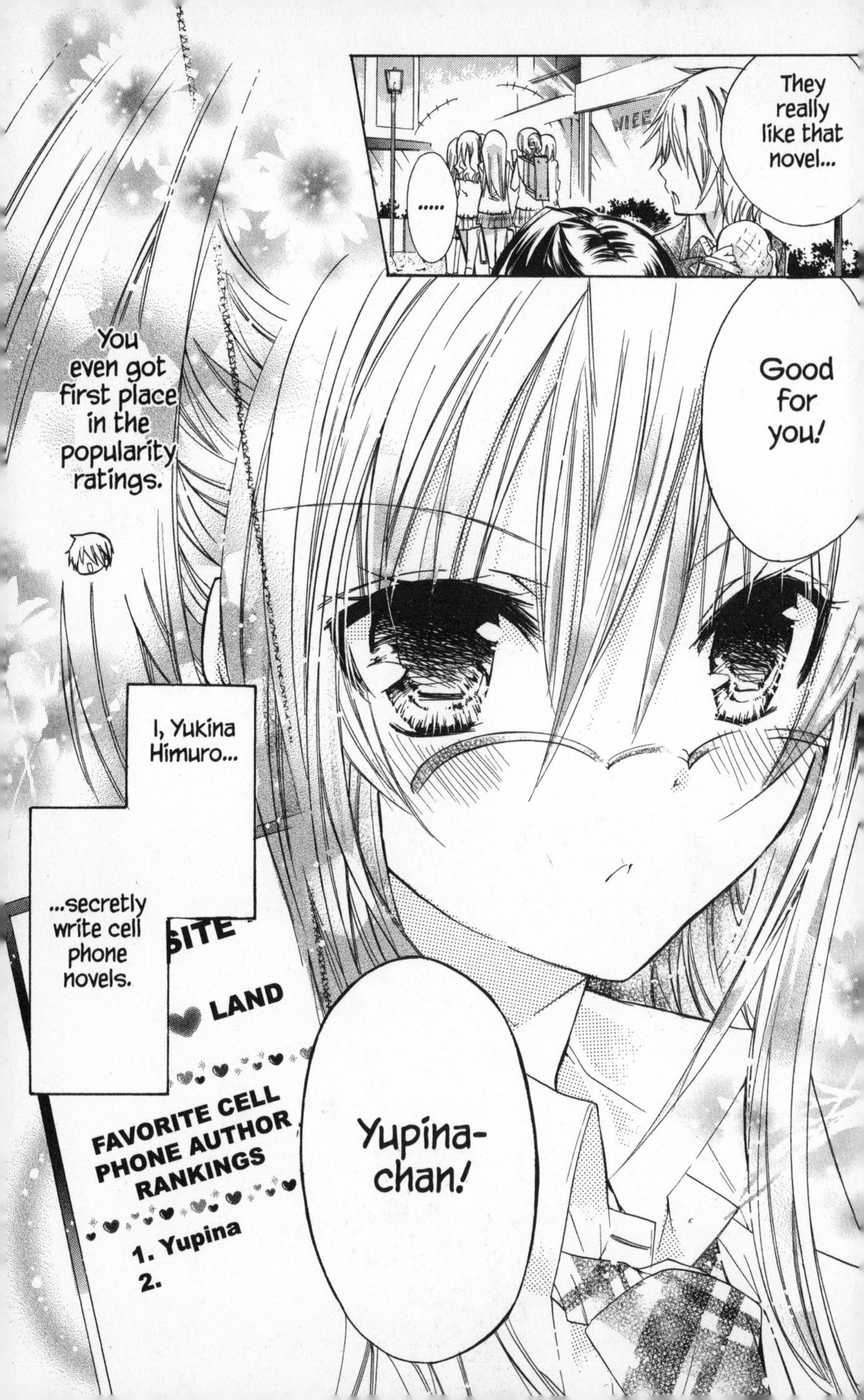
They really like that novel...
......
Good for you!
You even got first place in the popularity ratings.
Yupina-chan!
I, Yukina Himuro...
...secretly write cell phone novels.
SITE
LAND
FAVORITE CELL PHONE AUTHOR RANKINGS
1. Yupina
2.

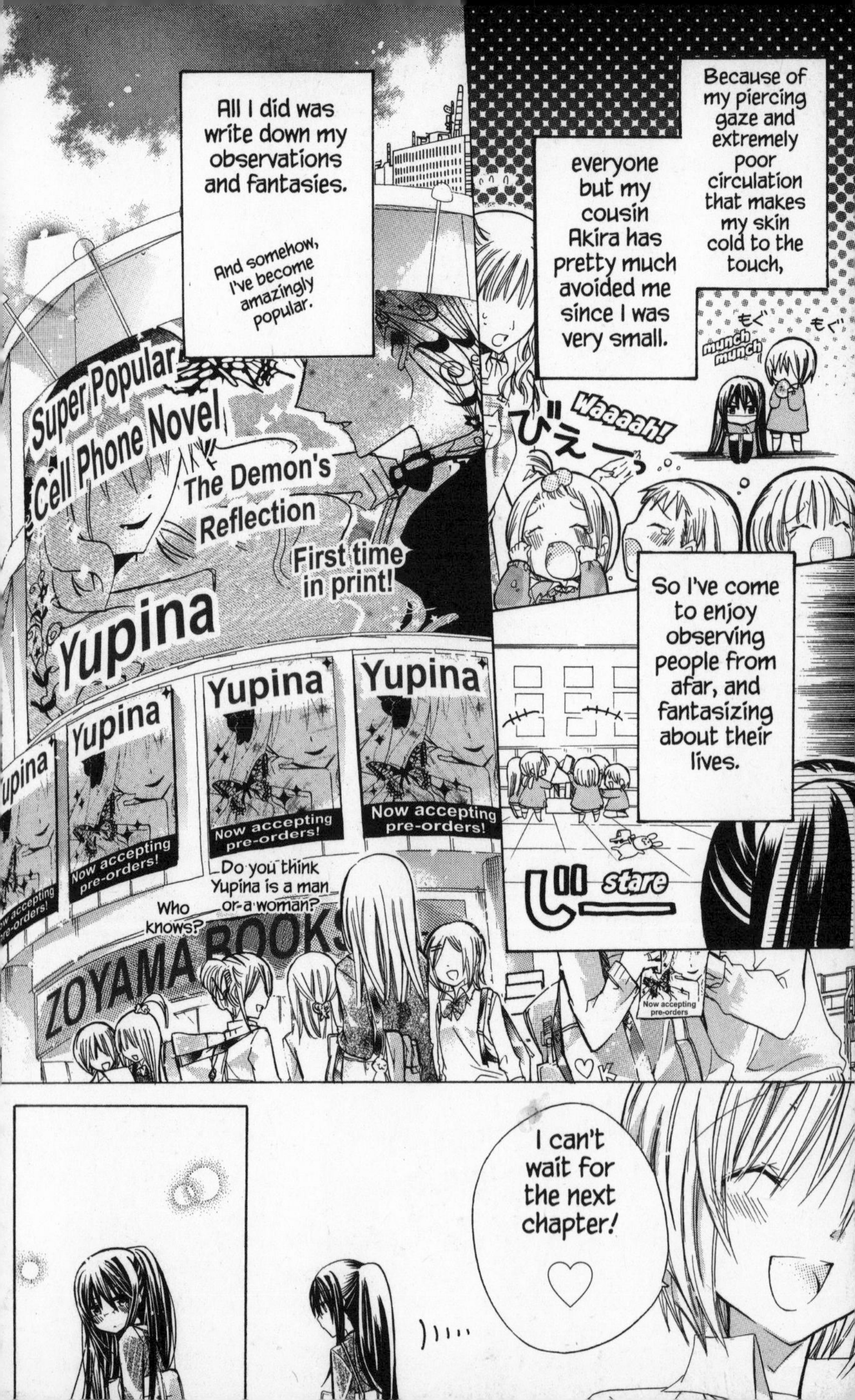
Because of my piercing gaze and extremely poor circulation that makes my skin cold to the touch,
everyone but my cousin Akira has pretty much avoided me since I was very small.
もぐ もぐ
munch munch
びえー
Waaaah!
So I've come to enjoy observing people from afar, and fantasizing about their lives.
stare
All I did was write down my observations and fantasies.
And somehow, I've become amazingly popular.
Super Popular Cell Phone Novel
The Demon's Reflection
First time in print!
Yupina
Yupina
Now accepting pre-orders!
Yupina
Now accepting pre-orders!
Yupina
Now accepting pre-orders!
Yupina
Now accepting pre-orders!
Do you think Yupina is a man or a woman?
Who knows?
ZOYAMA BOOKS
Now accepting pre-orders
I can't wait for the next chapter! ♡
!....

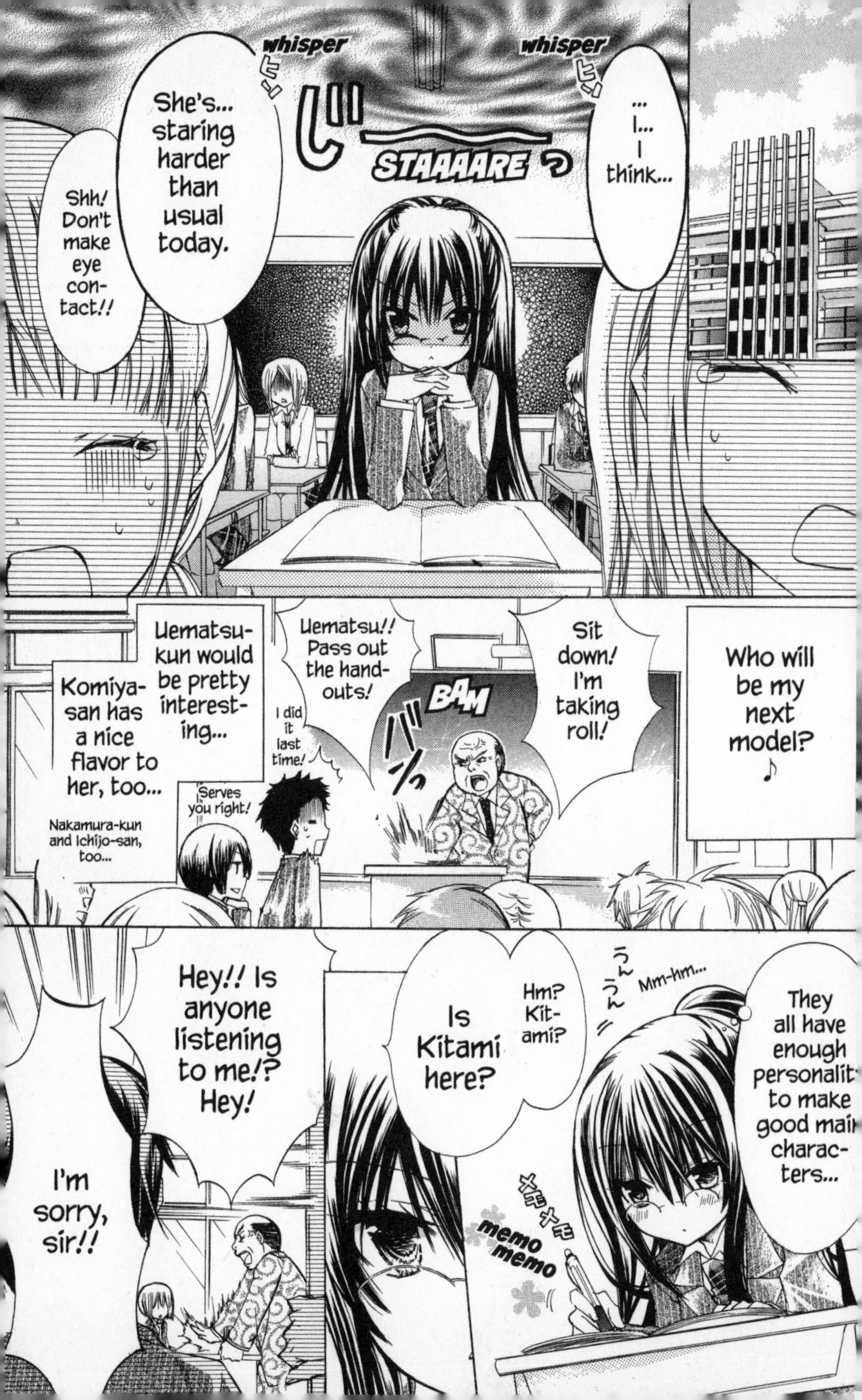

whisper
... I... I think...
じー STAAAARE
whisper
She's... staring harder than usual today.
Shh! Don't make eye contact!!
Who will be my next model? ♪
Sit down! I'm taking roll!
BAM
Uematsu!! Pass out the handouts!
I did it last time!
Serves you right!
Uematsu-kun would be pretty interesting...
Komiya-san has a nice flavor to her, too...
Nakamura-kun and Ichijo-san, too...
They all have enough personalit to make good mai characters...
Mm-hm...
memo memo
Hm? Kitami?
Is Kitami here?
Hey!! Is anyone listening to me!? Hey!
I'm sorry, sir!!

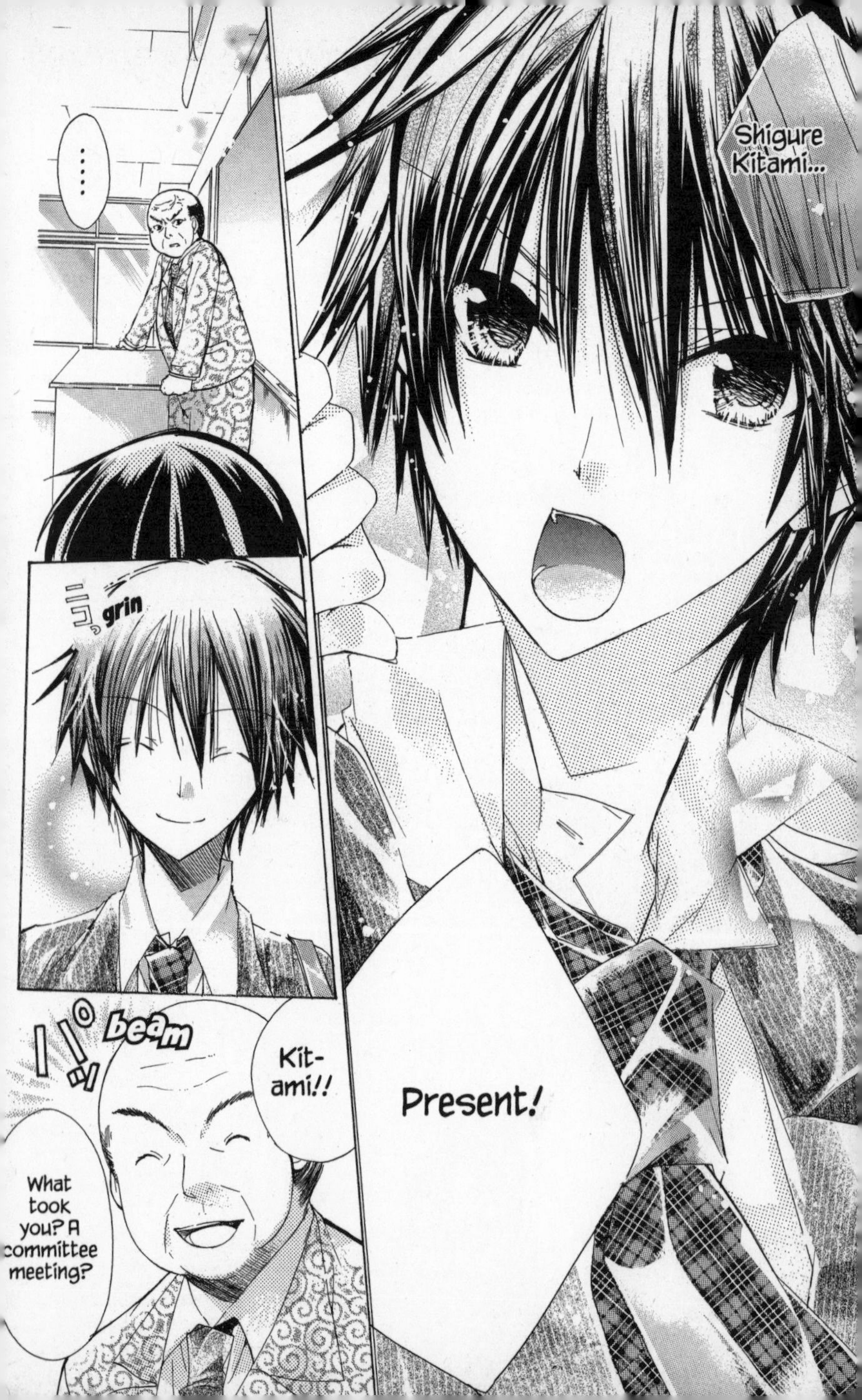

Shigure Kitami...
Present!
......
grin
beam
Kit-ami!!
What took you? A committee meeting?

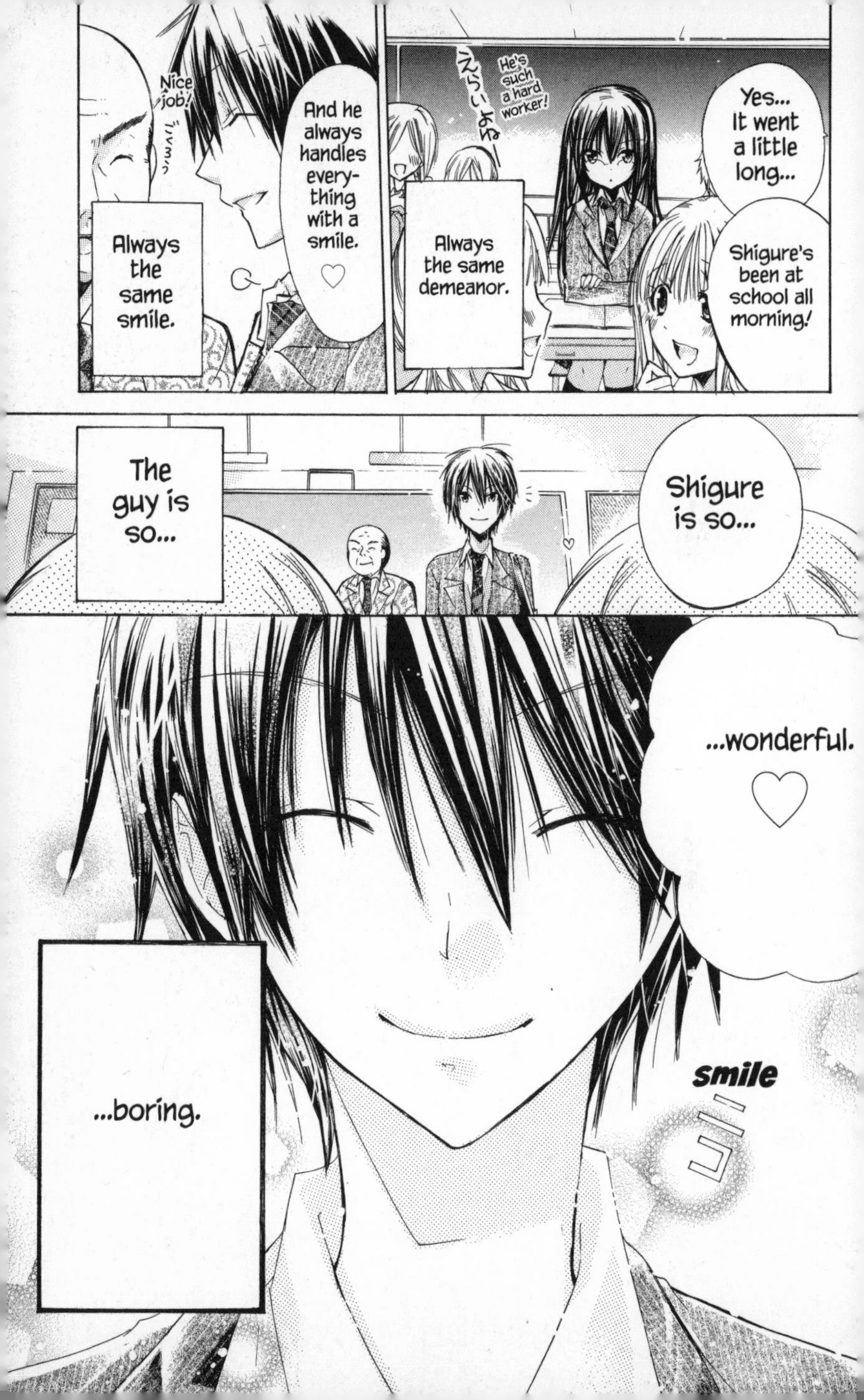

Yes... It went a little long...
Shigure's been at school all morning!
He's such a hard worker!
えらいよねー
Always the same demeanor.
And he always handles every-thing with a smile.
Nice job!
Always the same smile.
Shigure is so...
The guy is so...
...wonderful.
smile
...boring.

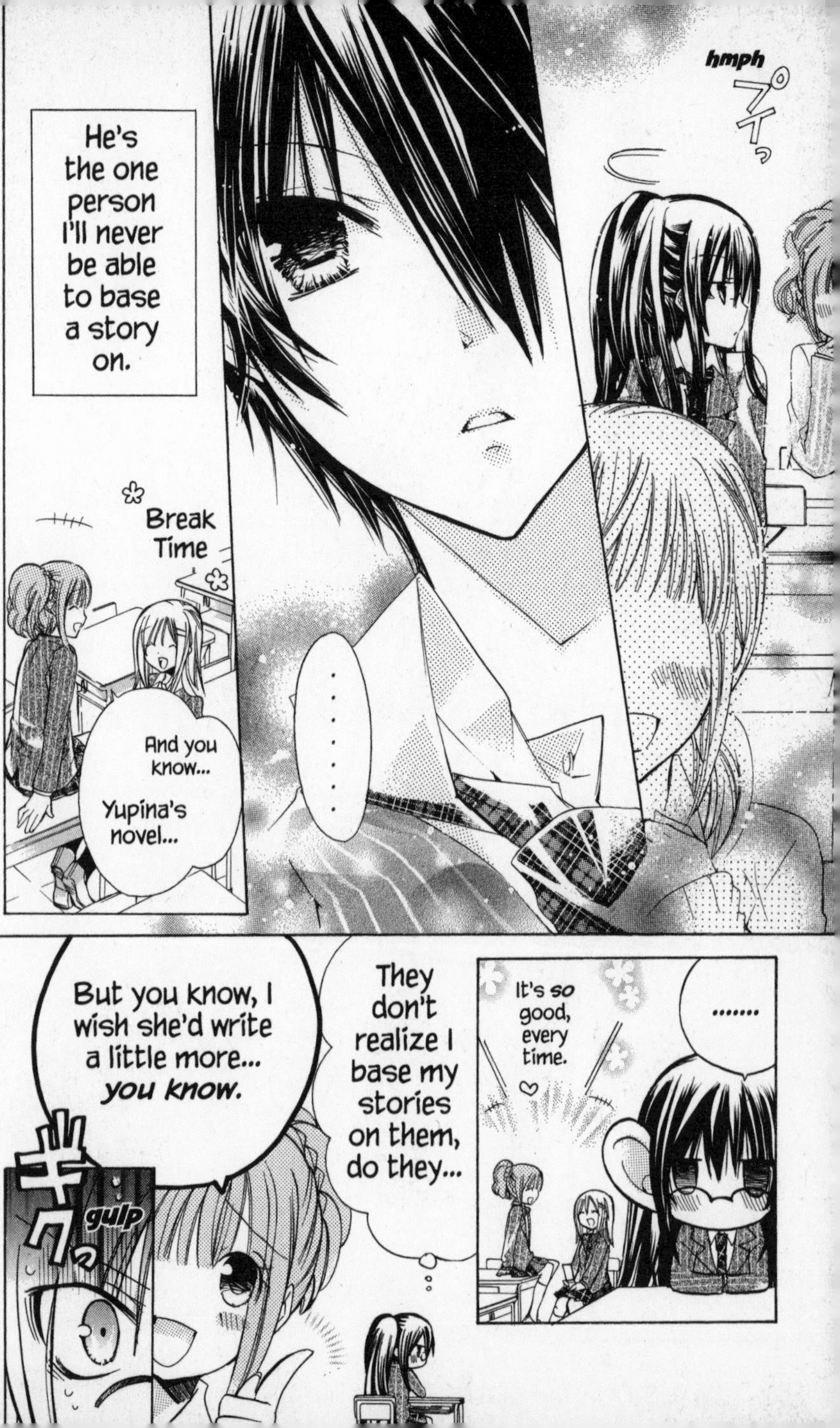

hmph
プイっ
....
He's the one person I'll never be able to base a story on.
Break Time
And you know...
Yupina's novel...
....
It's so good, every time.
They don't realize I base my stories on them, do they...
But you know, I wish she'd write a little more... *you know.*
ギクっ
gulp

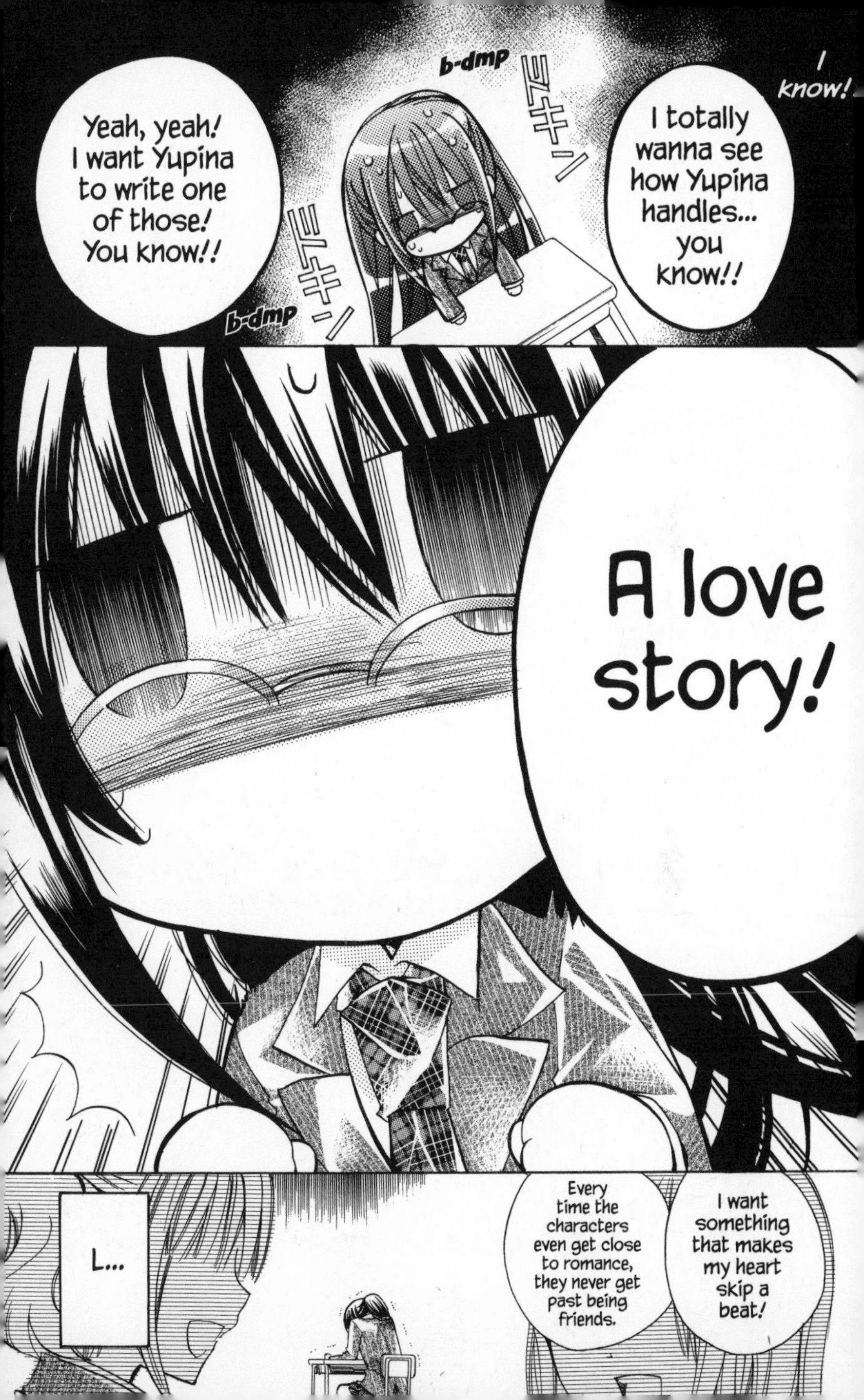
I know!
I totally wanna see how Yupina handles... you know!!
b-dmp
Yeah, yeah! I want Yupina to write one of those! You know!!
b-dmp
A love story!
I want something that makes my heart skip a beat!
Every time the characters even get close to romance, they never get past being friends.
L...

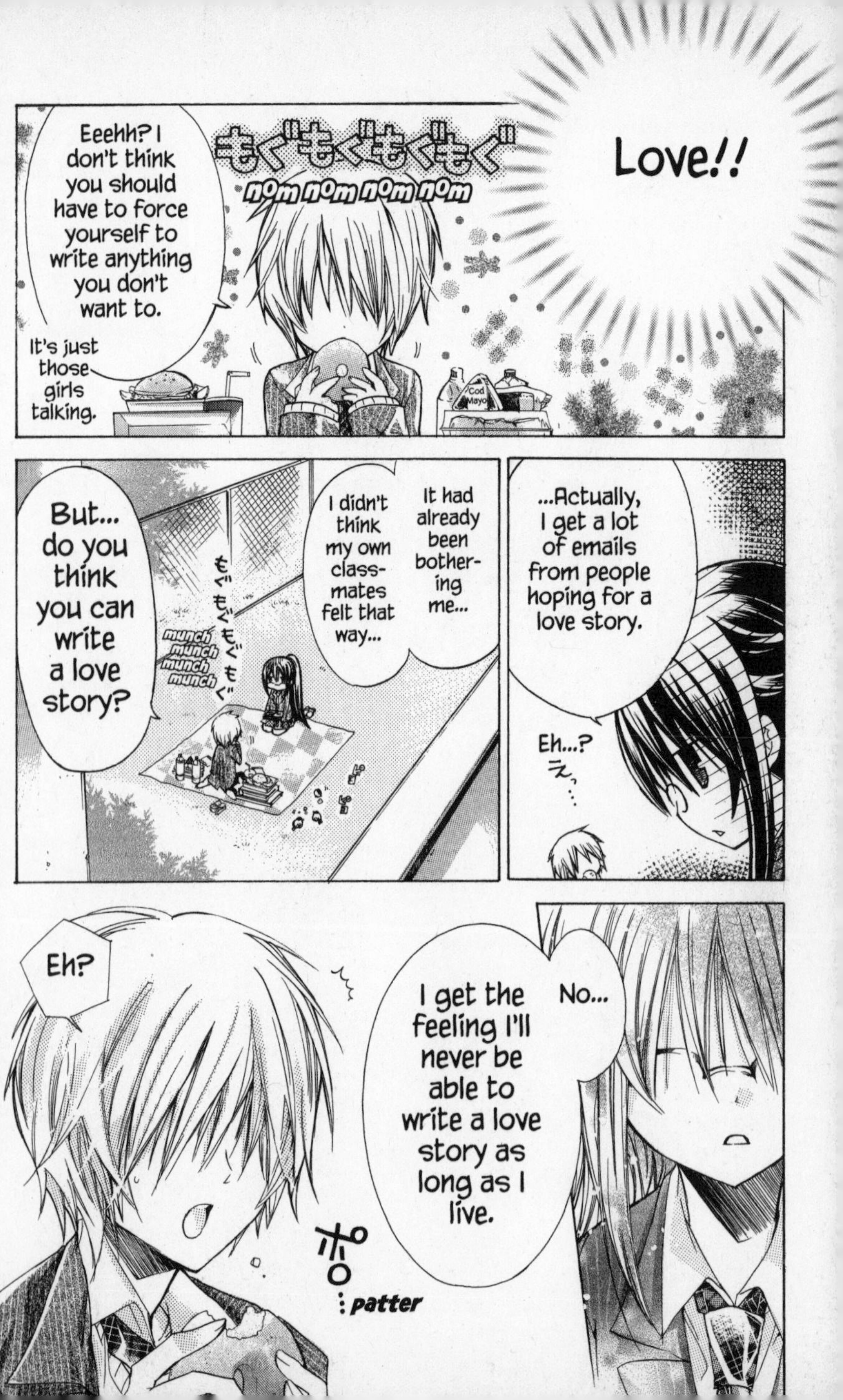
Love!!
もぐもぐもぐもぐ
nom nom nom nom
Eeehh? I don't think you should have to force yourself to write anything you don't want to.
It's just those girls talking.
...Actually, I get a lot of emails from people hoping for a love story.
Eh...?
It had already been bothering me...
I didn't think my own class-mates felt that way...
もぐもぐもぐもぐ
munch munch munch munch
But... do you think you can write a love story?
No...
I get the feeling I'll never be able to write a love story as long as I live.
patter
Eh?

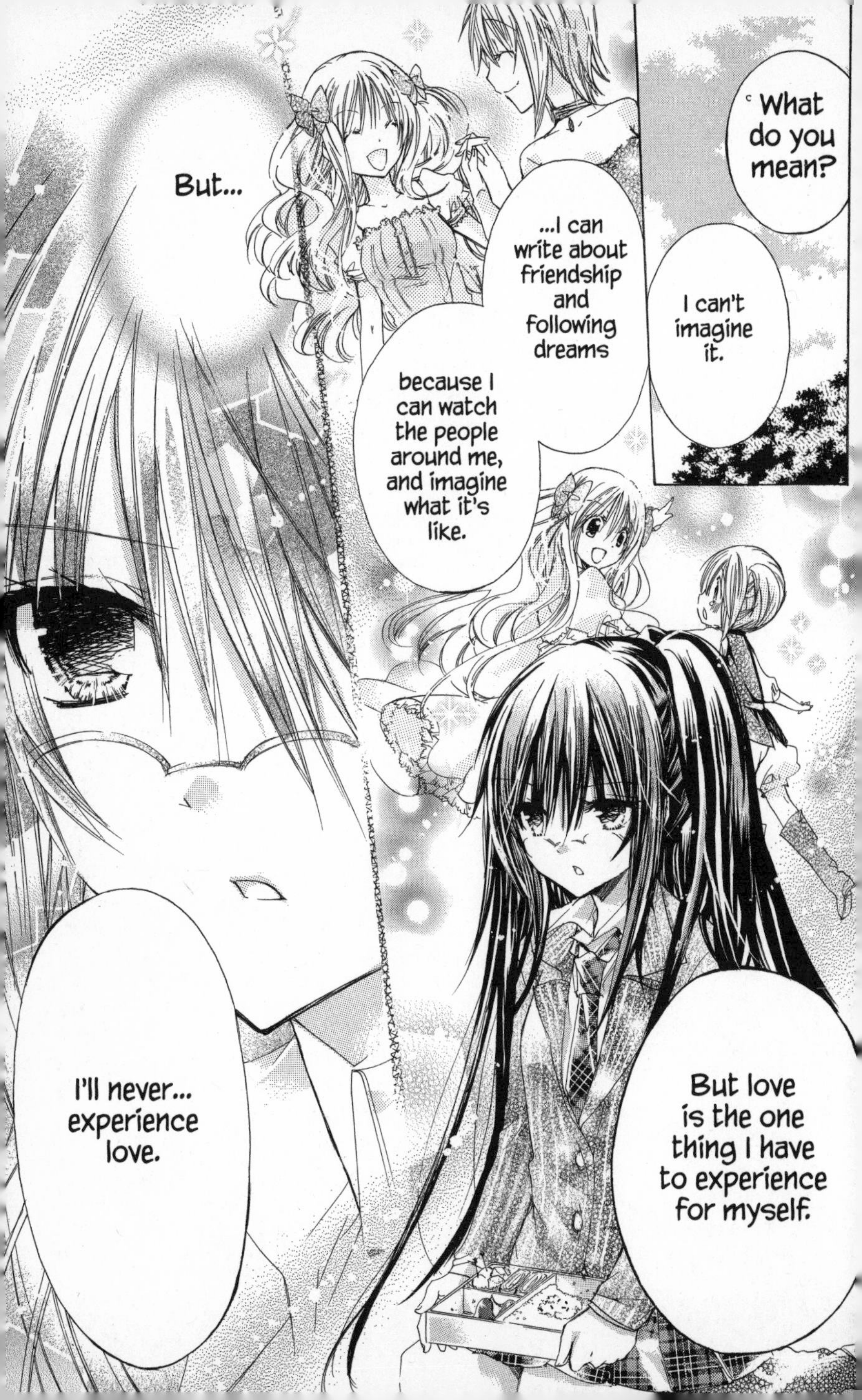
What do you mean?
I can't imagine it.
...I can write about friendship and following dreams
because I can watch the people around me, and imagine what it's like.
But love is the one thing I have to experience for myself.
But...
I'll never... experience love.

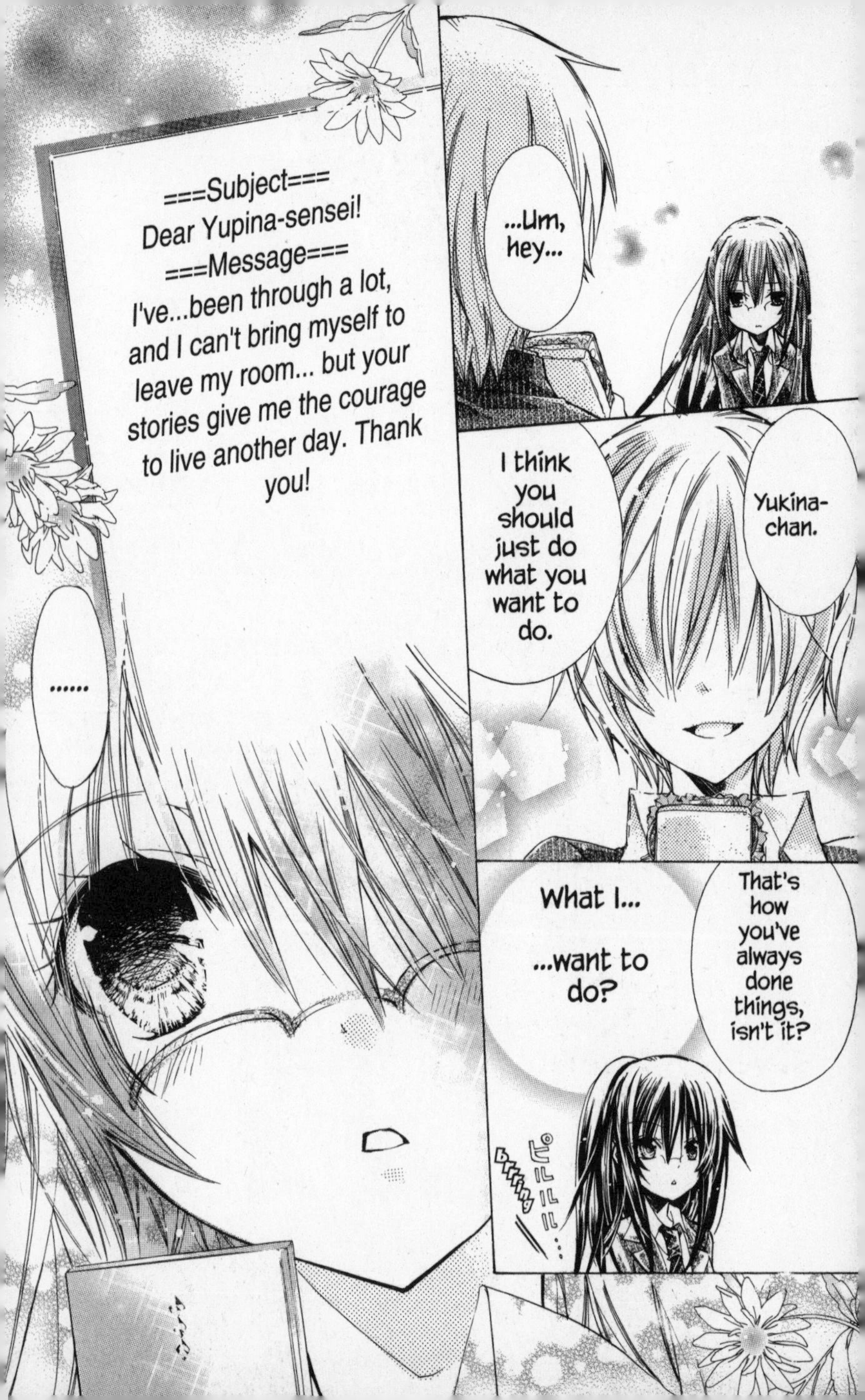
...Um, hey...
Yukina-chan.
I think you should just do what you want to do.
That's how you've always done things, isn't it?
What I...
...want to do?
ピルルル...
brrring
===Subject===
Dear Yupina-sensei!
===Message===
I've...been through a lot, and I can't bring myself to leave my room... but your stories give me the courage to live another day. Thank you!
......

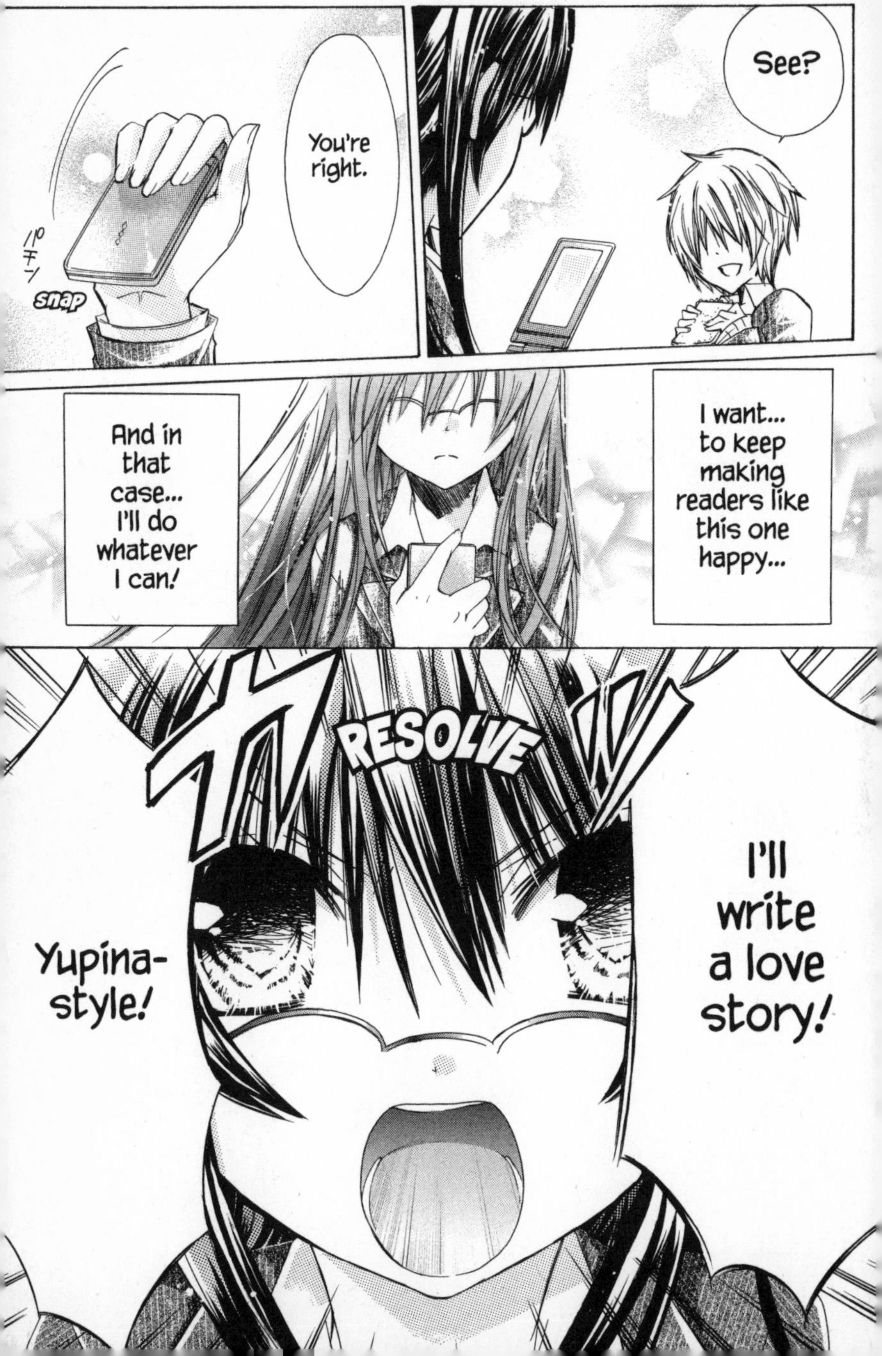
See?
You're right.
パチン
snap
I want... to keep making readers like this one happy...
And in that case... I'll do whatever I can!
RESOLVE
I'll write a love story!
Yupina-style!

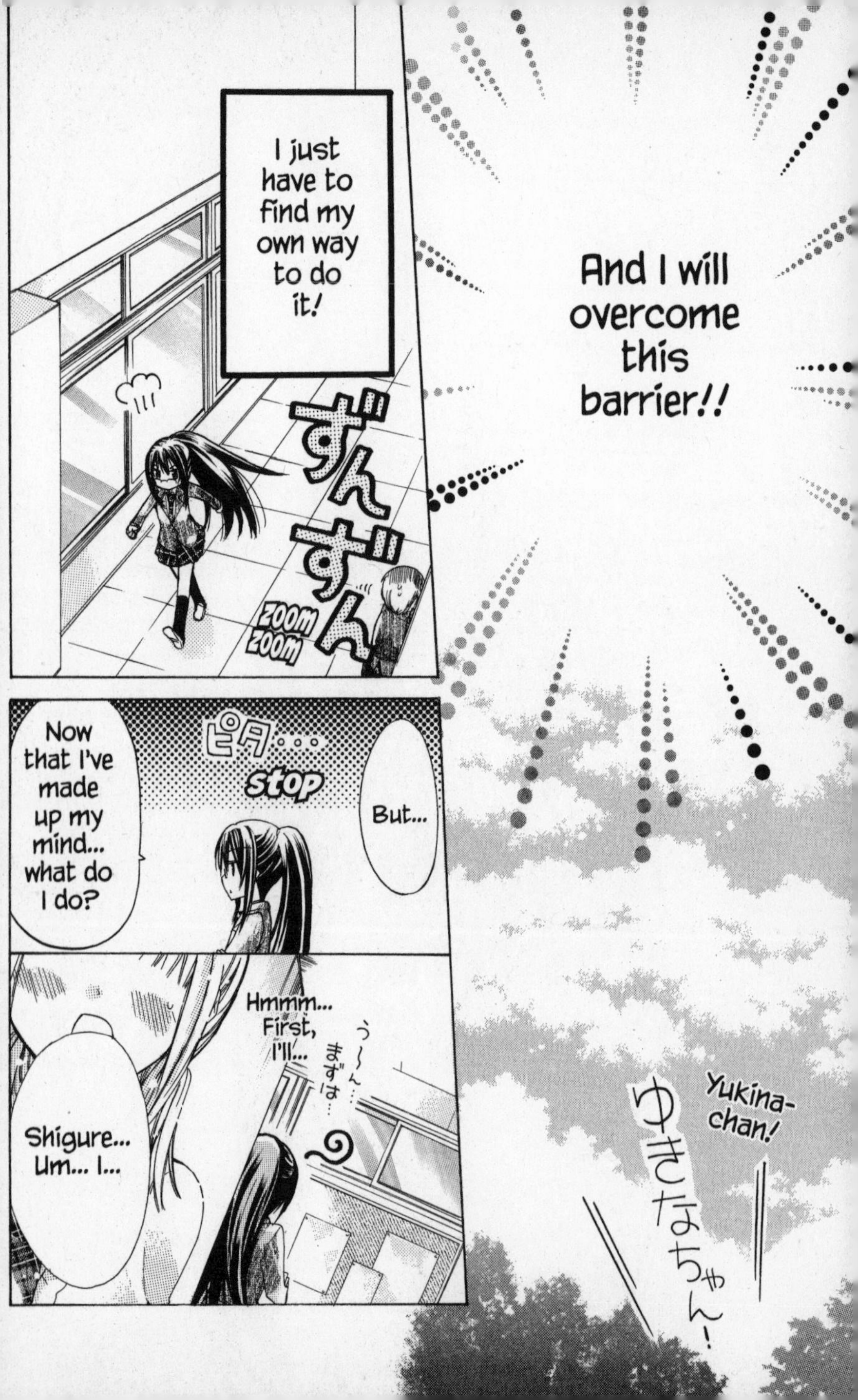
And I will overcome this barrier!!
ゆきなちゃん!
Yukina-chan!
I just have to find my own way to do it!
ずんずん
ZOOM ZOOM
ピタ…
STOP
But...
Now that I've made up my mind... what do I do?
うーん…まずは…
Hmmm... First, I'll...
Shigure... Um... I...

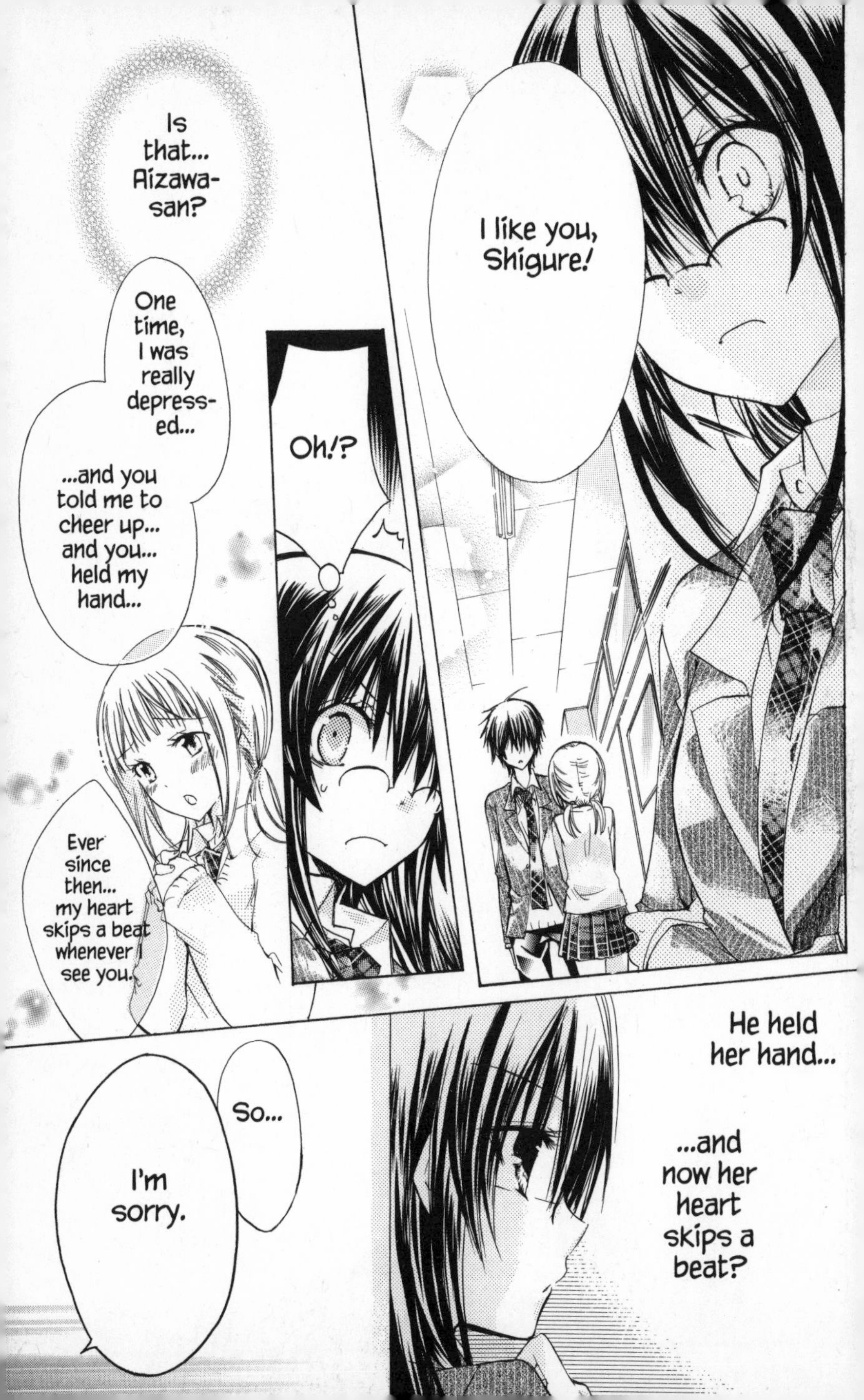
I like you, Shigure!
Oh!?
Is that... Aizawa-san?
One time, I was really depressed...
...and you told me to cheer up... and you... held my hand...
Ever since then... my heart skips a beat whenever I see you.
He held her hand...
...and now her heart skips a beat?
So...
I'm sorry.

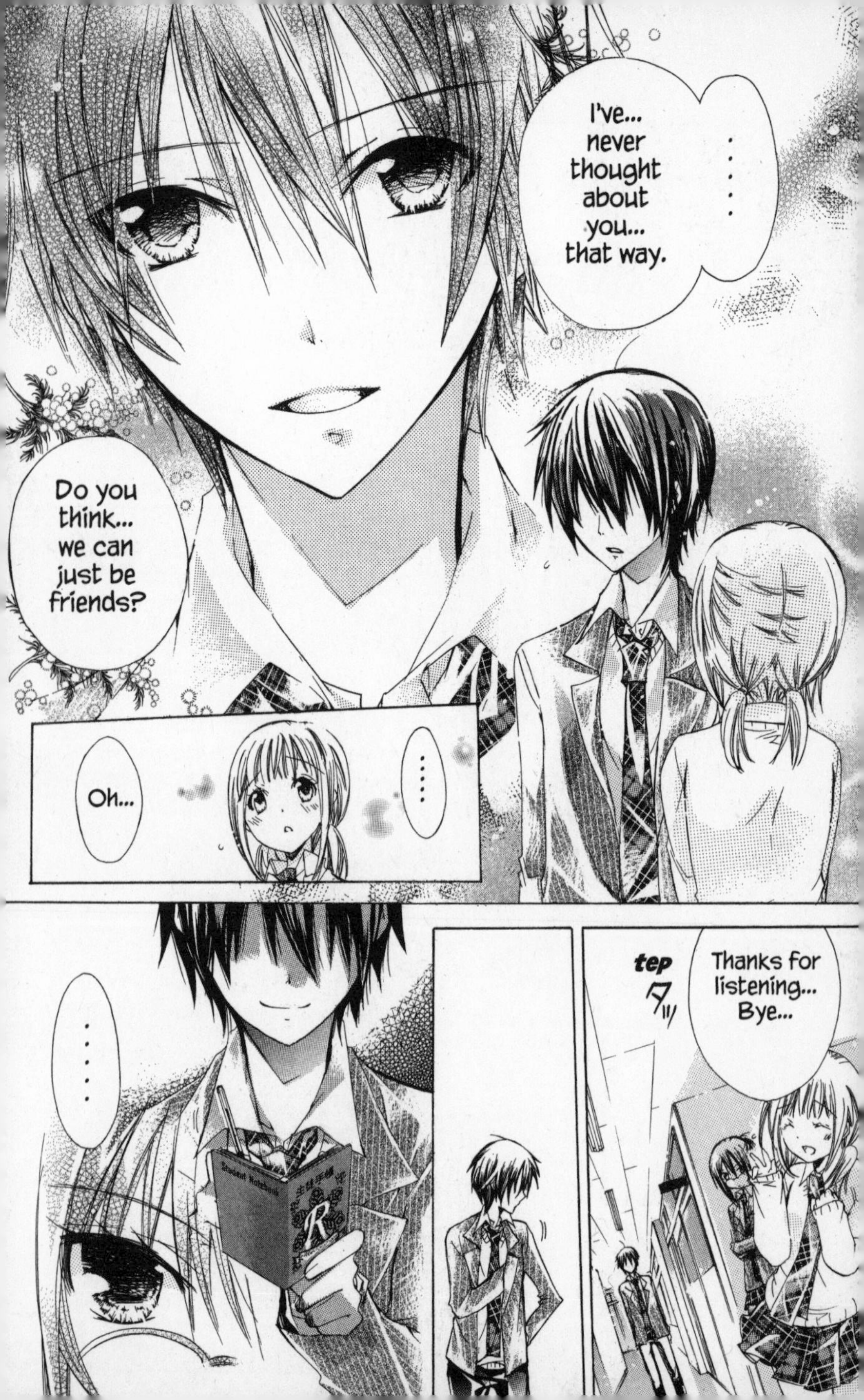
.....
I've... never thought about you... that way.
Do you think... we can just be friends?
.....
Oh...
tep
Thanks for listening... Bye...
.....

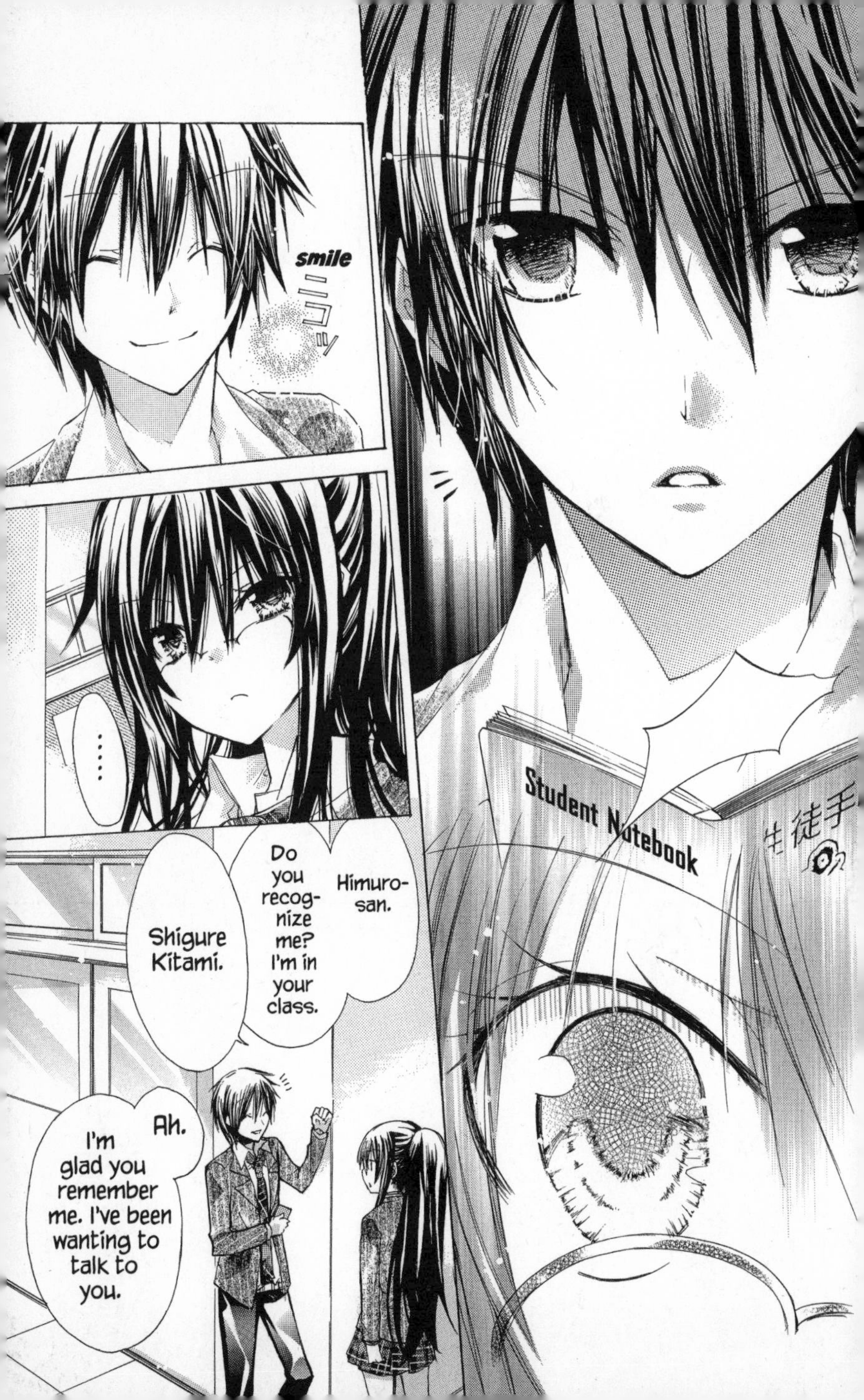
Student Notebook
生徒手
smile
ニコッ
......
Himuro-san.
Do you recognize me? I'm in your class.
Shigure Kitami.
Ah.
I'm glad you remember me. I've been wanting to talk to you.

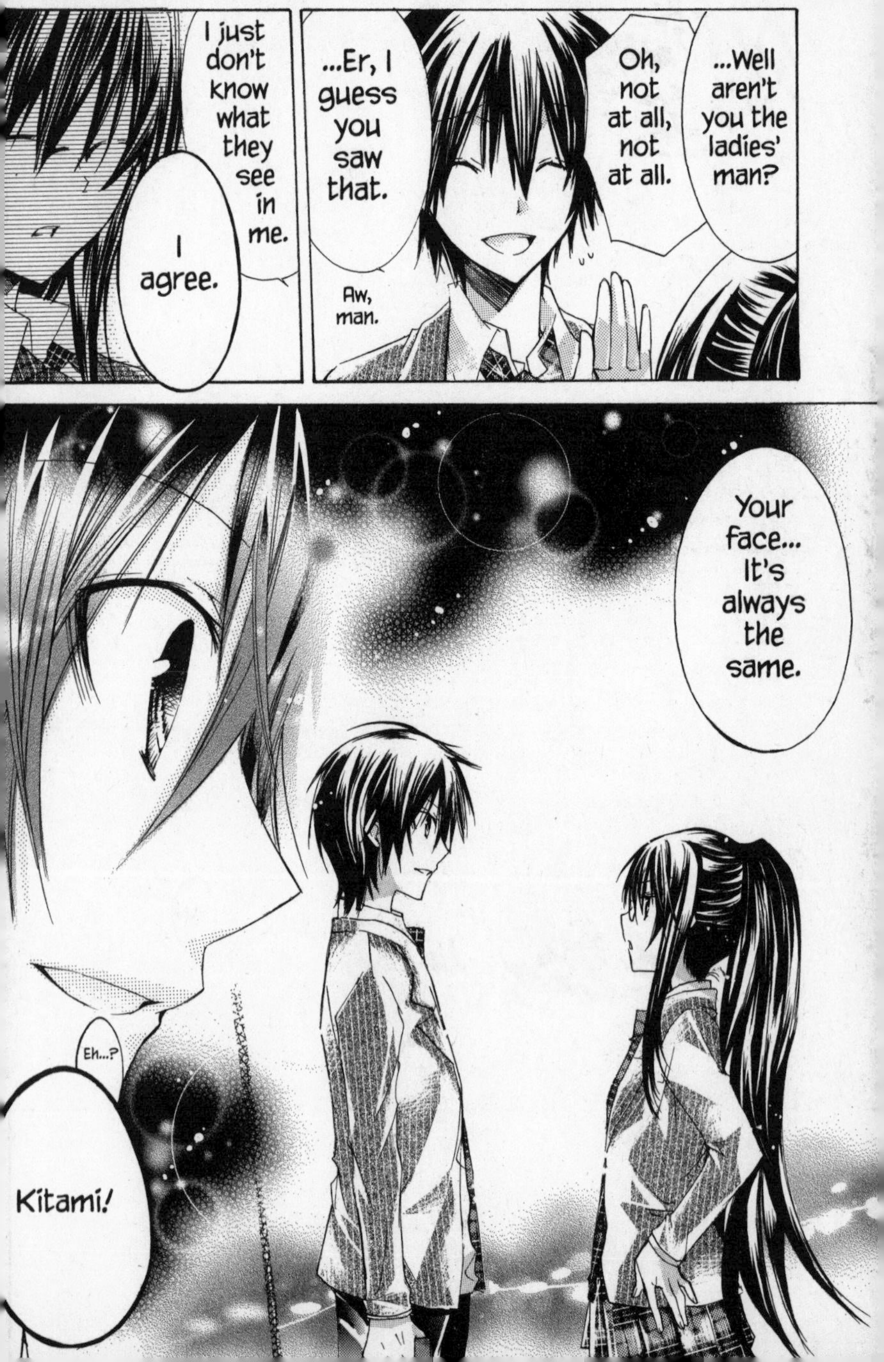
...Well aren't you the ladies' man?
Oh, not at all, not at all.
...Er, I guess you saw that.
Aw, man.
I just don't know what they see in me.
I agree.
Your face... It's always the same.
Eh...?
Kitami!

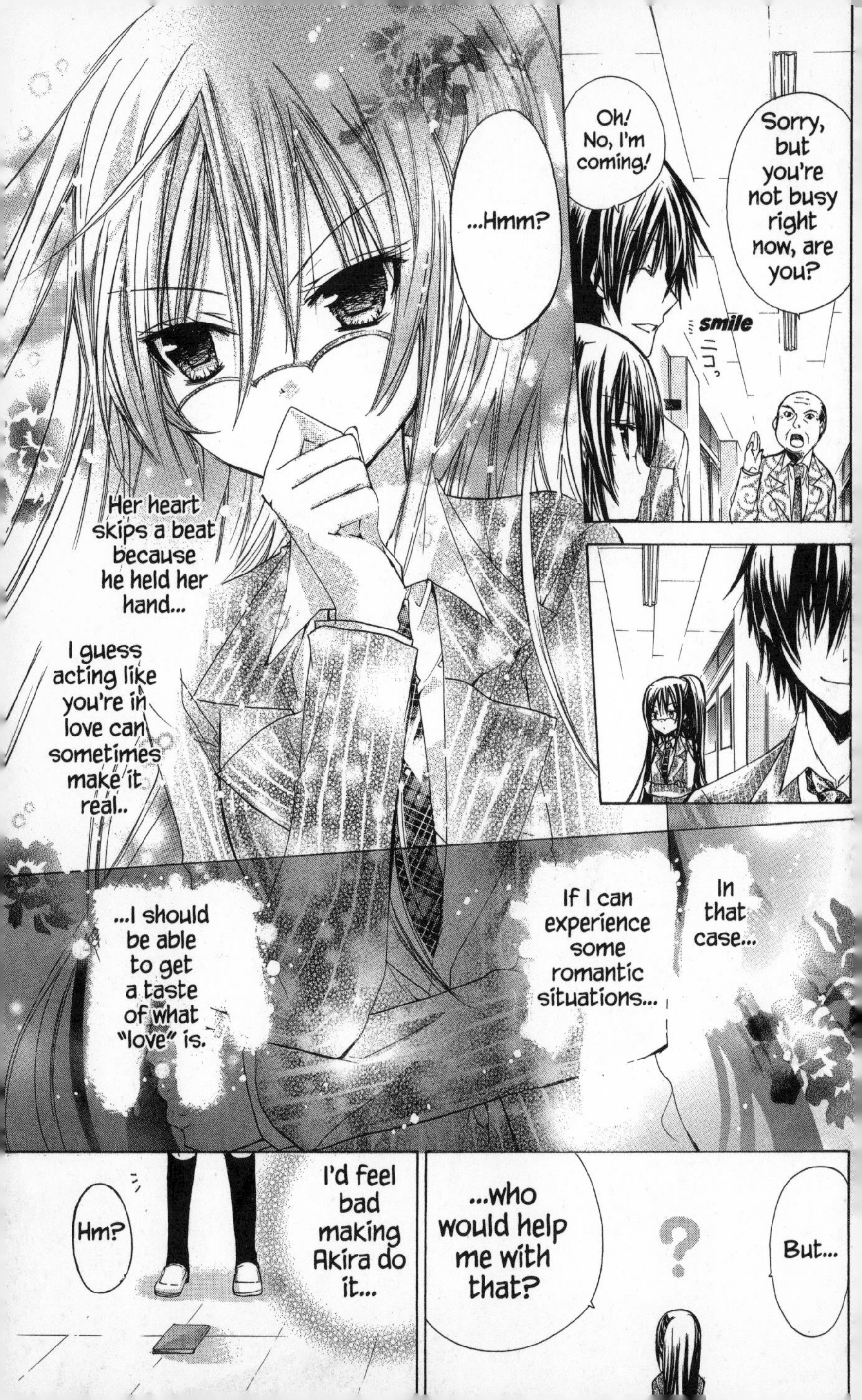

Sorry, but you're not busy right now, are you?
Oh! No, I'm coming!
smile
...Hmm?
Her heart skips a beat because he held her hand...
I guess acting like you're in love can sometimes make it real..
In that case...
If I can experience some romantic situations...
...I should be able to get a taste of what "love" is.
But...
...who would help me with that?
I'd feel bad making Akira do it...
Hm?

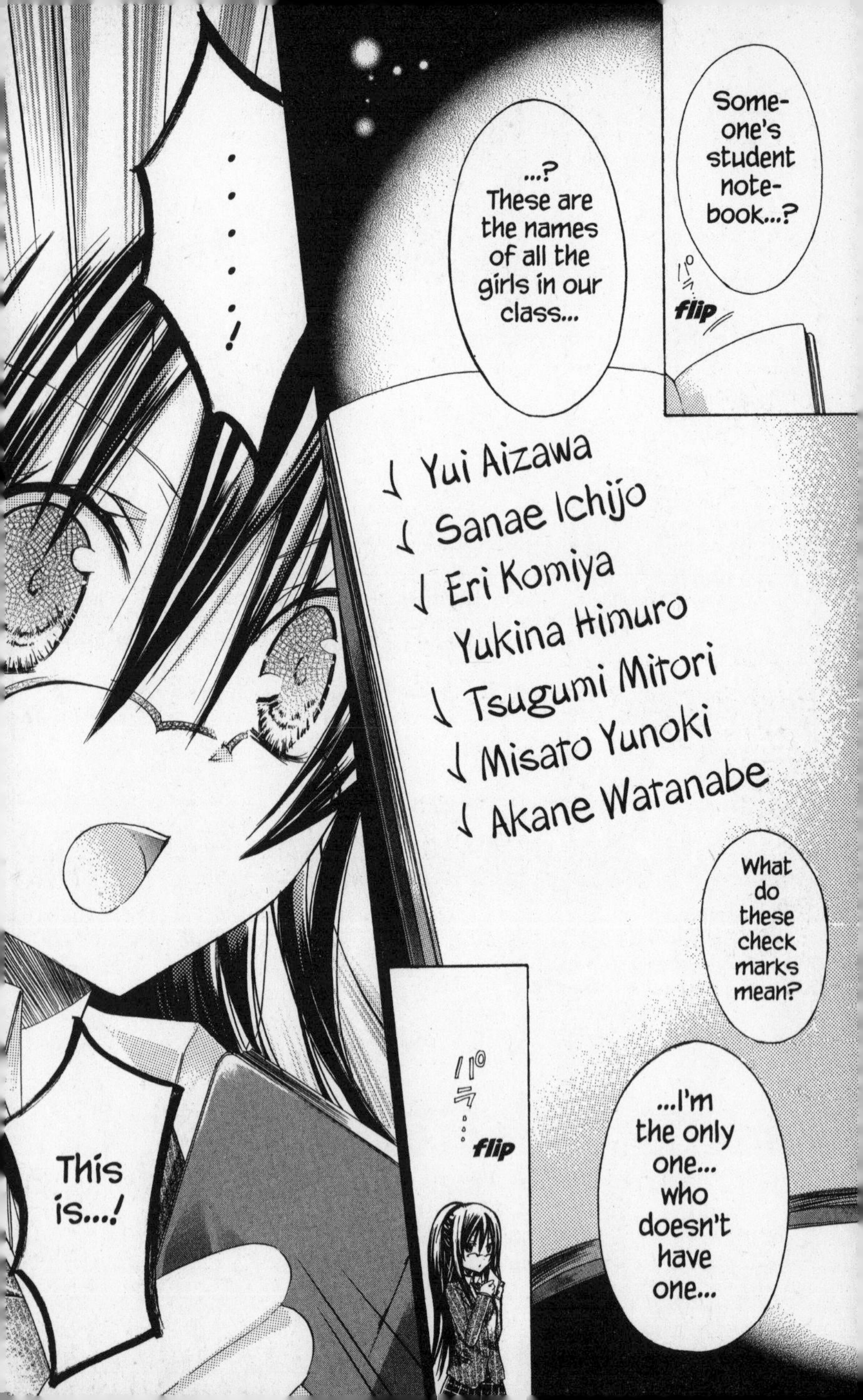

Some-one's student note-book...?
パラ
flip
...? These are the names of all the girls in our class...
.....!
✓ Yui Aizawa
✓ Sanae Ichijo
✓ Eri Komiya
Yukina Himuro
✓ Tsugumi Mitori
✓ Misato Yunoki
✓ Akane Watanabe
What do these check marks mean?
...I'm the only one... who doesn't have one...
パラ...
flip
This is...!

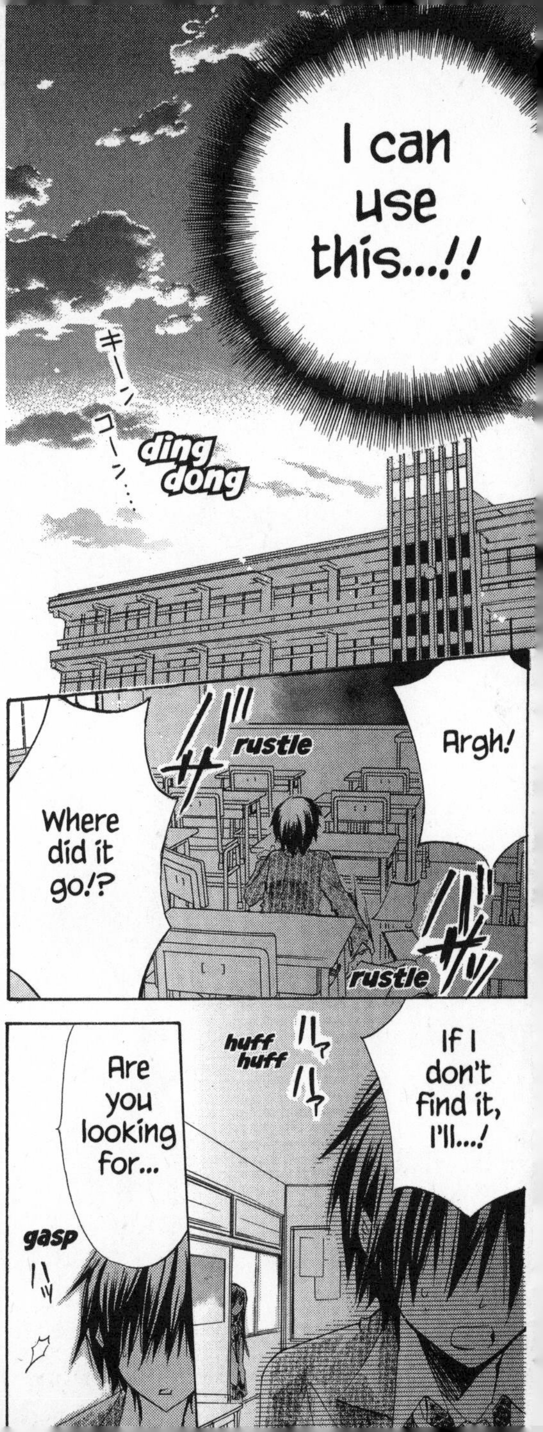
I can use this...!!
ding dong
Argh!
rustle
Where did it go!?
rustle
If I don't find it, I'll...!
huff huff
Are you looking for...
gasp

The Birth of Missions of Love

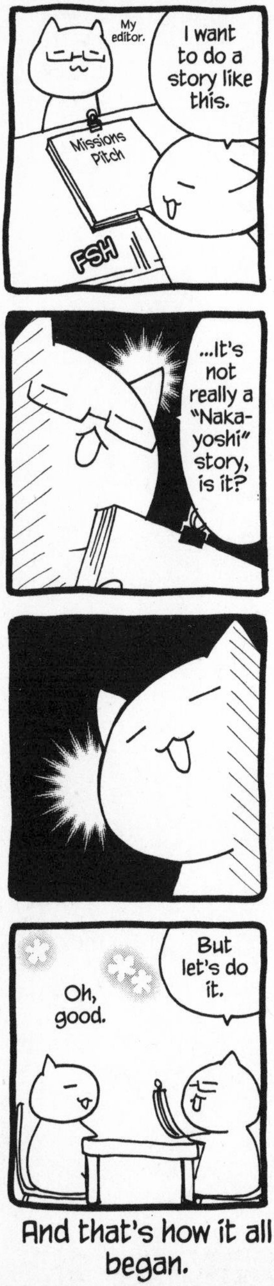
I want to do a story like this.
My editor.
Missions Pitch
FSH
...It's not really a "Naka-yoshi" story, is it?
But let's do it.
Oh, good.

And that's how it all began.

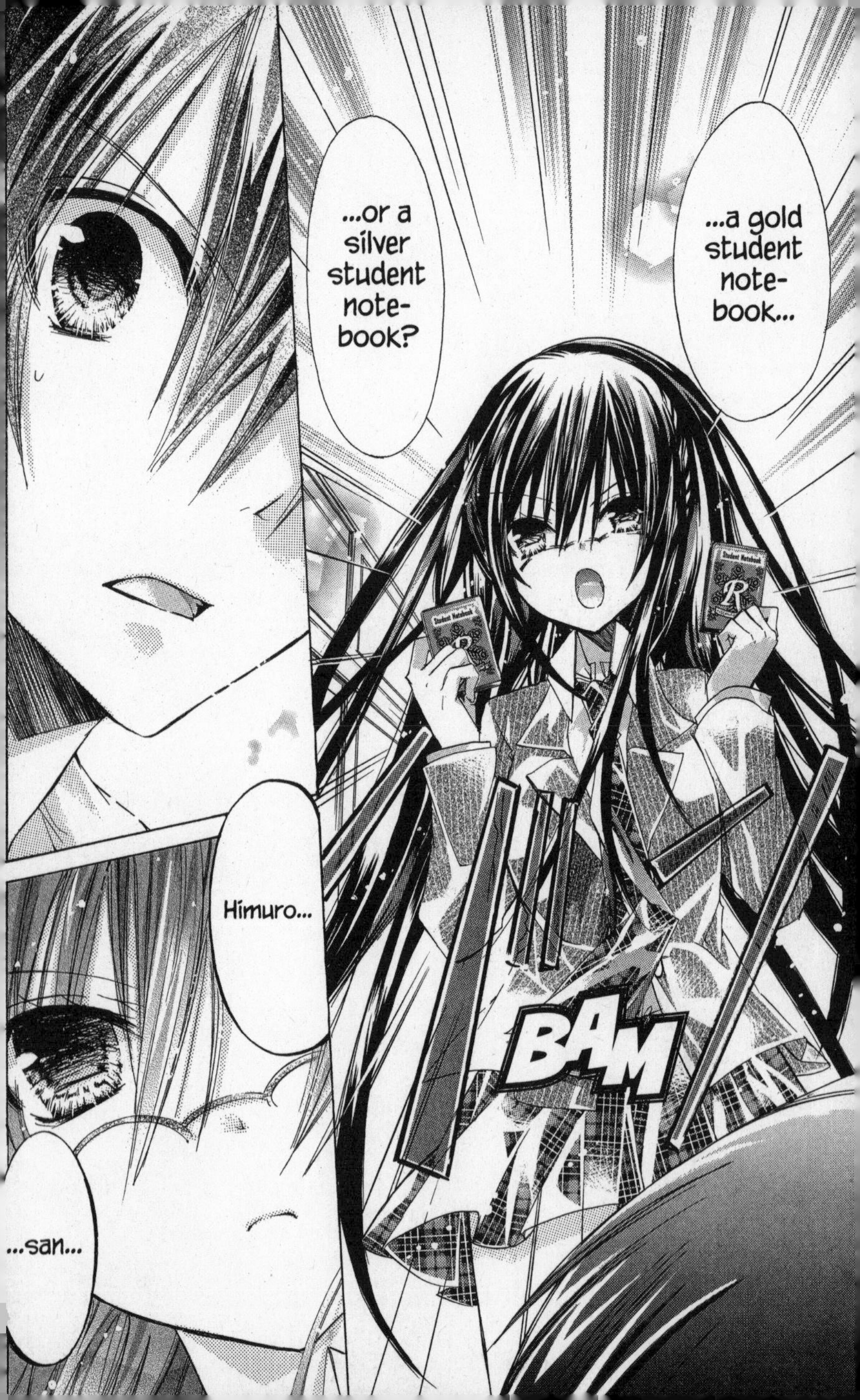
...a gold student note-book...
...or a silver student note-book?
BAM
Himuro...
...san...

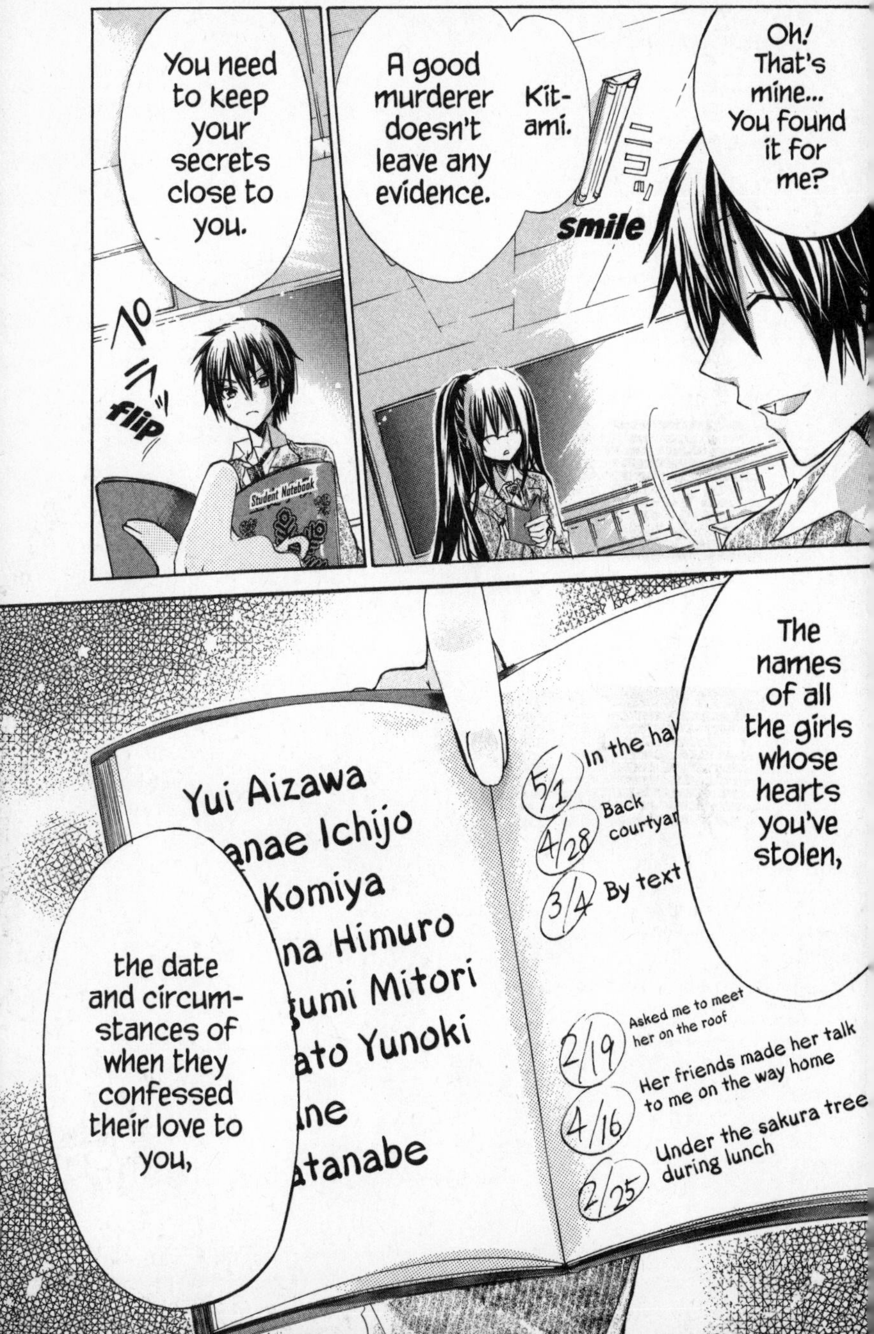
Oh! That's mine... You found it for me?
smile
Kit-ami.
A good murderer doesn't leave any evidence.
You need to keep your secrets close to you.
flip
Student Notebook
The names of all the girls whose hearts you've stolen,
5/1
4/28 Back
3/4 By text
2/19 Asked me to meet her on the roof
4/16 Her friends made her talk to me on the way home
2/25 Under the sakura tree during lunch
Yui Aizawa
Komiya
the date and circumstances of when they confessed their love to you,

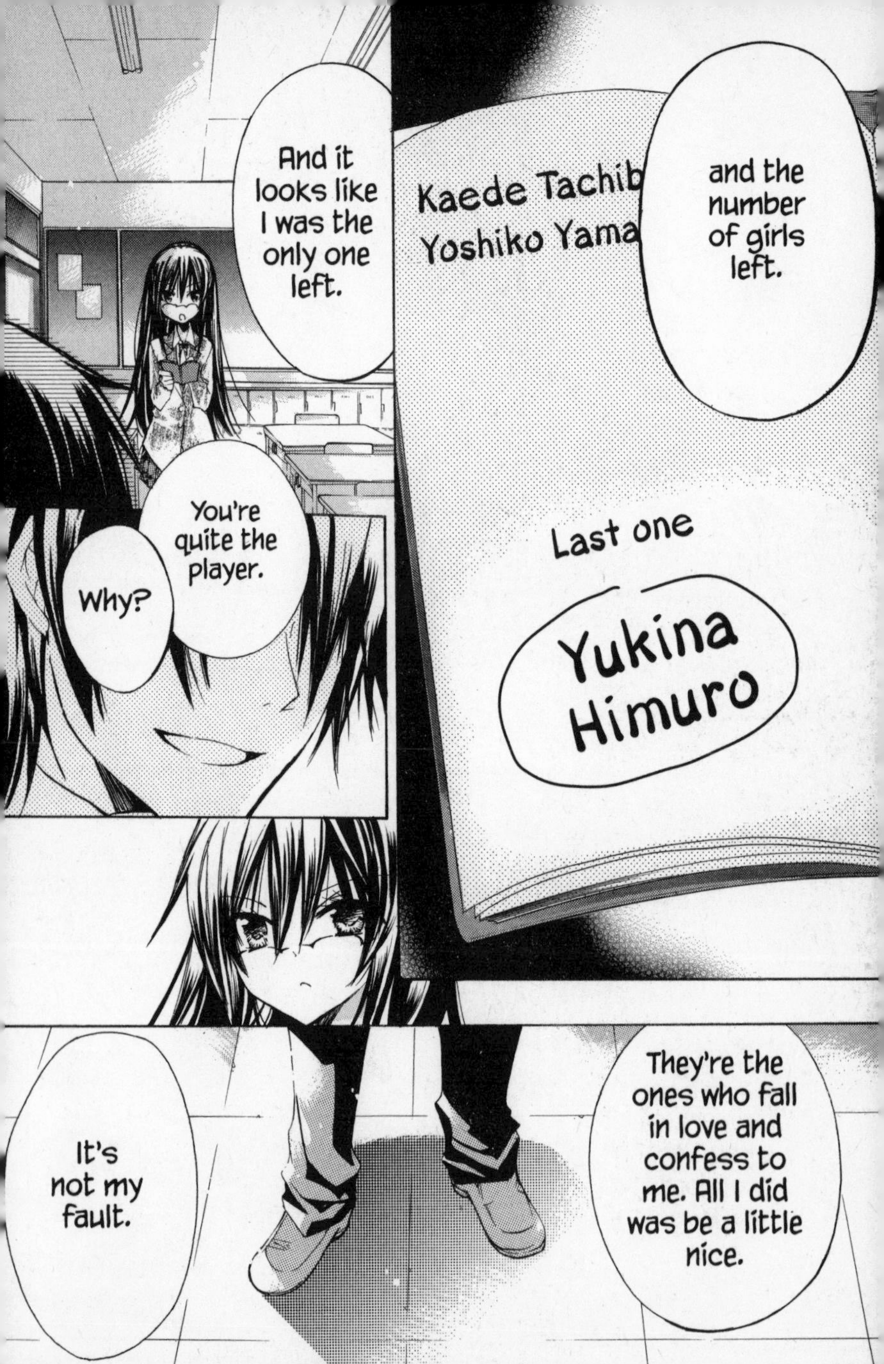
and the number of girls left.
Kaede Tachib
Yoshiko Yama
Last one
Yukina Himuro
And it looks like I was the only one left.
You're quite the player.
Why?
They're the ones who fall in love and confess to me. All I did was be a little nice.
It's not my fault.

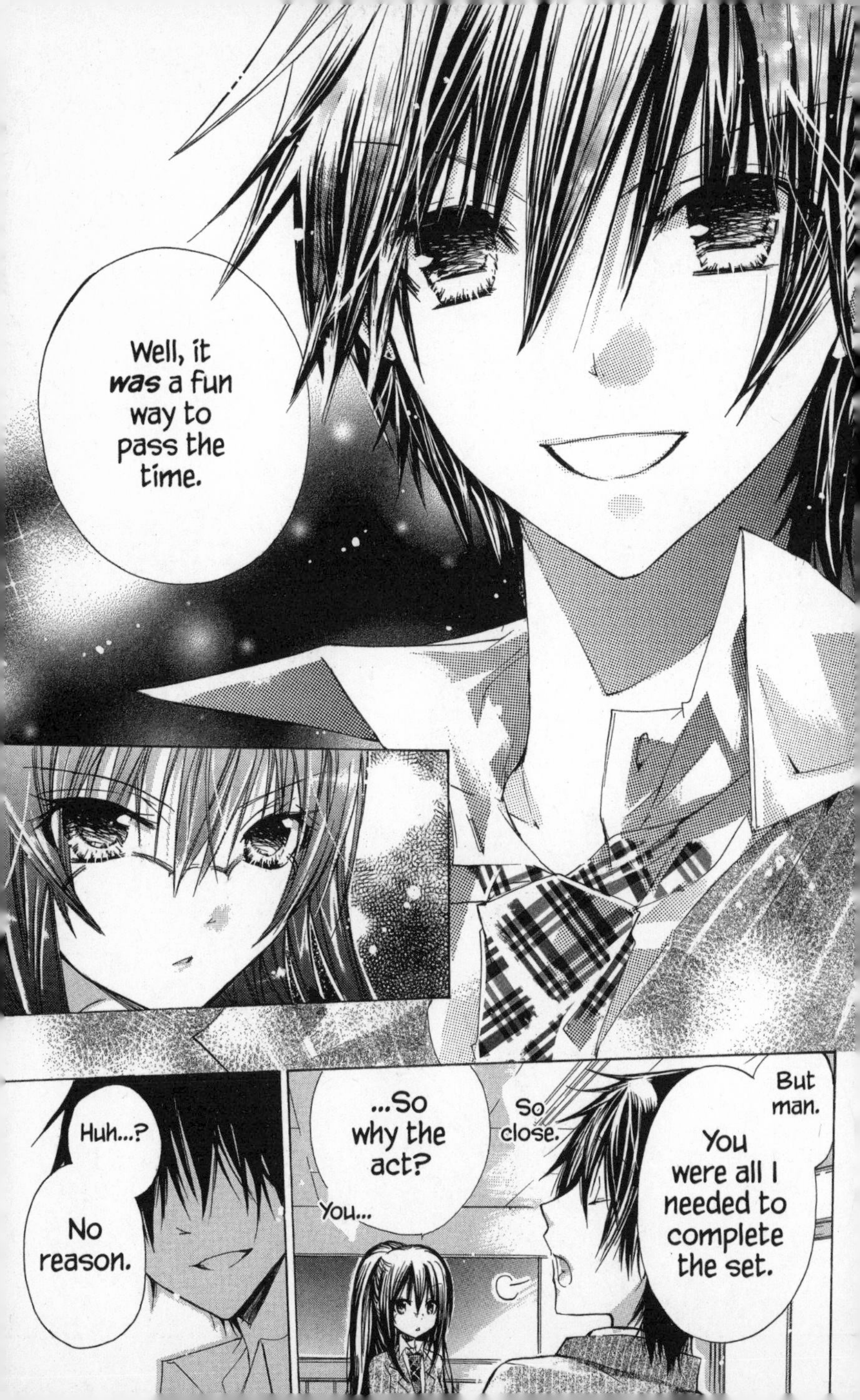

Well, it *was* a fun way to pass the time.
But man.
You were all I needed to complete the set.
So close.
You...
...So why the act?
Huh...?
No reason.

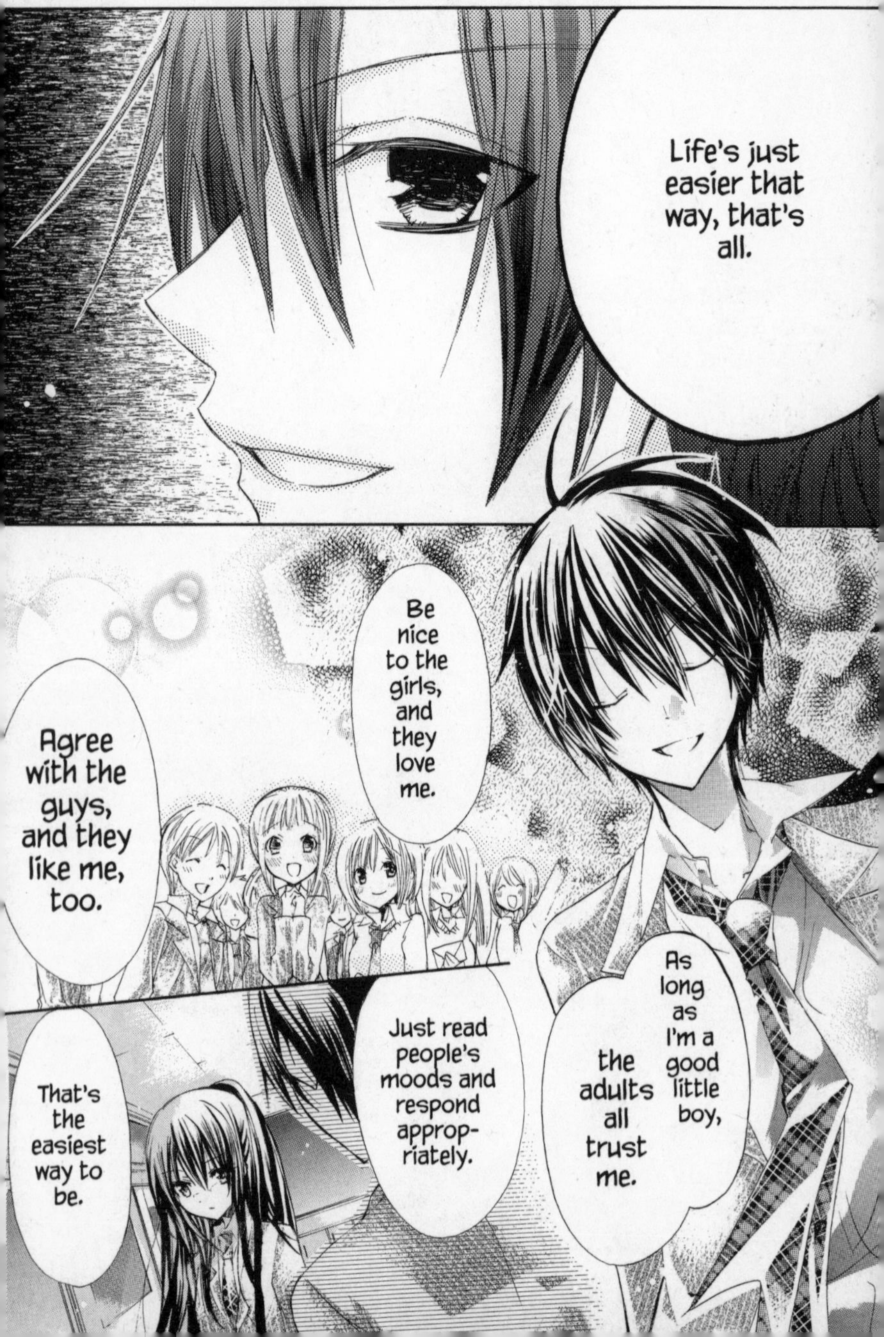
Life's just easier that way, that's all.
Be nice to the girls, and they love me.
Agree with the guys, and they like me, too.
As long as I'm a good little boy, the adults all trust me.
Just read people's moods and respond approp-riately.
That's the easiest way to be.

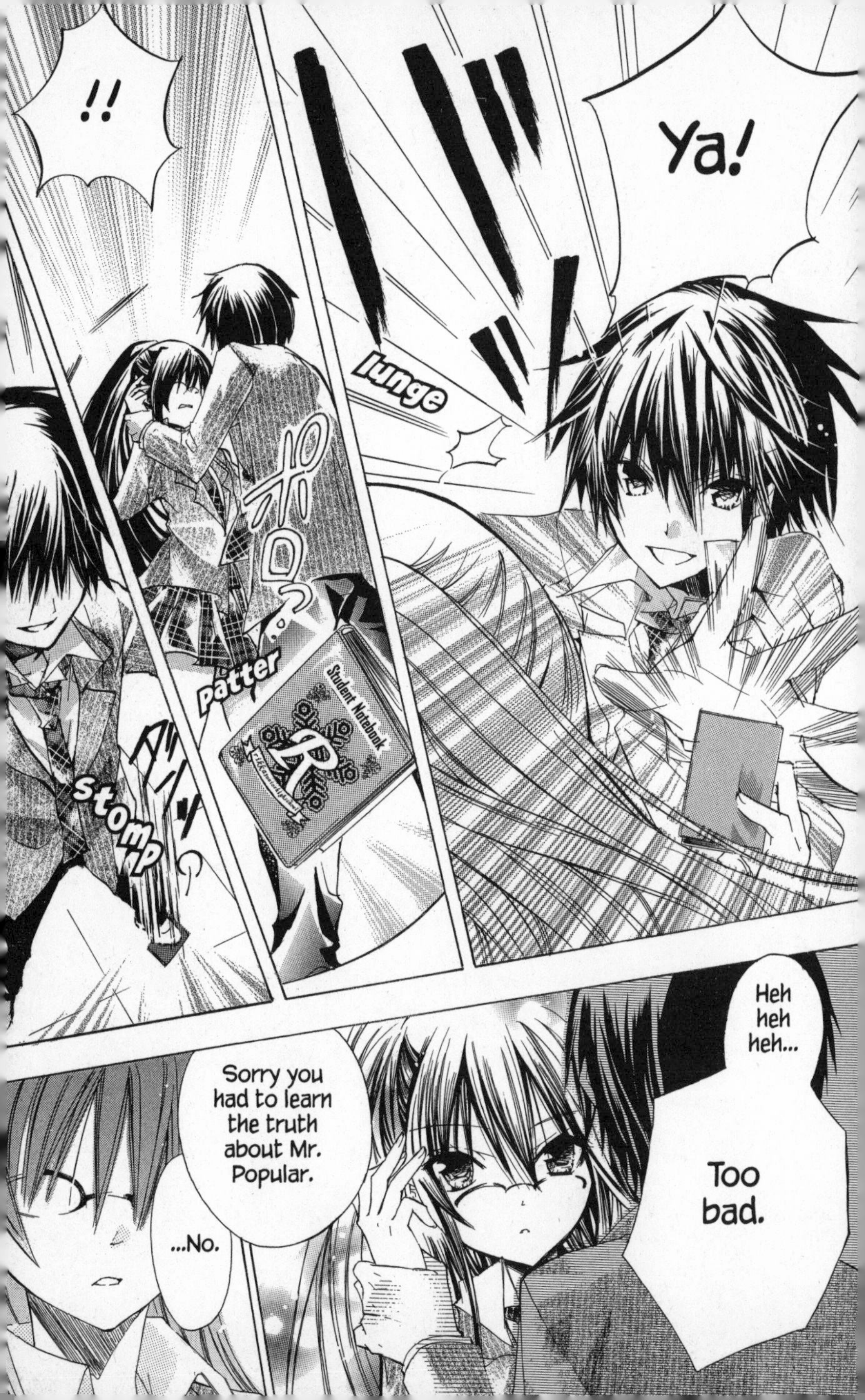

Ya!
lunge
Student Notebook
patter
!!
stomp
Heh heh heh...
Too bad.
Sorry you had to learn the truth about Mr. Popular.
...No.

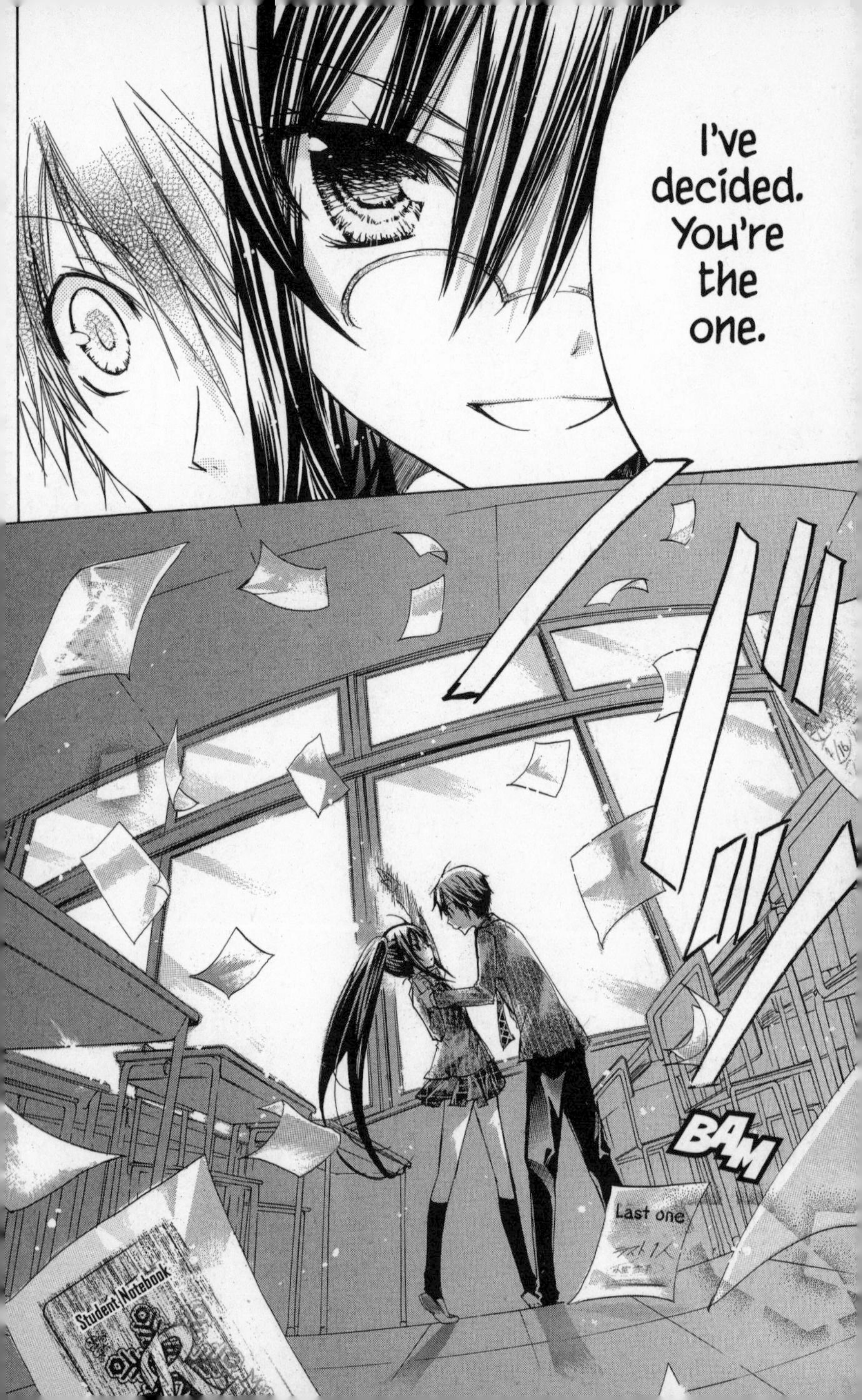
I've decided. You're the one.
BAM
Last one
Student Notebook

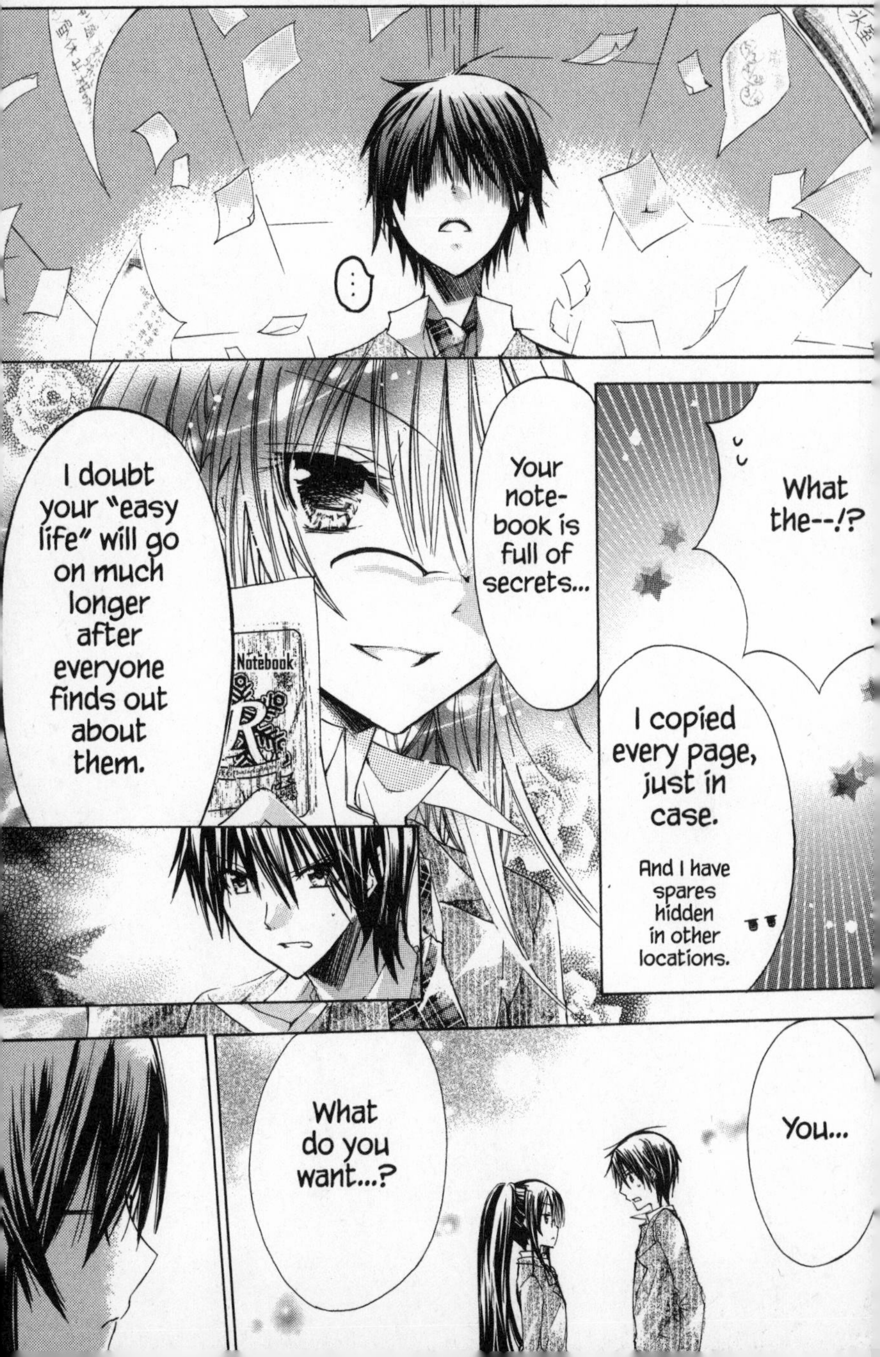
...
What the--!?
I copied every page, just in case.
And I have spares hidden in other locations.
Your notebook is full of secrets...
I doubt your "easy life" will go on much longer after everyone finds out about them.
Notebook
You...
What do you want...?

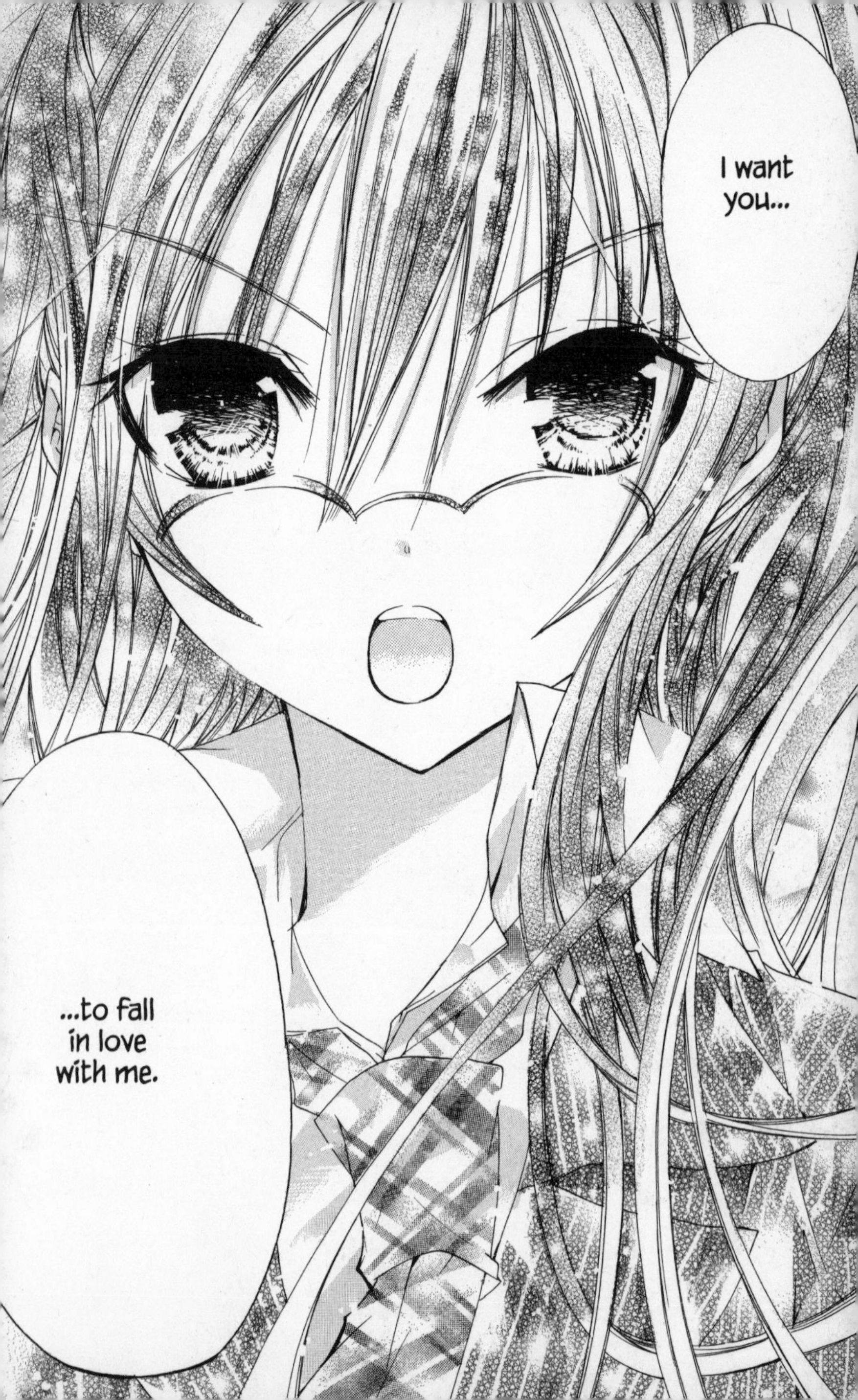
I want you...
...to fall in love with me.

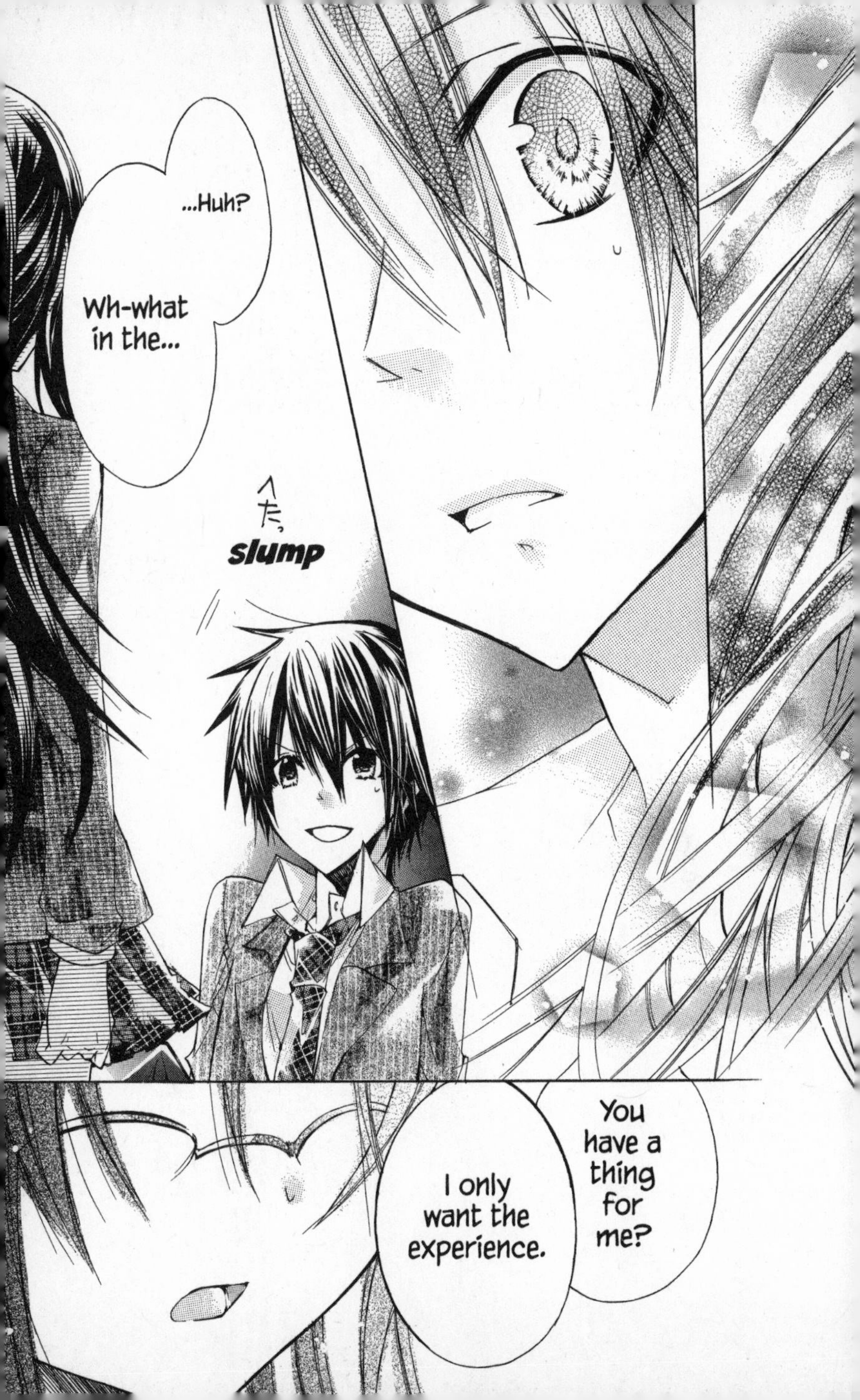
...Huh?
Wh-what in the...
へたっ
slump
You have a thing for me?
I only want the experience.

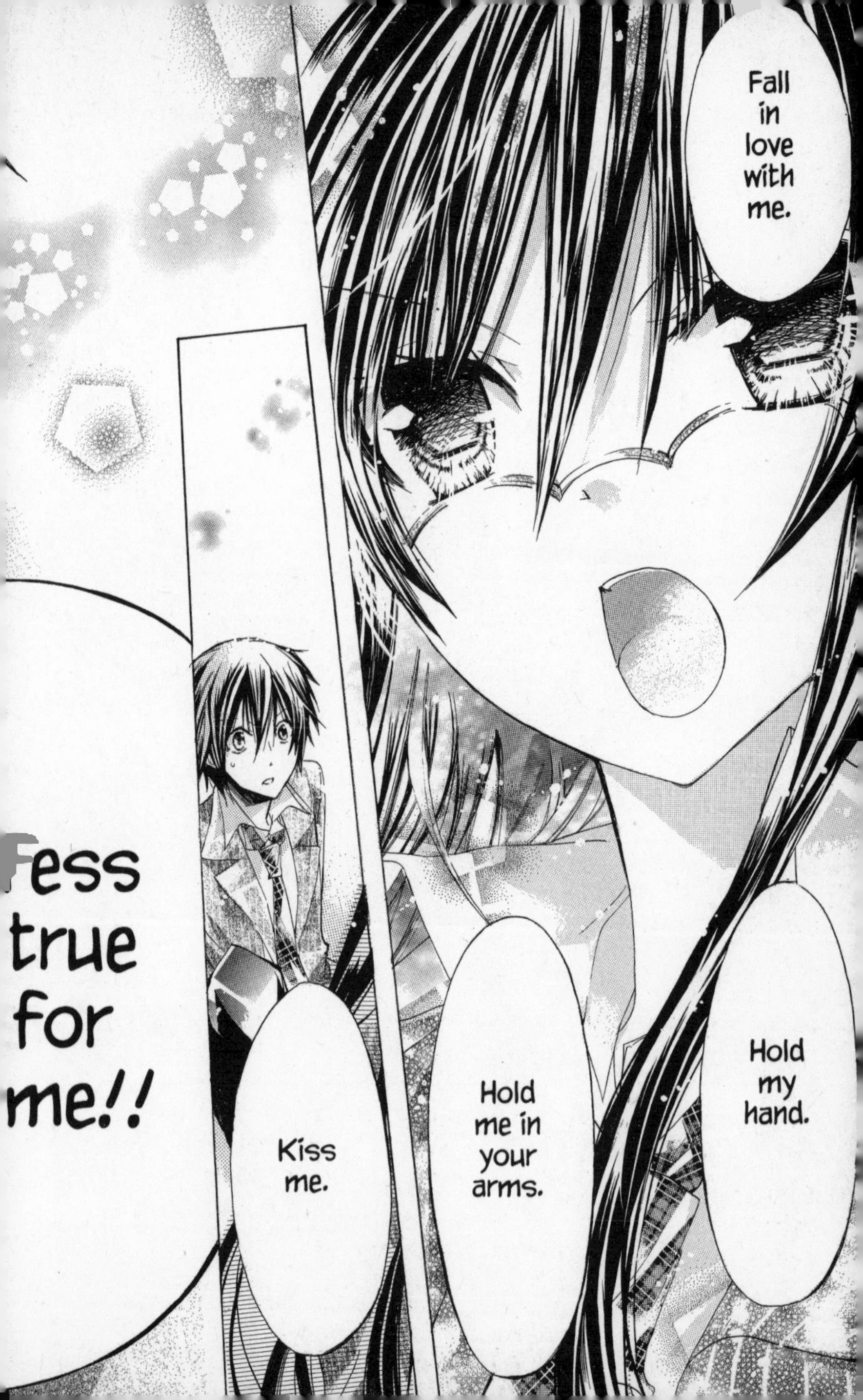

Fall in love with me.
Hold my hand.
Hold me in your arms.
Kiss me.
Fess true for me!!

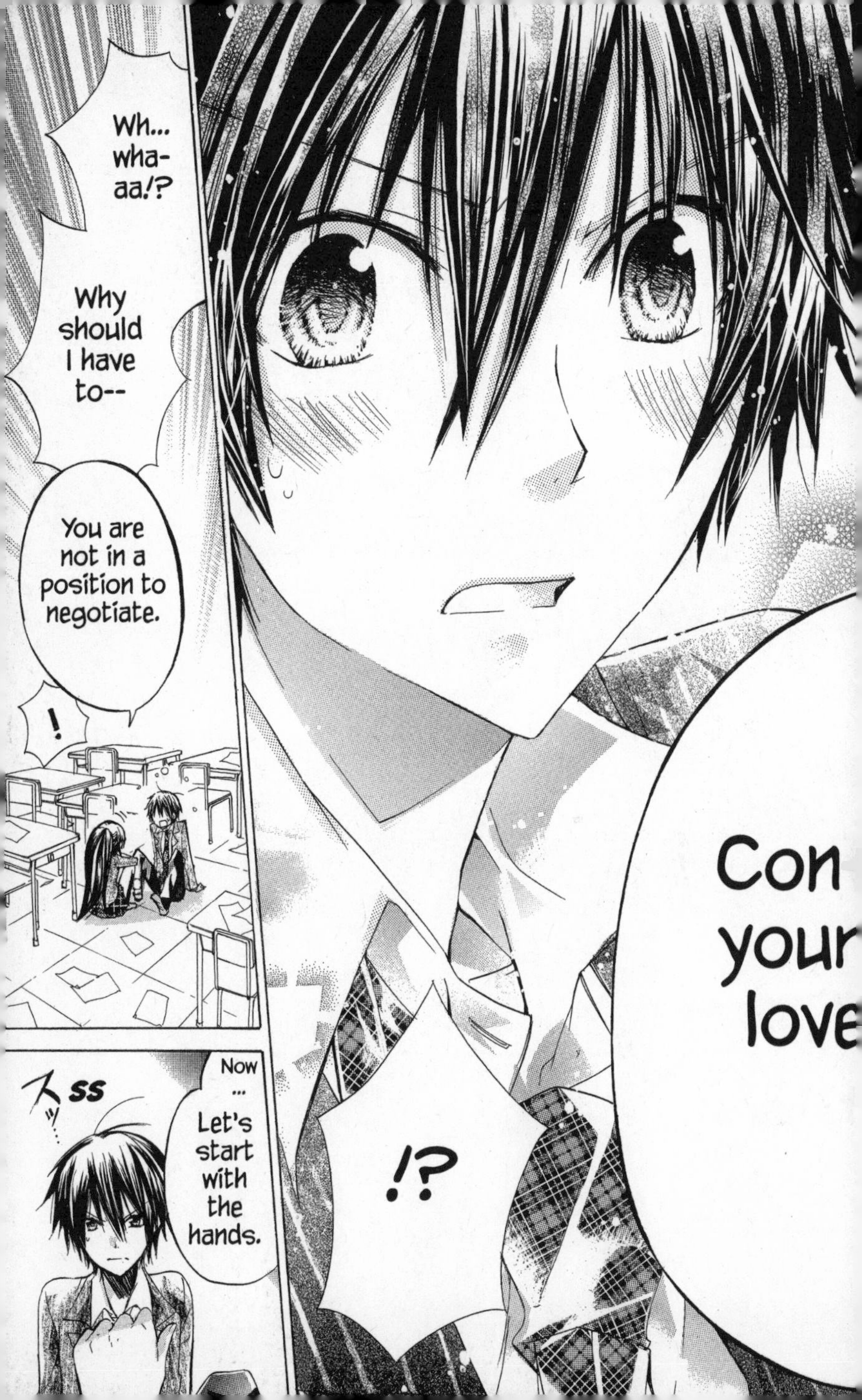

Con your love
!?
Wh... wha-aa!?
Why should I have to--
You are not in a position to negotiate.
!
Now...
Let's start with the hands.
ss

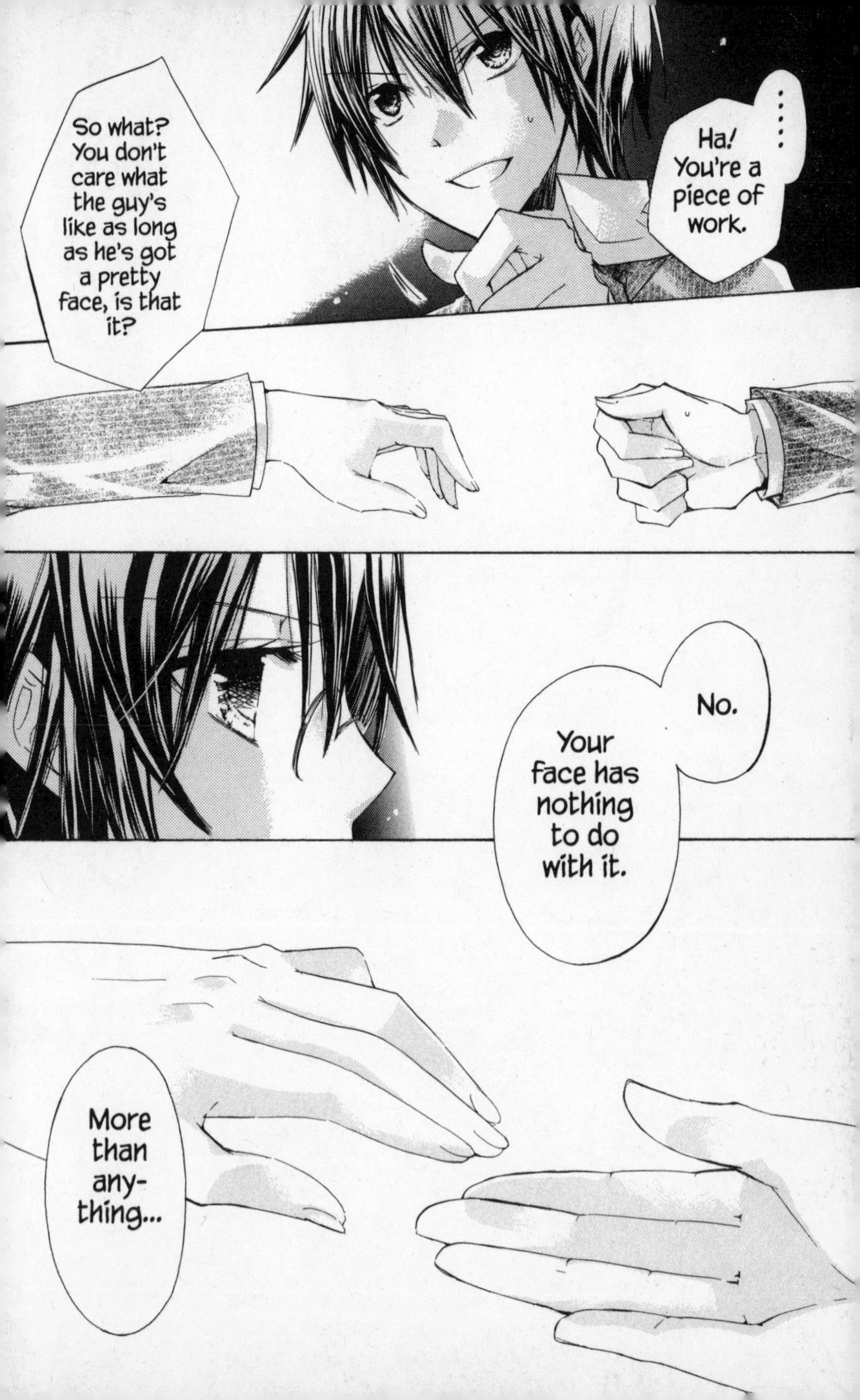
.....
Ha! You're a piece of work.
So what? You don't care what the guy's like as long as he's got a pretty face, is that it?
No.
Your face has nothing to do with it.
More than anything...

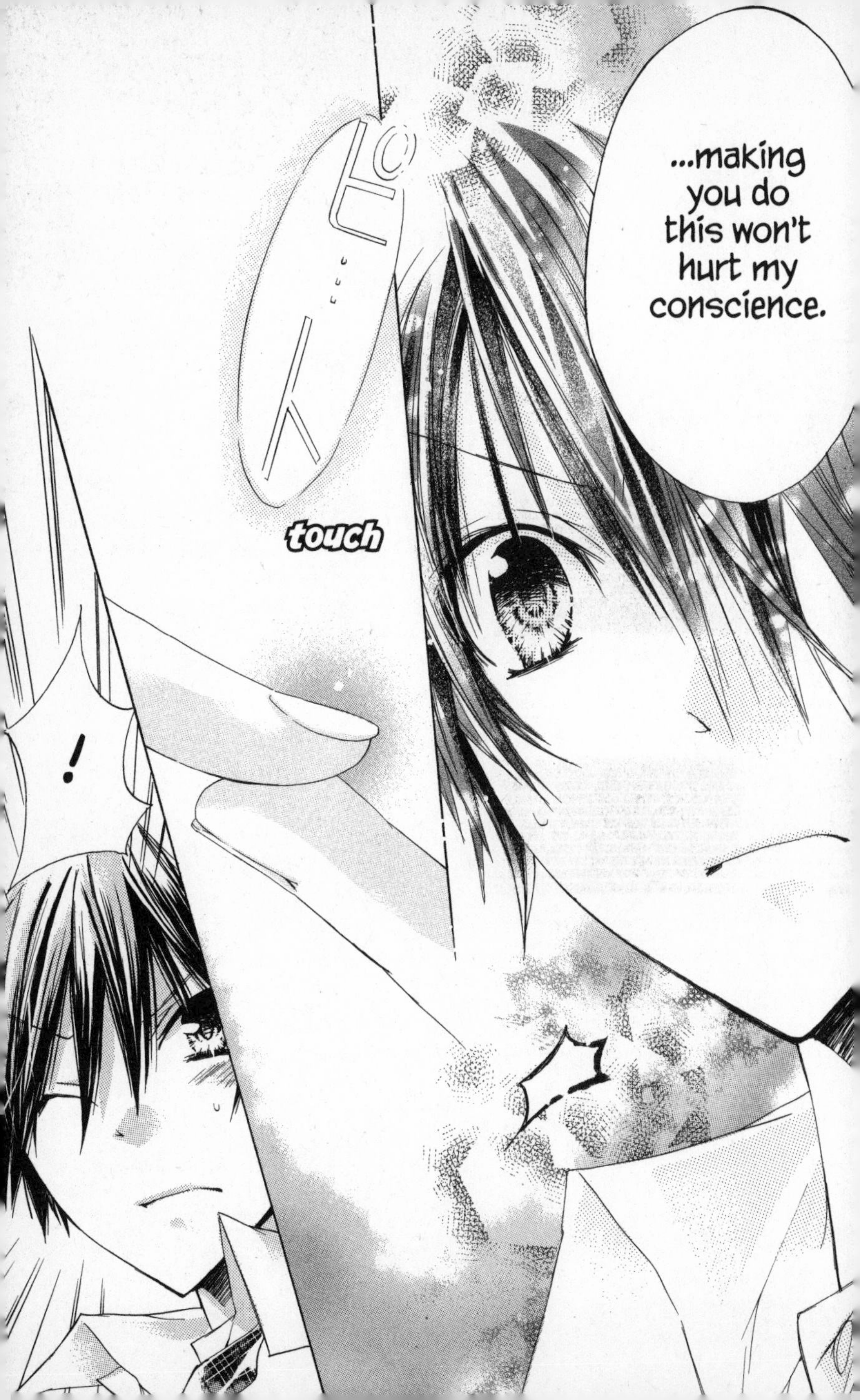
...making you do this won't hurt my conscience.
touch
!

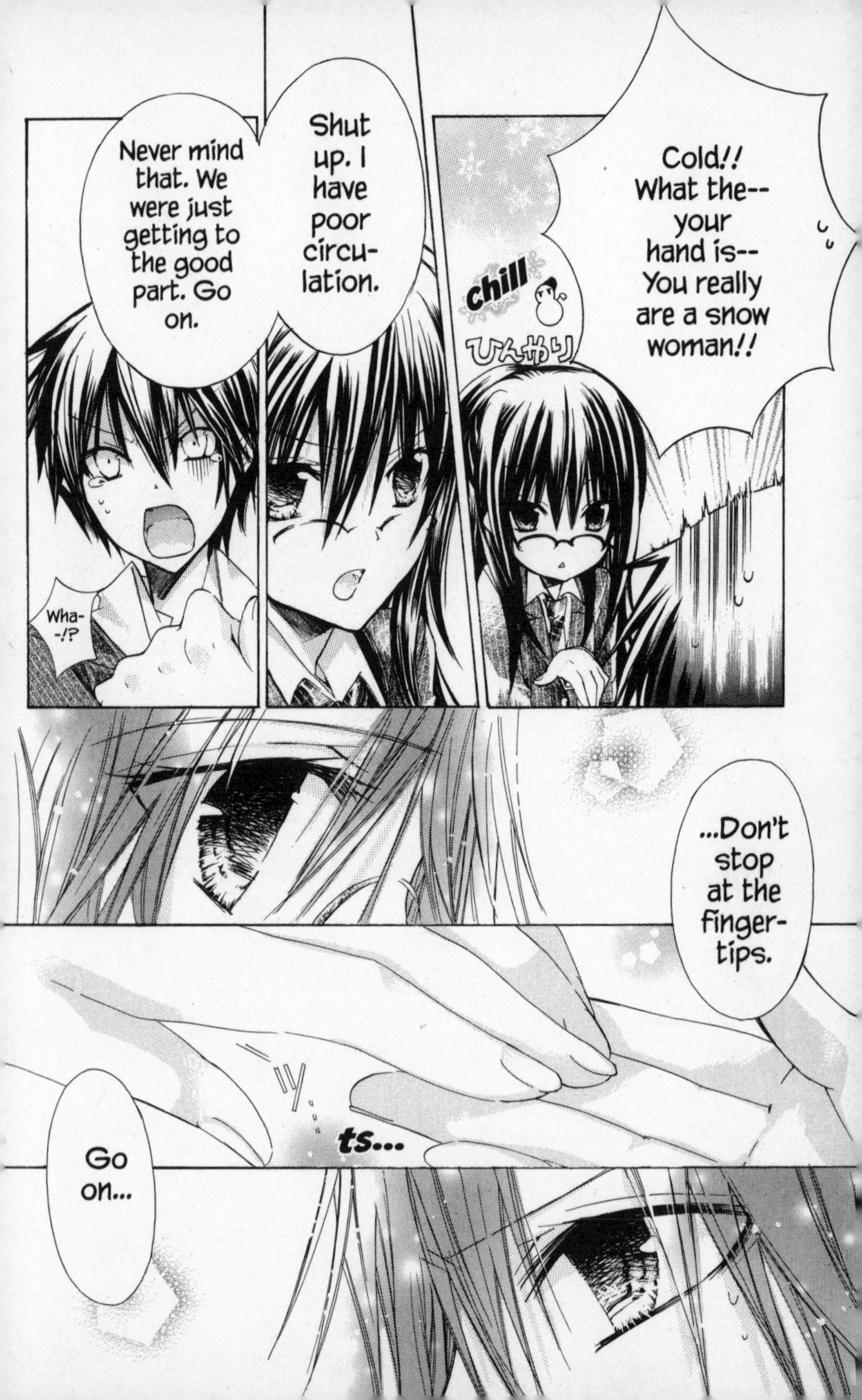
Cold!! What the-- your hand is-- You really are a snow woman!!
Chill
ひんやり
Shut up. I have poor circulation.
Never mind that. We were just getting to the good part. Go on.
Wha- -!?
...Don't stop at the finger-tips.
ts...
Go on...

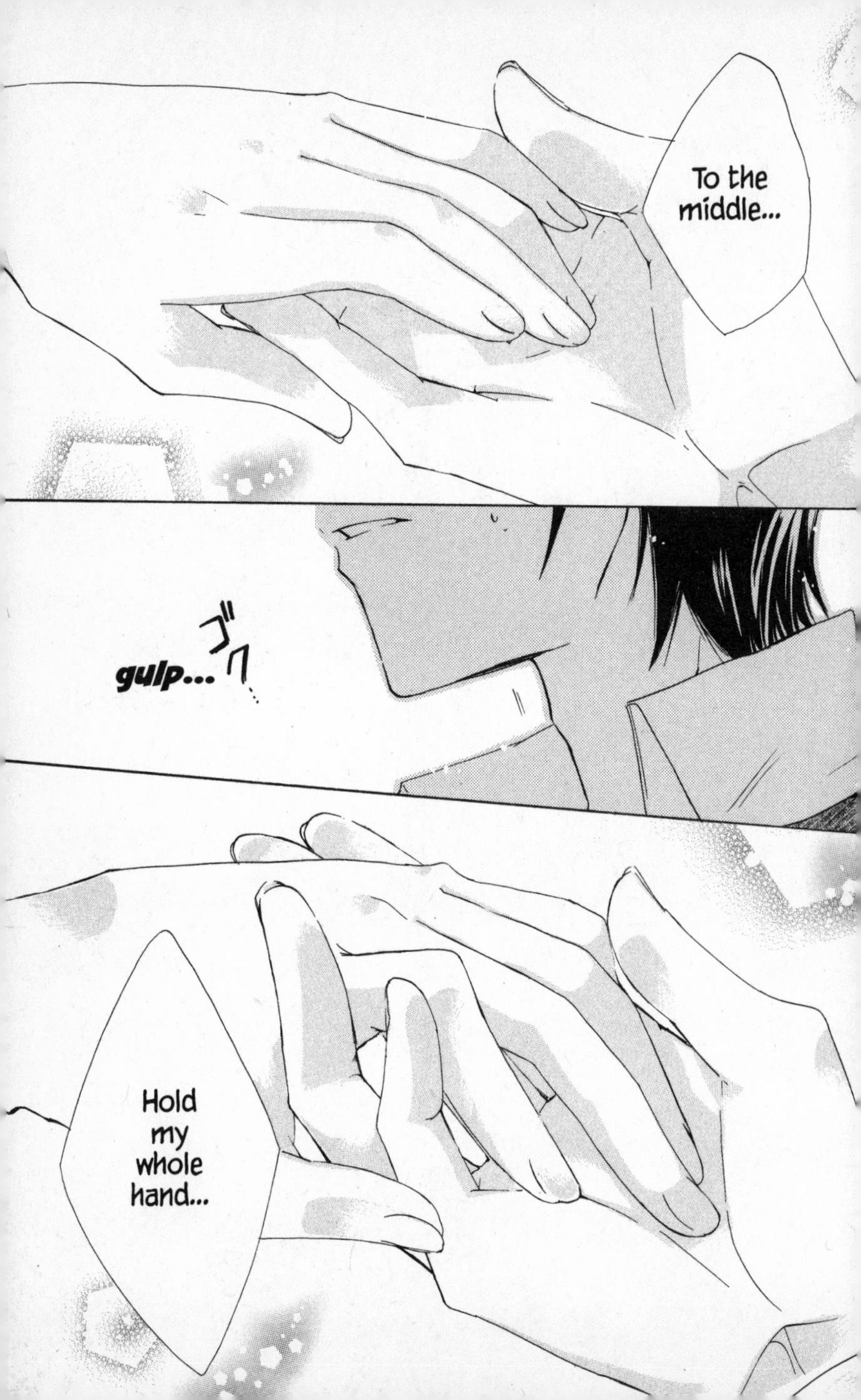
To the middle...
gulp... ゴク...
Hold my whole hand...

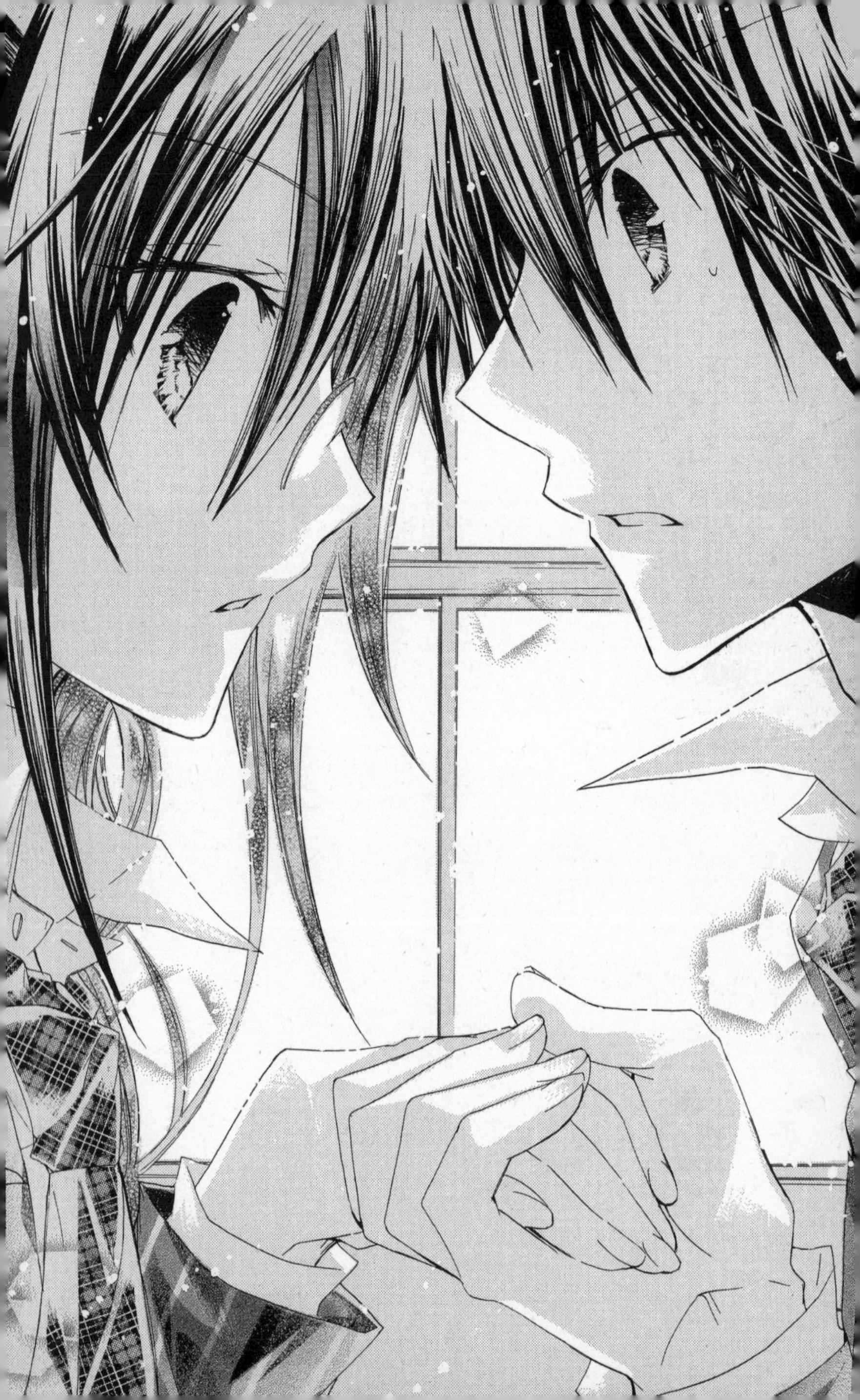

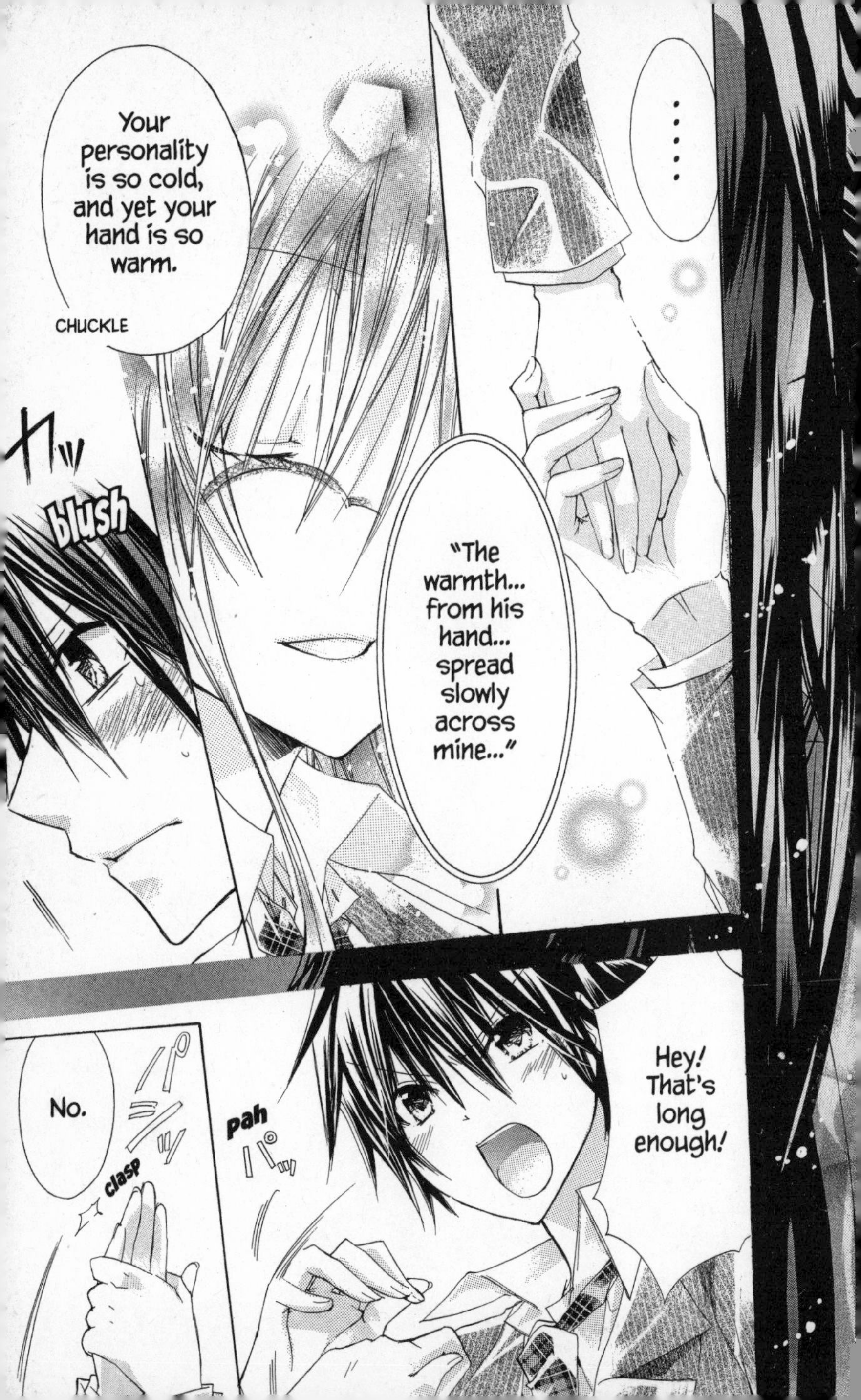
....
Your personality is so cold, and yet your hand is so warm.
CHUCKLE
"The warmth... from his hand... spread slowly across mine..."
blush
Hey! That's long enough!
pah
No.
clasp

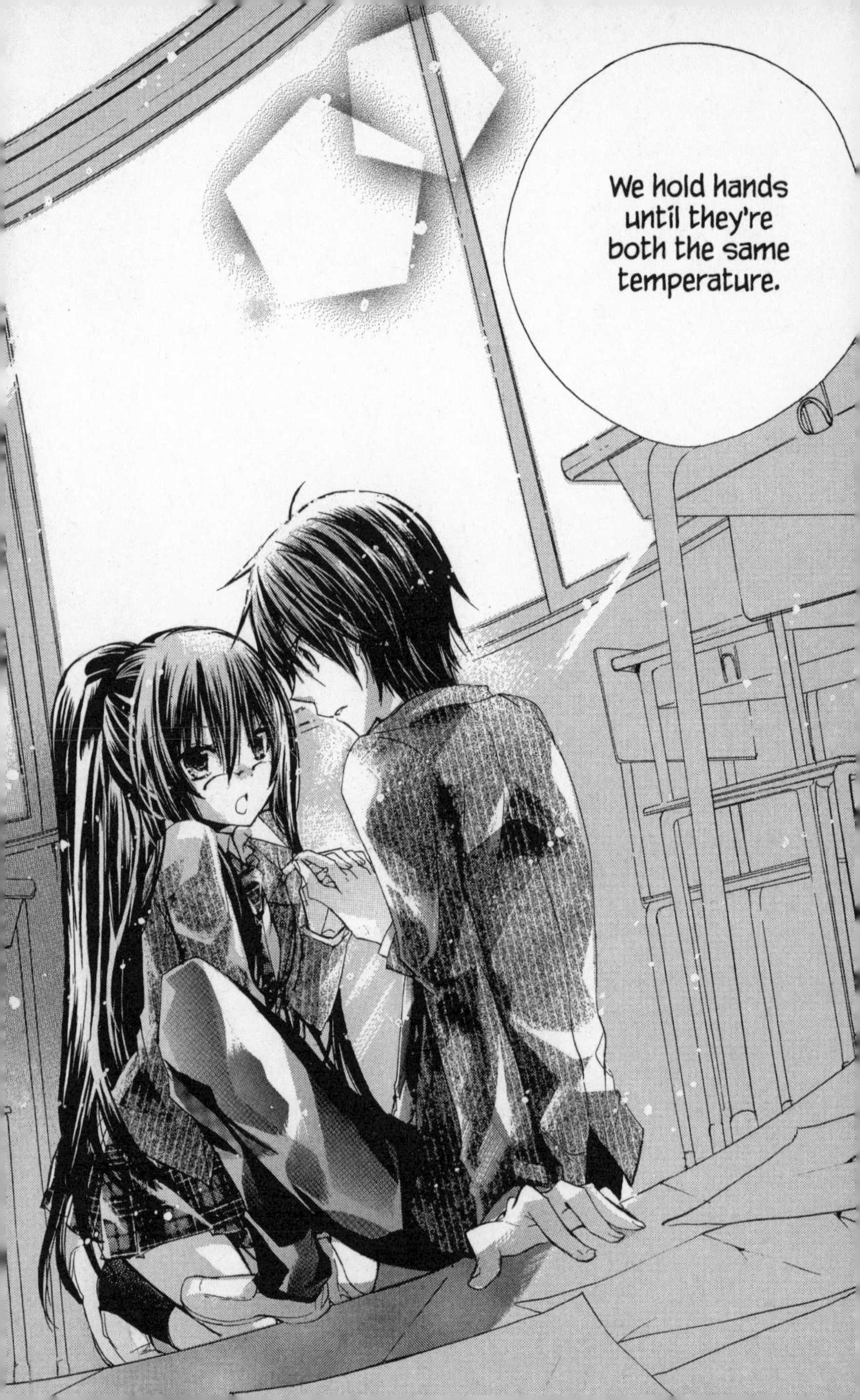
We hold hands until they're both the same temperature.

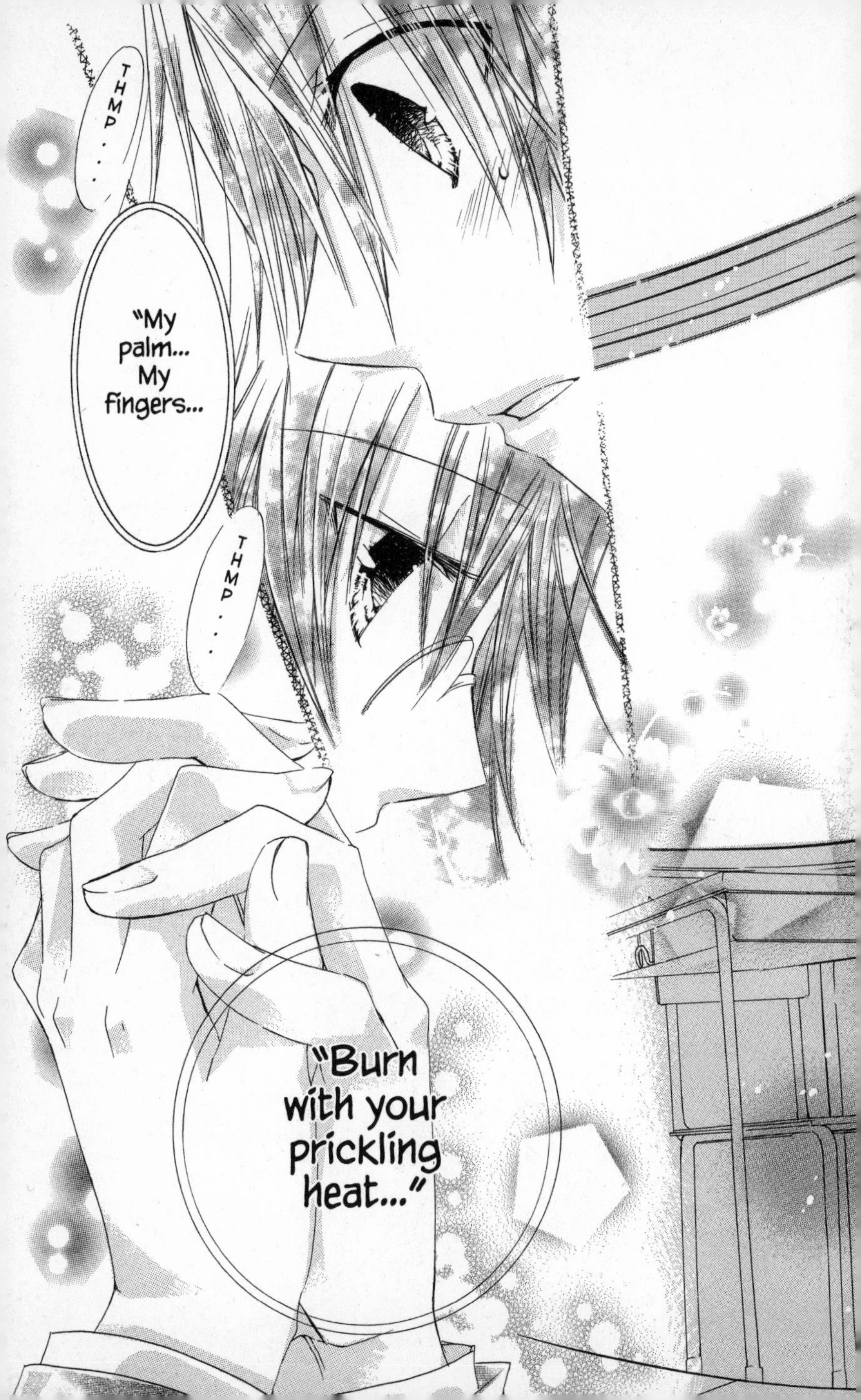
THMP...
"My palm... My fingers...
THMP...
"Burn with your prickling heat..."

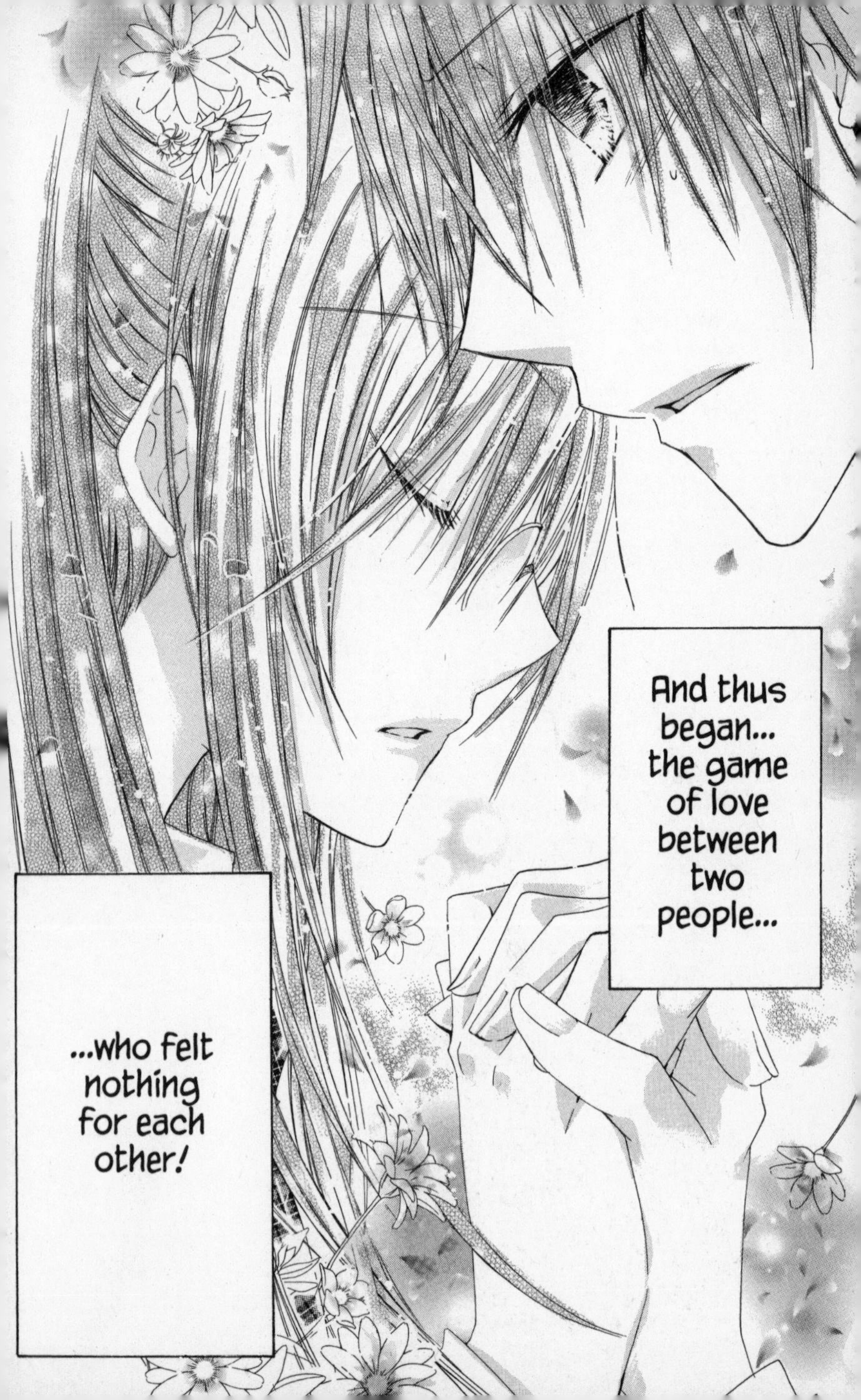
And thus began... the game of love between two people...
...who felt nothing for each other!

Missions of Love

**It is time for love.
Secret cell phone
novelist vs. the most
popular boy in school.
A mission of love for
absolute servitude.**

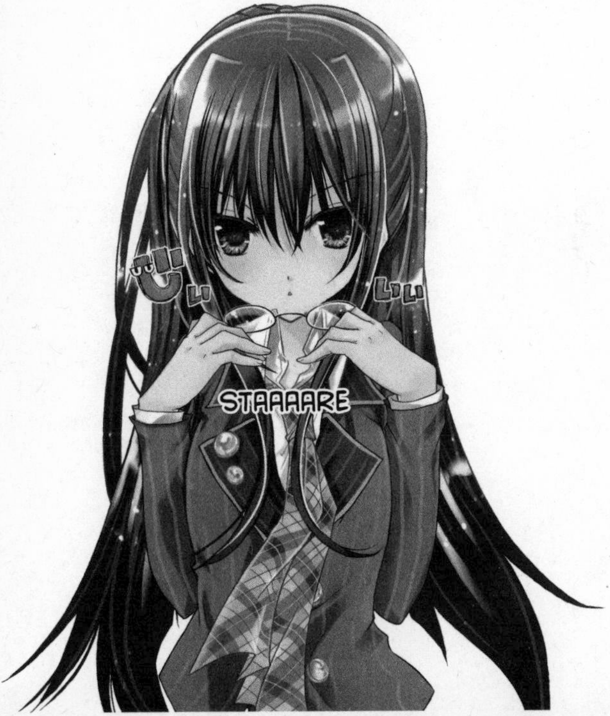
STAAAARE

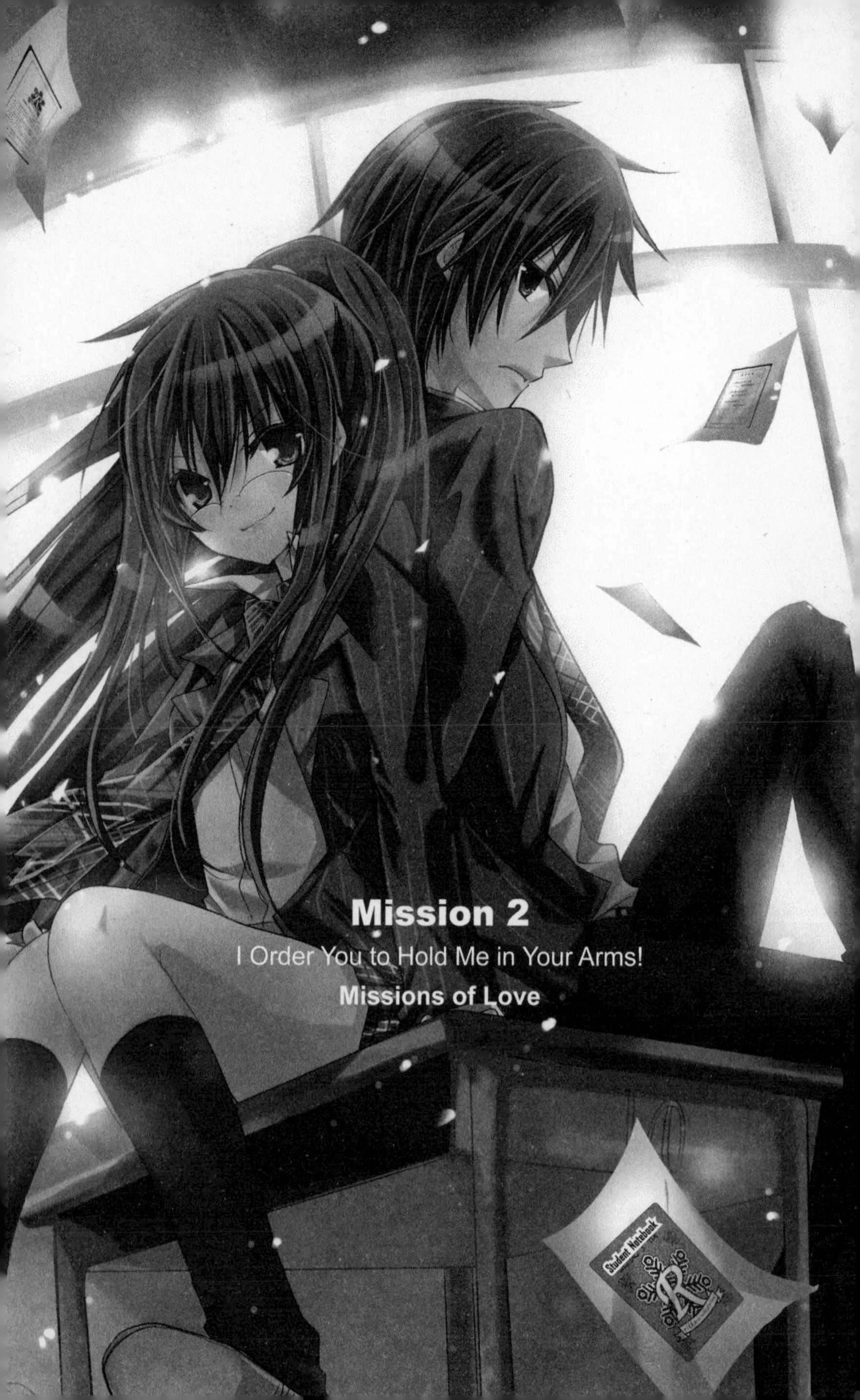
Student Notebook

Mission 2

I Order You to Hold Me in Your Arms!

Missions of Love

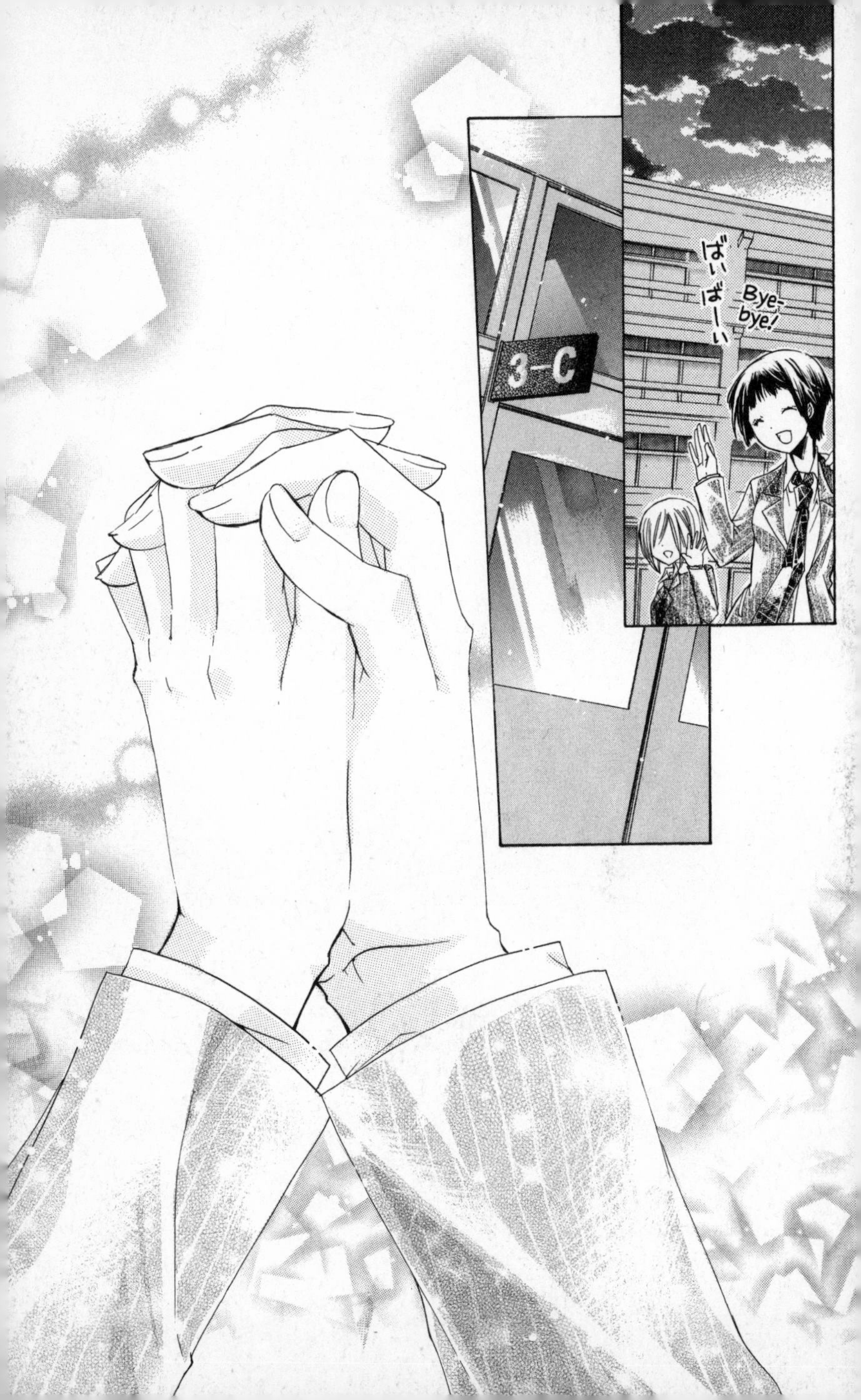
3-C
ばいばーい
Bye-bye!

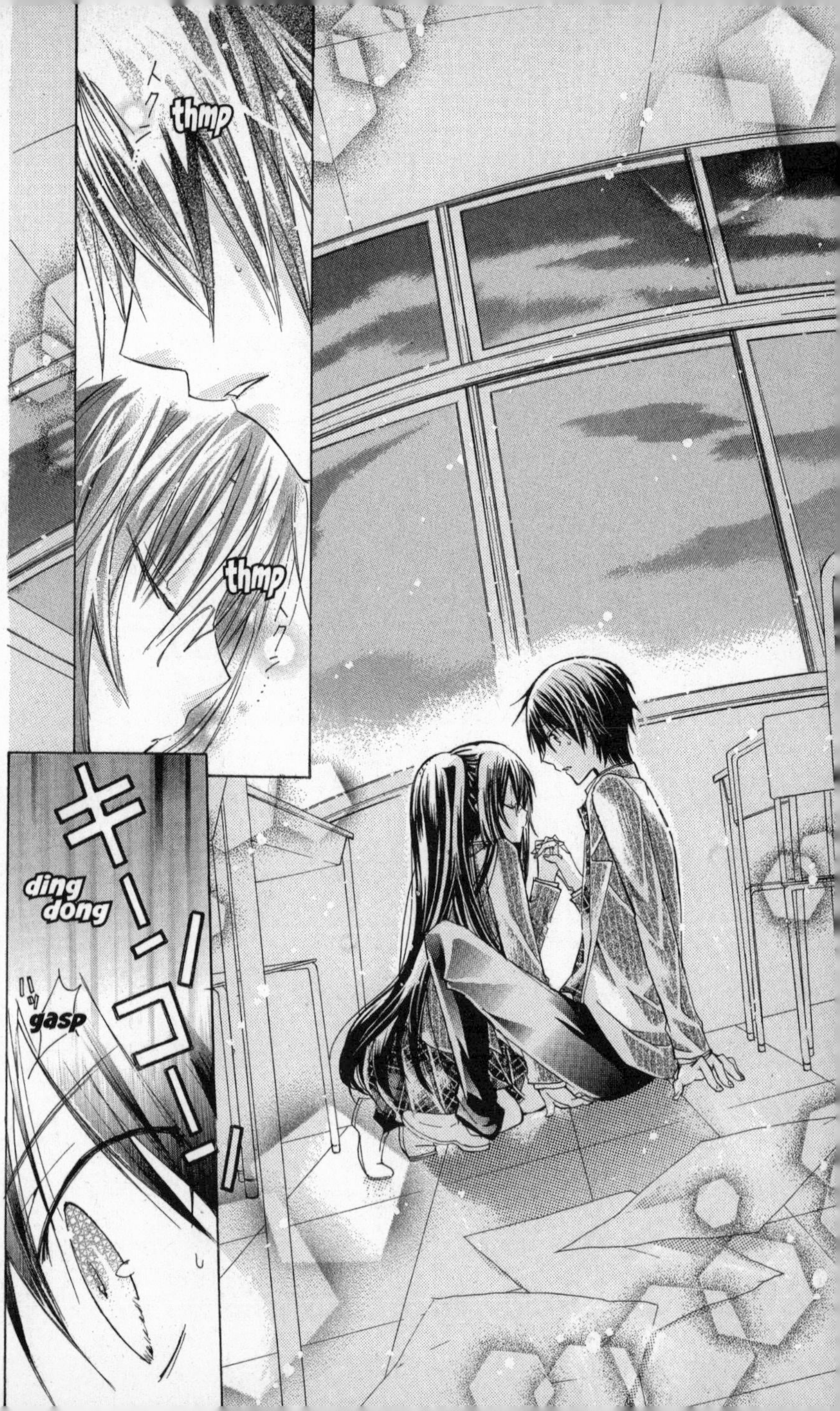
thmp
thmp
キーンコーン
ding dong
ハッ
gasp

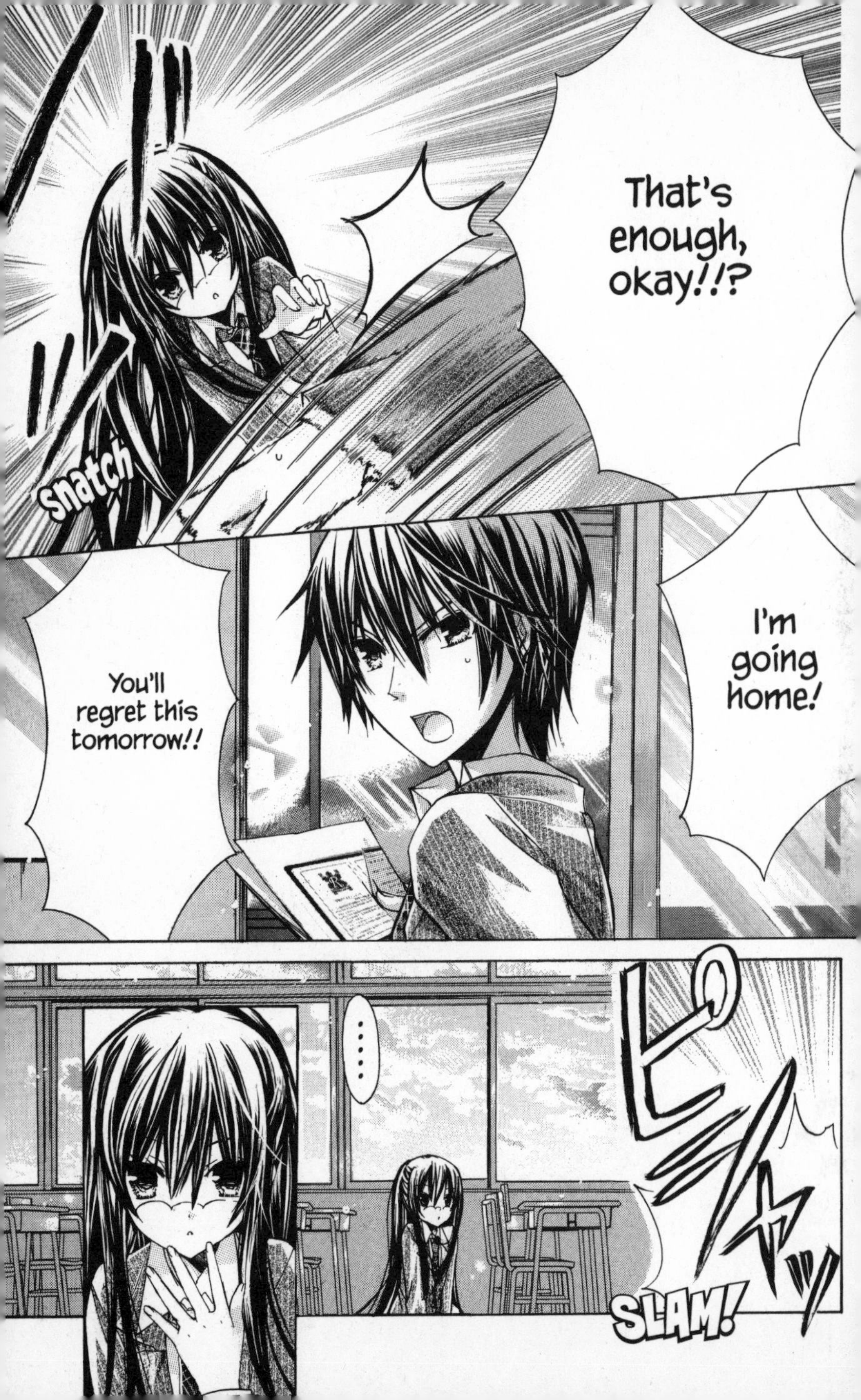
That's enough, okay!!?
snatch
I'm going home!
You'll regret this tomorrow!!
SLAM!
……

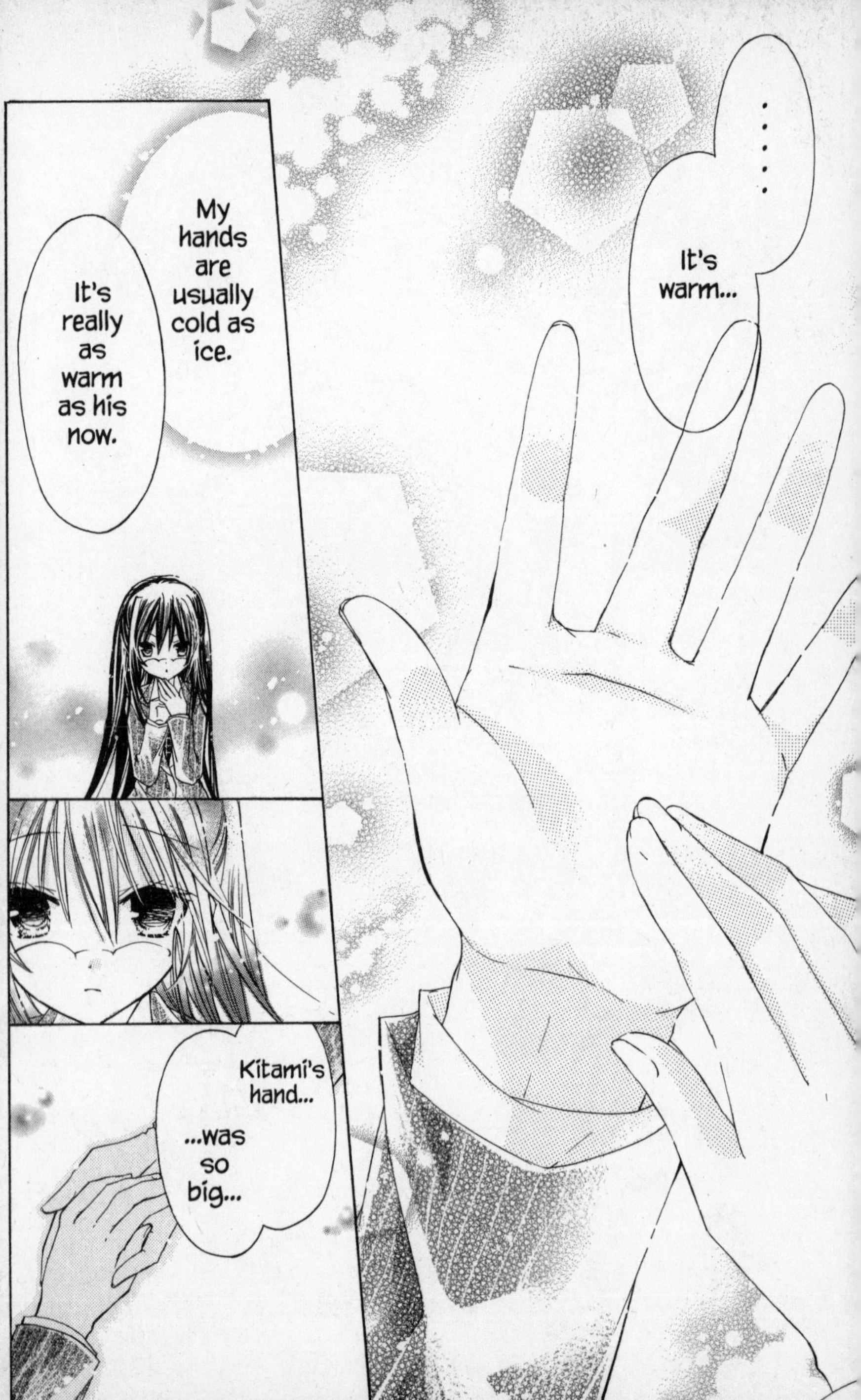
......
It's warm...
My hands are usually cold as ice.
It's really as warm as his now.
Kitami's hand...
...was so big...

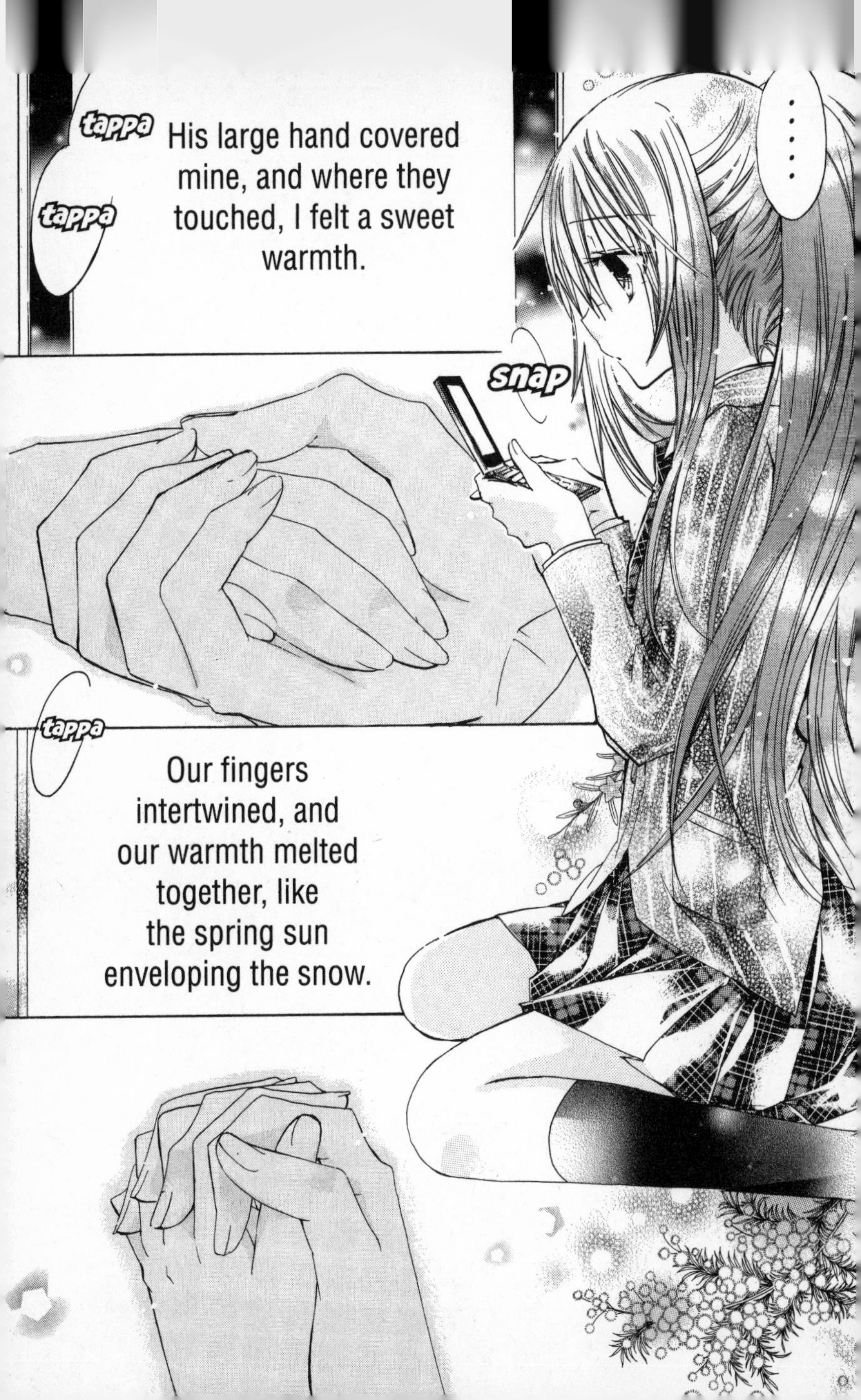

......
snap
His large hand covered mine, and where they touched, I felt a sweet warmth.
tappa
tappa
tappa
Our fingers intertwined, and our warmth melted together, like the spring sun enveloping the snow.

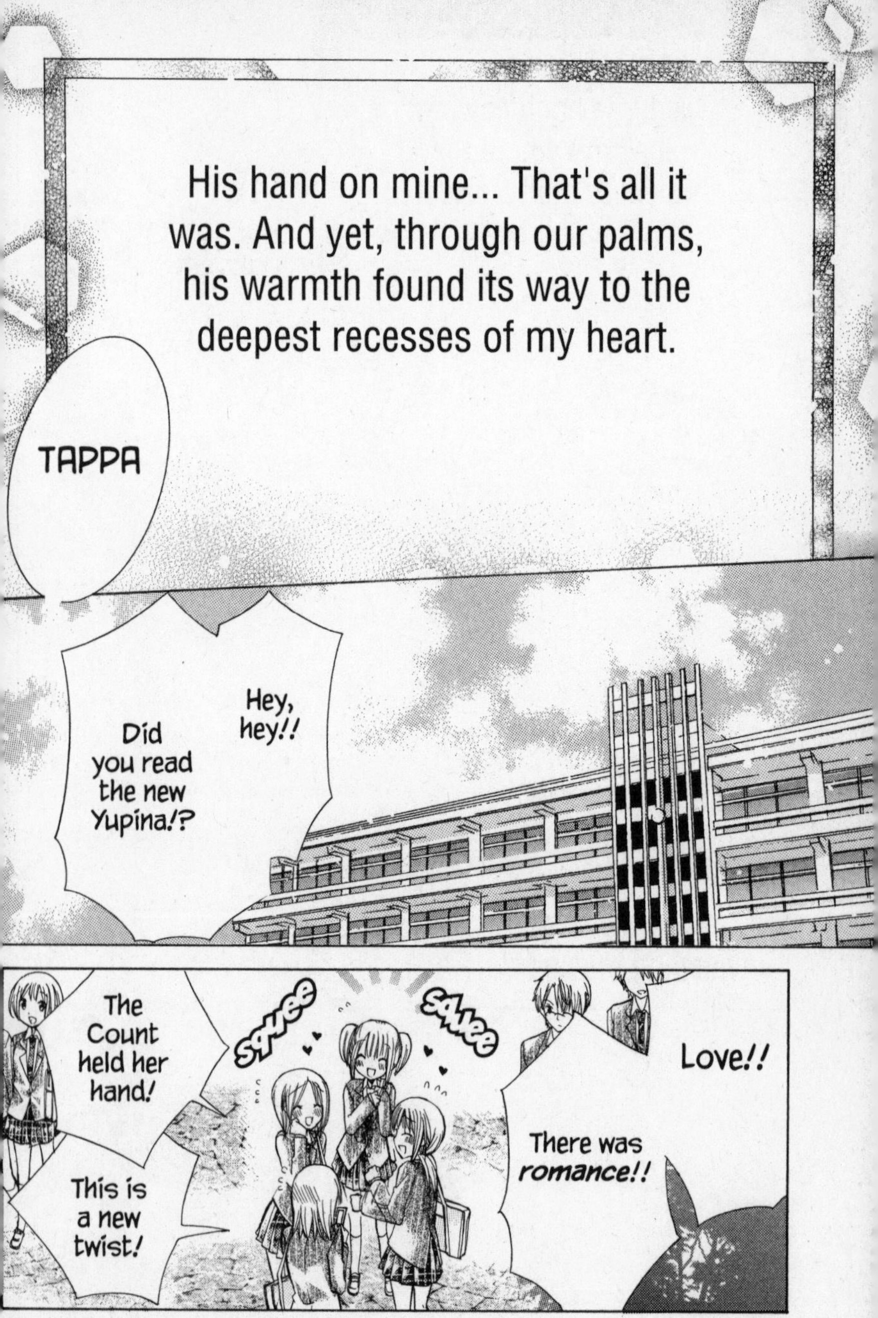
His hand on mine... That's all it was. And yet, through our palms, his warmth found its way to the deepest recesses of my heart.
TAPPA
Hey, hey!!
Did you read the new Yupina!?
Love!!
There was *romance*!!
Squee
Squee
The Count held her hand!
This is a new twist!

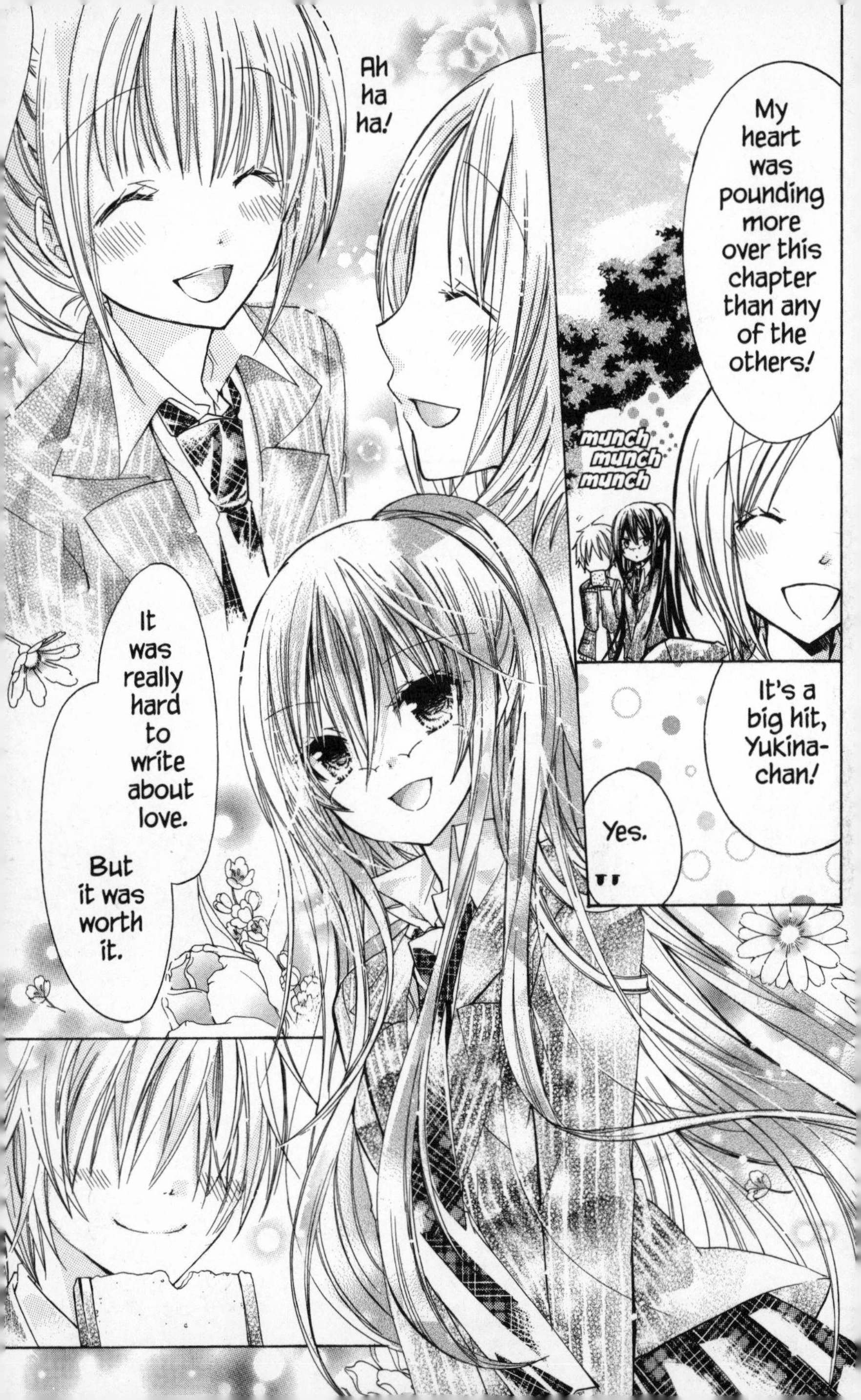
My heart was pounding more over this chapter than any of the others!
munch munch munch
It's a big hit, Yukina-chan!
Yes.
Ah ha ha!
It was really hard to write about love.
But it was worth it.

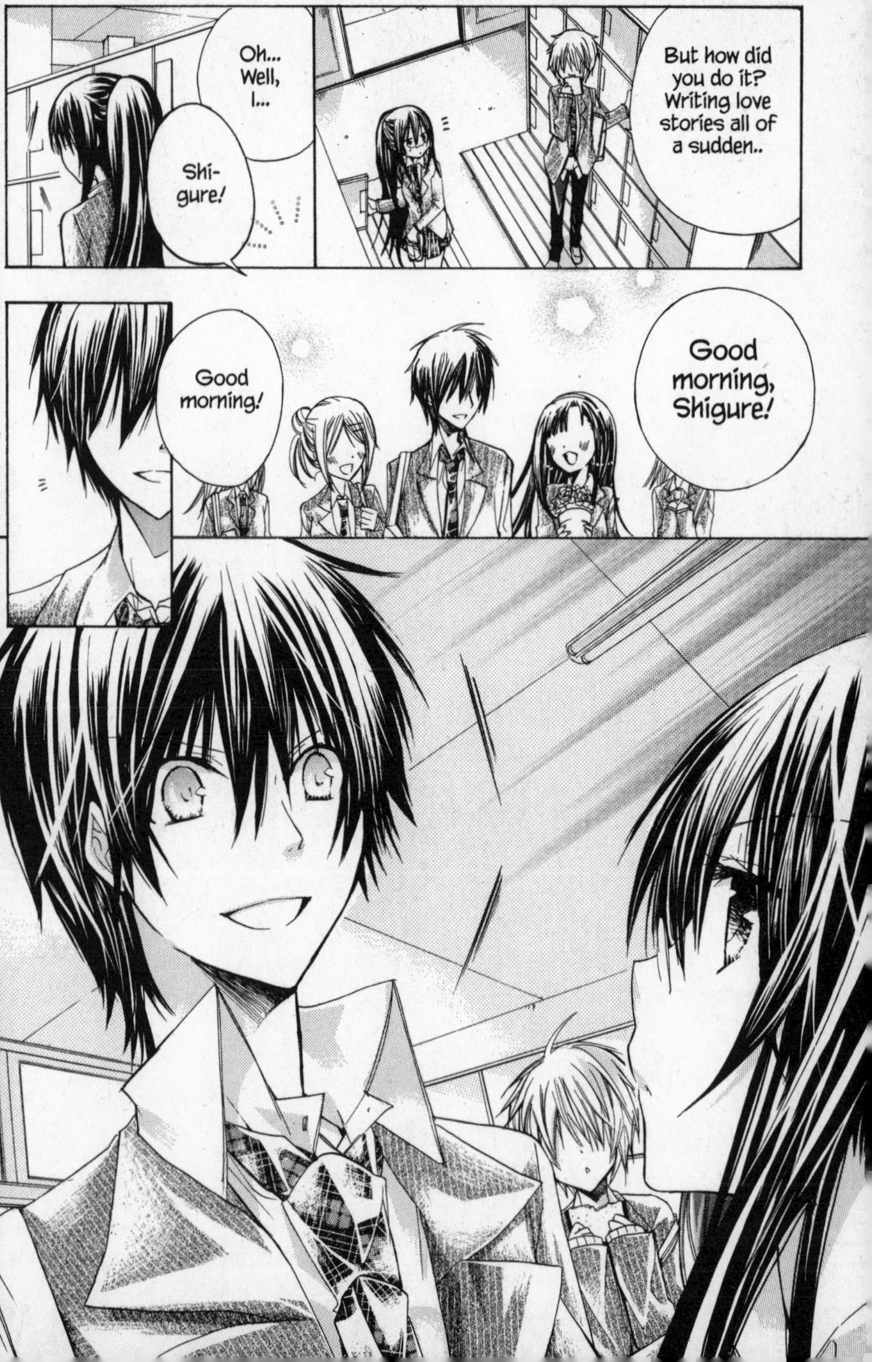
But how did you do it? Writing love stories all of a sudden..
Oh... Well, I...
Shi-gure!
Good morning, Shigure!
Good morning!

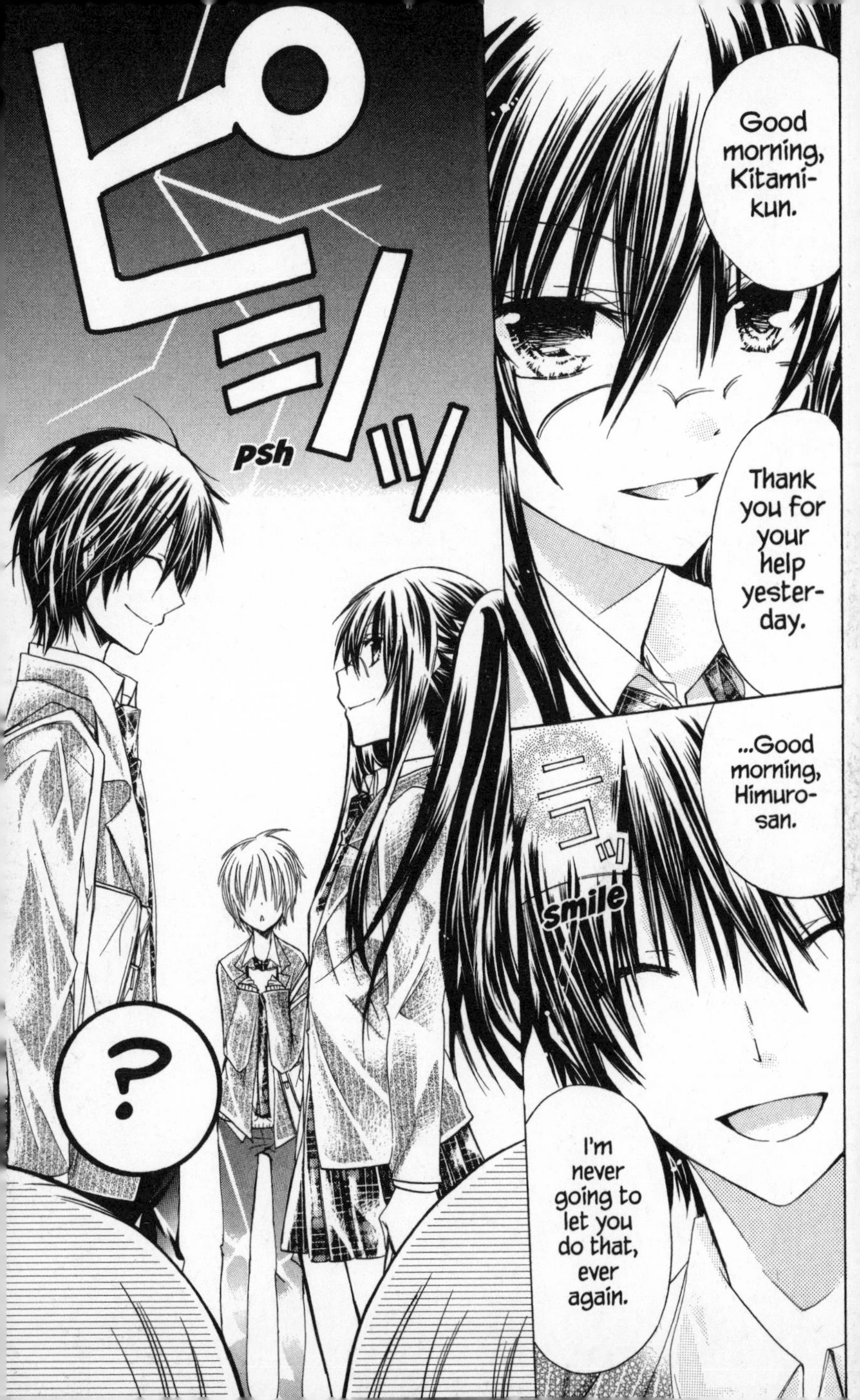
Good morning, Kitami-kun.
Thank you for your help yesterday.
...Good morning, Himuro-san.
smile
I'm never going to let you do that, ever again.
Psh
?

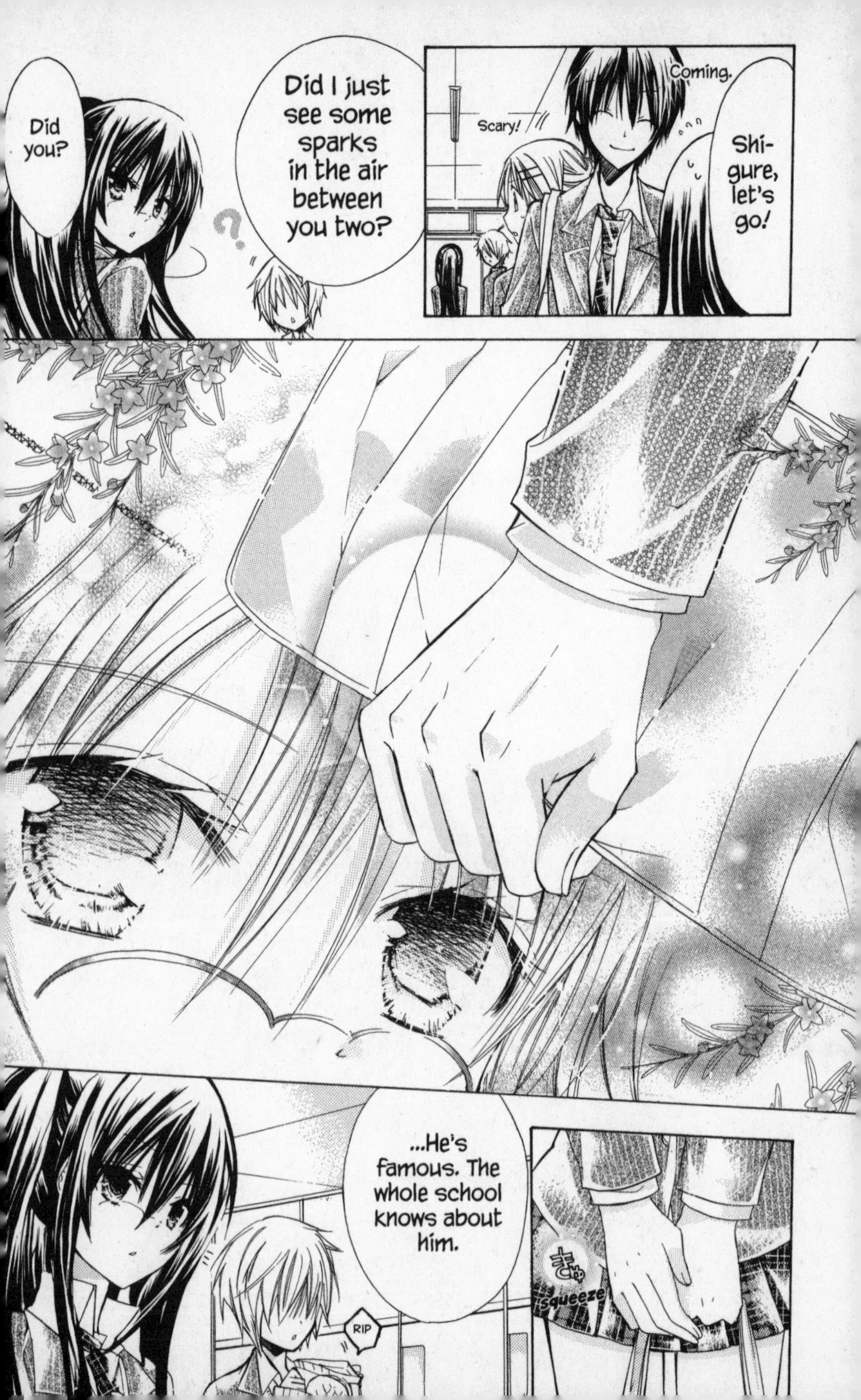
Shigure, let's go!
Coming.
Scary!
Did I just see some sparks in the air between you two?
Did you?
squeeze
...He's famous. The whole school knows about him.
RIP

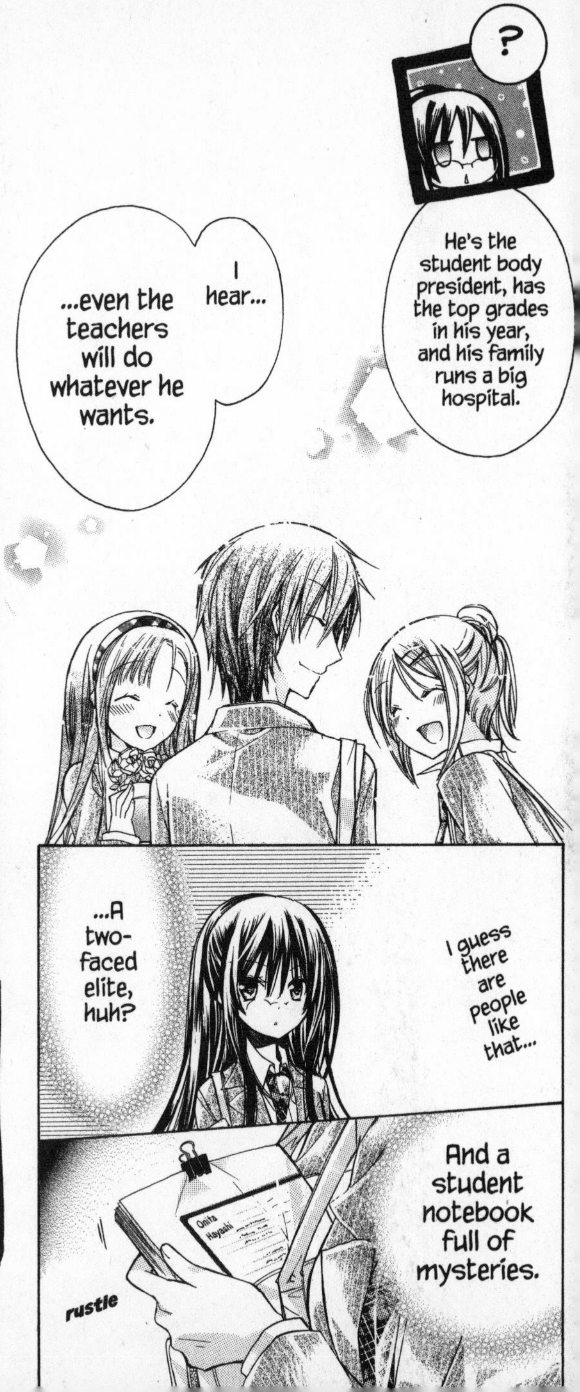
?
He's the student body president, has the top grades in his year, and his family runs a big hospital.
I hear...
...even the teachers will do whatever he wants.
I guess there are people like that...
...A two-faced elite, huh?
And a student notebook full of mysteries.
Onita
Hayashi
rustle

Mini Character

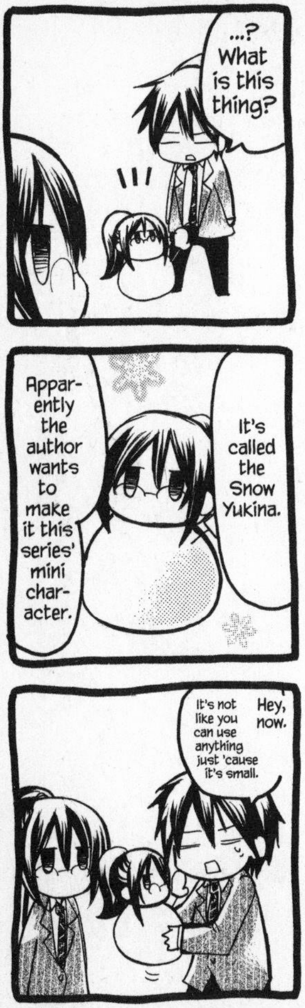
...? What is this thing?
It's called the Snow Yukina.
Apparently the author wants to make it this series' mini character.
Hey, now.
It's not like you can use anything just 'cause it's small.
!
fzh

Special Feature: It melts fast

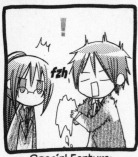

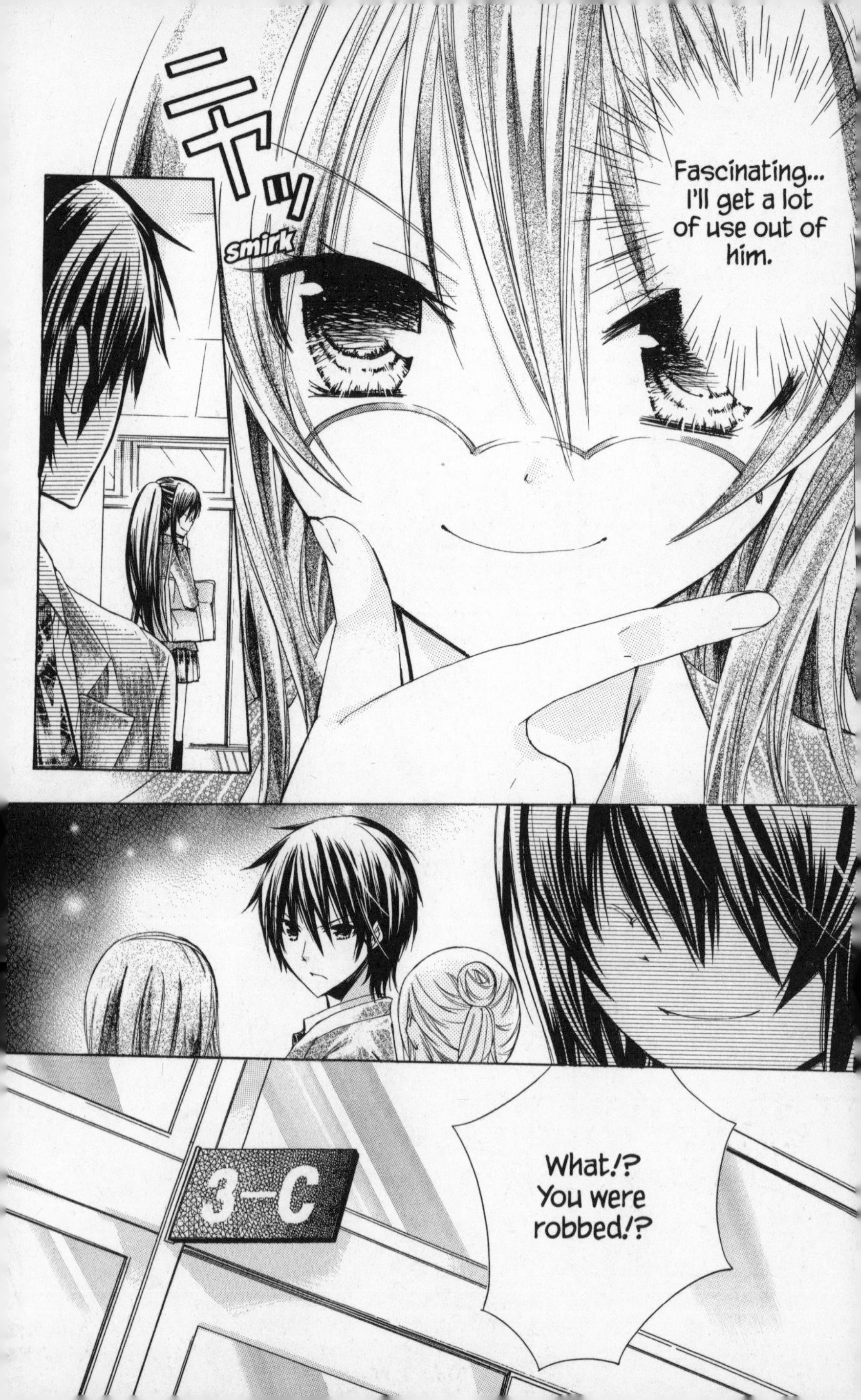
Fascinating... I'll get a lot of use out of him.
ニヤッ
smirk
3-C
What!? You were robbed!?

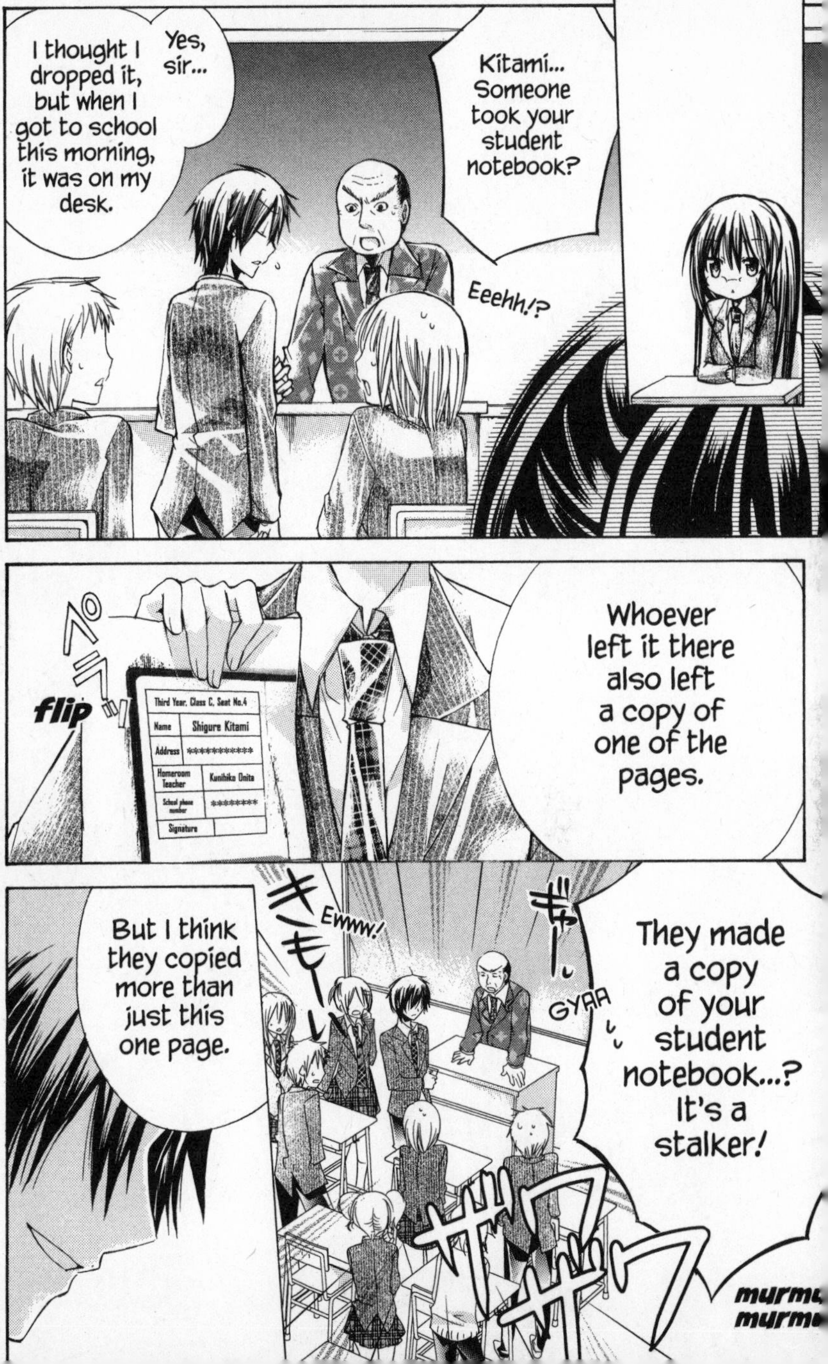
Kitami... Someone took your student notebook?
Eeehh!?
Yes, sir...
I thought I dropped it, but when I got to school this morning, it was on my desk.
Whoever left it there also left a copy of one of the pages.
flip
Third Year, Class C, Seat No.4
Name Shigure Kitami
Address ***********
Homeroom Teacher Kunihiko Onita
School phone number ********
Signature
They made a copy of your student notebook...? It's a stalker!
murmu
murmu
GYAA
EWWW!
But I think they copied more than just this one page.

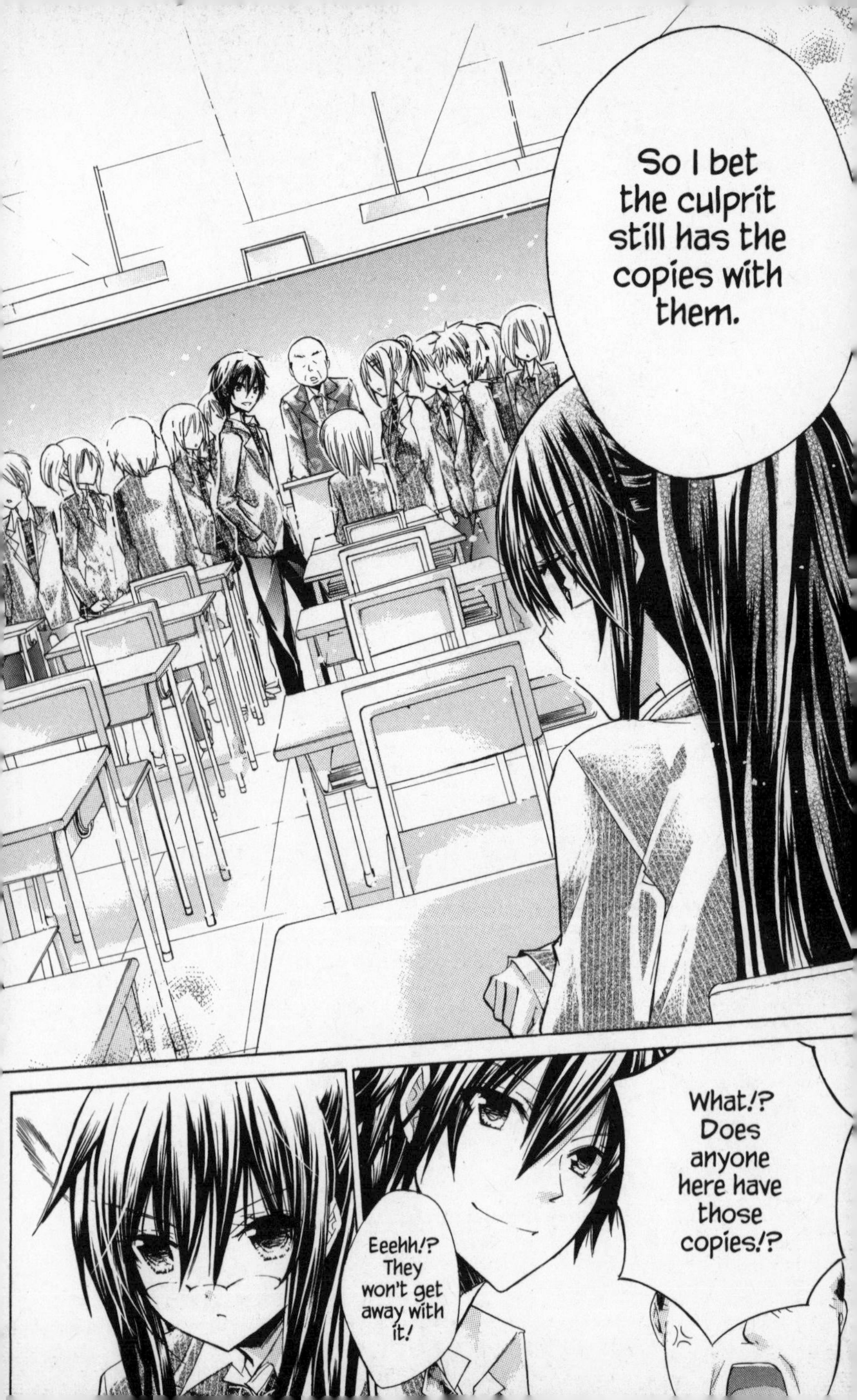
So I bet the culprit still has the copies with them.
What!? Does anyone here have those copies!?
Eeehh!? They won't get away with it!

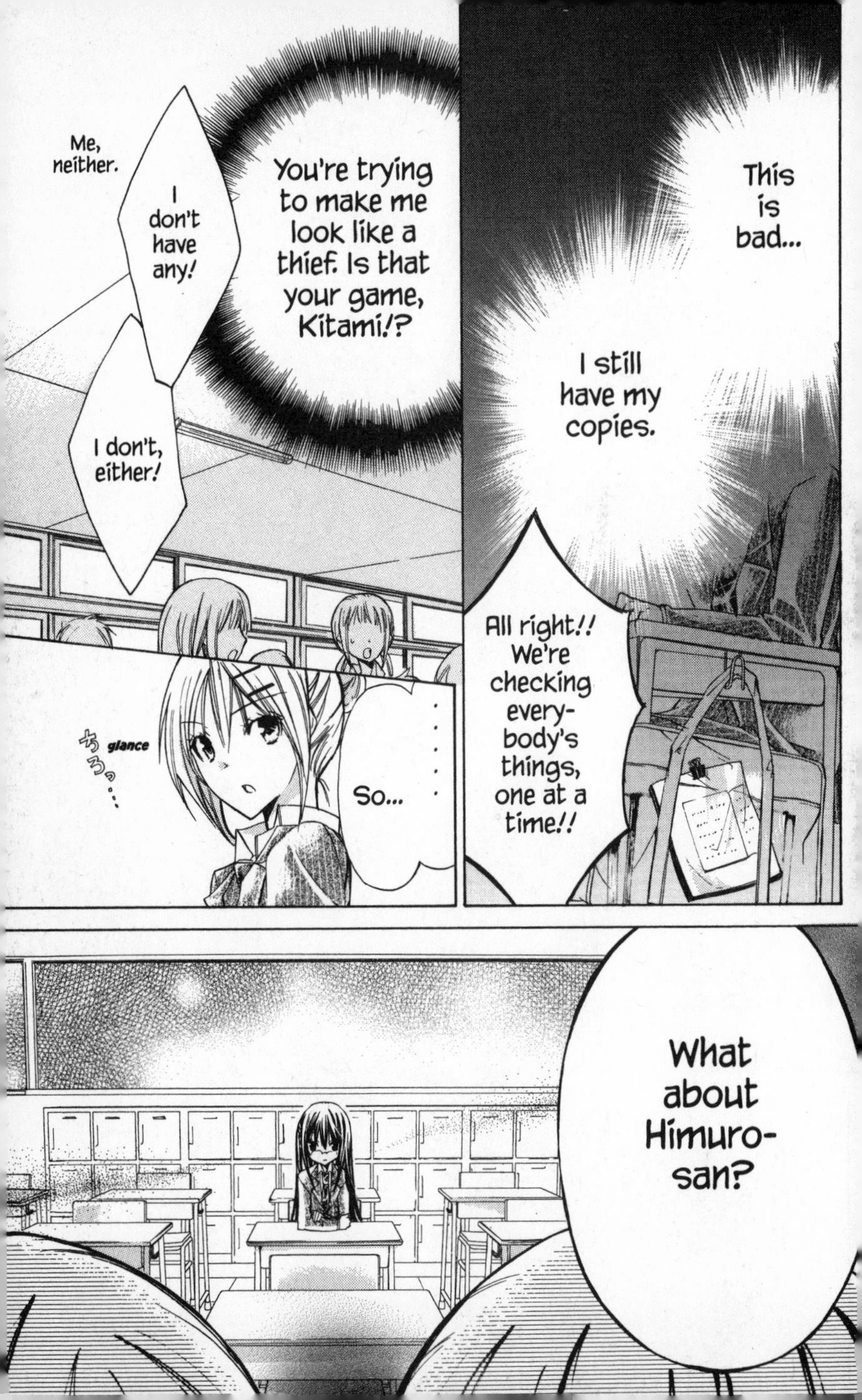
This is bad...
I still have my copies.
All right!! We're checking everybody's things, one at a time!!
You're trying to make me look like a thief. Is that your game, Kitami!?
I don't have any!
Me, neither.
I don't, either!
......
So...
glance
What about Himuro-san?

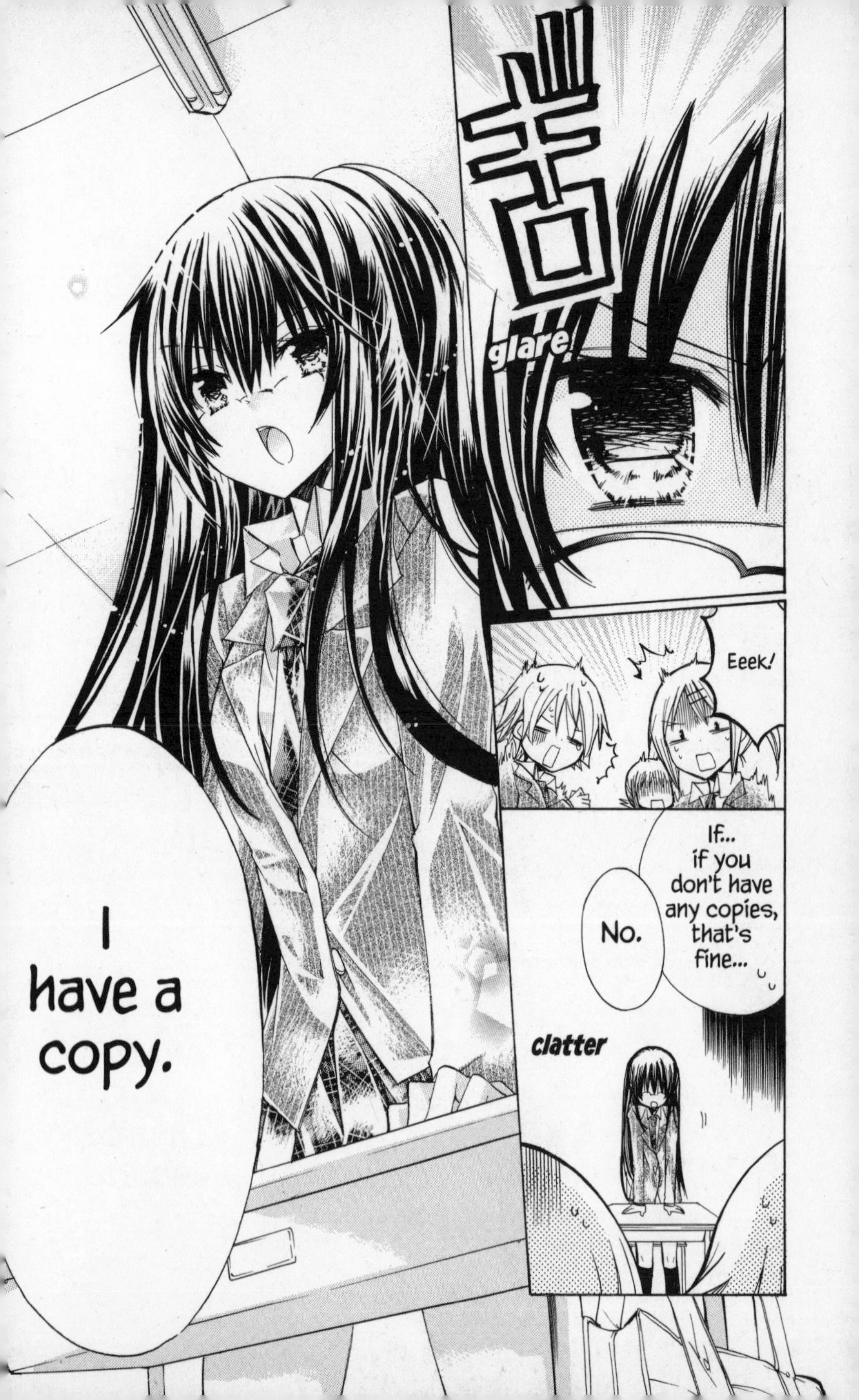

ギロ
glare!
Eeek!
If... if you don't have any copies, that's fine...
No.
clatter
I have a copy.

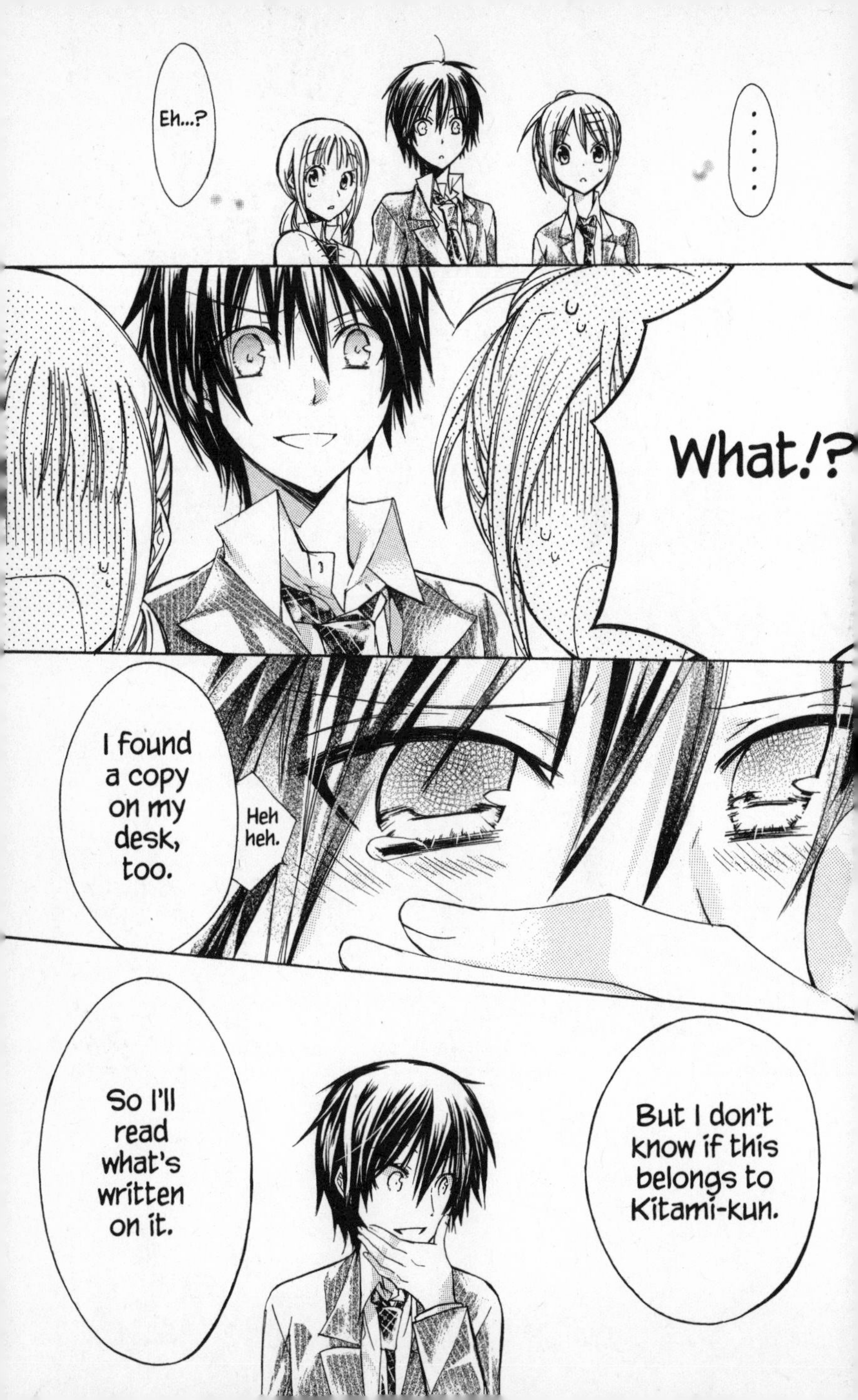
......
Eh...?
What!?
Heh heh.
I found a copy on my desk, too.
But I don't know if this belongs to Kitami-kun.
So I'll read what's written on it.

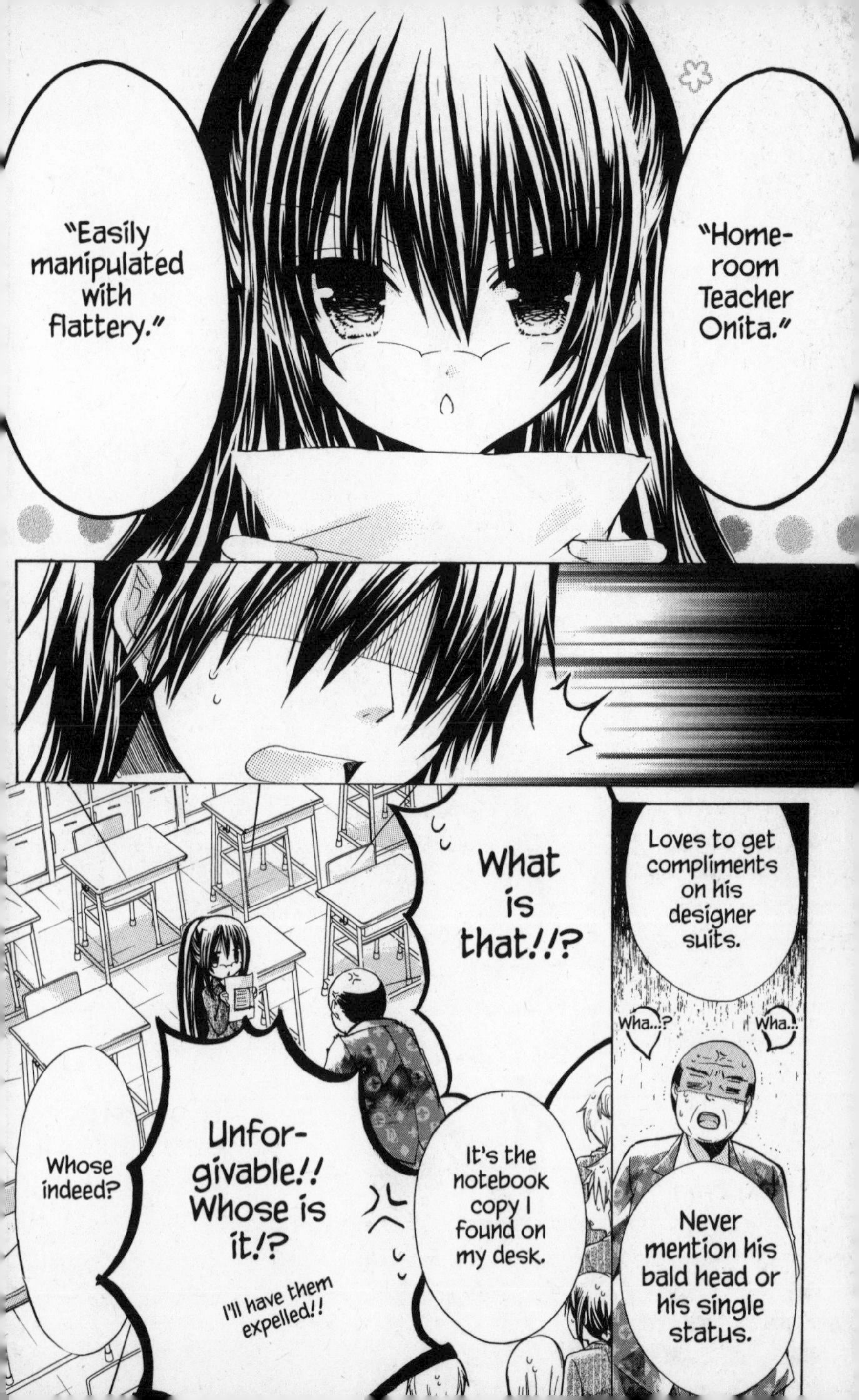
"Home-room Teacher Onita."
"Easily manipulated with flattery."
Loves to get compliments on his designer suits.
Wha...
Wha...?
Never mention his bald head or his single status.
What is that!!?
It's the notebook copy I found on my desk.
Unfor-givable!! Whose is it!?
I'll have them expelled!!
Whose indeed?

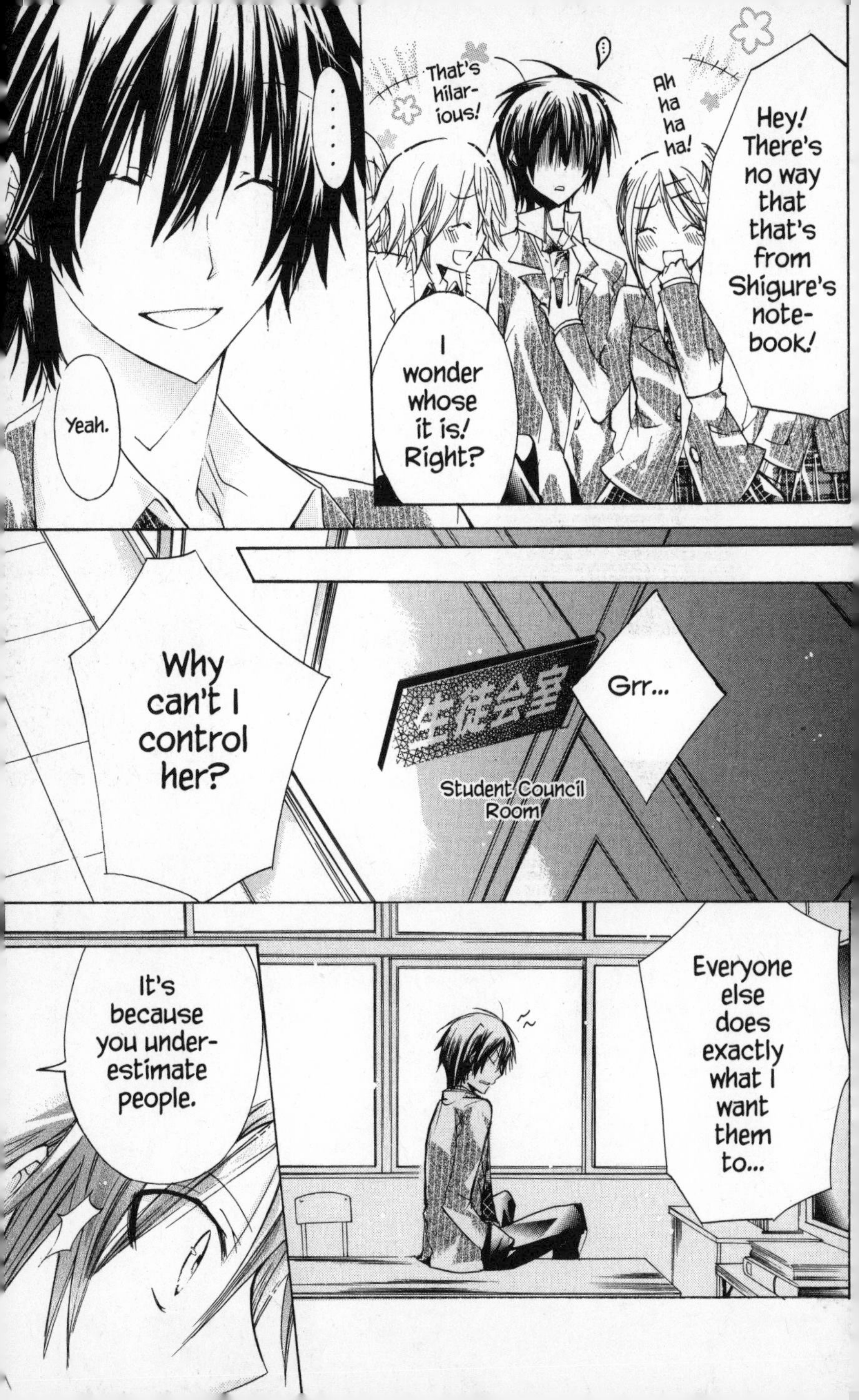
Hey! There's no way that that's from Shigure's notebook!
Ah ha ha ha!
That's hilarious!
...
I wonder whose it is! Right?
......
Yeah.
Grr...
Student Council Room
Why can't I control her?
Everyone else does exactly what I want them to...
It's because you under-estimate people.

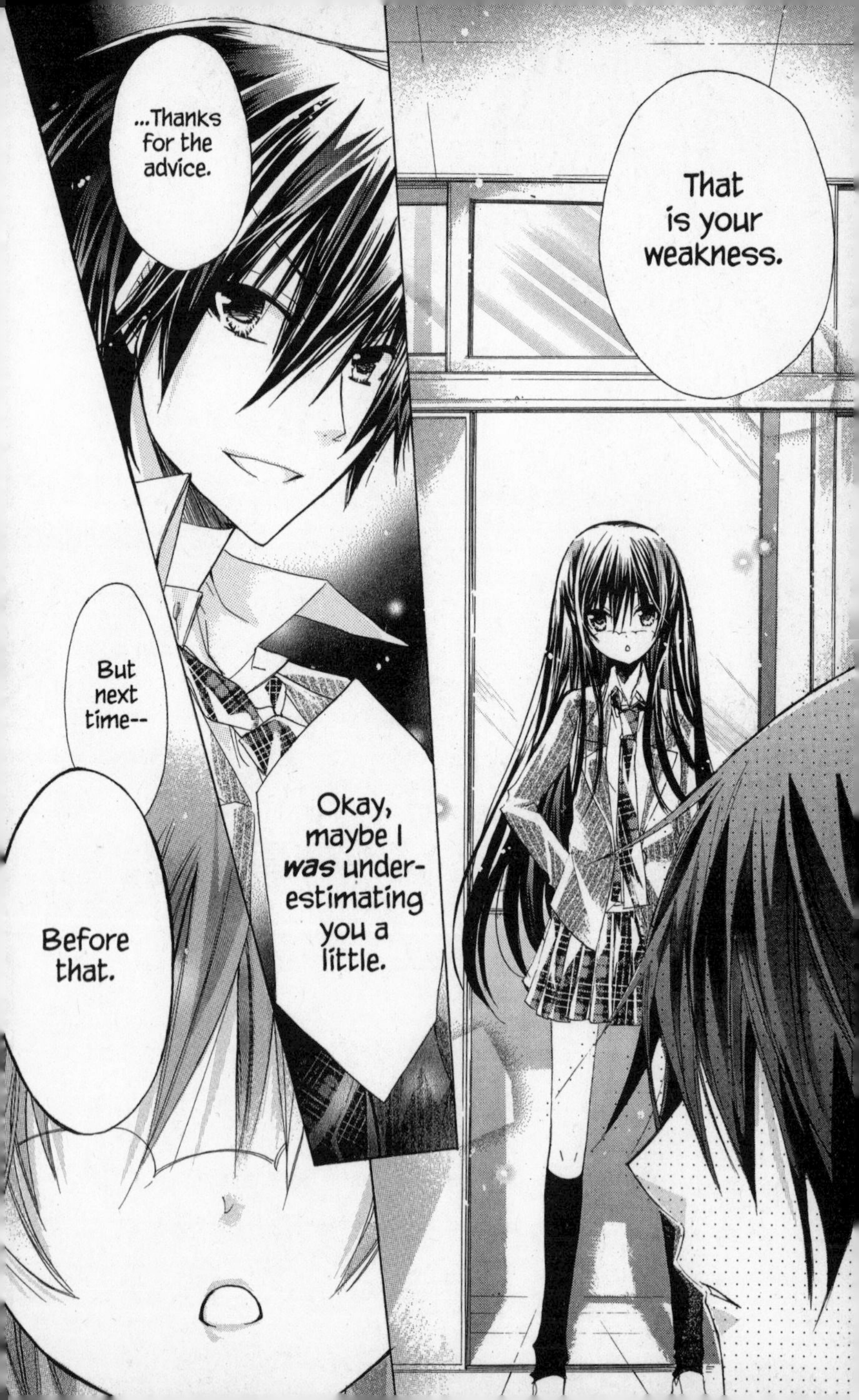
That is your weakness.
...Thanks for the advice.
Okay, maybe I *was* under-estimating you a little.
But next time--
Before that.

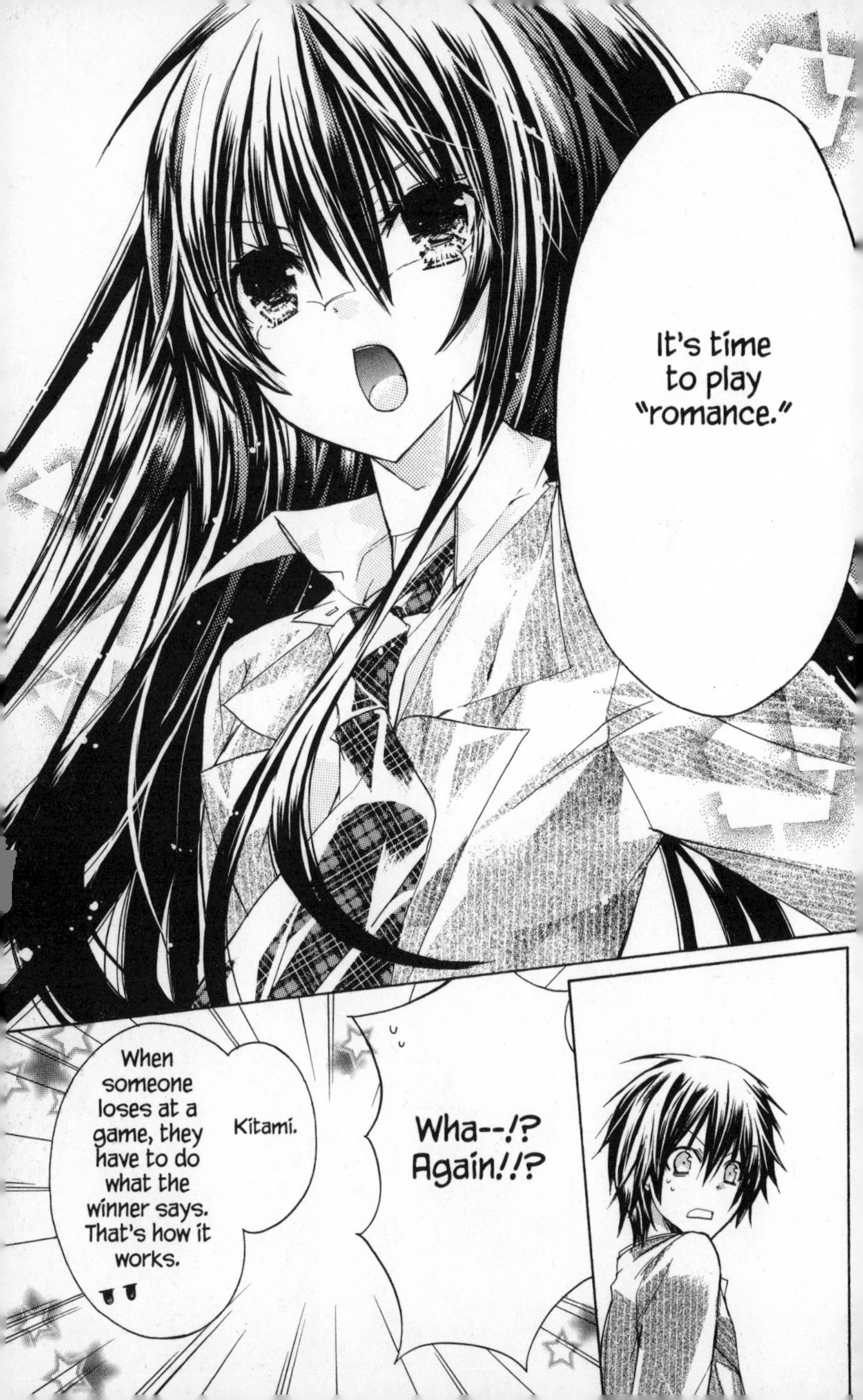
It's time to play "romance."
Wha--!? Again!!?
Kitami.
When someone loses at a game, they have to do what the winner says. That's how it works.

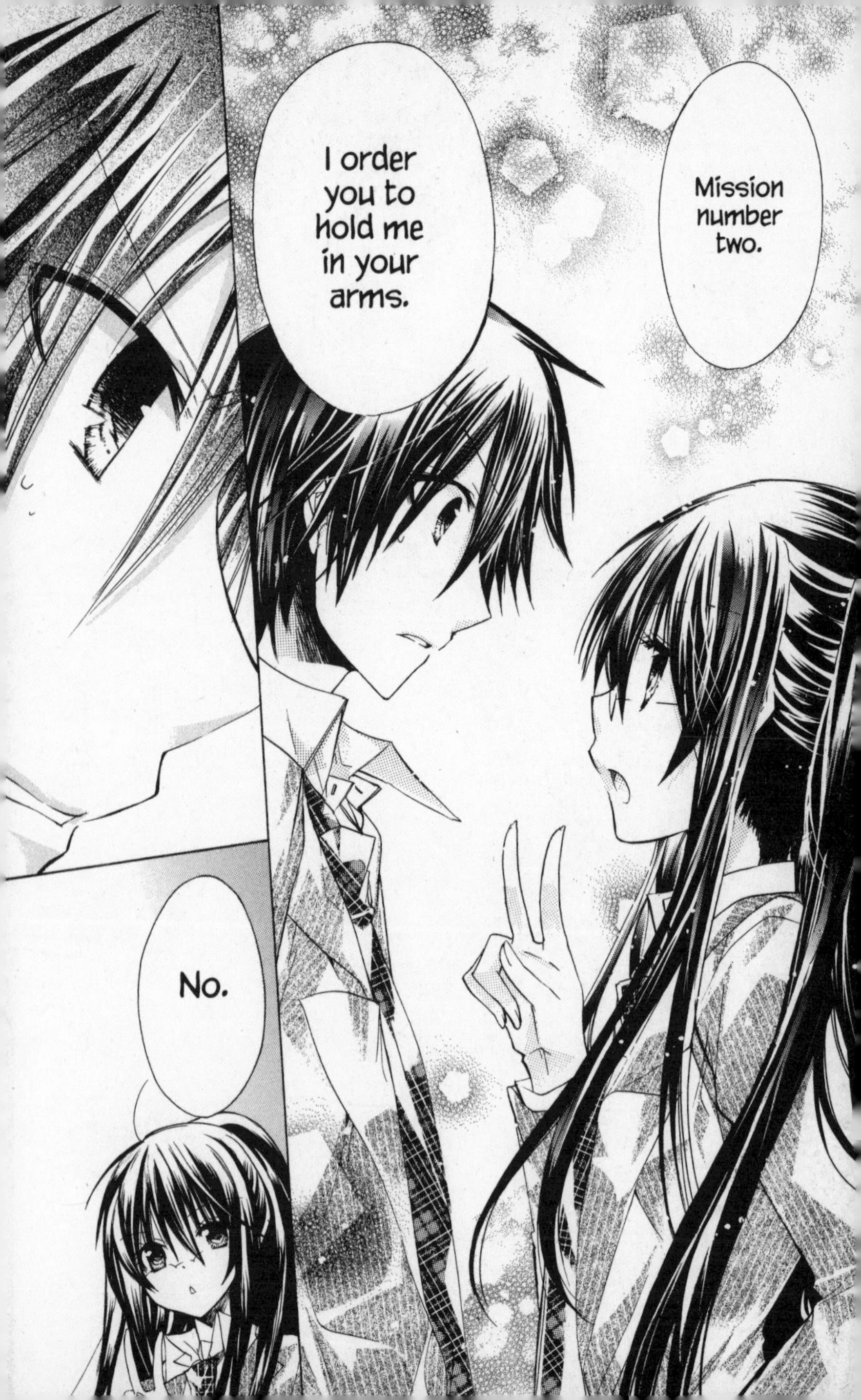
Mission number two.
I order you to hold me in your arms.
No.

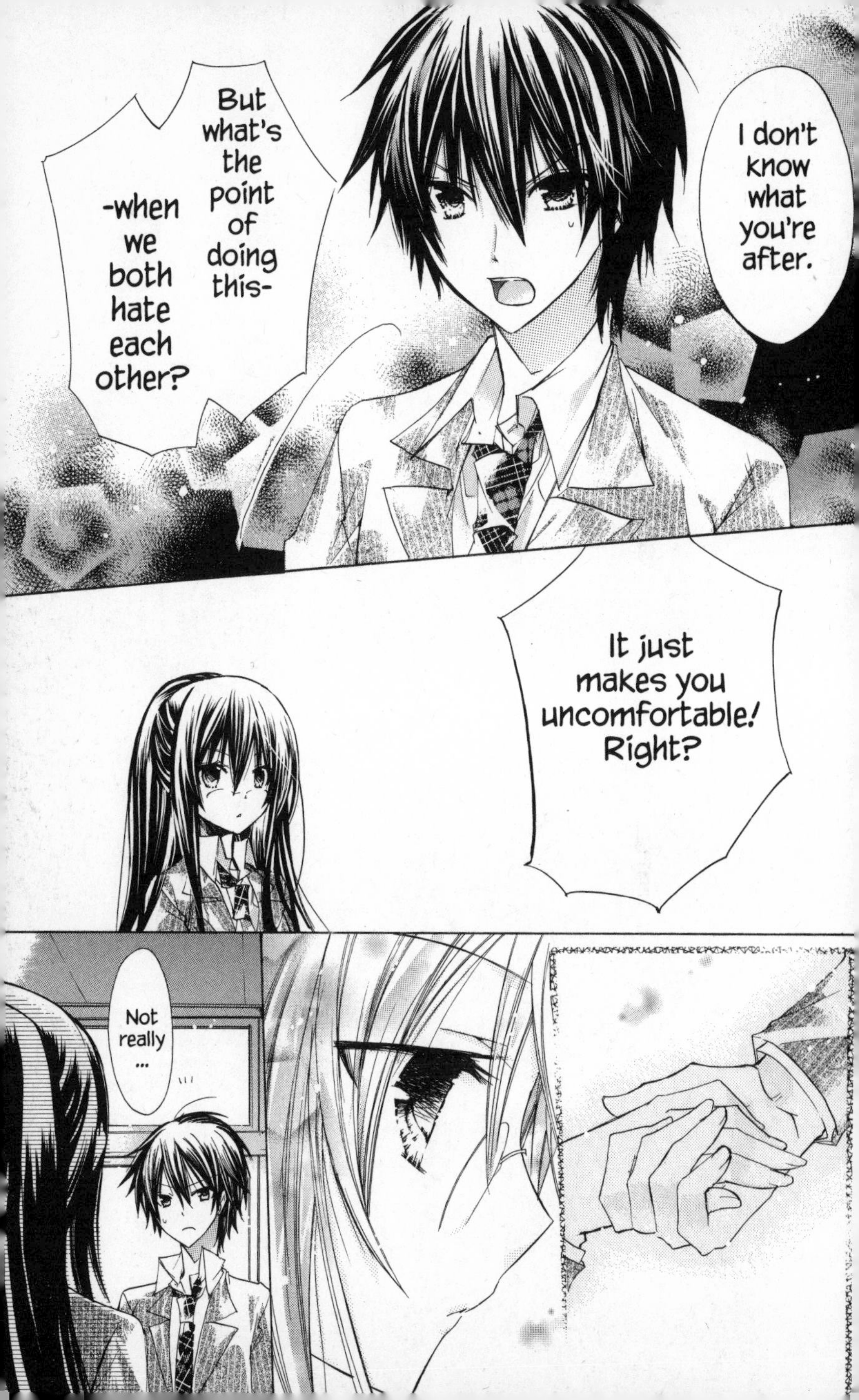
I don't know what you're after.
But what's the point of doing this-
-when we both hate each other?
It just makes you uncomfortable! Right?
Not really ...

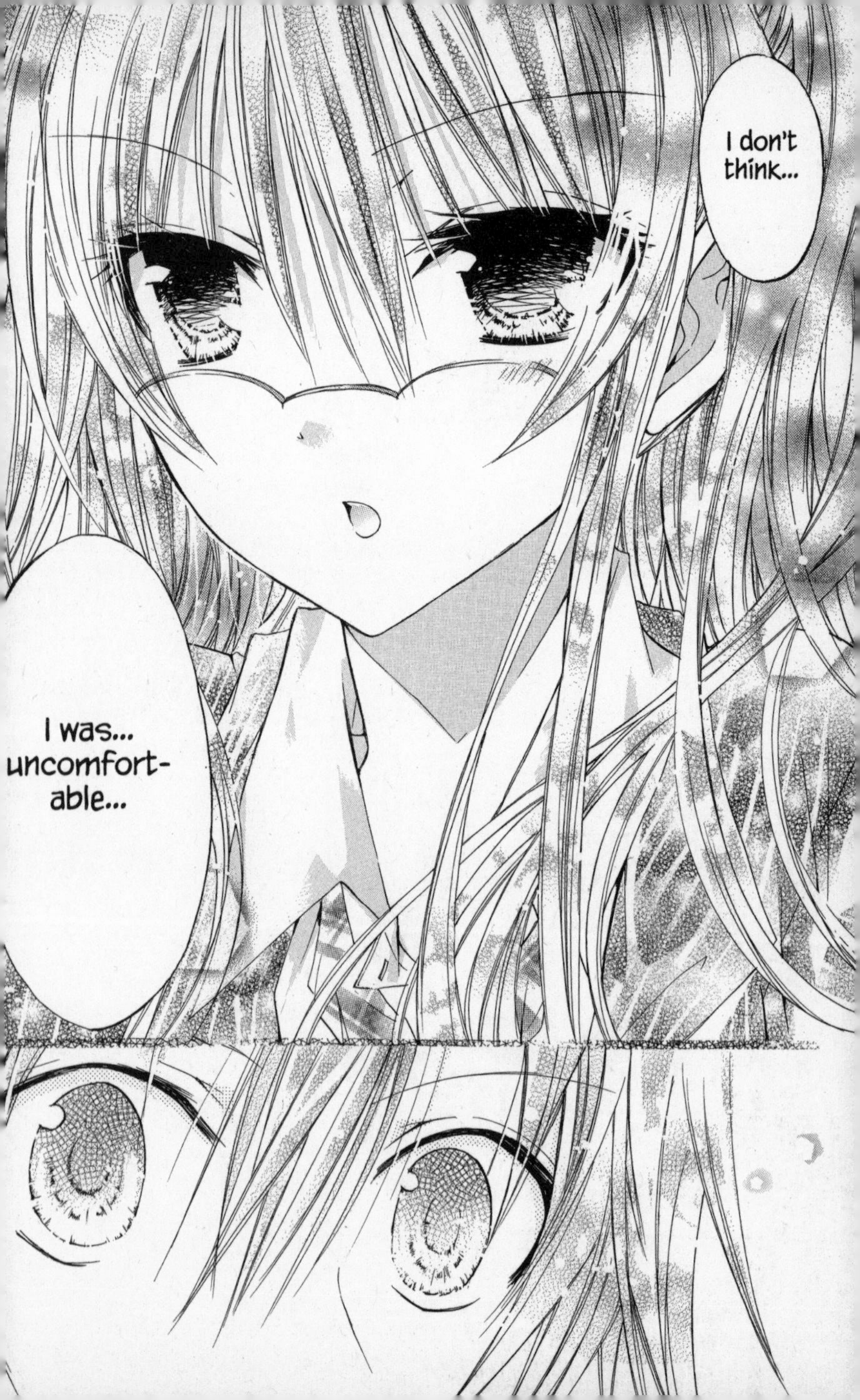
I don't think...
I was... uncomfort-able...

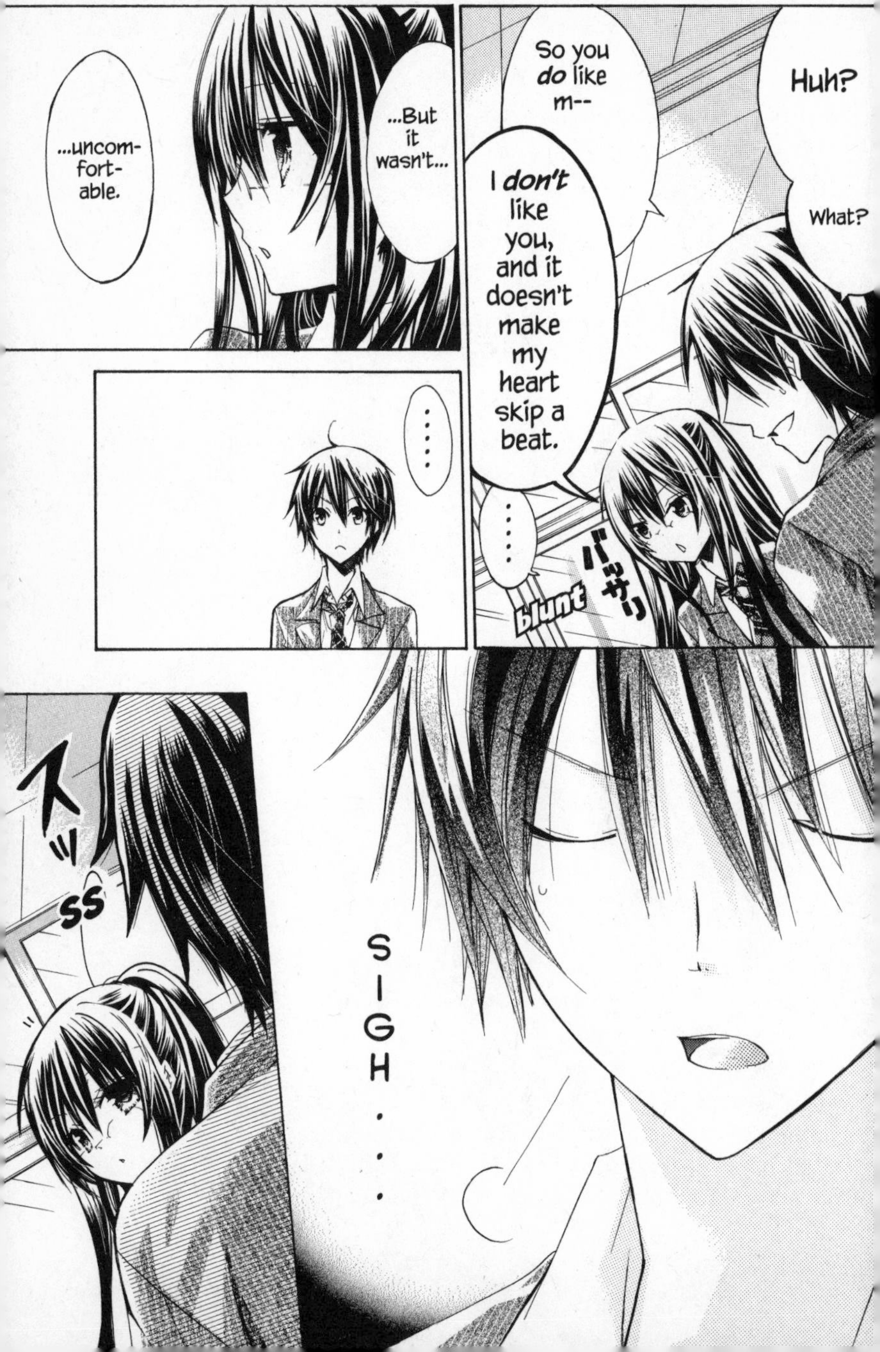

Huh?
What?
So you *do* like m--
I *don't* like you, and it doesn't make my heart skip a beat.
......
バッサリ
blunt
...But it wasn't...
...uncomfortable.
......
SIGH...
スッ
SS

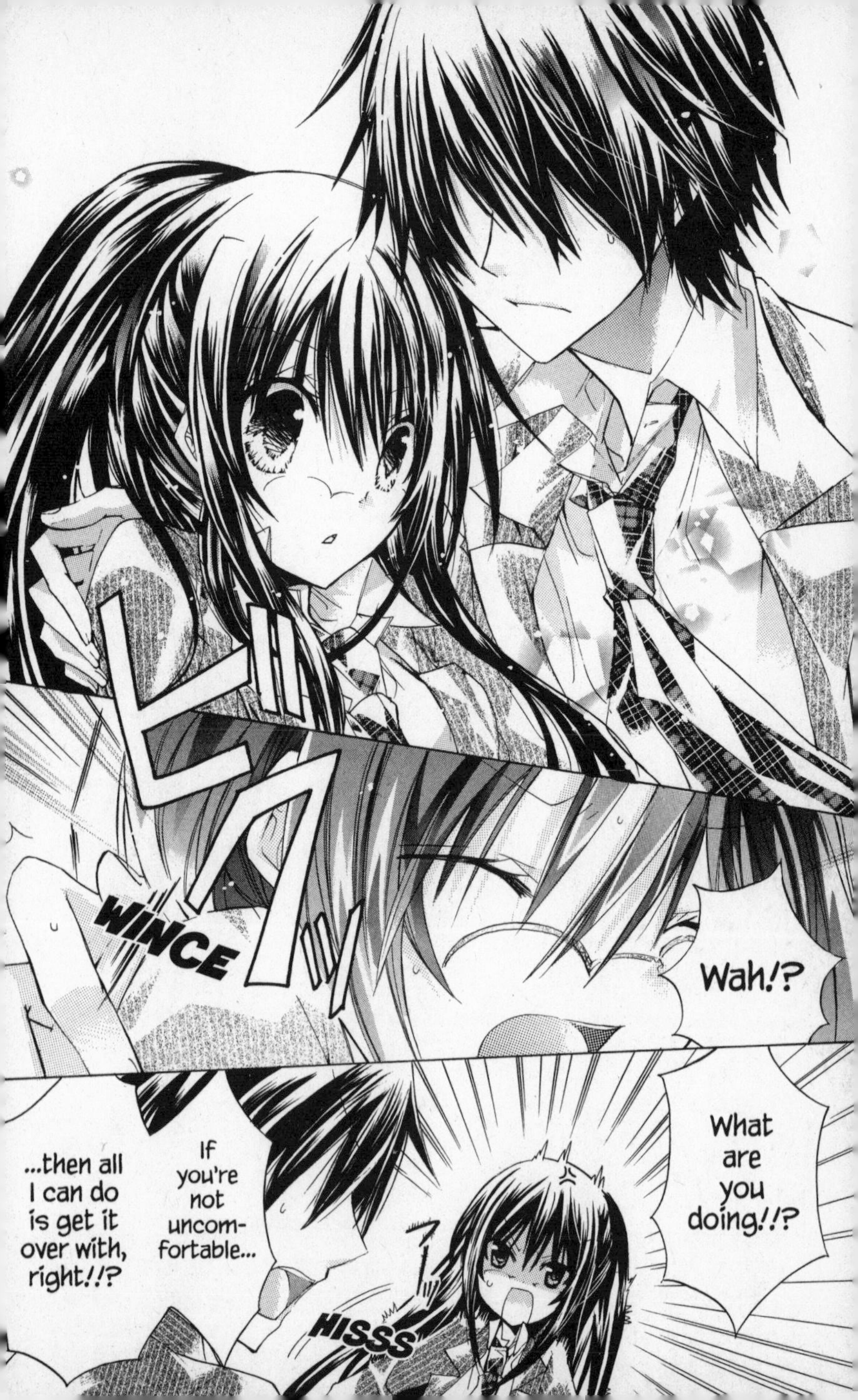
Wah!?
WINCE
What are you doing!!?
HISSS
If you're not uncomfortable...
...then all I can do is get it over with, right!!?

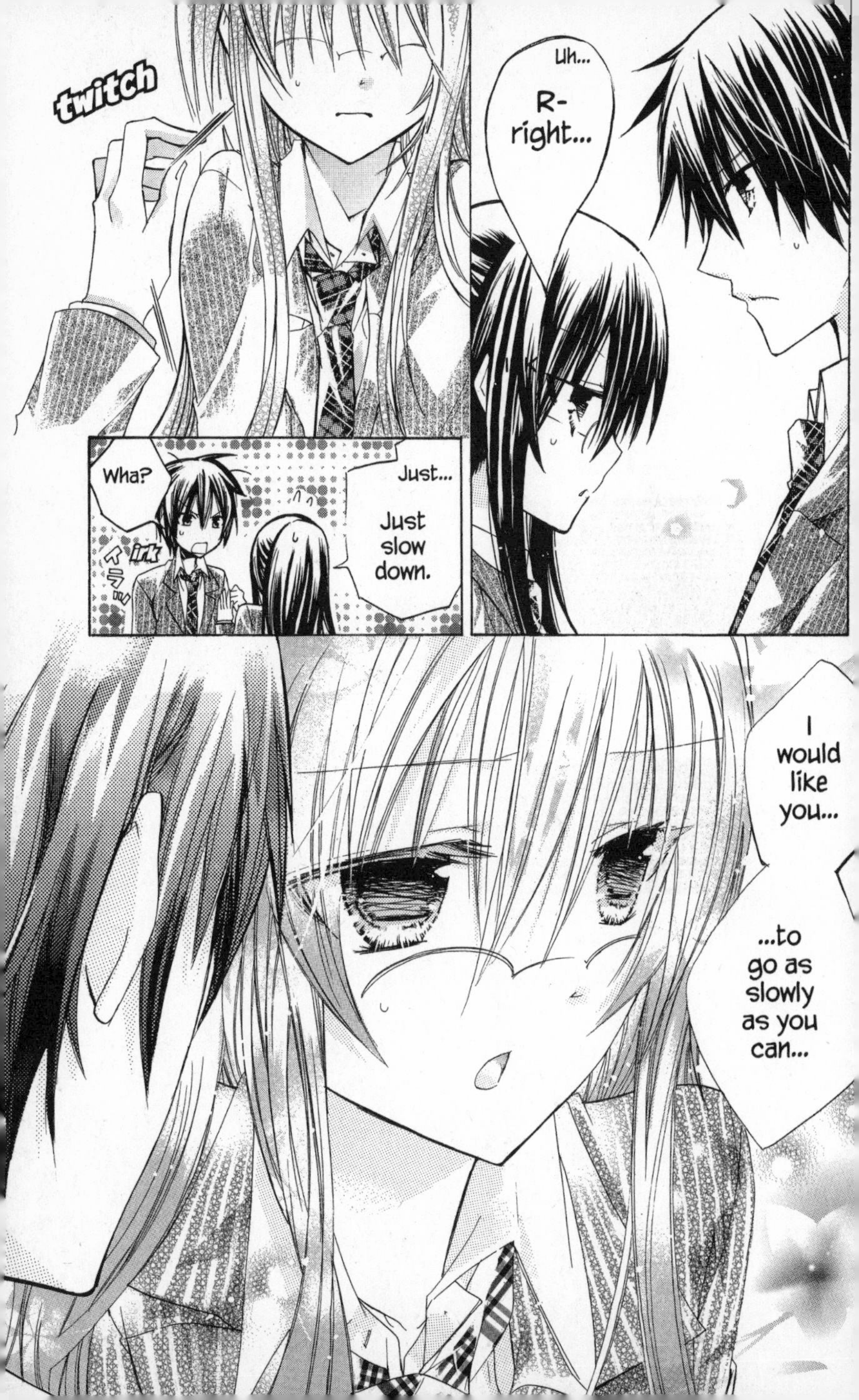
Uh...
R- right...
twitch
Just...
Just slow down.
Wha?
irk
イラッ
I would like you...
...to go as slowly as you can...

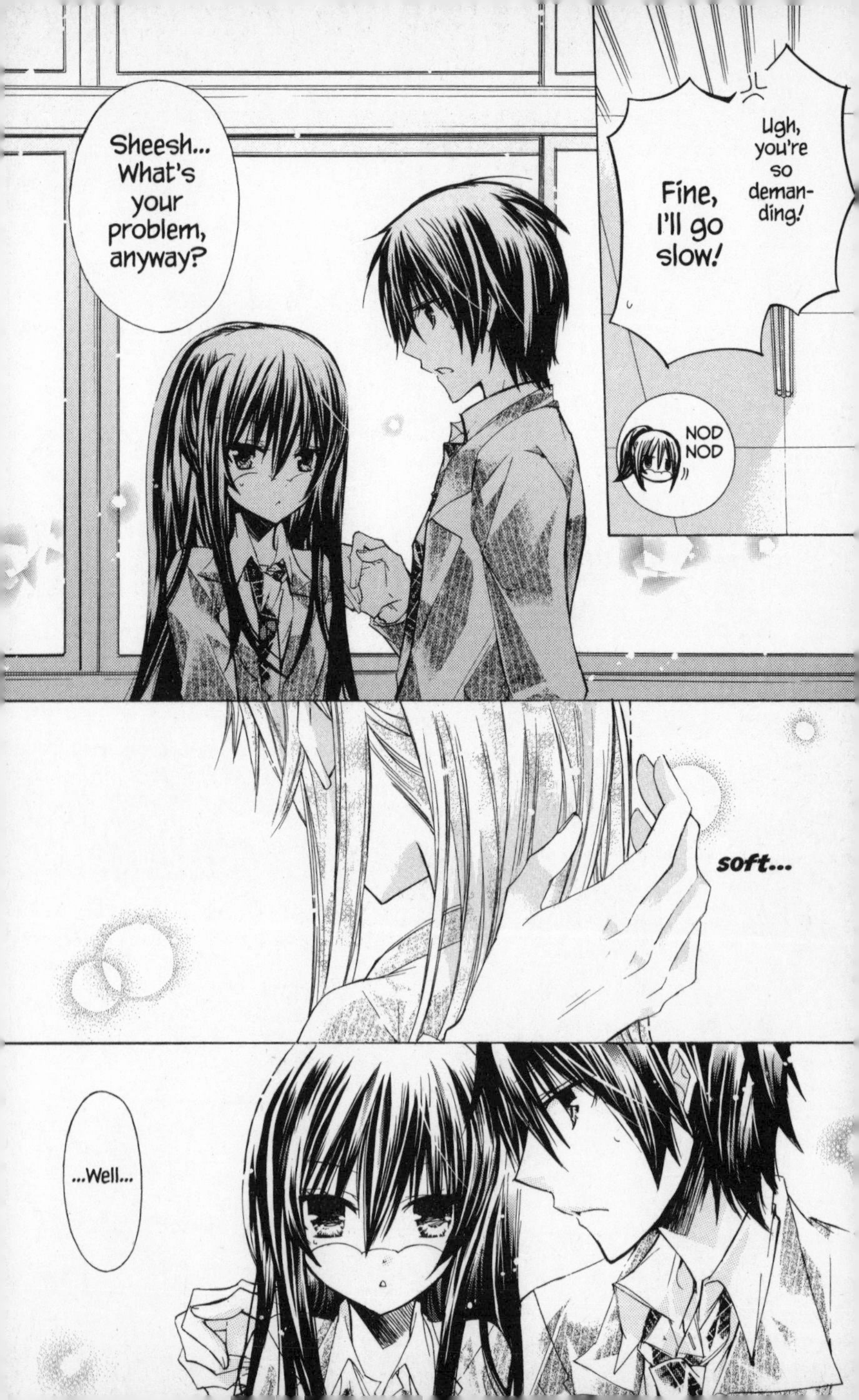
Ugh, you're so deman-ding!
Fine, I'll go slow!
NOD NOD
Sheesh... What's your problem, anyway?
soft...
...Well...

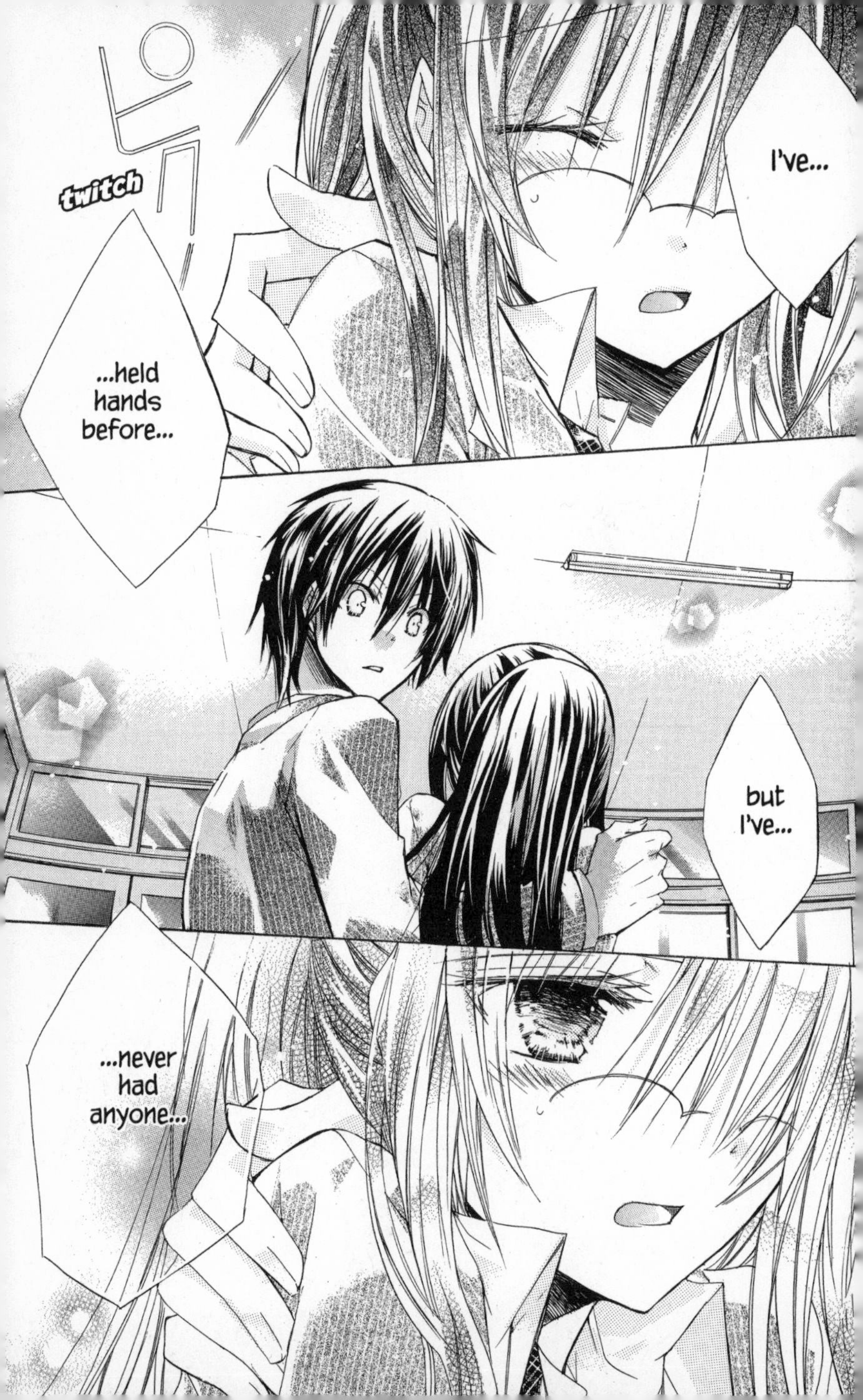
I've...
ピク
twitch
...held hands before...
but I've...
...never had anyone...

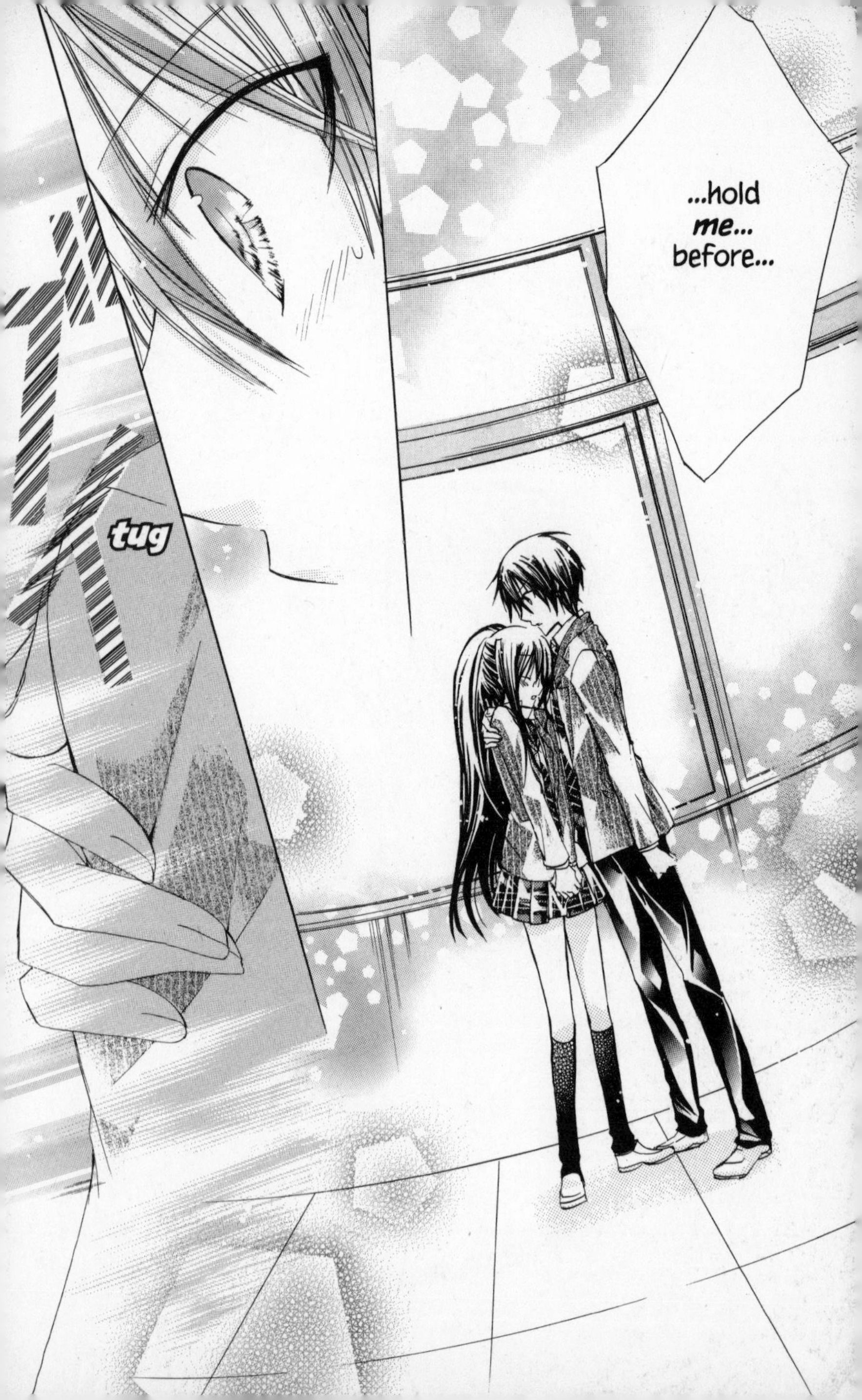
...hold *me*... before...
tug

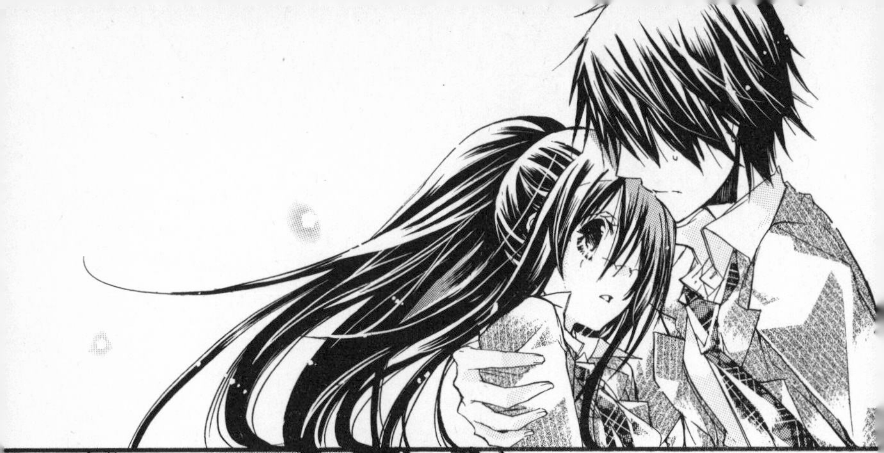
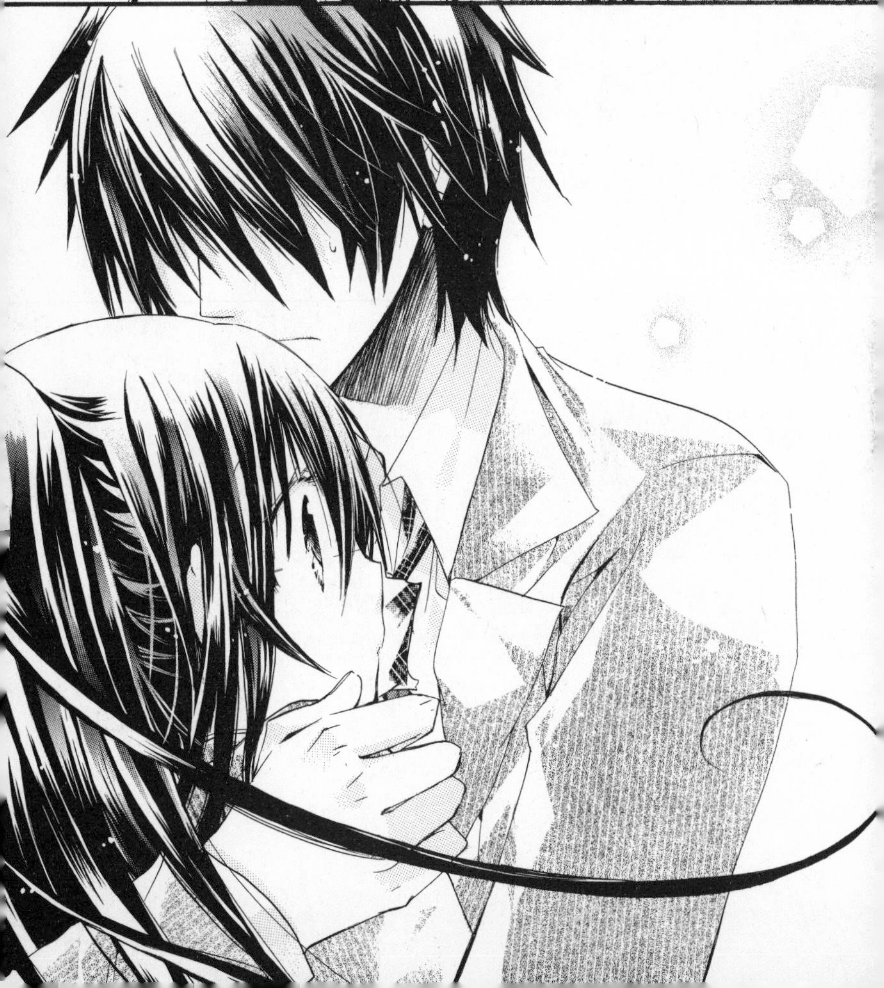

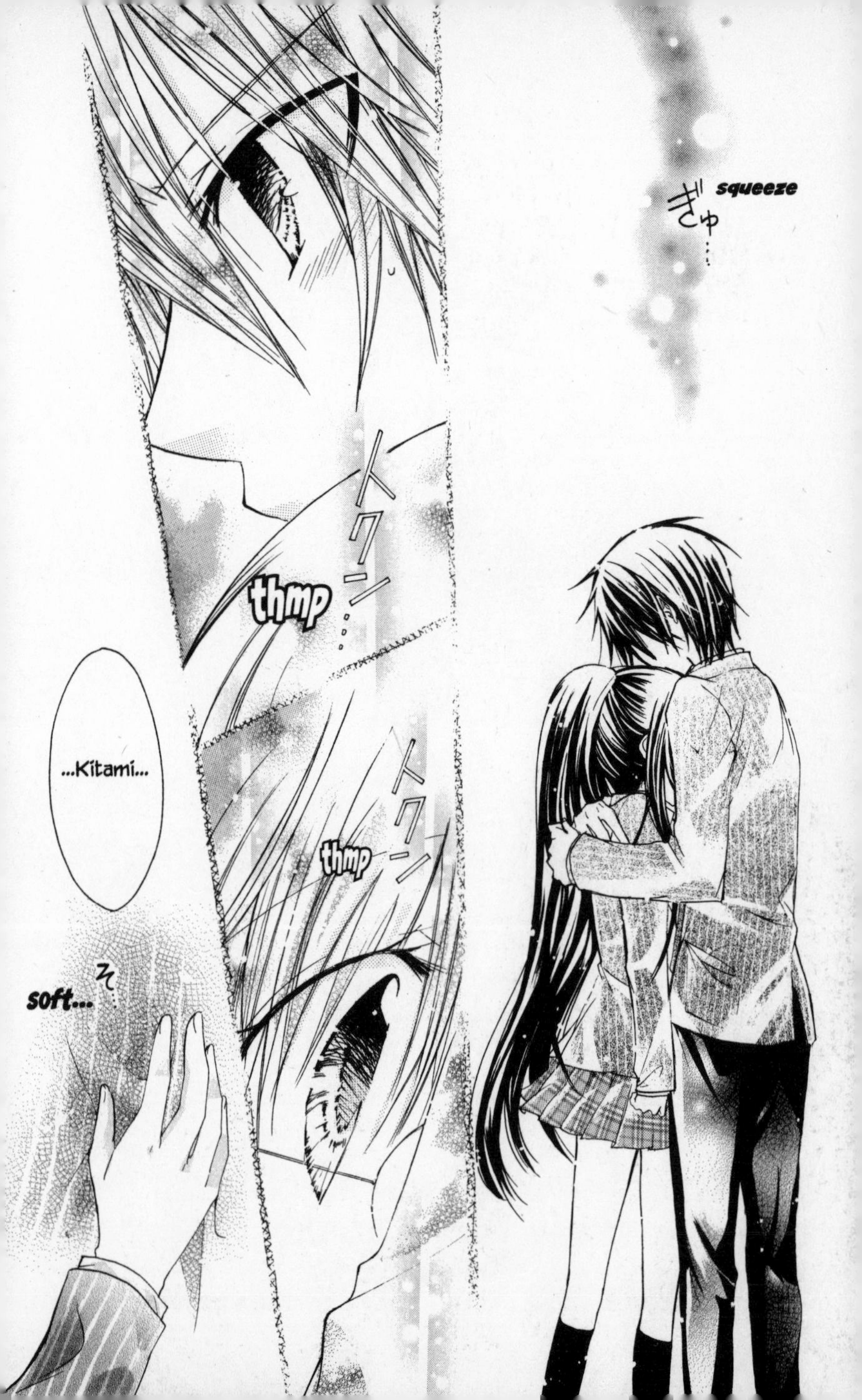
ぎゅ…
squeeze
トクン…
thmp
トクン
thmp
...Kitami...
soft...

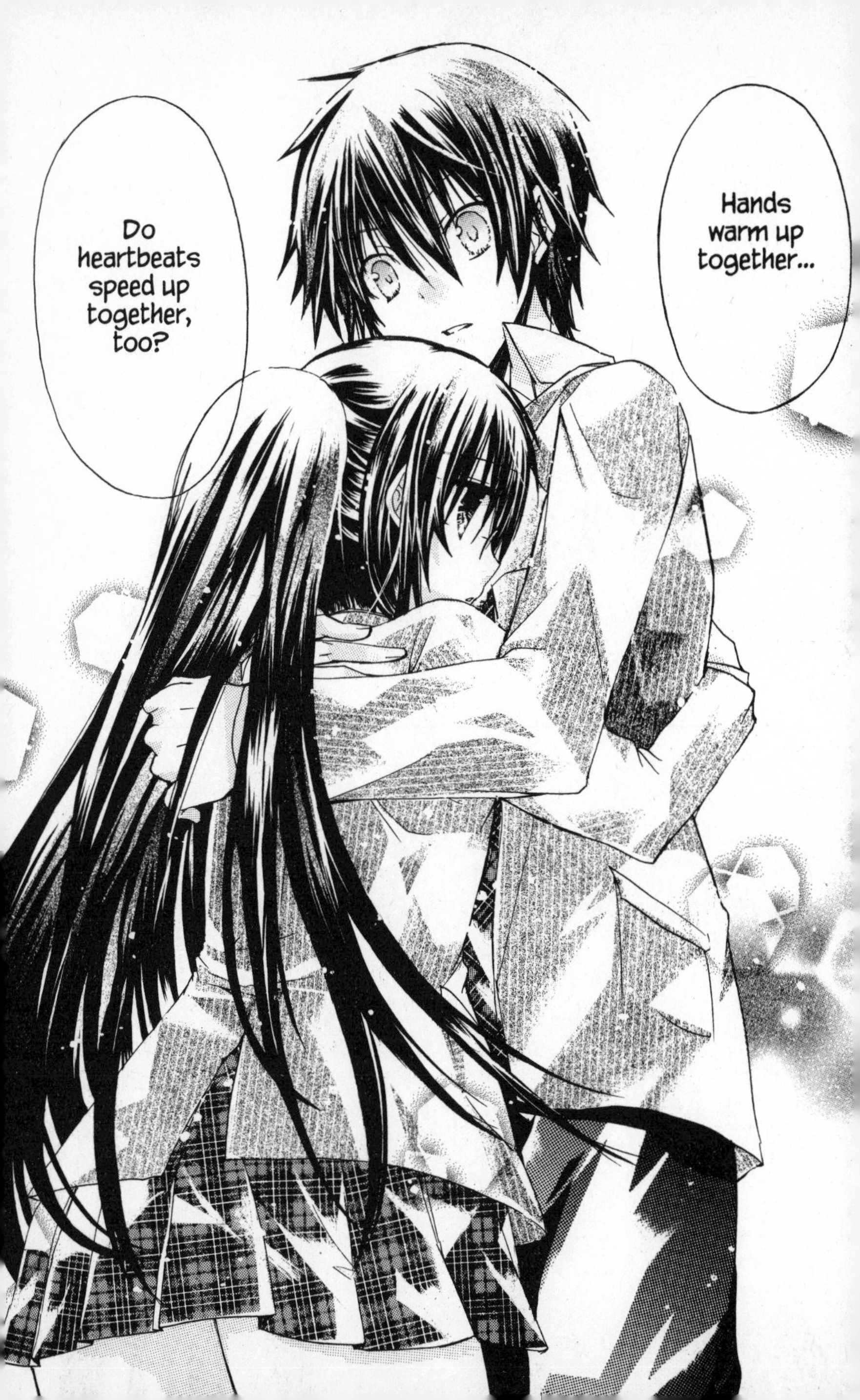
Hands warm up together...
Do heartbeats speed up together, too?

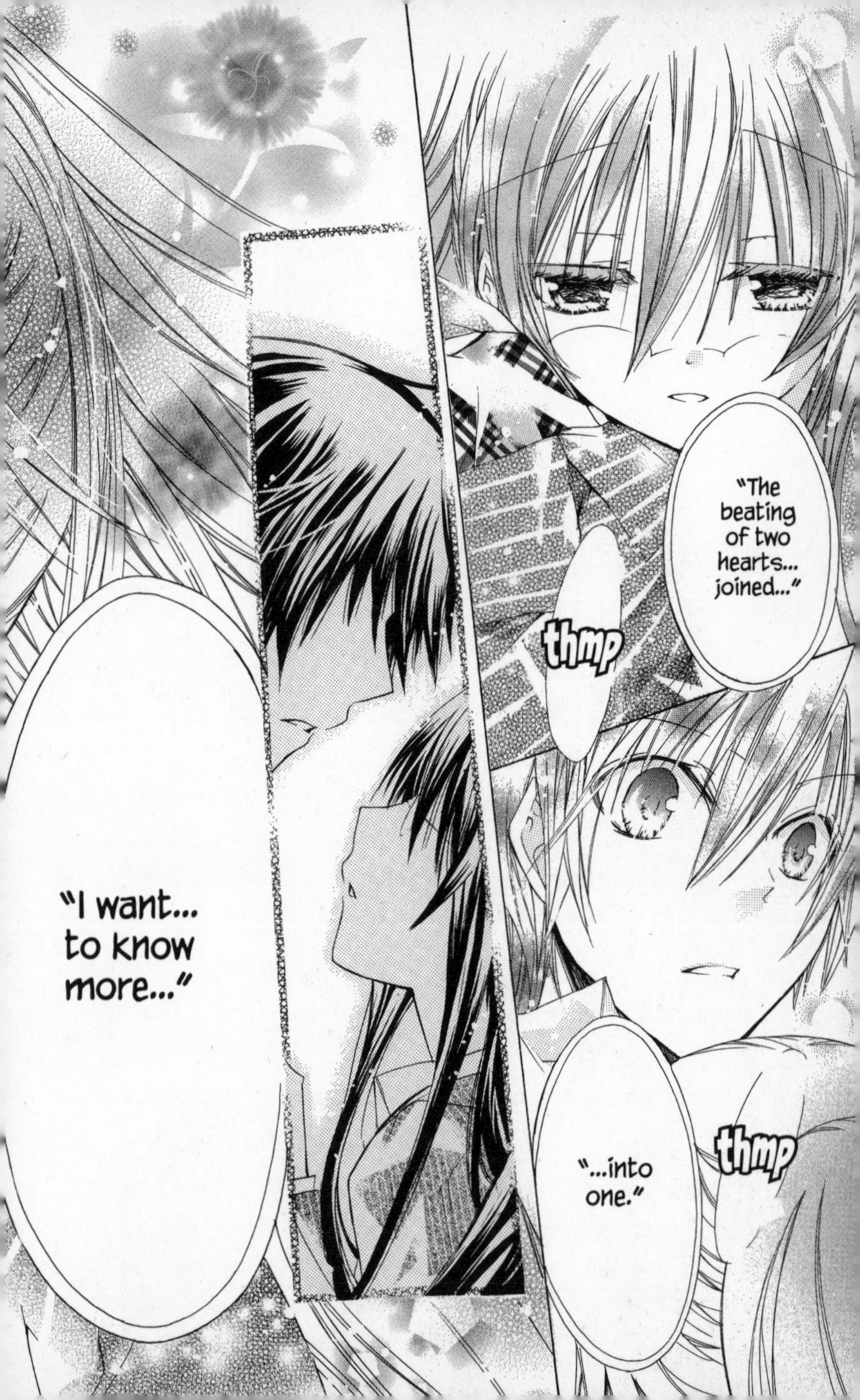
"The beating of two hearts... joined..."
thmp
"...into one."
thmp
"I want... to know more..."

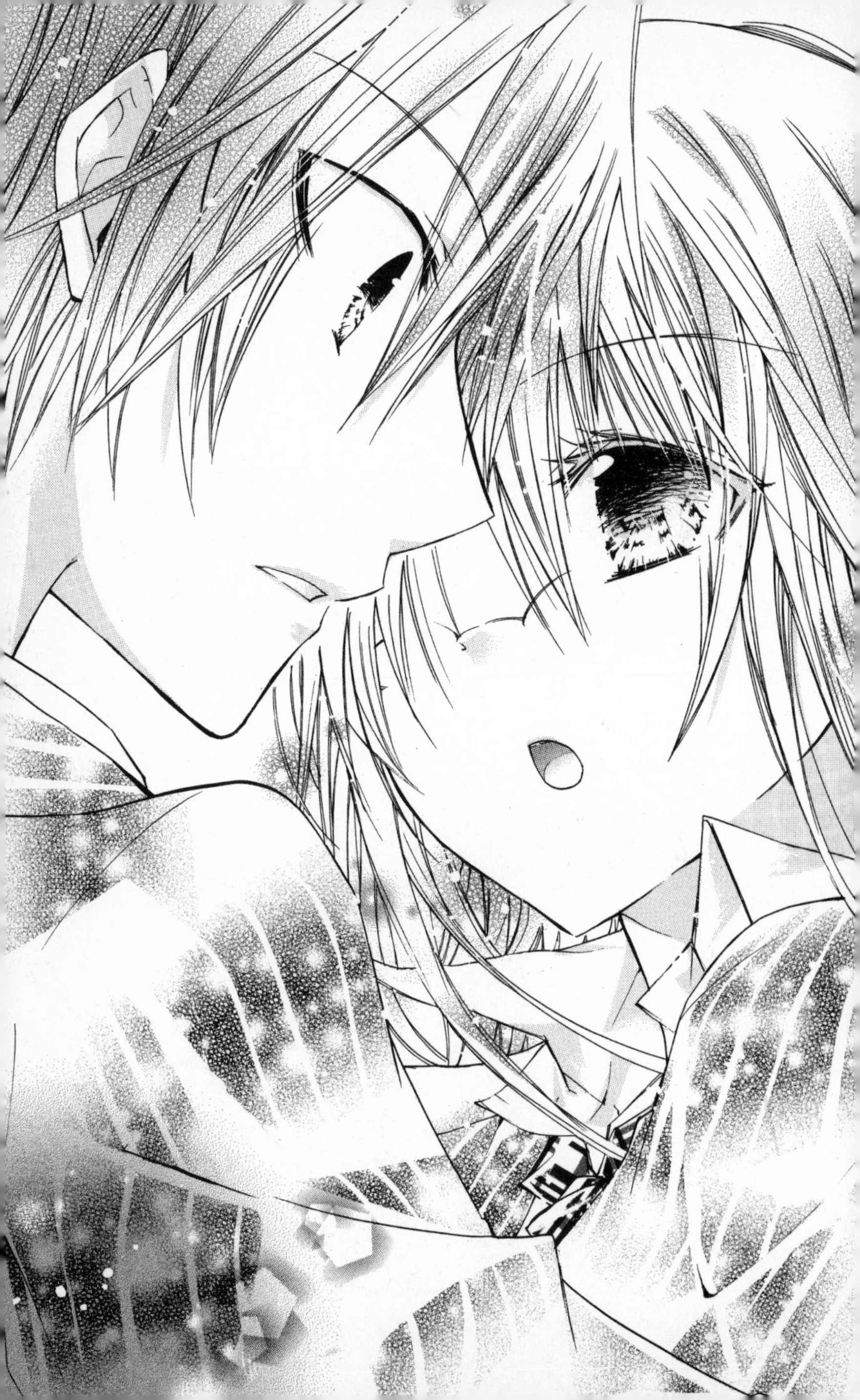

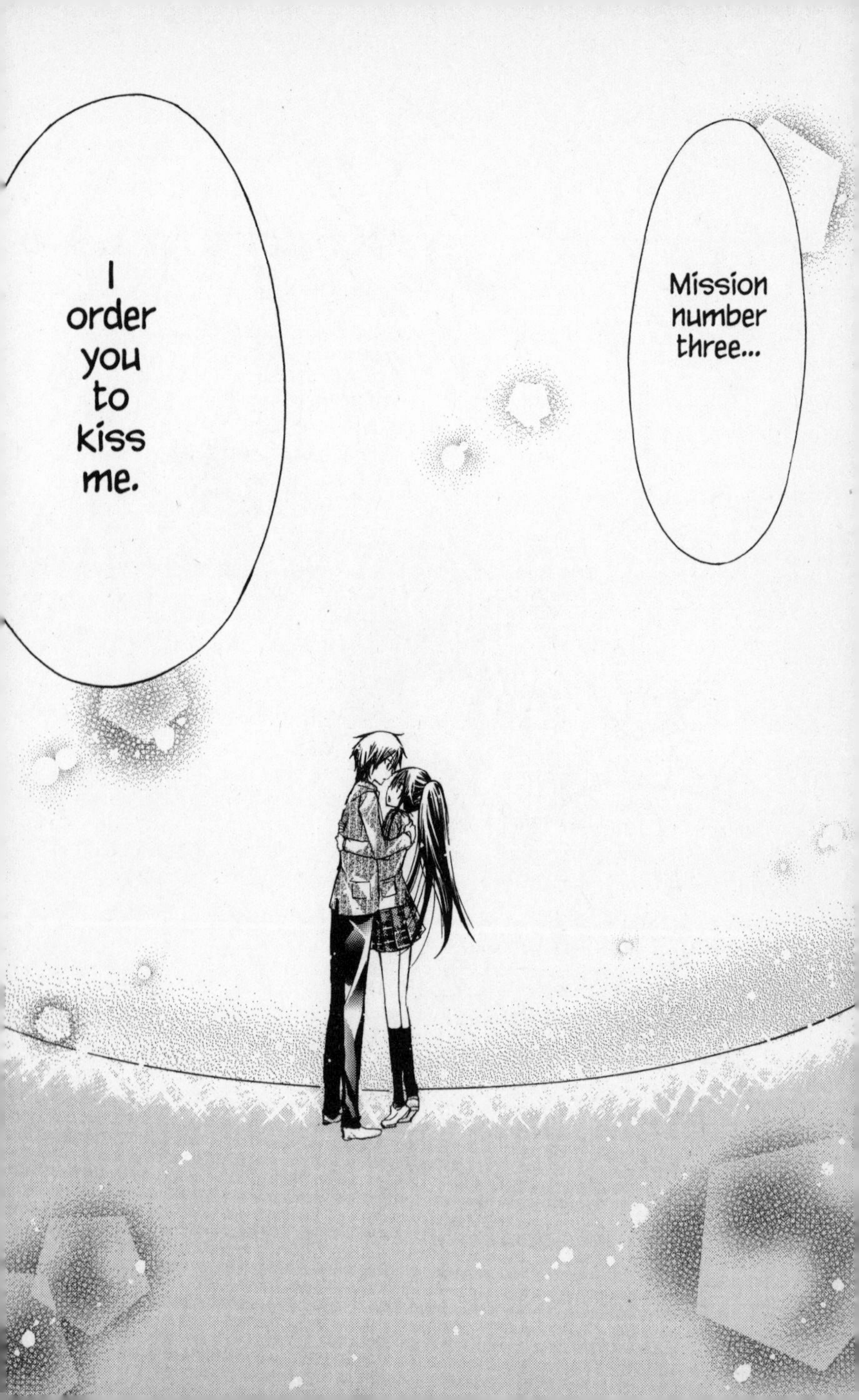
Mission number three...
I order you to kiss me.

Missions of Love

**It is time for love.
Secret cell phone
novelist vs. the most
popular boy in school.
A mission of love for
absolute servitude.**

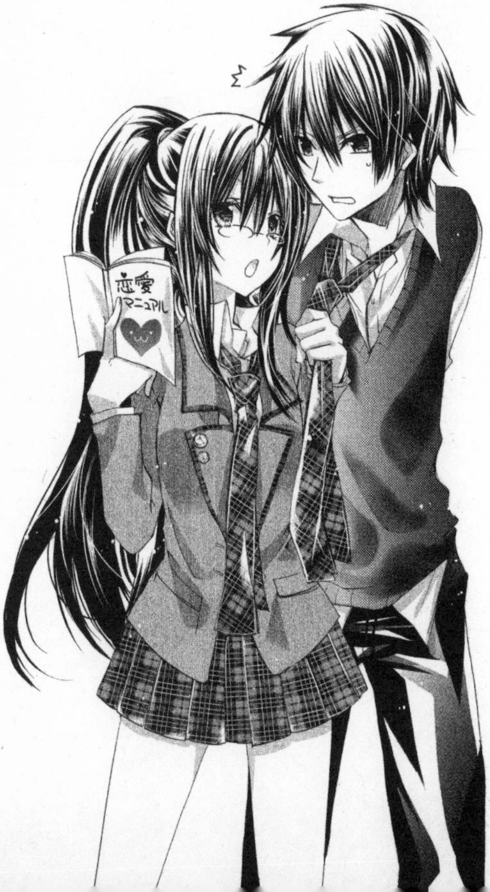
恋愛
マニュアル

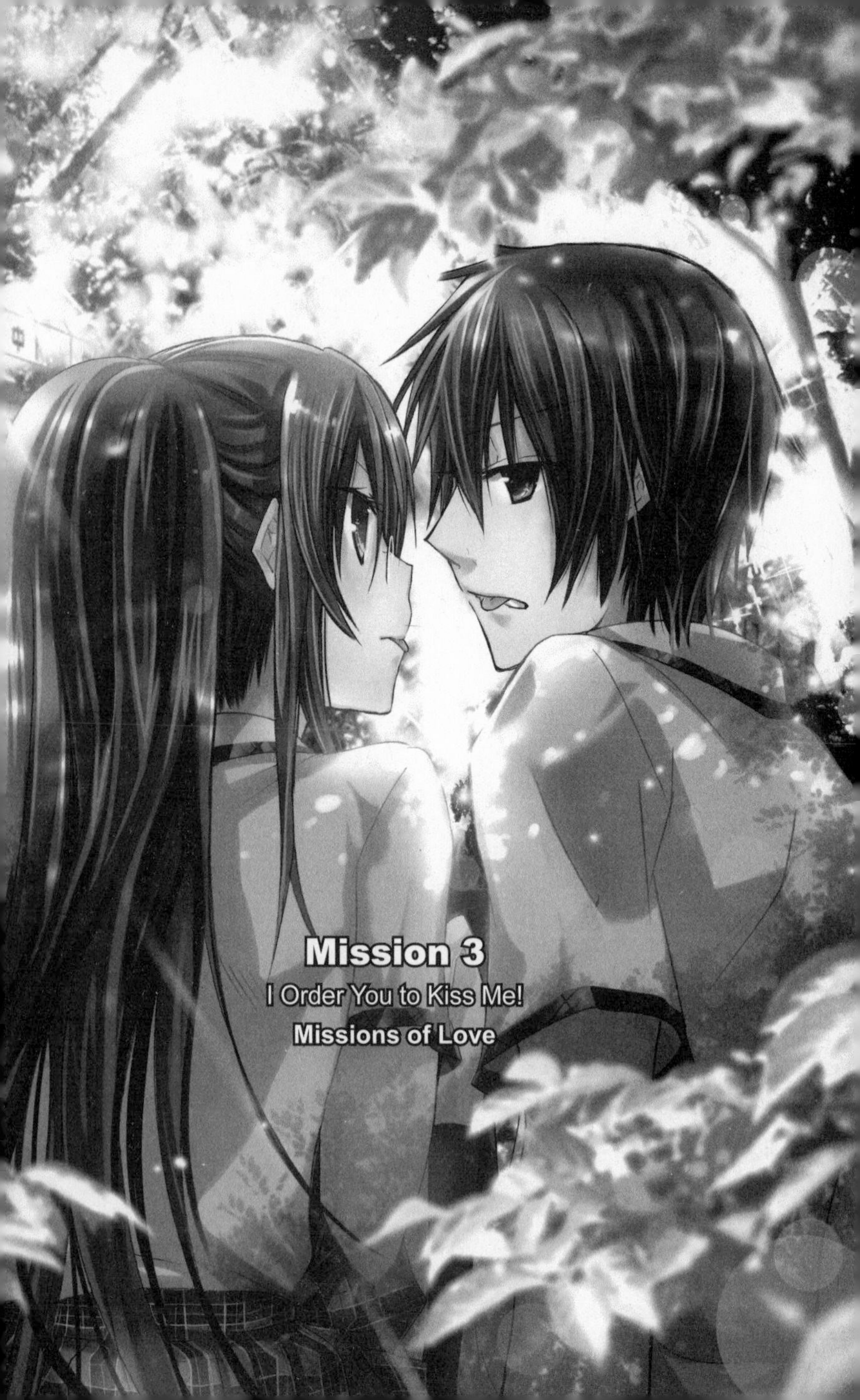

Mission 3

I Order You to Kiss Me!

Missions of Love

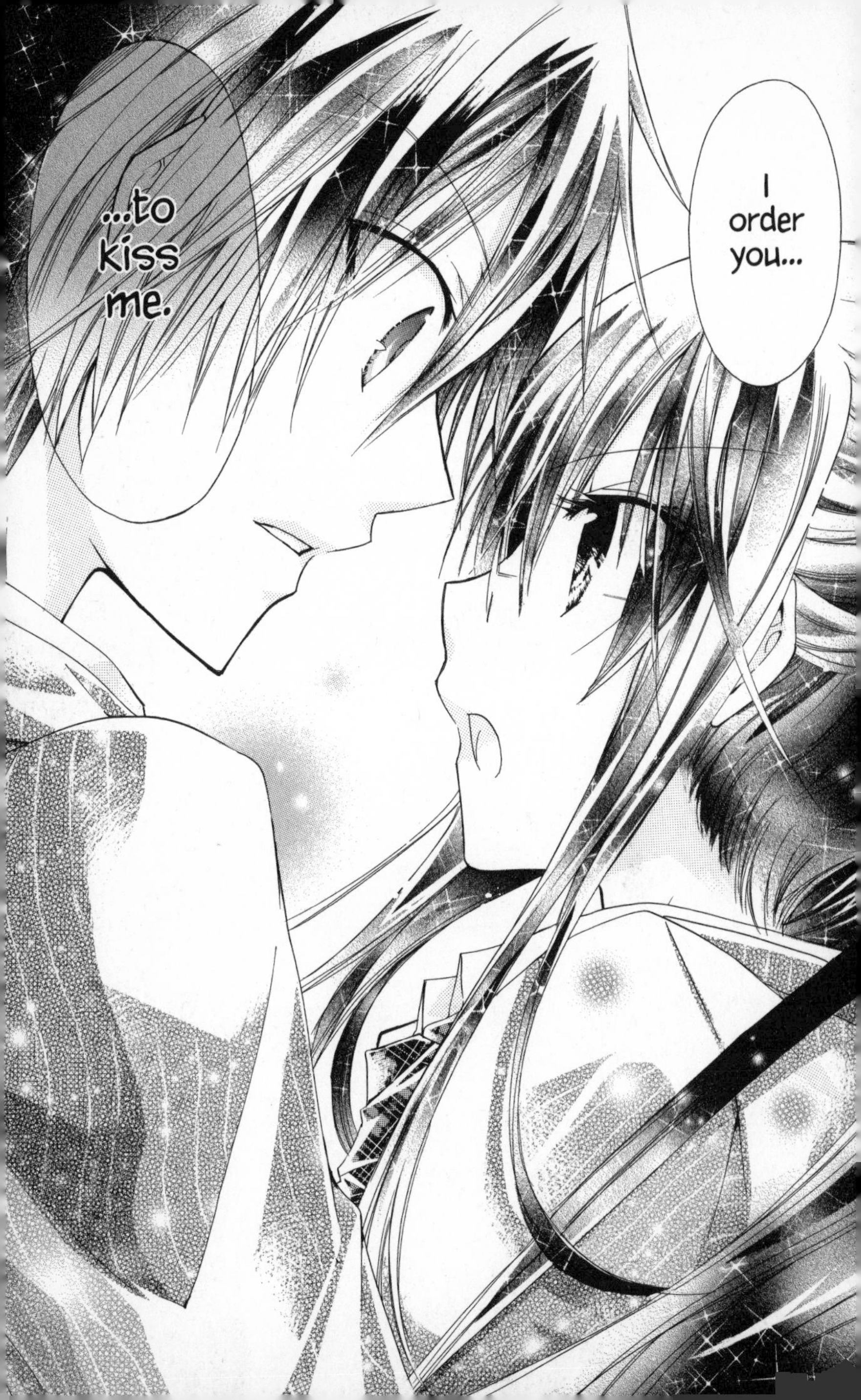
I order you...
...to kiss me.

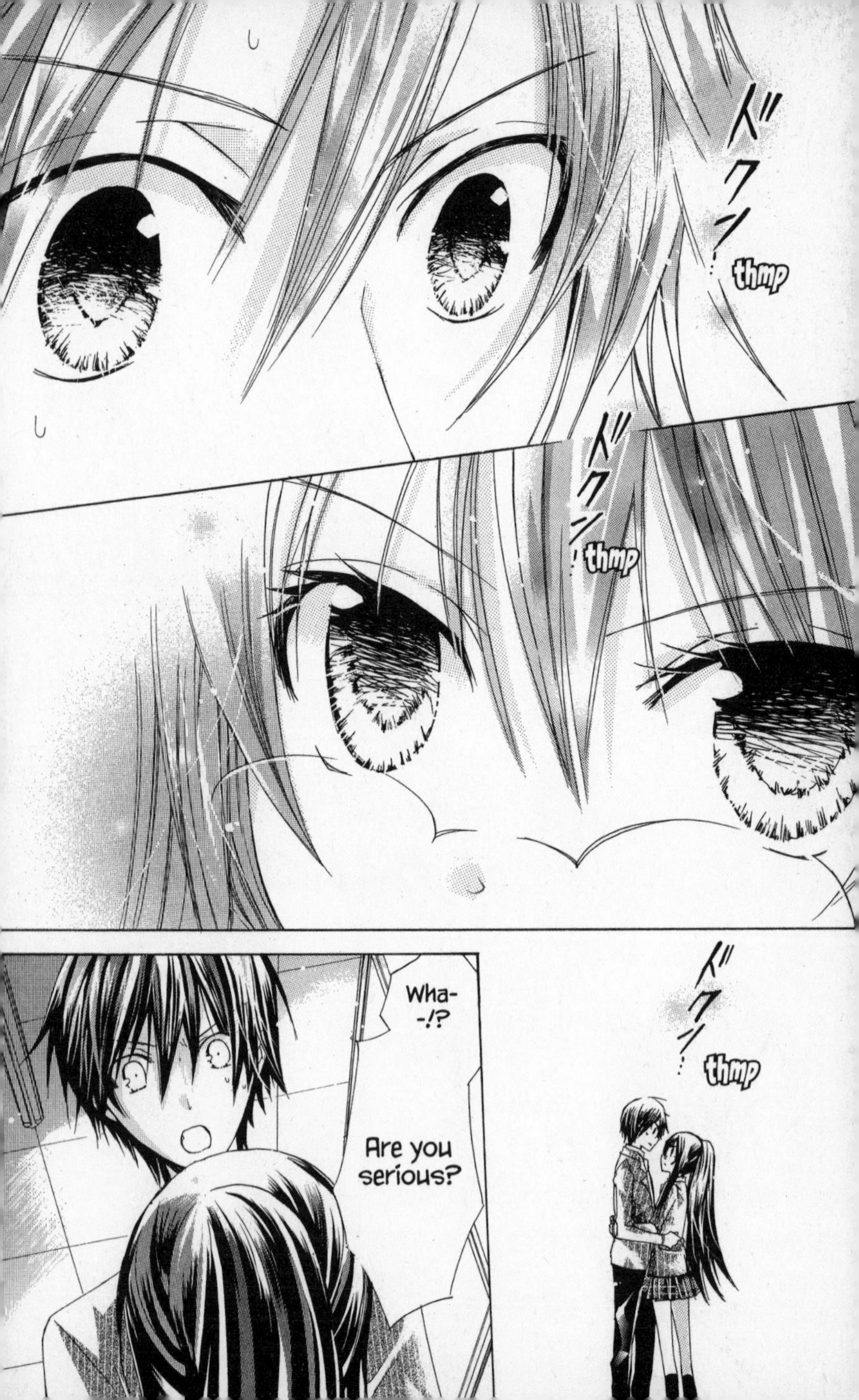
ドクン…
thmp
ドクン…
thmp
ドクン…
thmp
Wha-
-!?
Are you
serious?

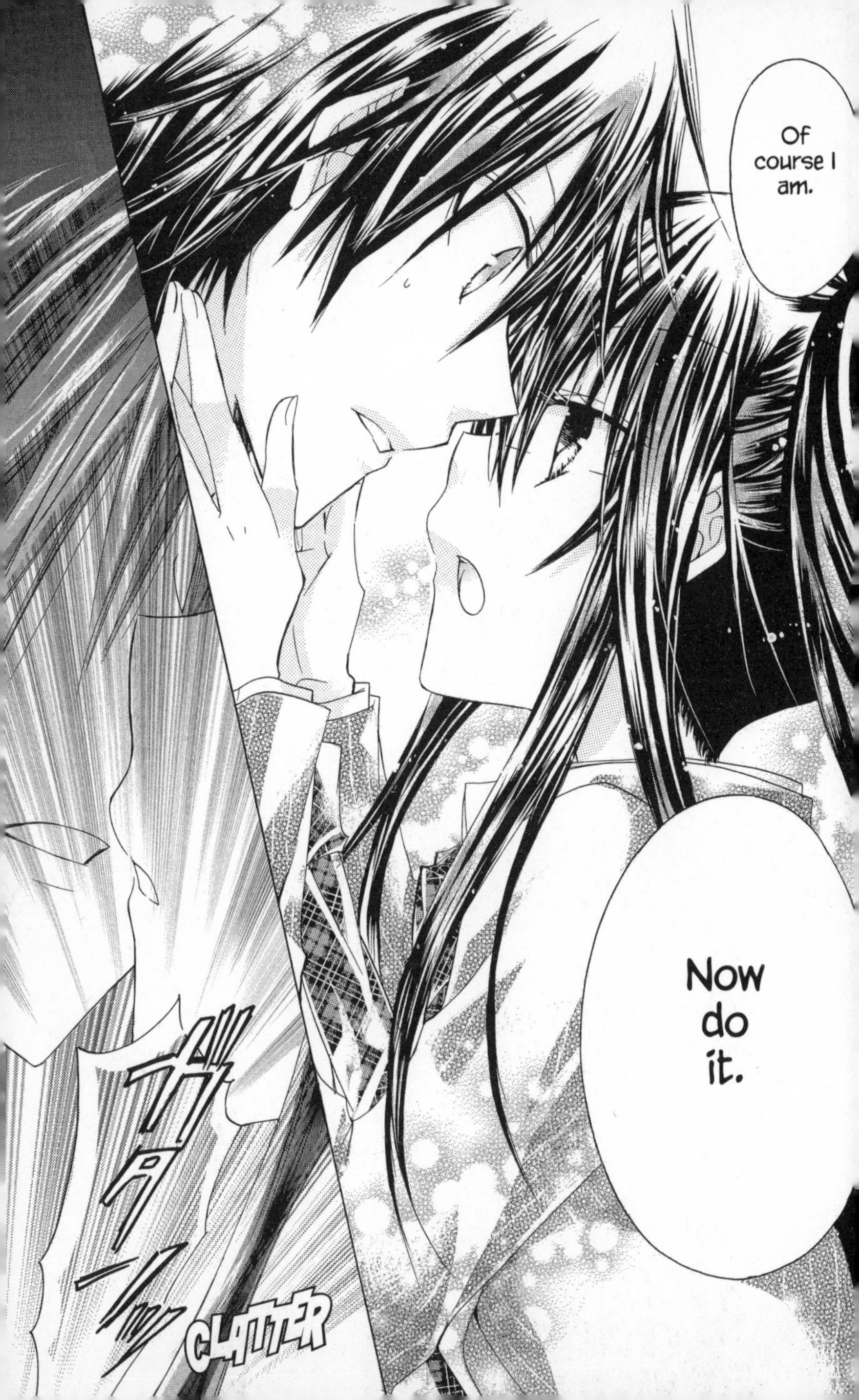
Of course I am.
Now do it.
CLATTER

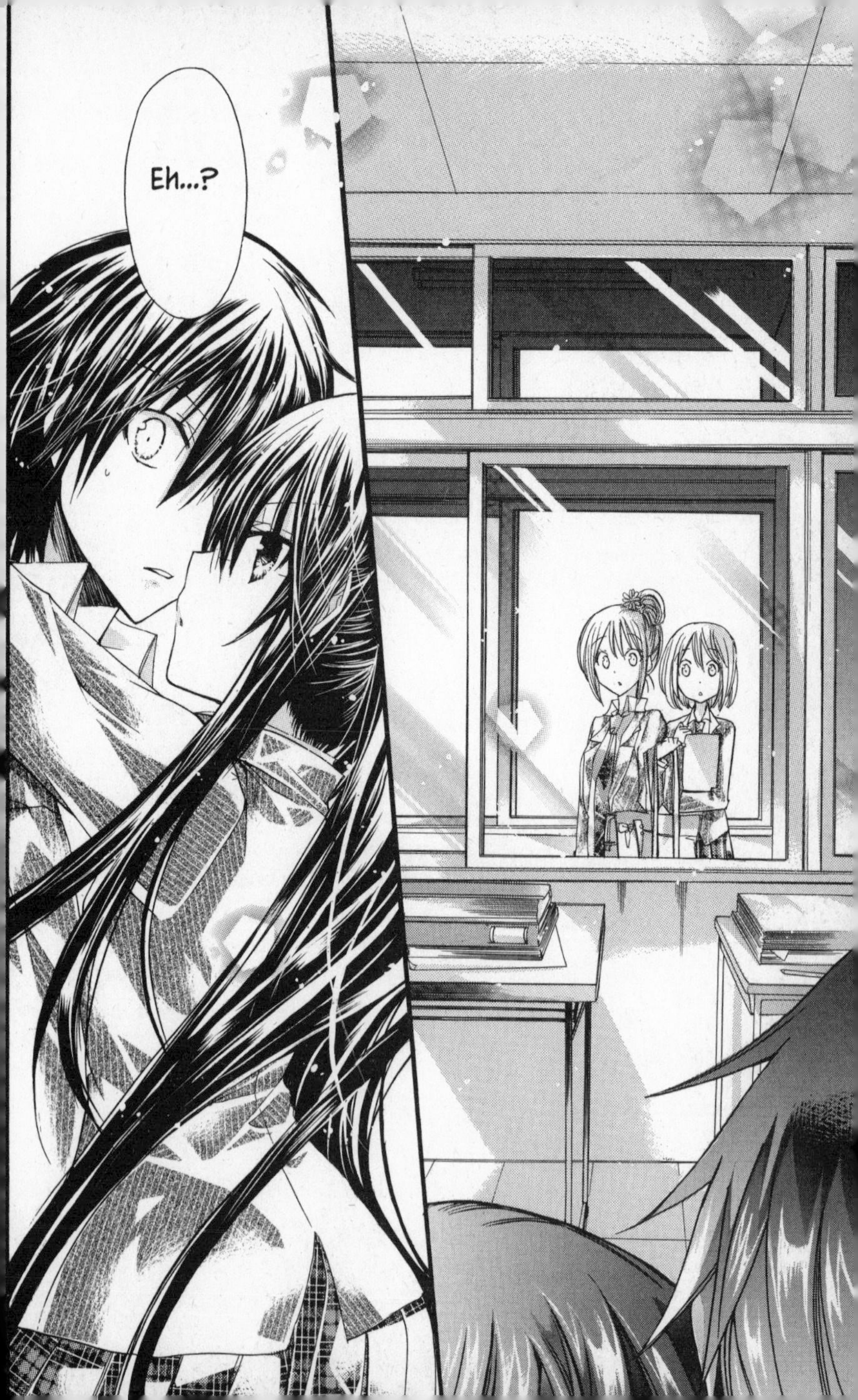
Eh...?

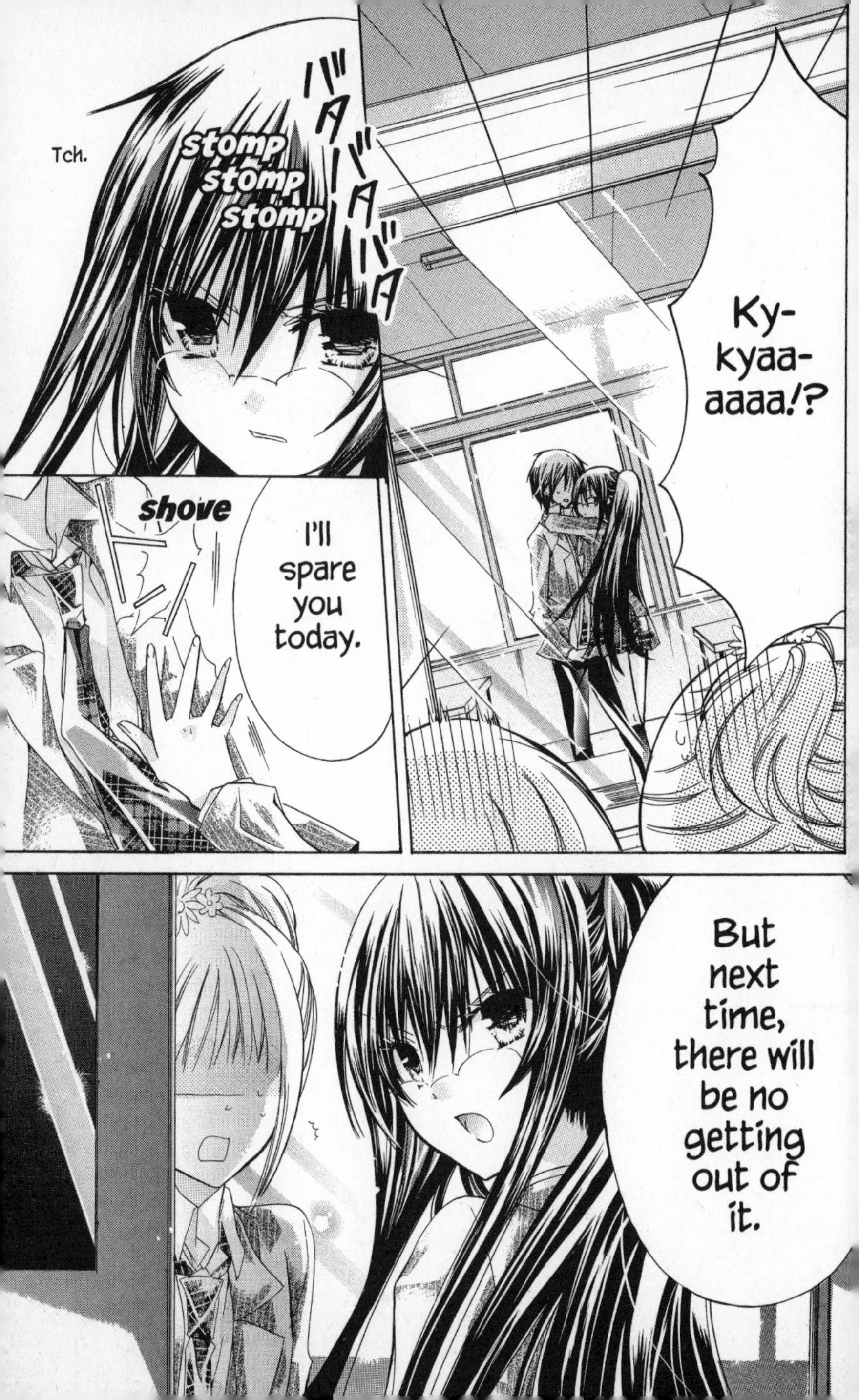

Ky-kyaa-aaaa!?
Tch.
stomp stomp stomp
バタバタバタ
shove
I'll spare you today.
But next time, there will be no getting out of it.

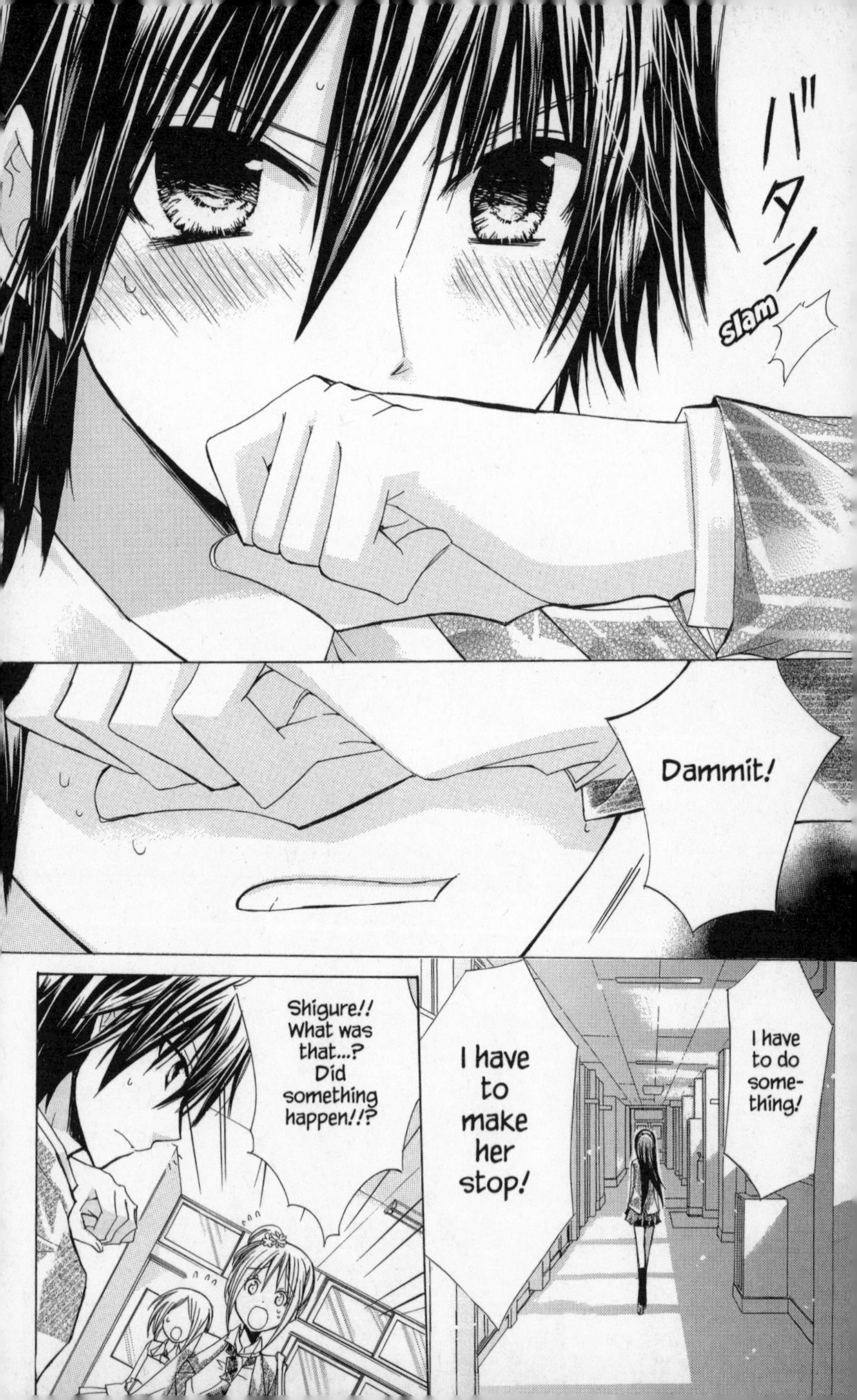

バタン
slam
Dammit!
I have to do some-thing!
I have to make her stop!
Shigure!! What was that...? Did something happen!!?

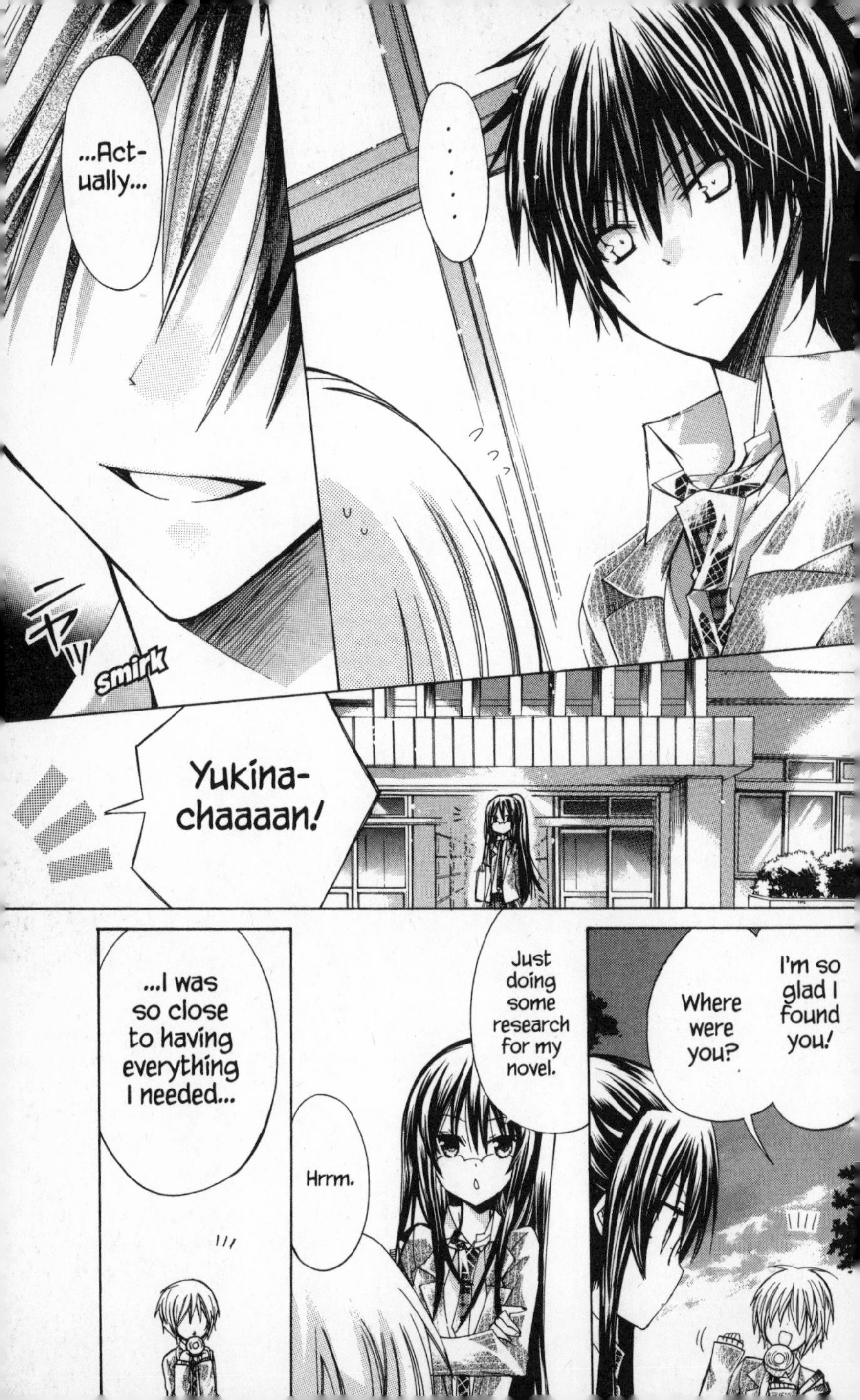

......
...Act-ually...
ニヤッ
smirk
Yukina-chaaaan!
I'm so glad I found you!
Where were you?
Just doing some research for my novel.
Hrrm.
...I was so close to having everything I needed...

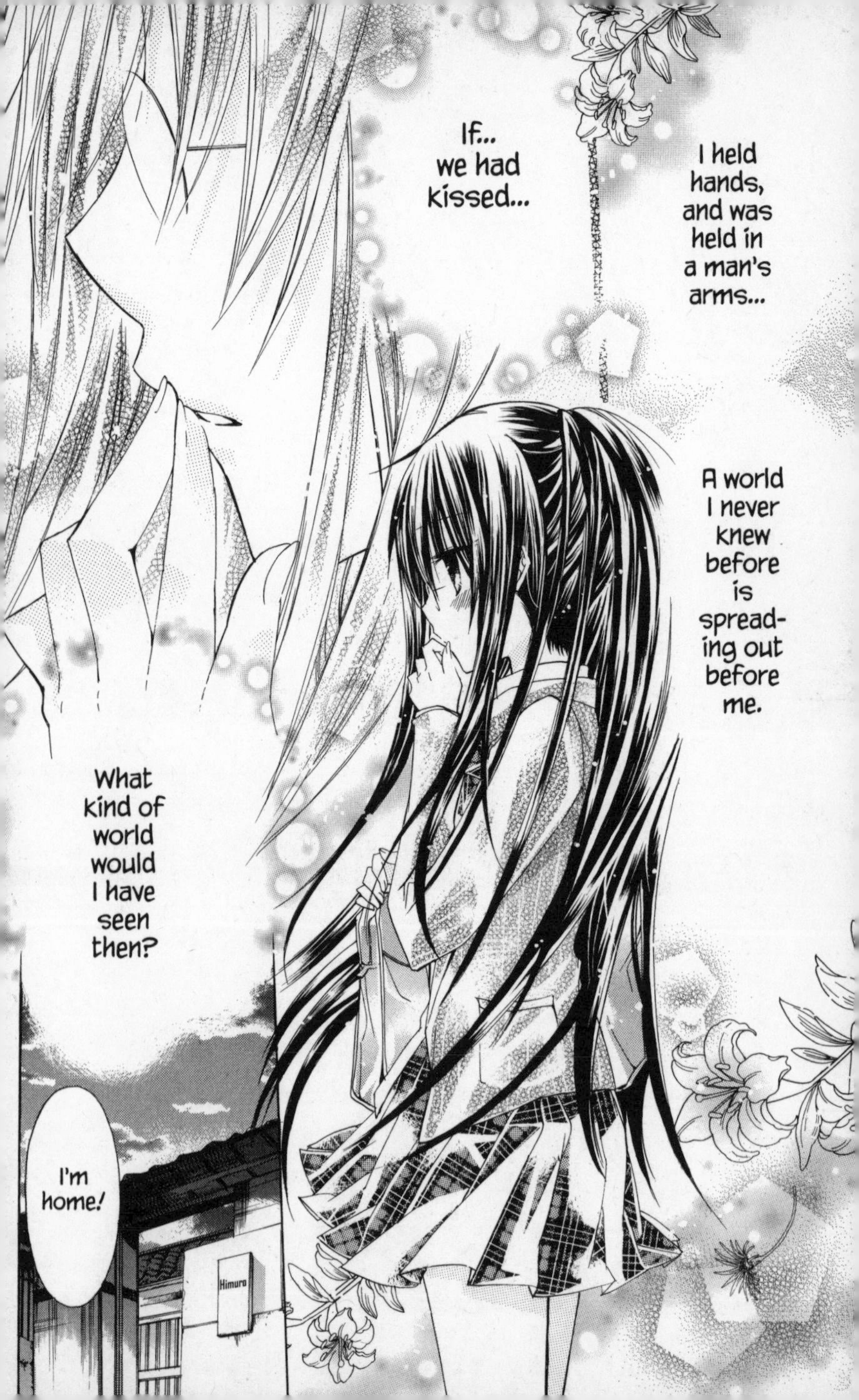
I held hands, and was held in a man's arms...
If... we had kissed...
A world I never knew before is spreading out before me.
What kind of world would I have seen then?
I'm home!
Himura

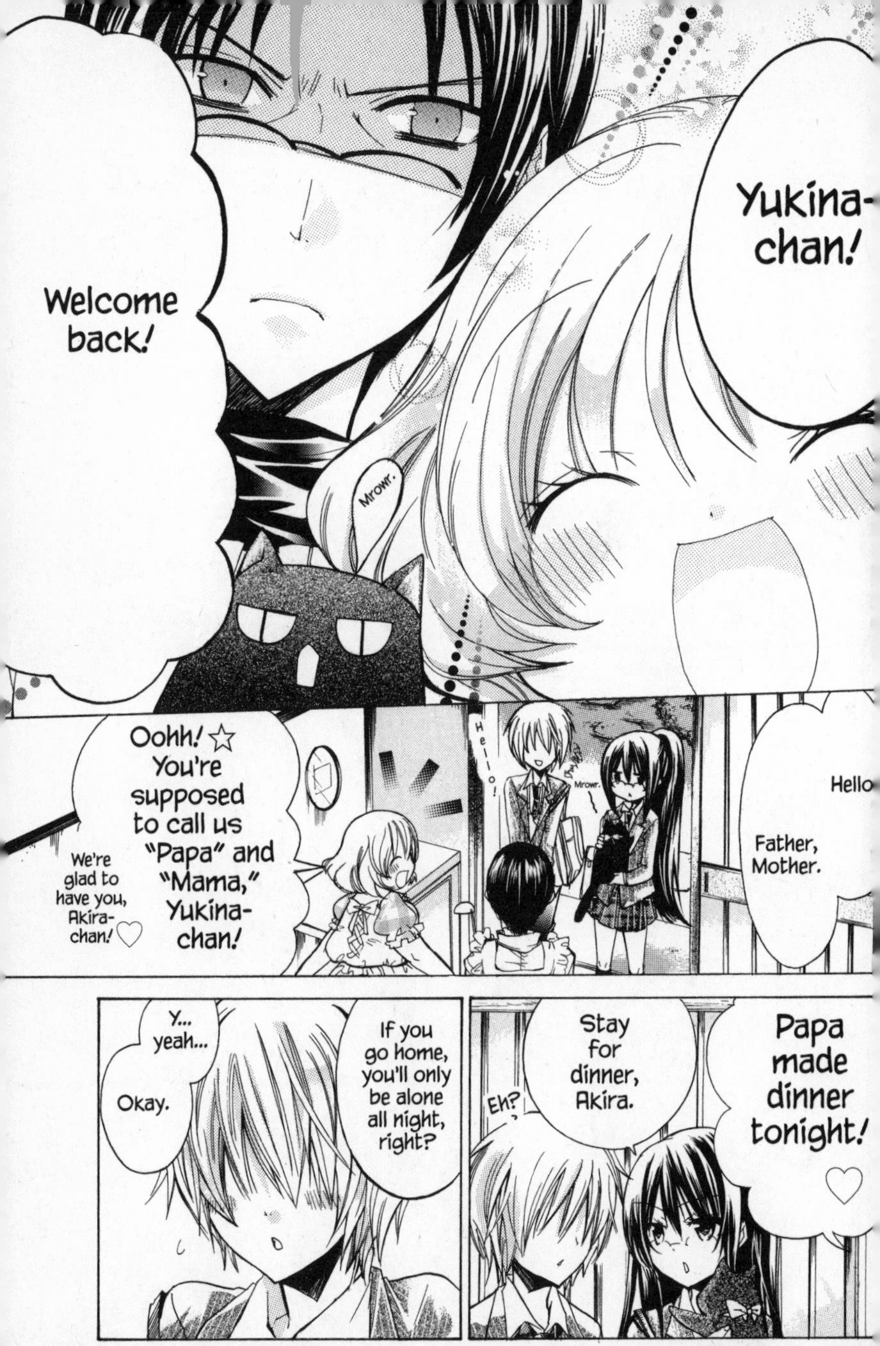

Yukina-chan!
Welcome back!
Mrowr.
Hello
Father, Mother.
Hello!
Mrowr.
Oohh! ☆ You're supposed to call us "Papa" and "Mama," Yukina-chan!
We're glad to have you, Akira-chan! ♡
Papa made dinner tonight! ♡
Stay for dinner, Akira.
Eh?
If you go home, you'll only be alone all night, right?
Y... yeah...
Okay.

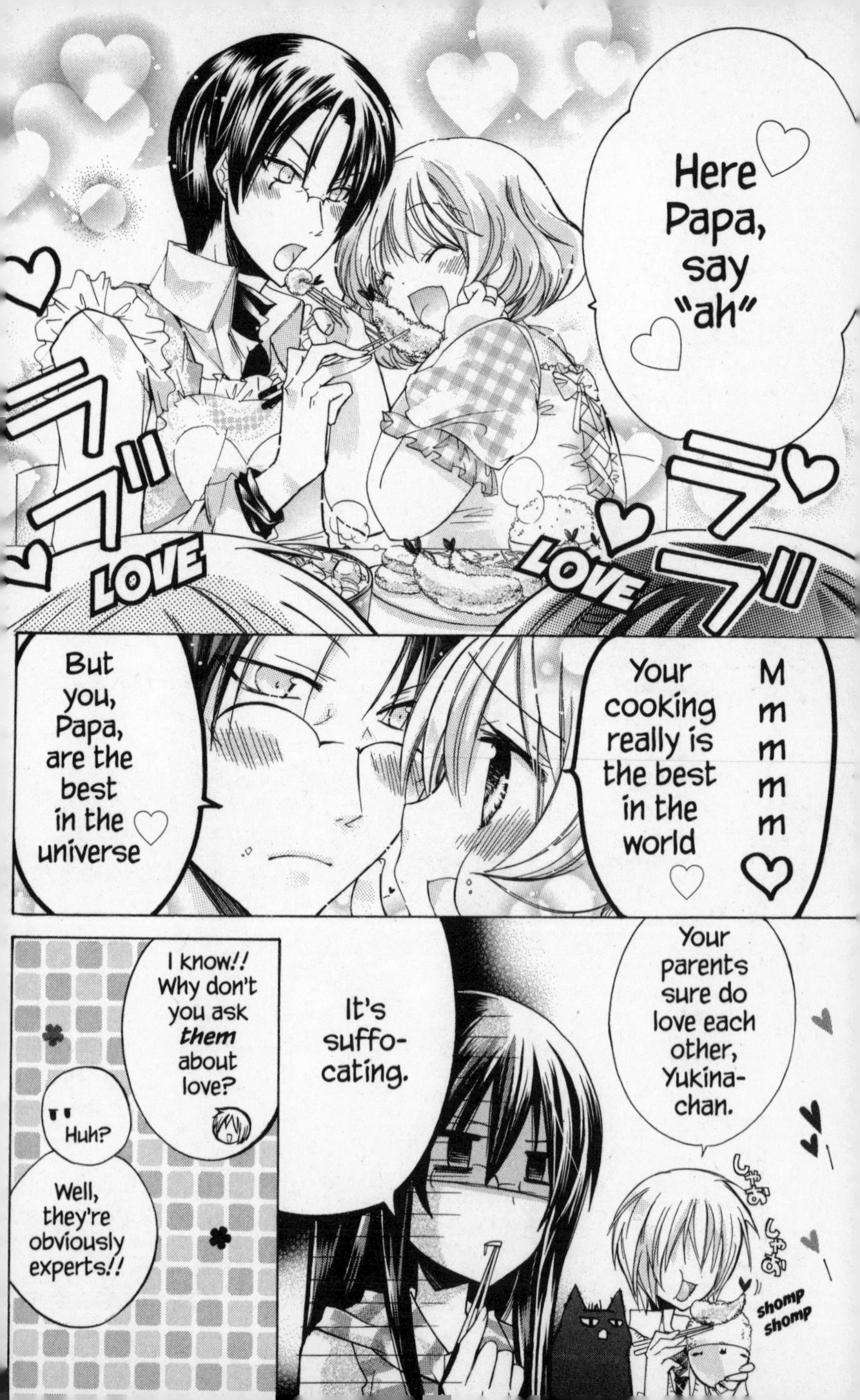
Here Papa, say "ah"
ラブ
LOVE
ラブ
LOVE
Mmmmmm
Your cooking really is the best in the world
But you, Papa, are the best in the universe
Your parents sure do love each other, Yukina-chan.
shomp shomp
It's suffo-cating.
I know!! Why don't you ask *them* about love?
Huh?
Well, they're obviously experts!!

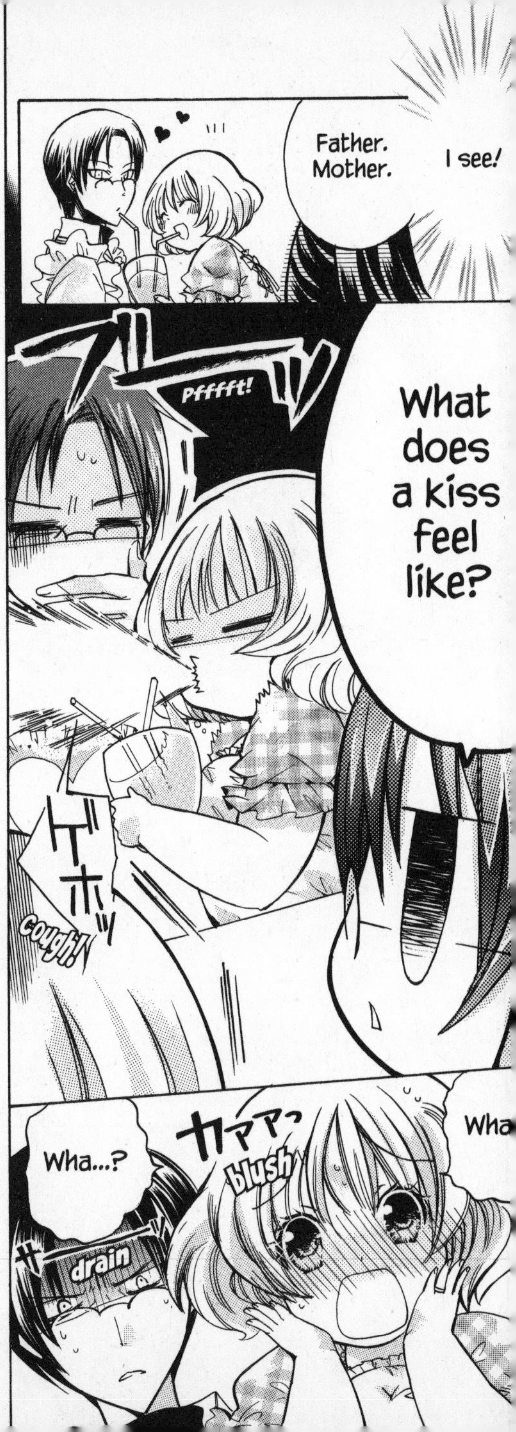
I see!
Father. Mother.
What does a kiss feel like?
Pfffft!
Cough!
Wha
blush
Wha...?
drain

Pronunciation

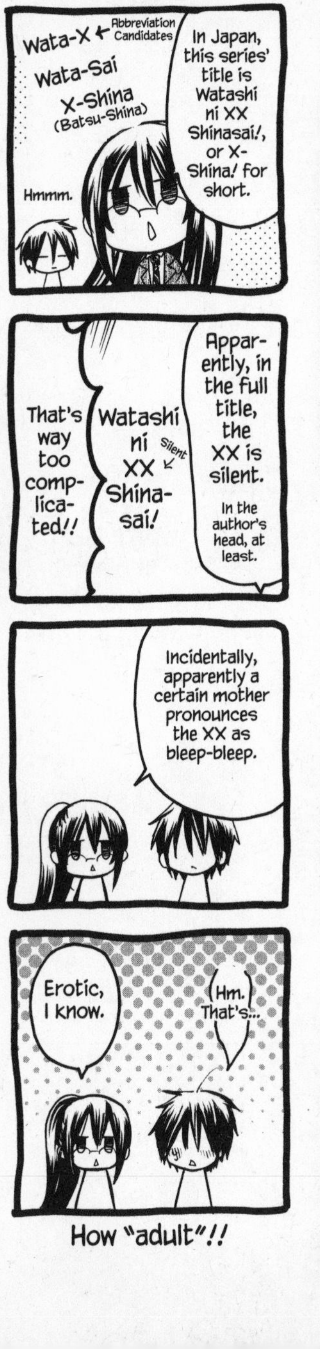
In Japan, this series' title is Watashi ni XX Shinasai!, or X-Shina! for short.
Wata-X ← Abbreviation Candidates
Wata-Sai
X-Shina (Batsu-Shina)
Hmmm.
Apparently, in the full title, the XX is silent.
In the author's head, at least.
Watashi ni XX Shinasai!
silent
That's way too complicated!!
Incidentally, apparently a certain mother pronounces the XX as bleep-bleep.
Hm. That's...
Erotic, I know.

How "adult"!!

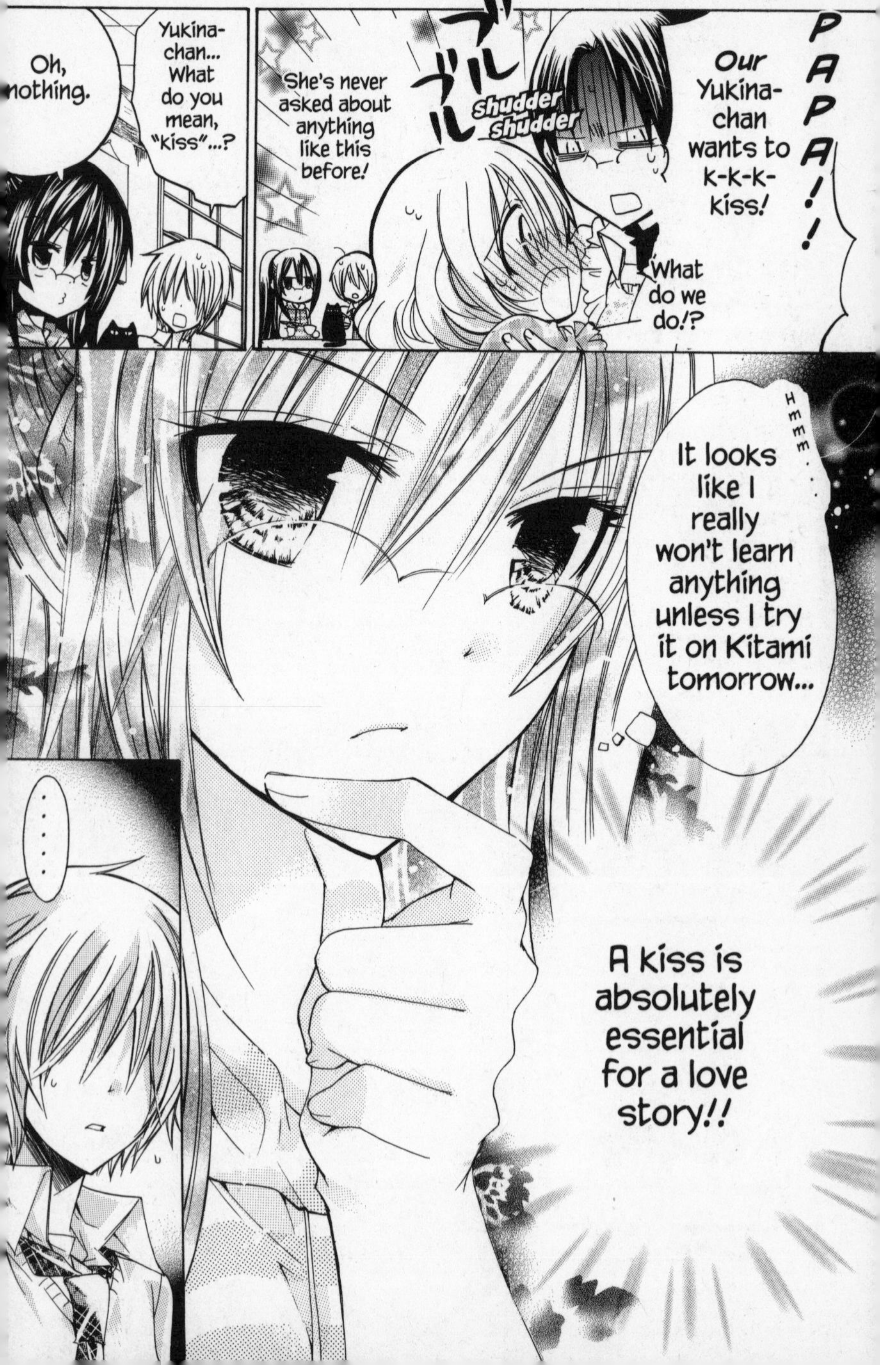
PAPA!!
Our Yukina-chan wants to k-k-k-kiss!
What do we do!?
ブルブル
Shudder shudder
She's never asked about anything like this before!
Yukina-chan... What do you mean, "kiss"...?
Oh, nothing.
Hmmm...
It looks like I really won't learn anything unless I try it on Kitami tomorrow...
A kiss is absolutely essential for a love story!!
.....

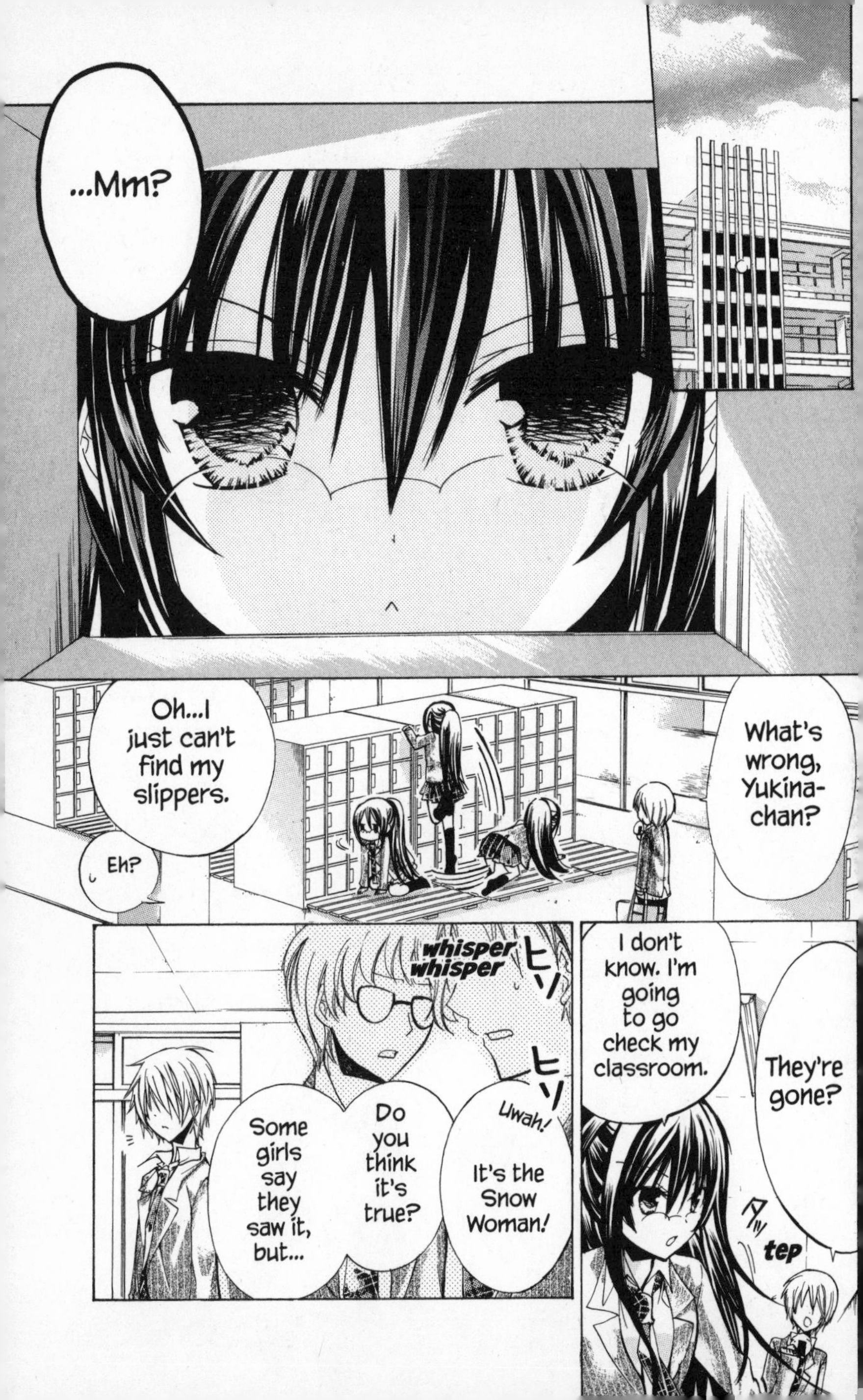
...Mm?
What's wrong, Yukina-chan?
Oh...I just can't find my slippers.
Eh?
They're gone?
I don't know. I'm going to go check my classroom.
tep
whisper whisper
Uwah!
It's the Snow Woman!
Do you think it's true?
Some girls say they saw it, but...

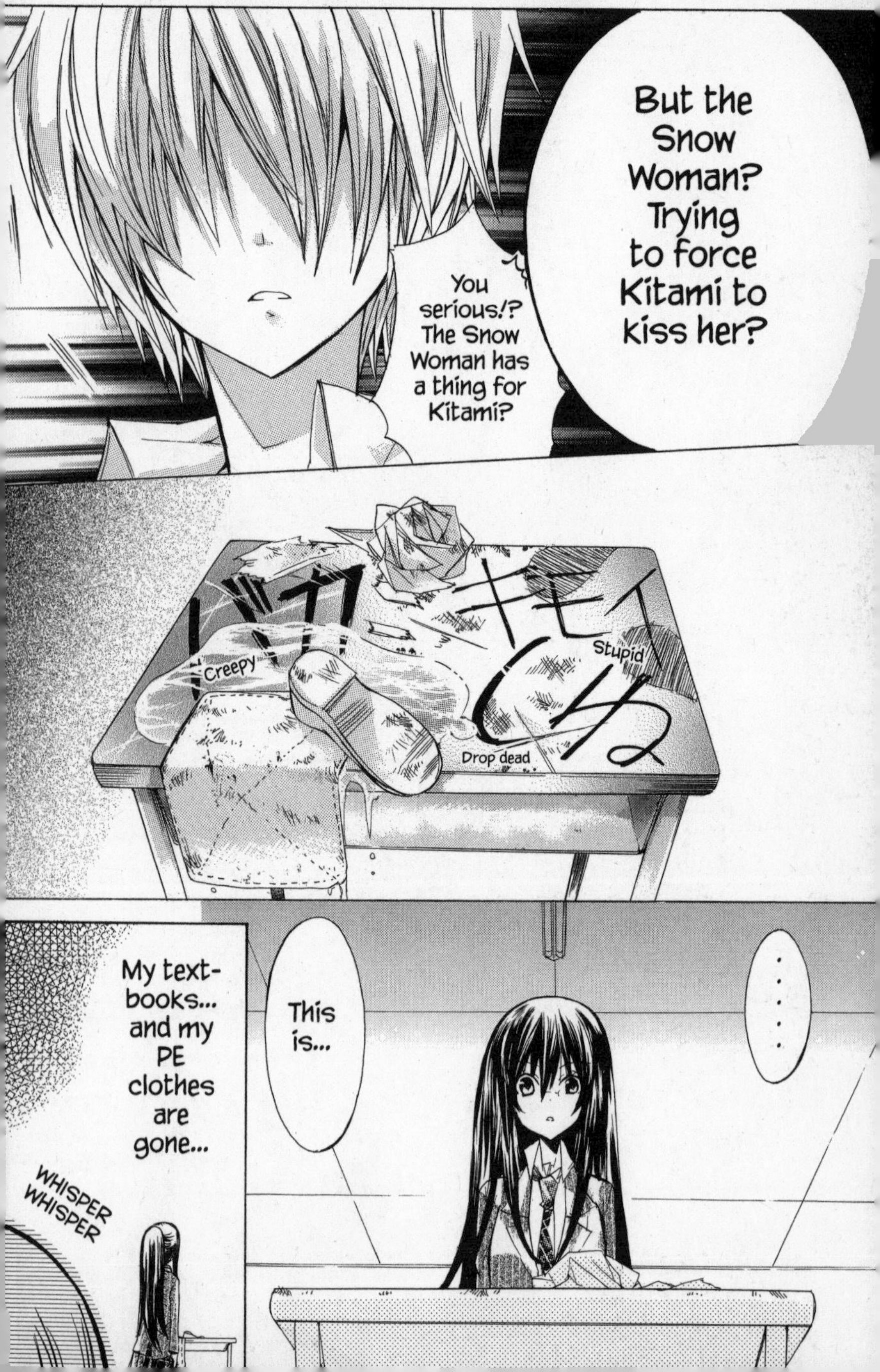
But the Snow Woman? Trying to force Kitami to kiss her?
You serious!? The Snow Woman has a thing for Kitami?
Stupid
Creepy
Drop dead
. . . . .
This is...
My text-books... and my PE clothes are gone...
WHISPER WHISPER

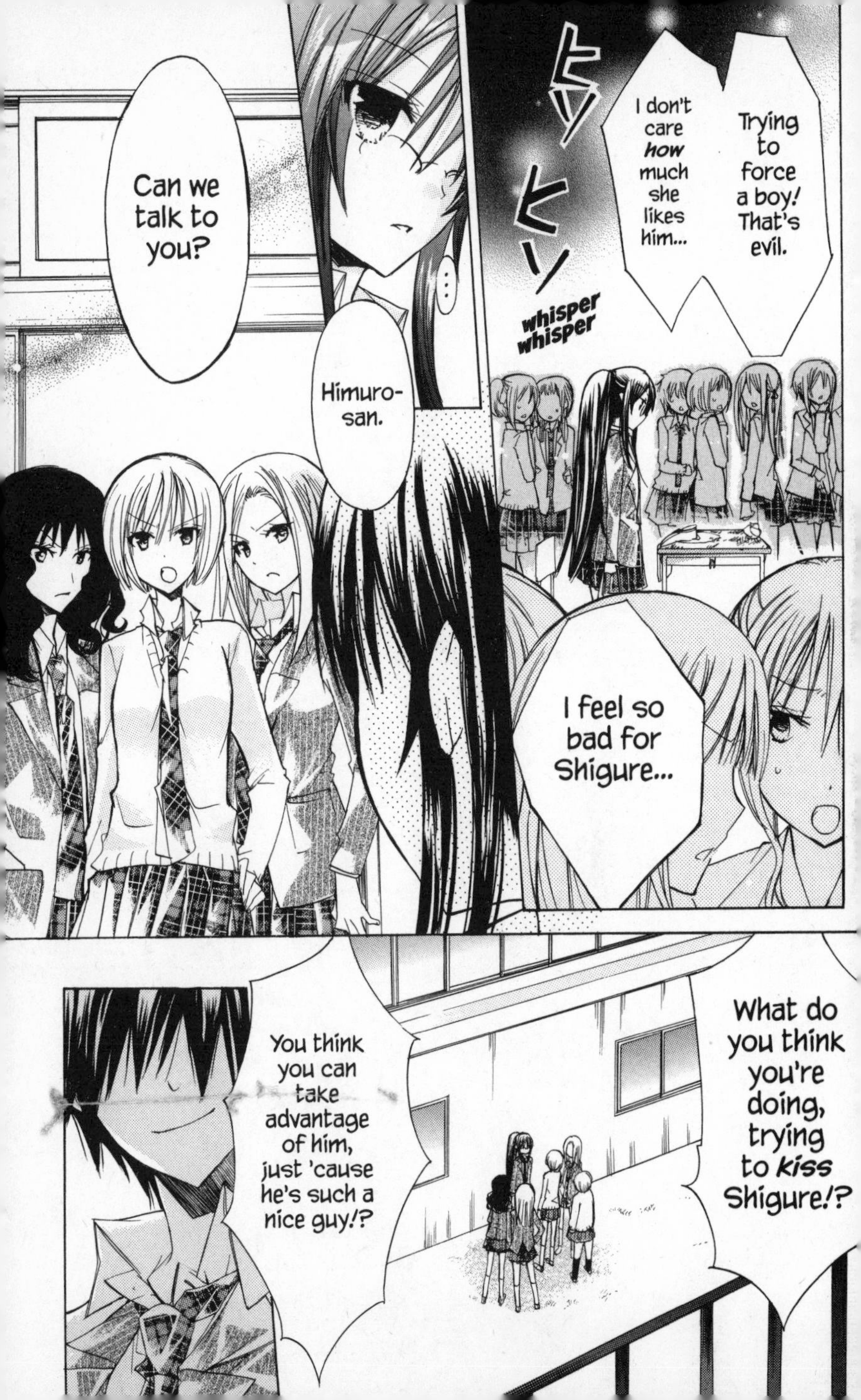

Trying to force a boy! That's evil.
I don't care *how* much she likes him...
whisper whisper
I feel so bad for Shigure...
...
Himuro-san.
Can we talk to you?
What do you think you're doing, trying to *kiss* Shigure!?
You think you can take advantage of him, just 'cause he's such a nice guy!?

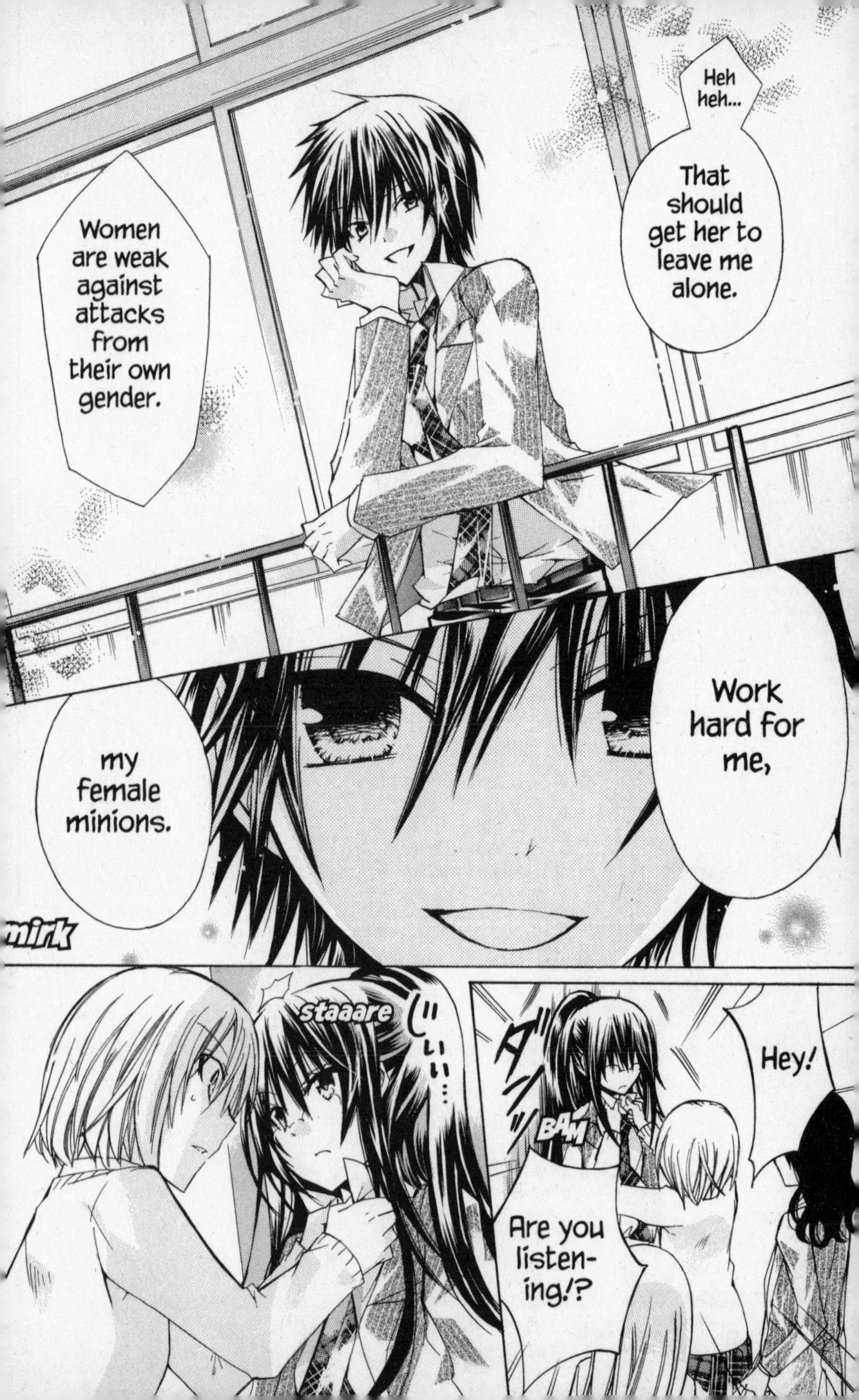
Heh heh...
That should get her to leave me alone.
Women are weak against attacks from their own gender.
Work hard for me,
my female minions.
smirk
Hey!
BAM
Are you listening!?
staaare

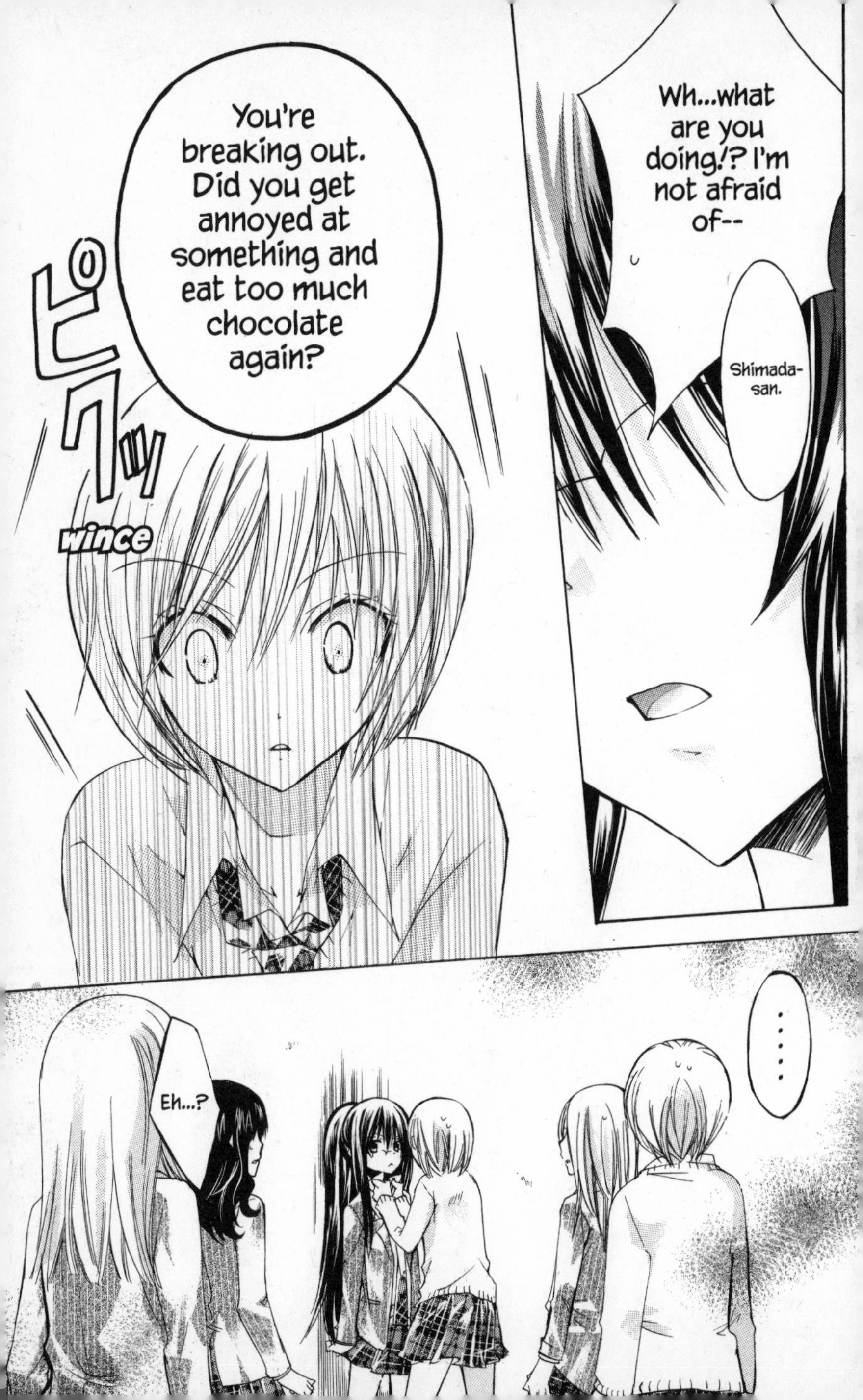
Wh...what are you doing!? I'm not afraid of--
Shimada-san.
You're breaking out. Did you get annoyed at something and eat too much chocolate again?
wince
......
Eh...?

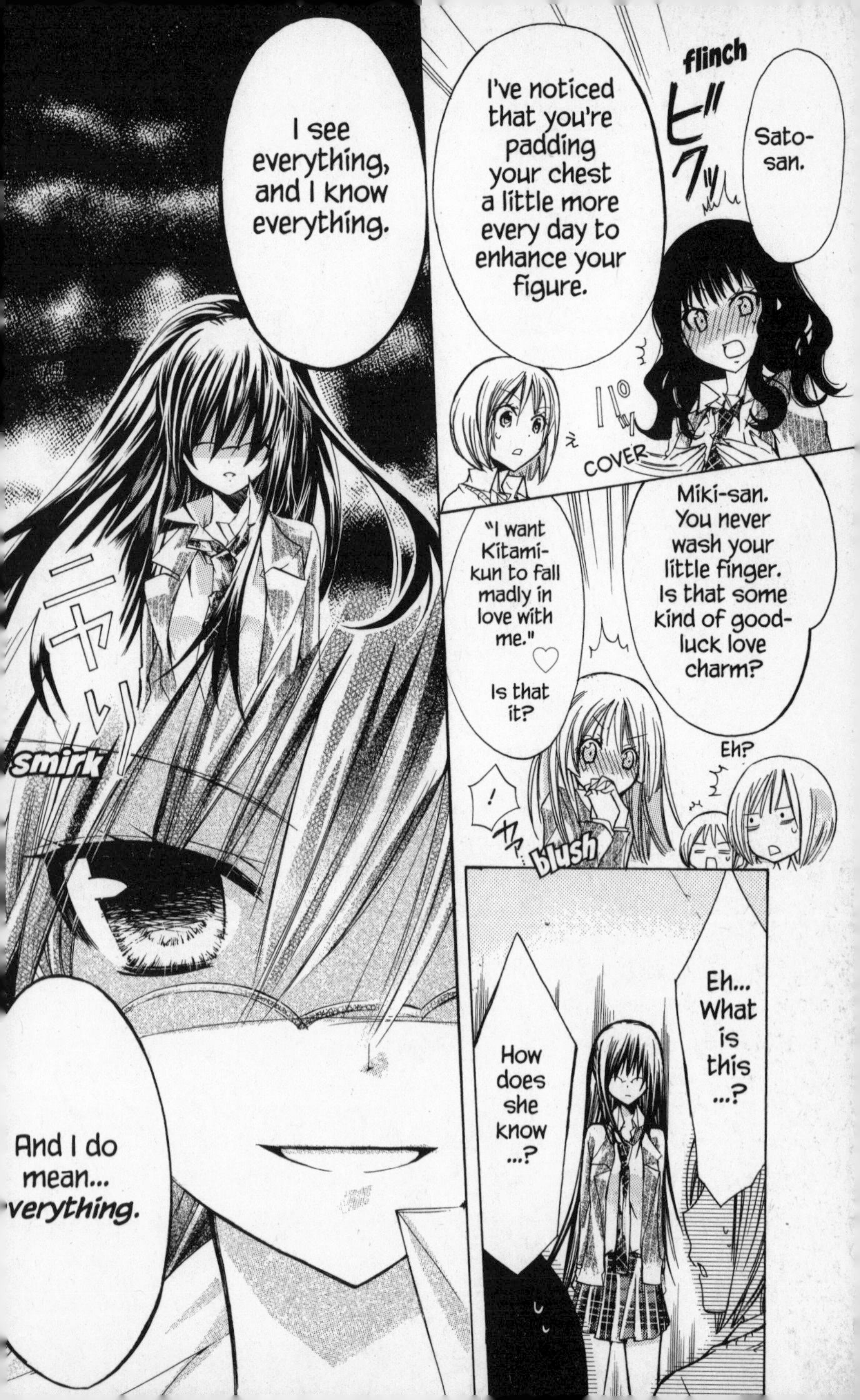
Sato-san.
flinch
I've noticed that you're padding your chest a little more every day to enhance your figure.
COVER
Miki-san. You never wash your little finger. Is that some kind of good-luck love charm?
"I want Kitami-kun to fall madly in love with me." ♡ Is that it?
Eh?
!
blush
Eh... What is this...?
How does she know...?
I see everything, and I know everything.
smirk
And I do mean... verything.

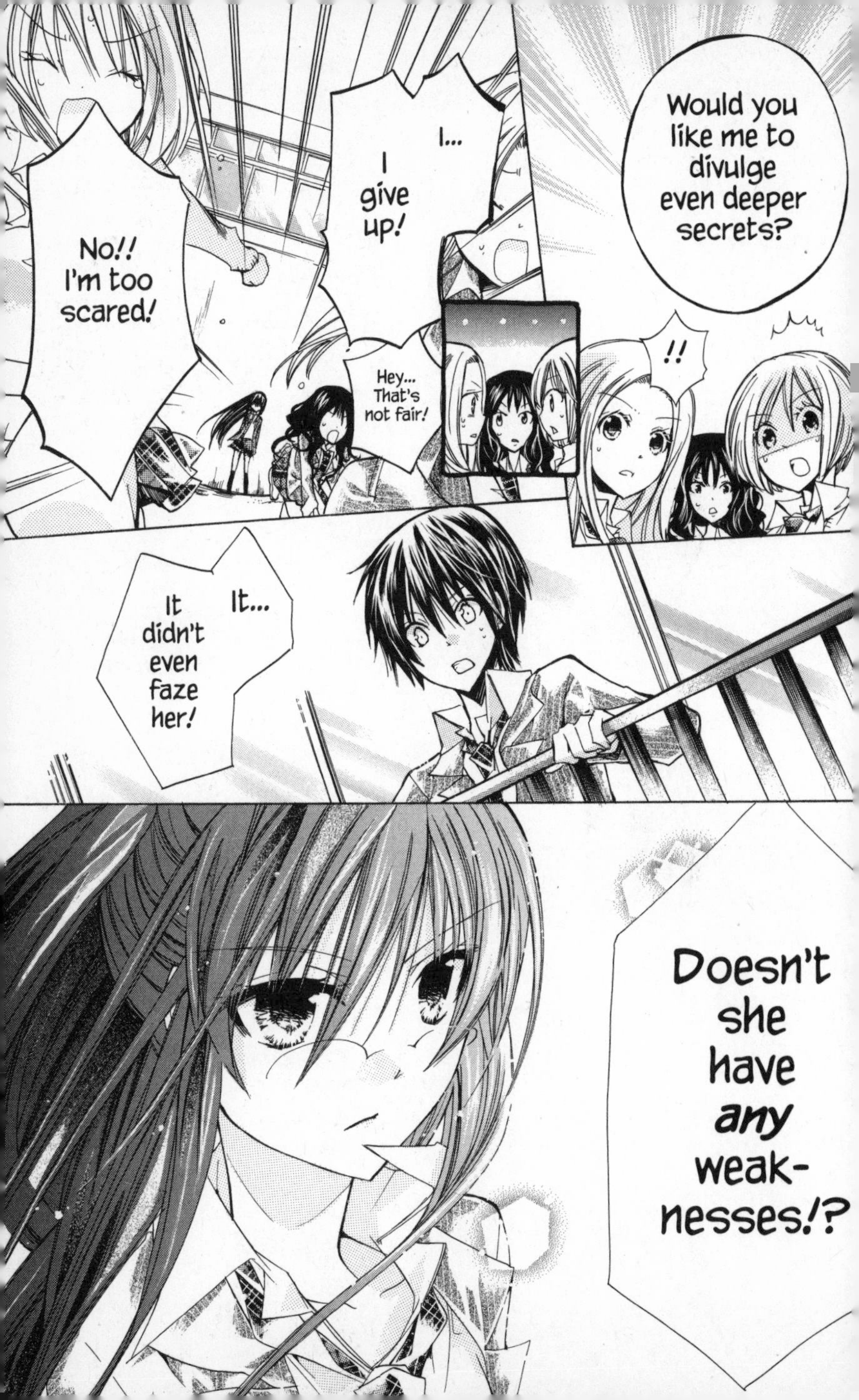
Would you like me to divulge even deeper secrets?
I... I give up!
No!! I'm too scared!
Hey... That's not fair!
!!
It... It didn't even faze her!
Doesn't she have *any* weak-nesses!?

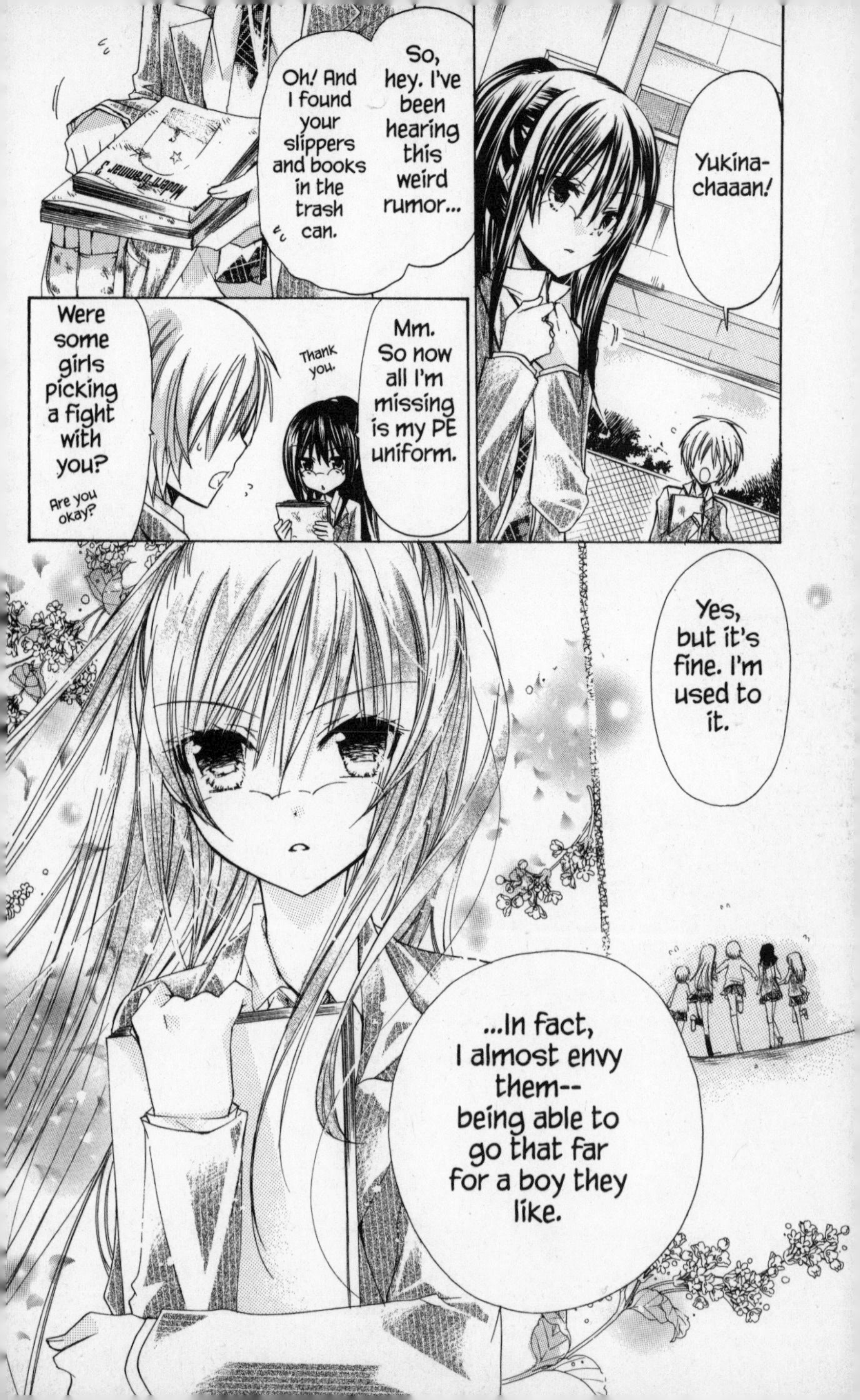
Yukina-chaaan!
So, hey. I've been hearing this weird rumor...
Oh! And I found your slippers and books in the trash can.
Mm. So now all I'm missing is my PE uniform.
Thank you.
Were some girls picking a fight with you?
Are you okay?
Yes, but it's fine. I'm used to it.
...In fact, I almost envy them--being able to go that far for a boy they like.

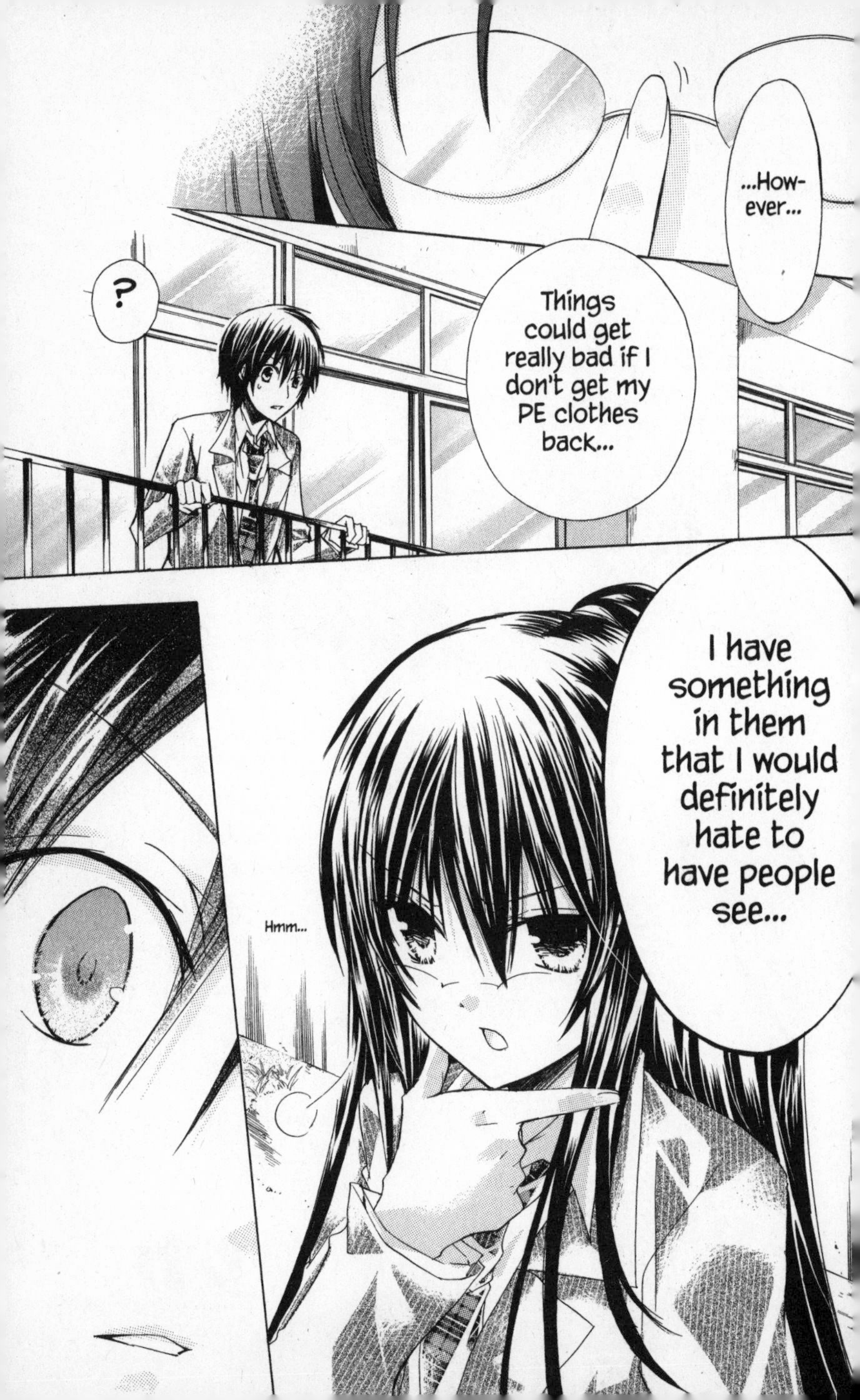
...How-ever...
Things could get really bad if I don't get my PE clothes back...
?
I have something in them that I would definitely hate to have people see...
Hmm...

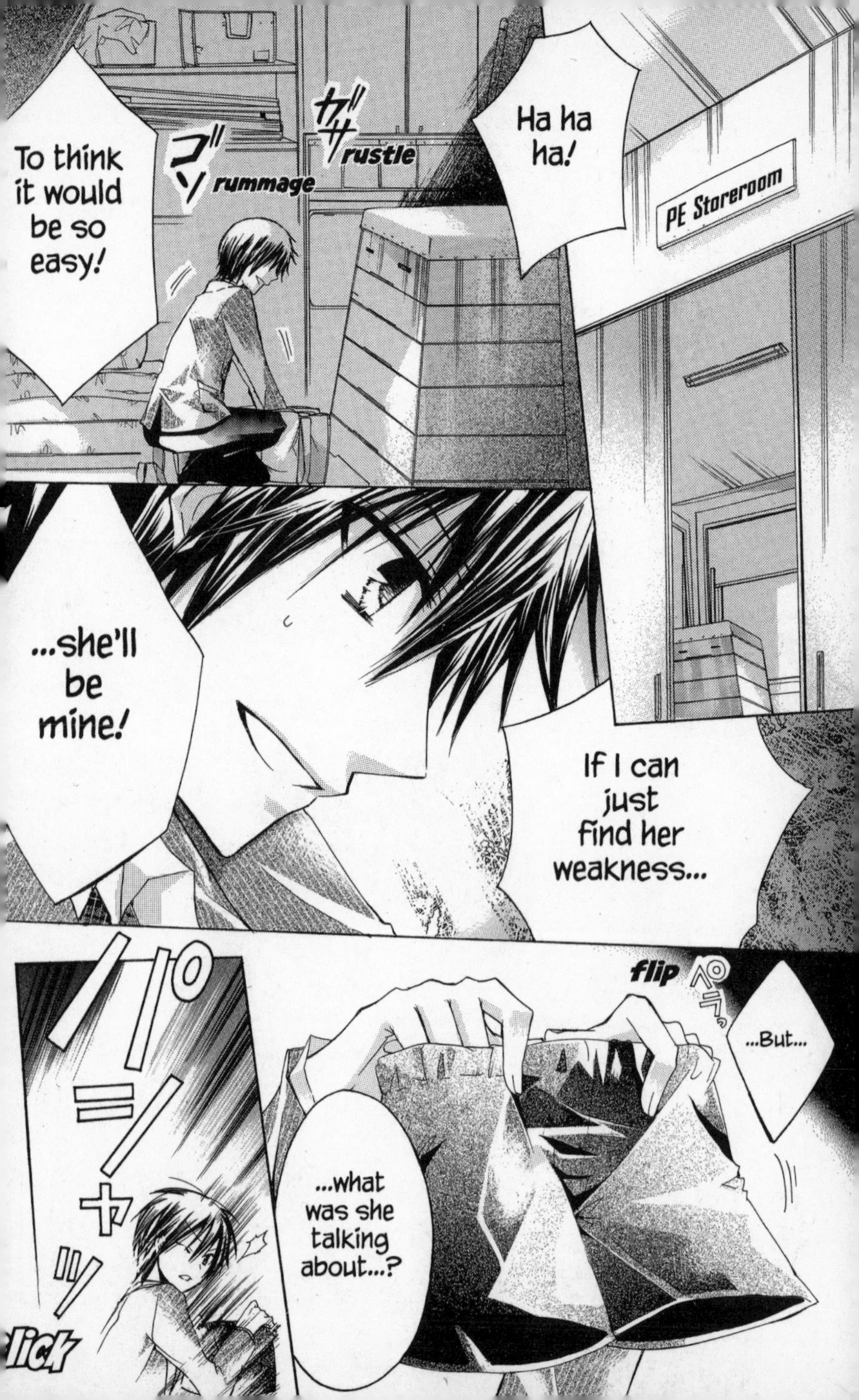
Ha ha ha!
PE Storeroom
To think it would be so easy!
rustle
rummage
If I can just find her weakness...
...she'll be mine!
flip
...But...
...what was she talking about...?
lick

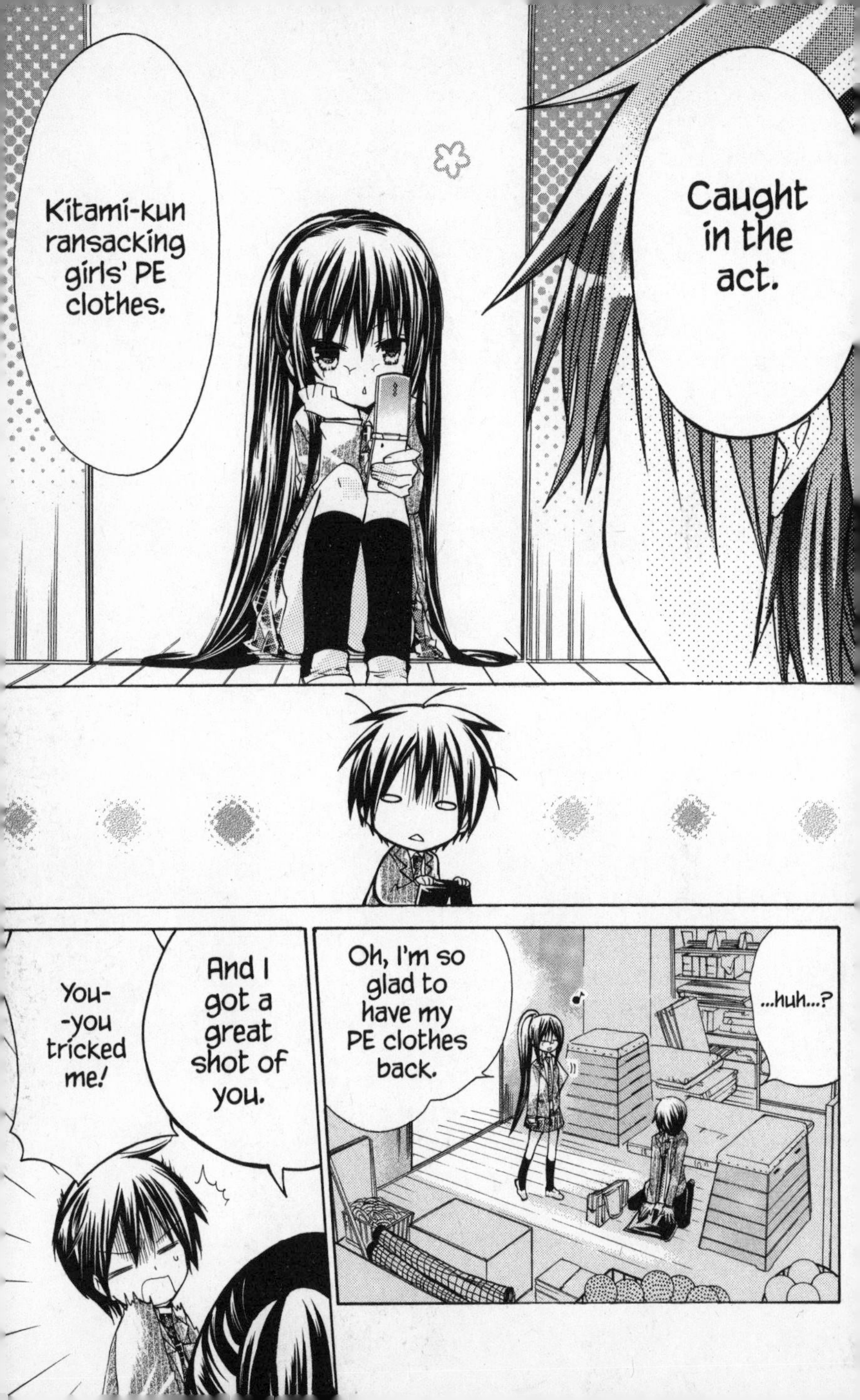
Caught in the act.
Kitami-kun ransacking girls' PE clothes.
...huh...?
Oh, I'm so glad to have my PE clothes back.
And I got a great shot of you.
You- -you tricked me!

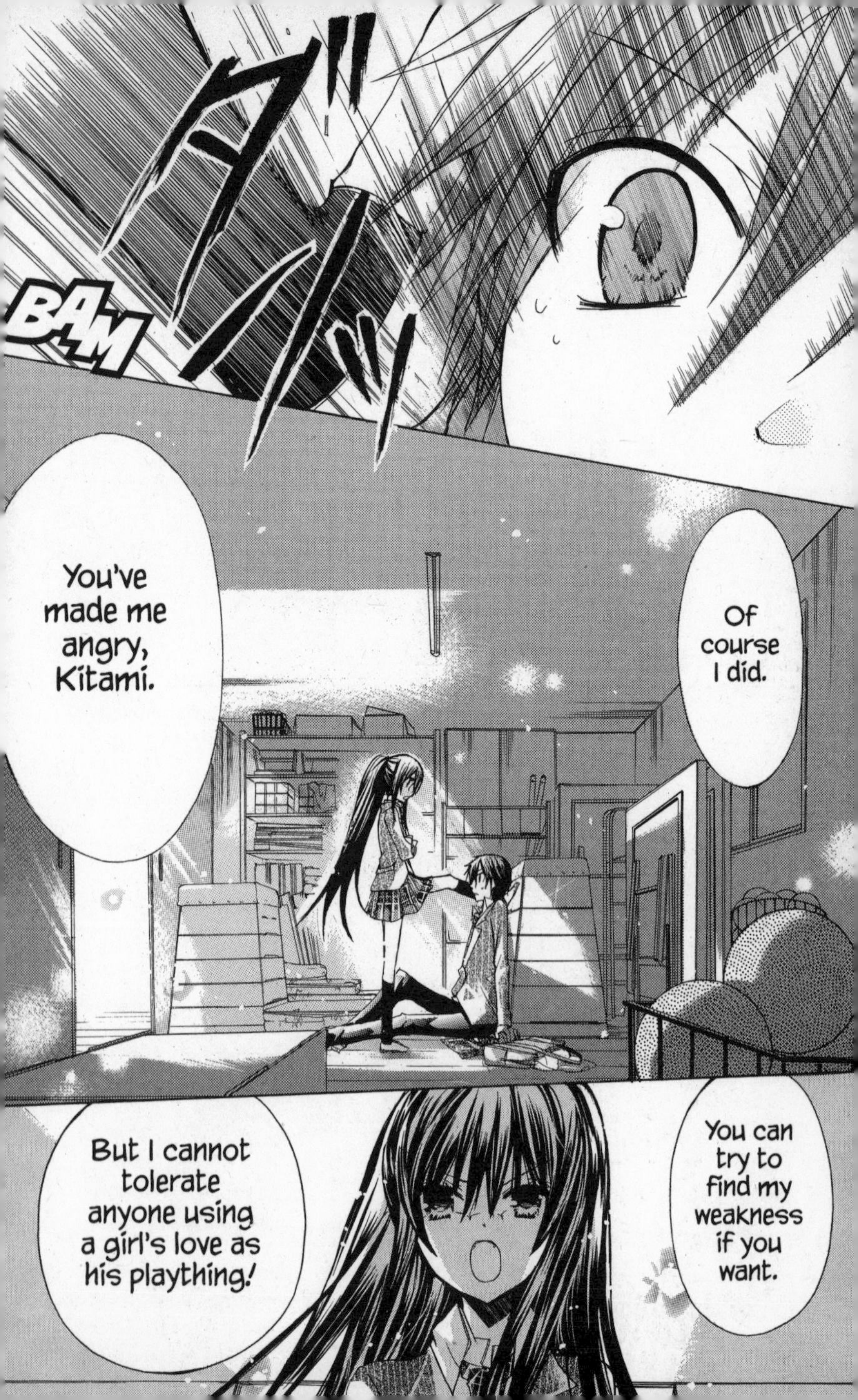
BAM
Of course I did.
You've made me angry, Kitami.
You can try to find my weakness if you want.
But I cannot tolerate anyone using a girl's love as his plaything!

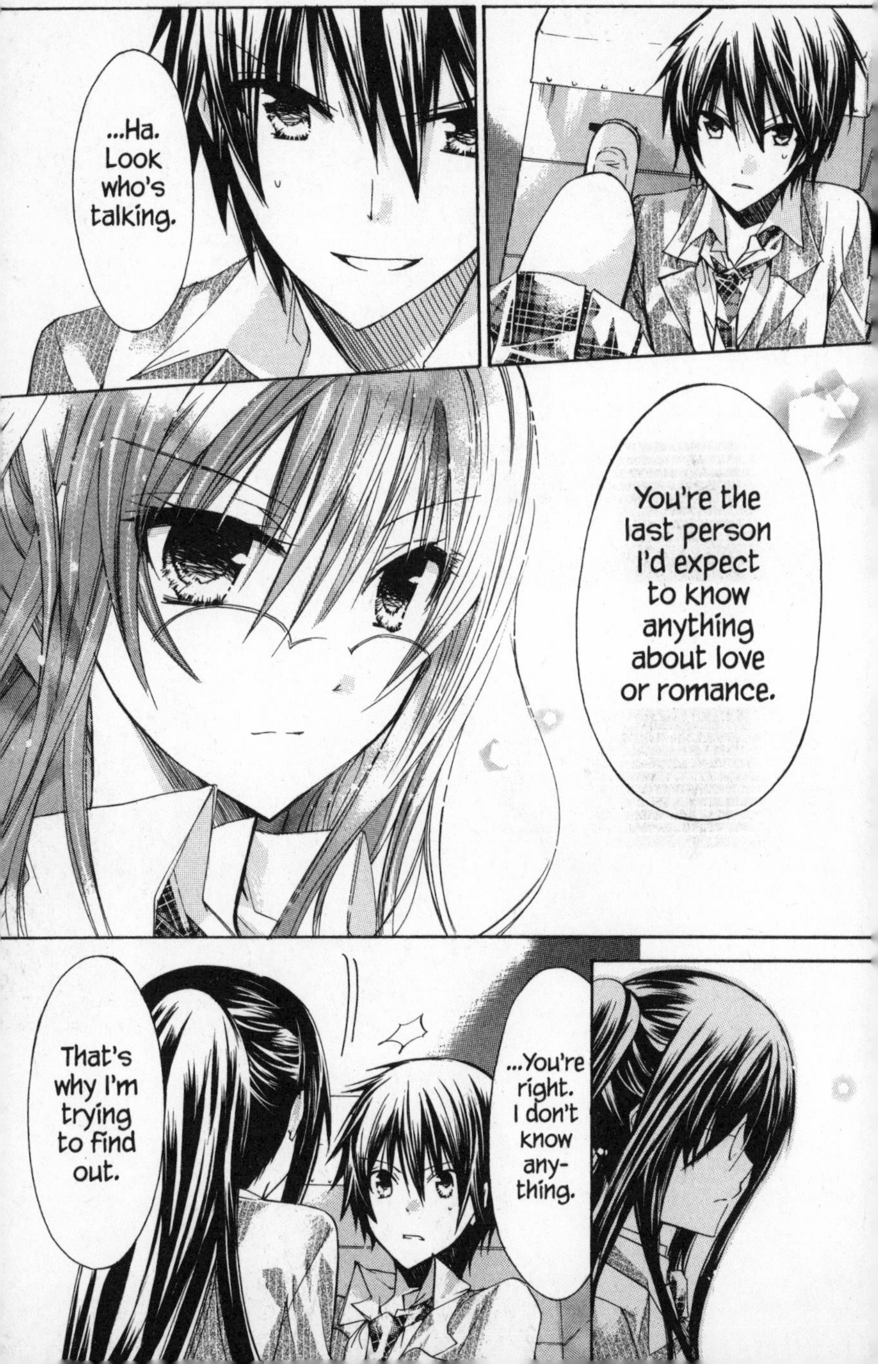
...Ha. Look who's talking.
You're the last person I'd expect to know anything about love or romance.
...You're right. I don't know any-thing.
That's why I'm trying to find out.

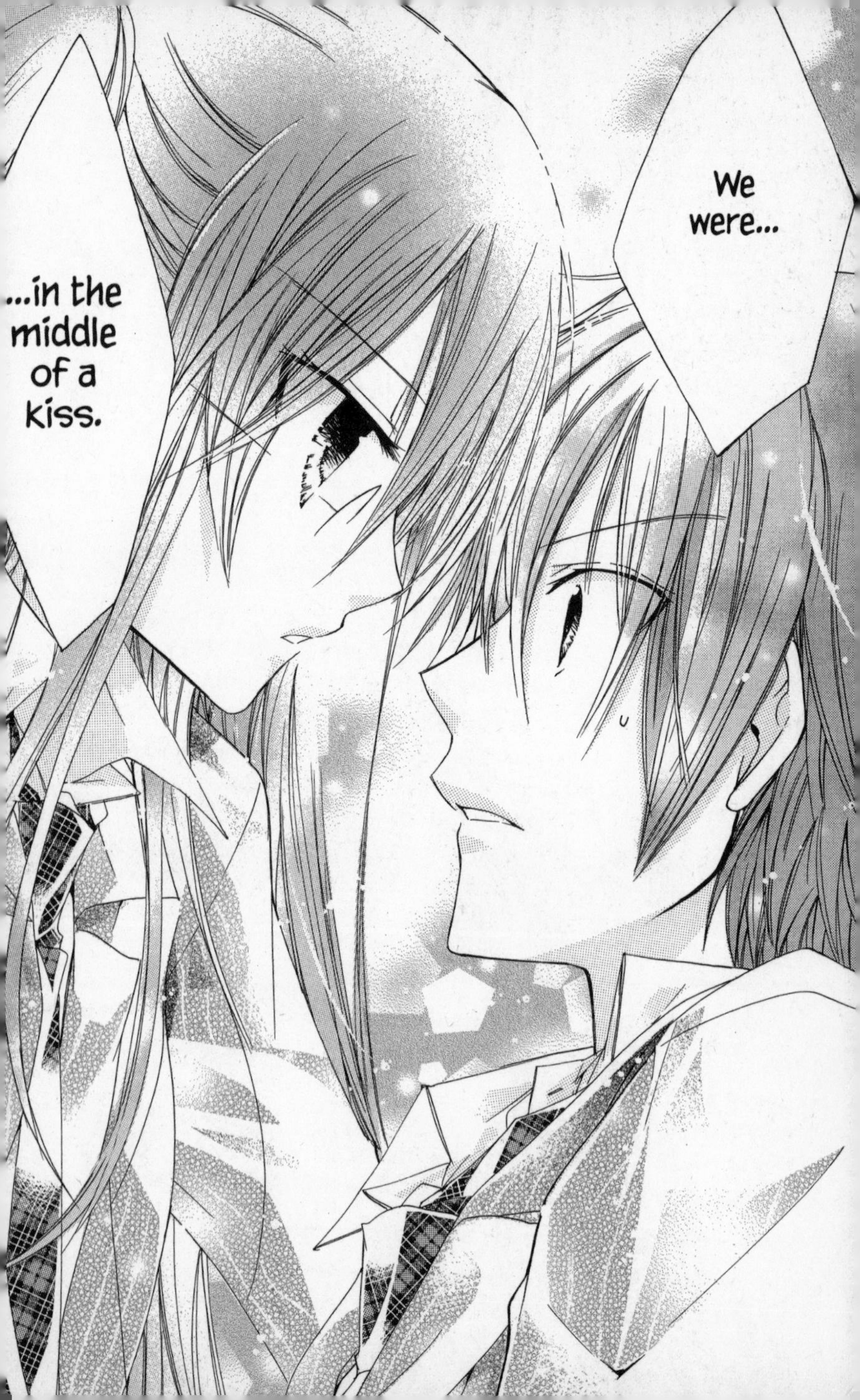
We were...
...in the middle of a kiss.

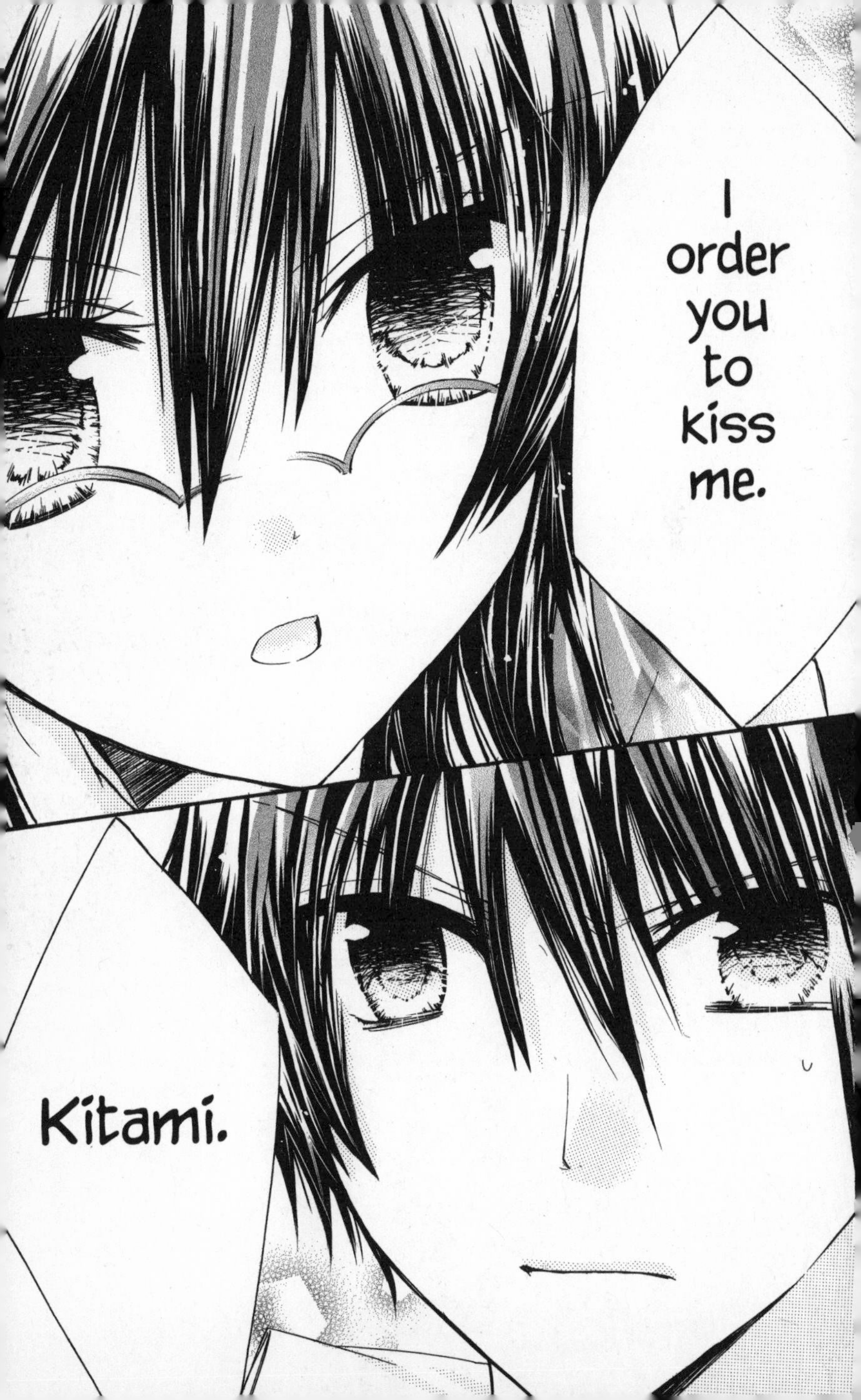
I order you to kiss me.
Kitami.

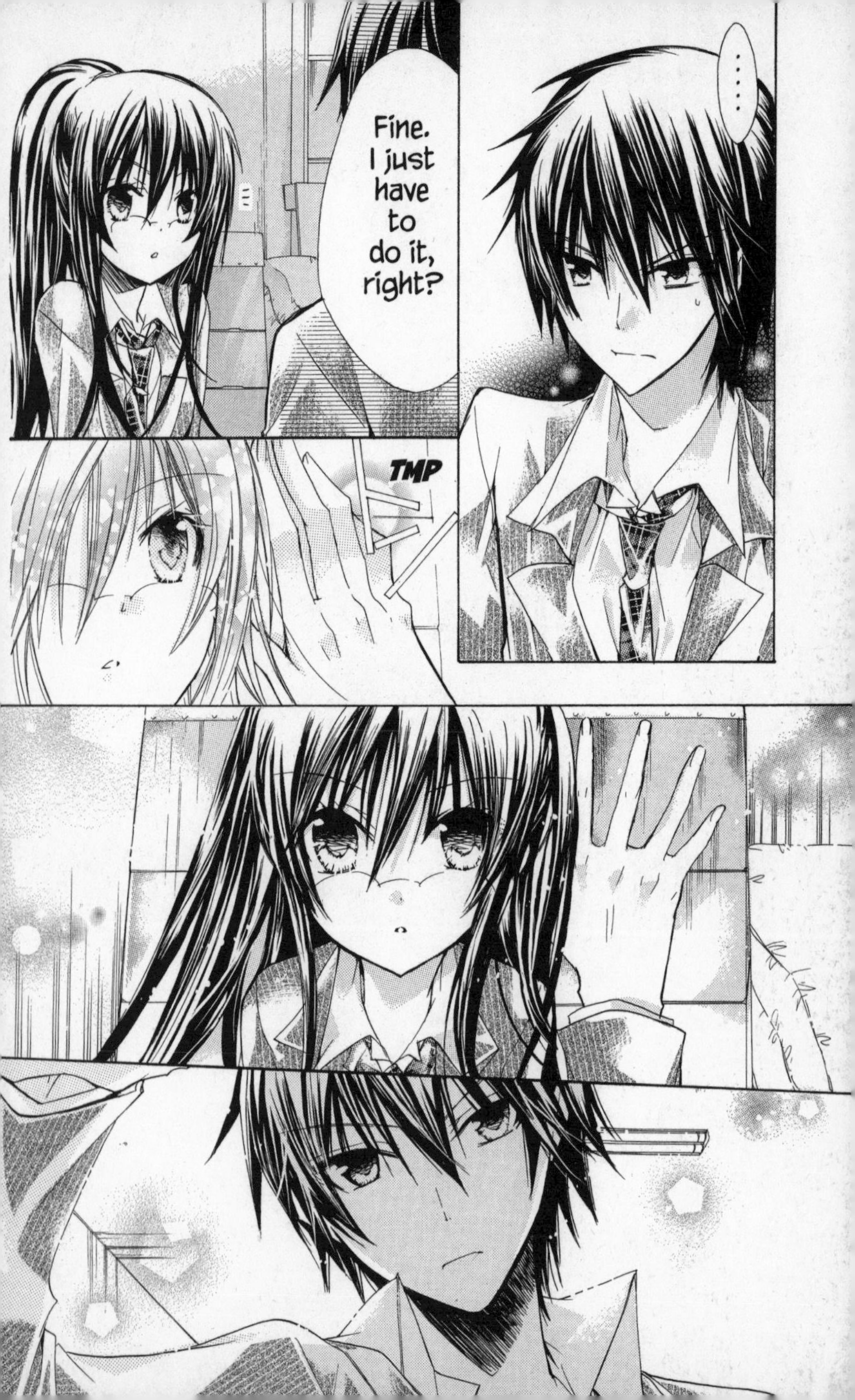
......
Fine. I just have to do it, right?
TMP

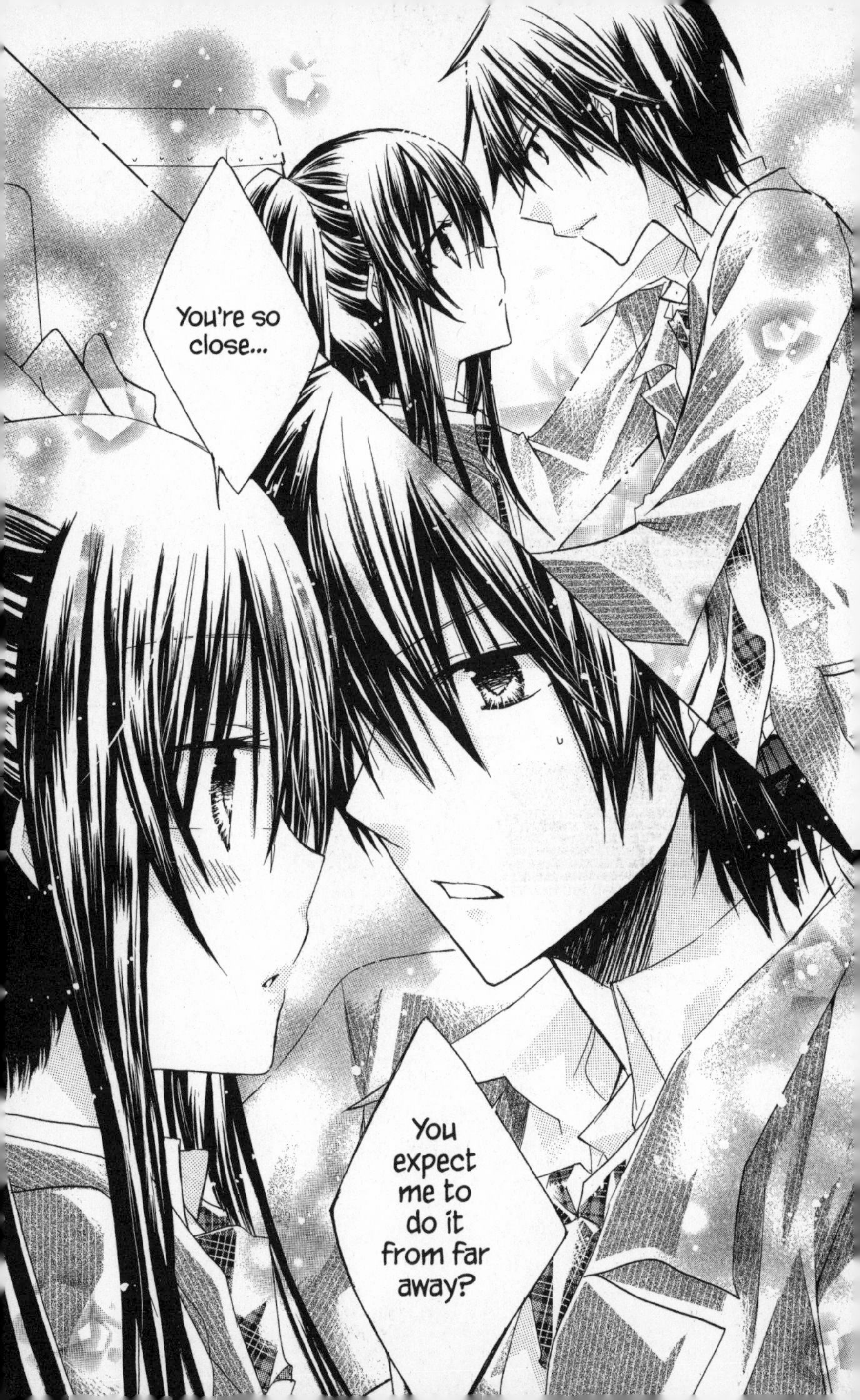
You're so close...
You expect me to do it from far away?

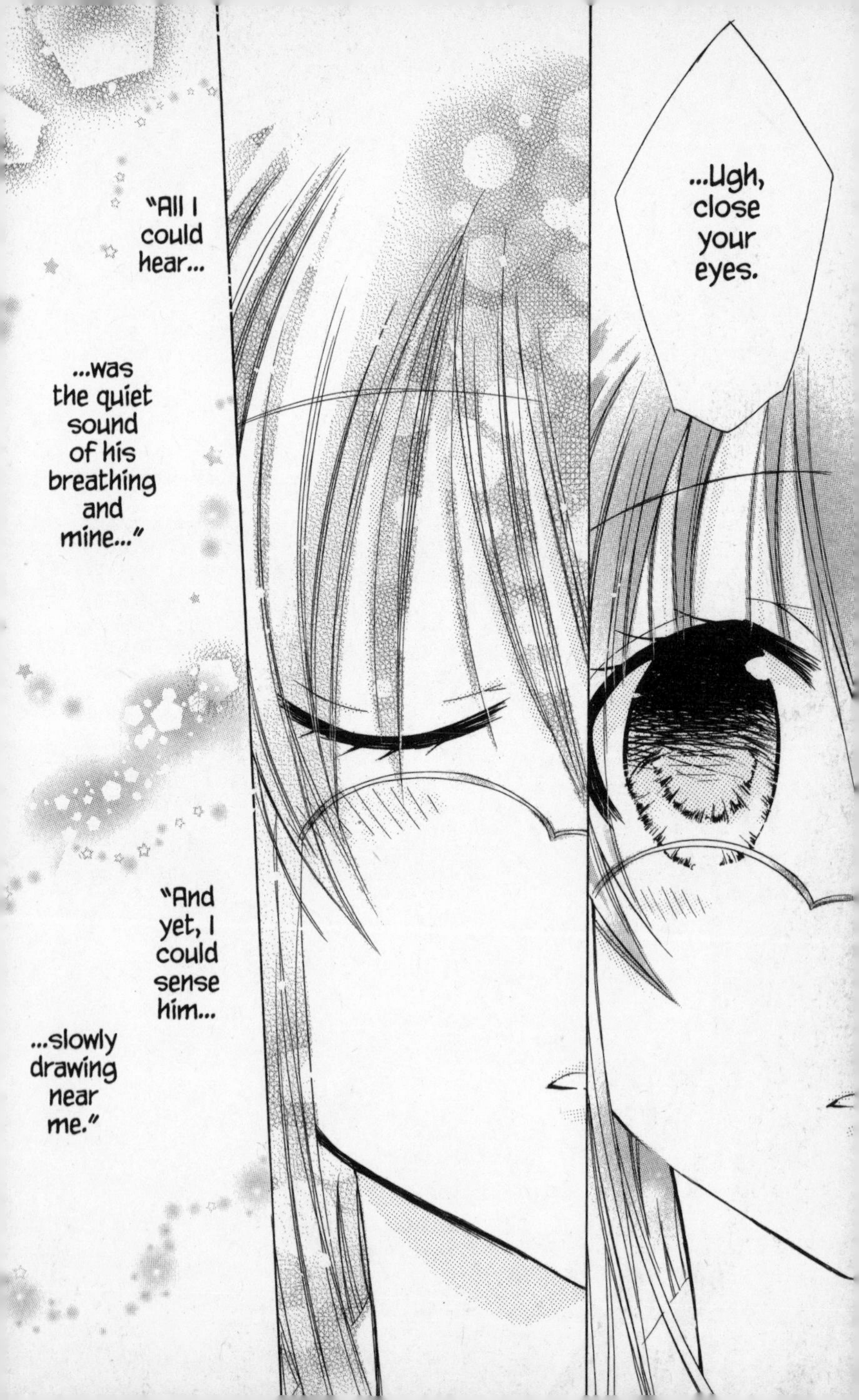
...Ugh, close your eyes.
"All I could hear...
...was the quiet sound of his breathing and mine..."
"And yet, I could sense him...
...slowly drawing near me."

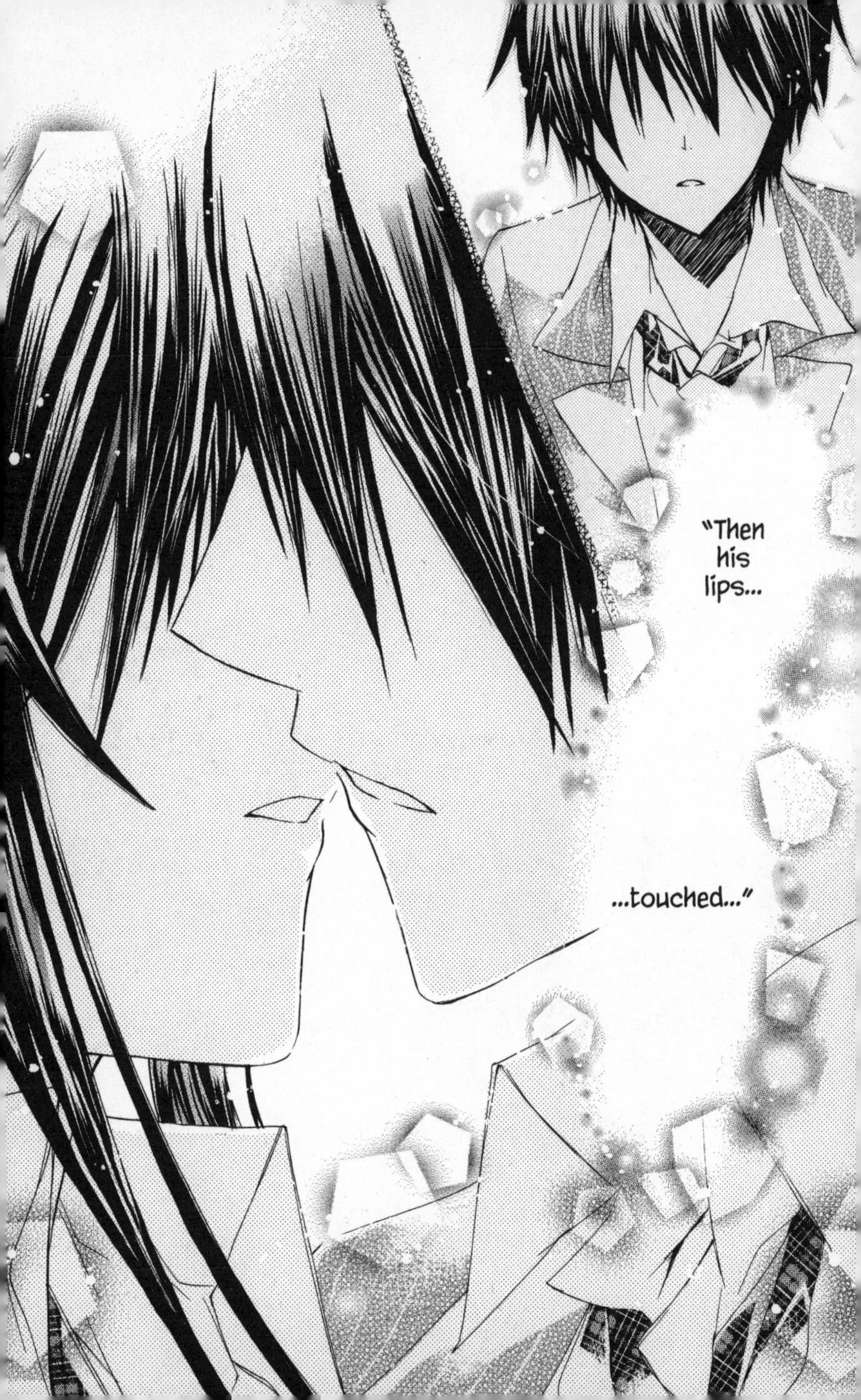
"Then his lips...
...touched..."

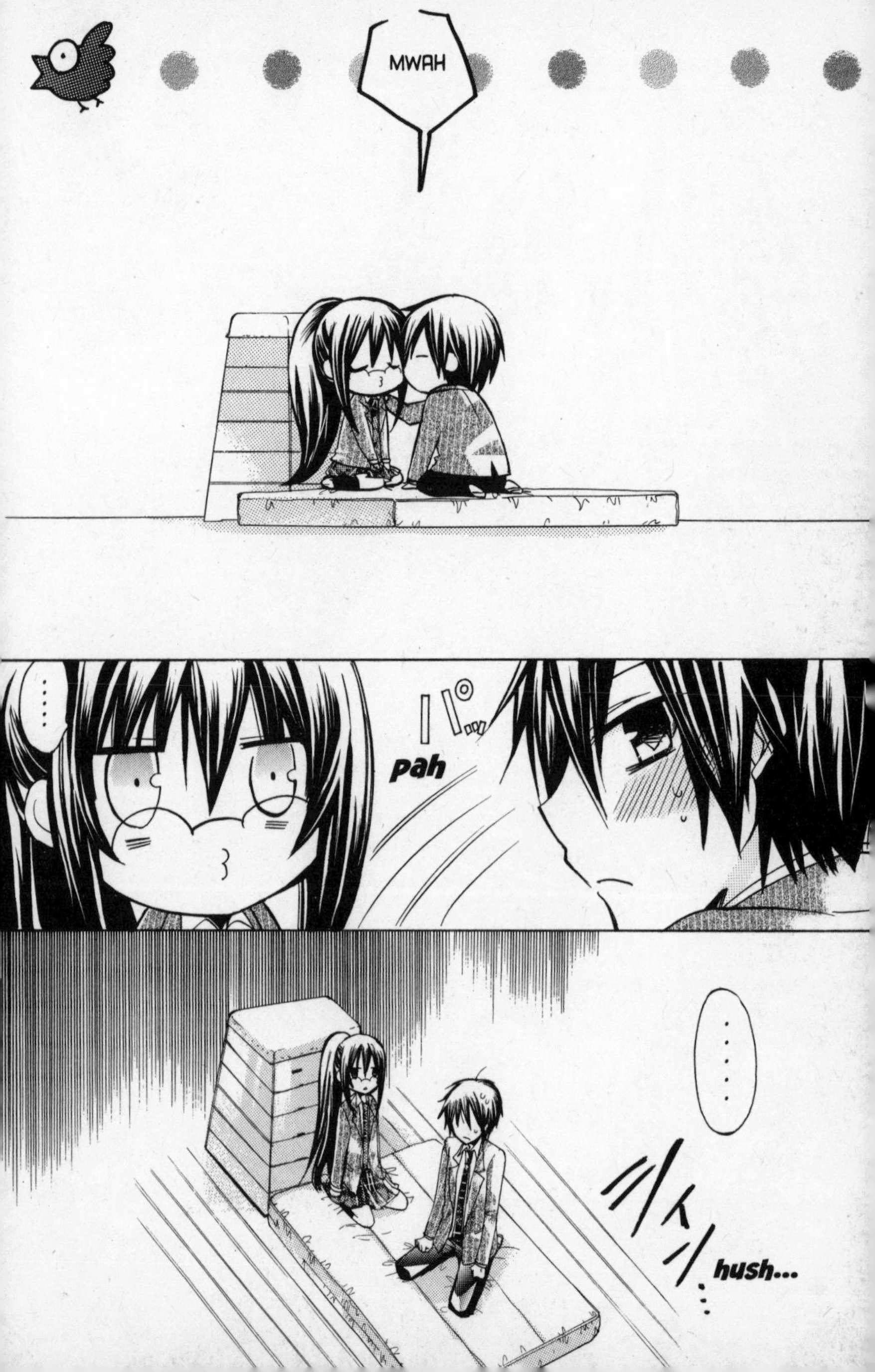
MWAH
pah
……
……
hush…

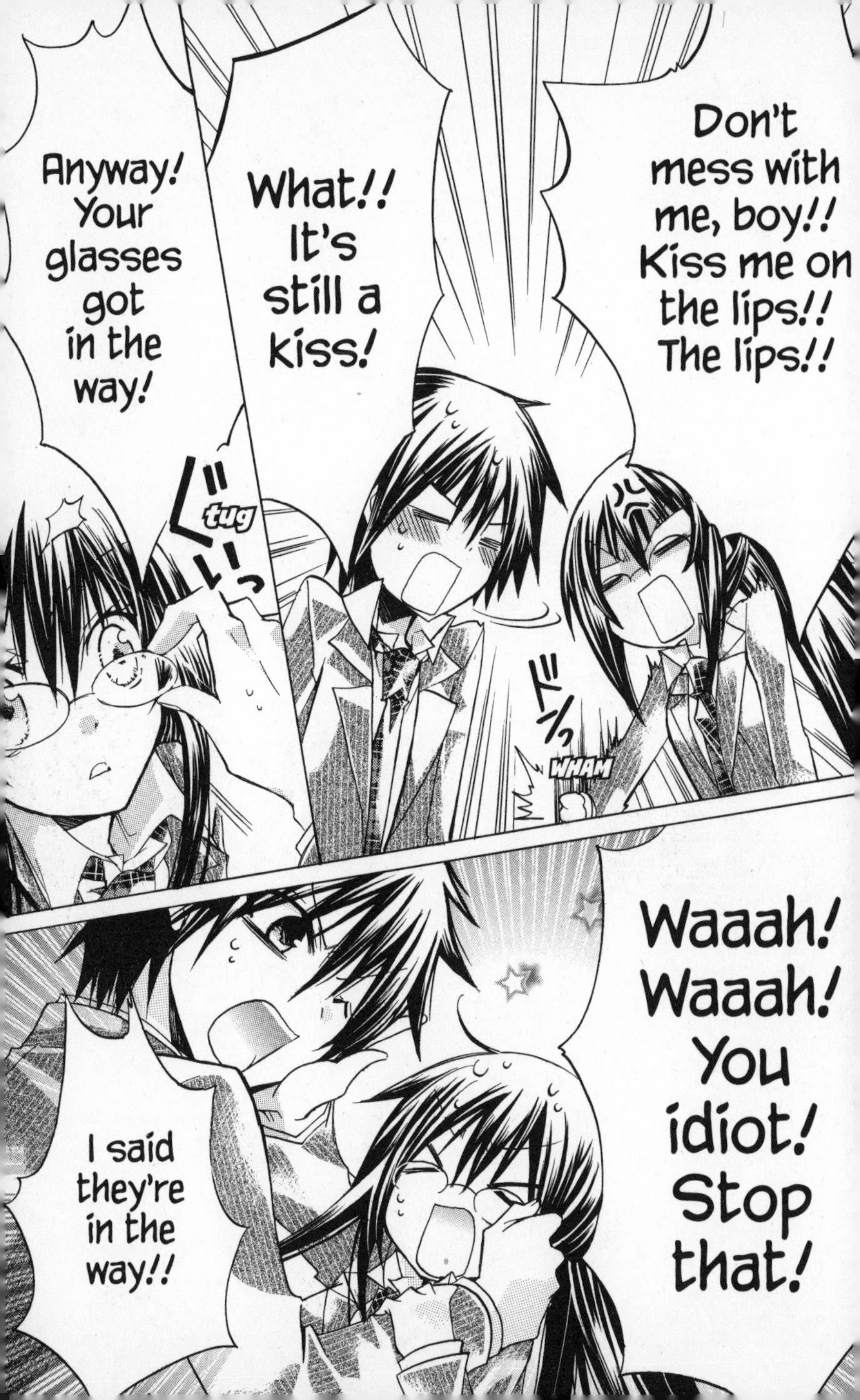

Don't mess with me, boy!! Kiss me on the lips!! The lips!!
What!! It's still a kiss!
ドンッ
WHAM
Anyway! Your glasses got in the way!
ぐいっ
tug
Waaah! Waaah! You idiot! Stop that!
I said they're in the way!!

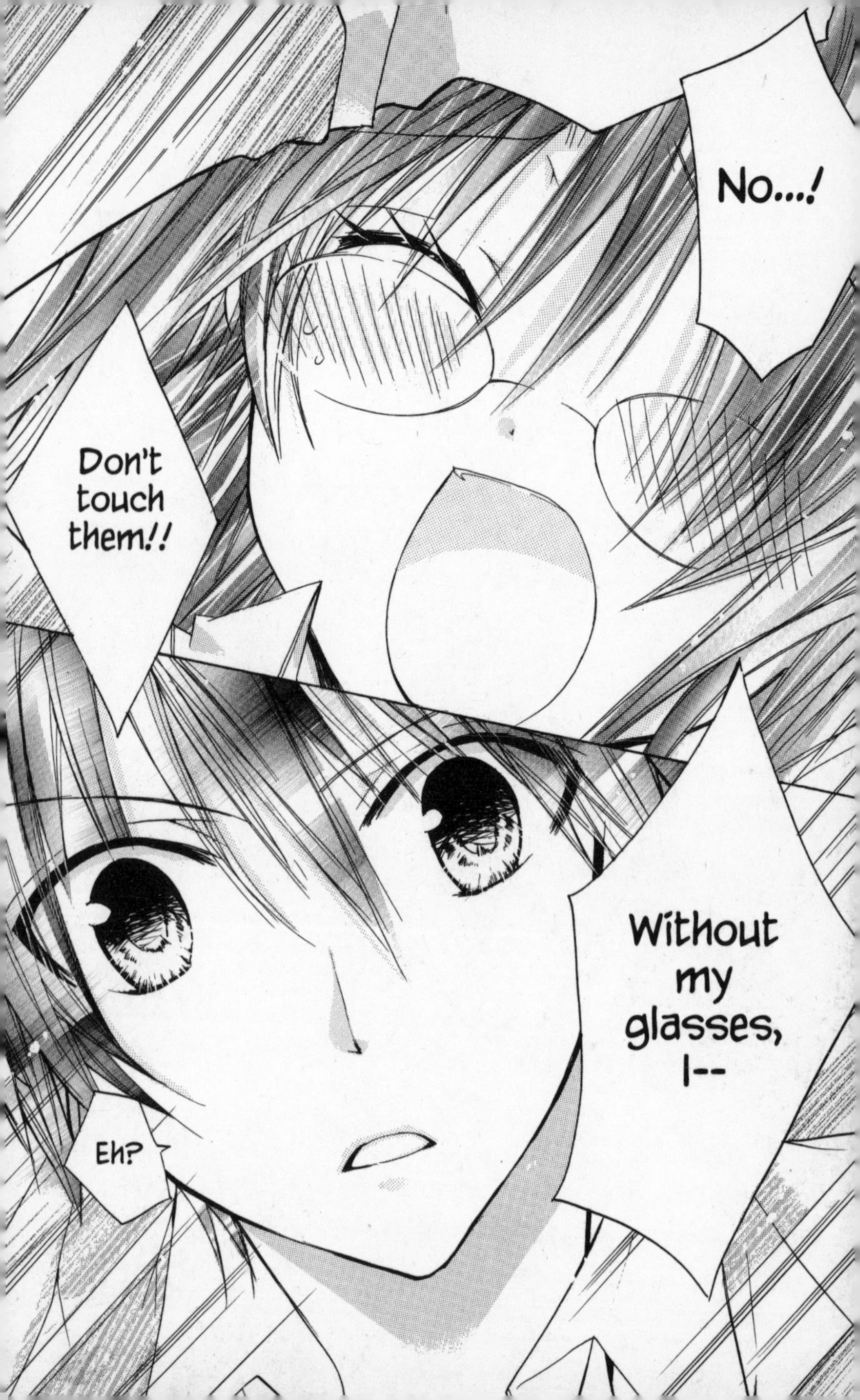
No...!
Don't touch them!!
Without my glasses, I--
Eh?

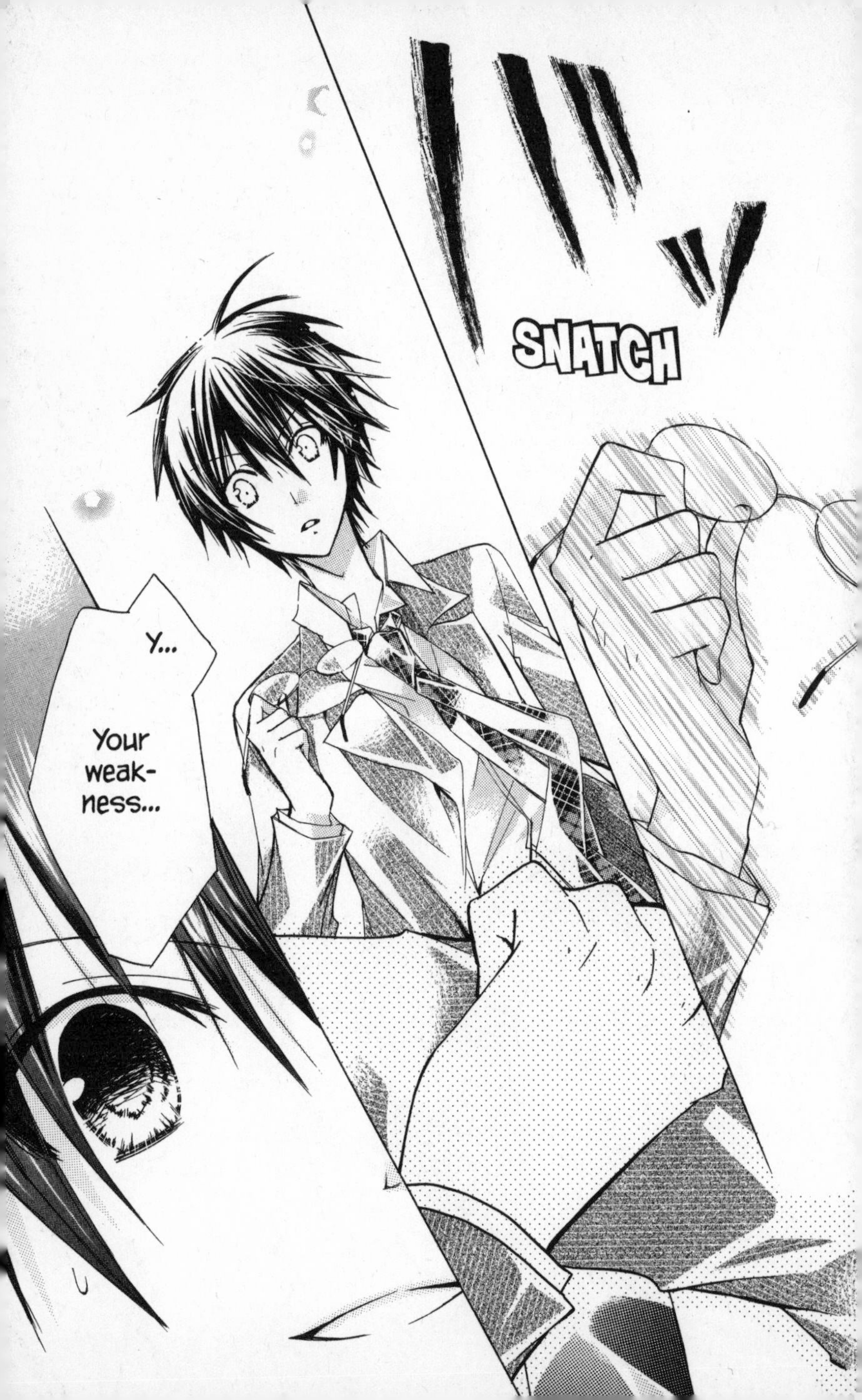
SNATCH
Y...
Your weak-ness...

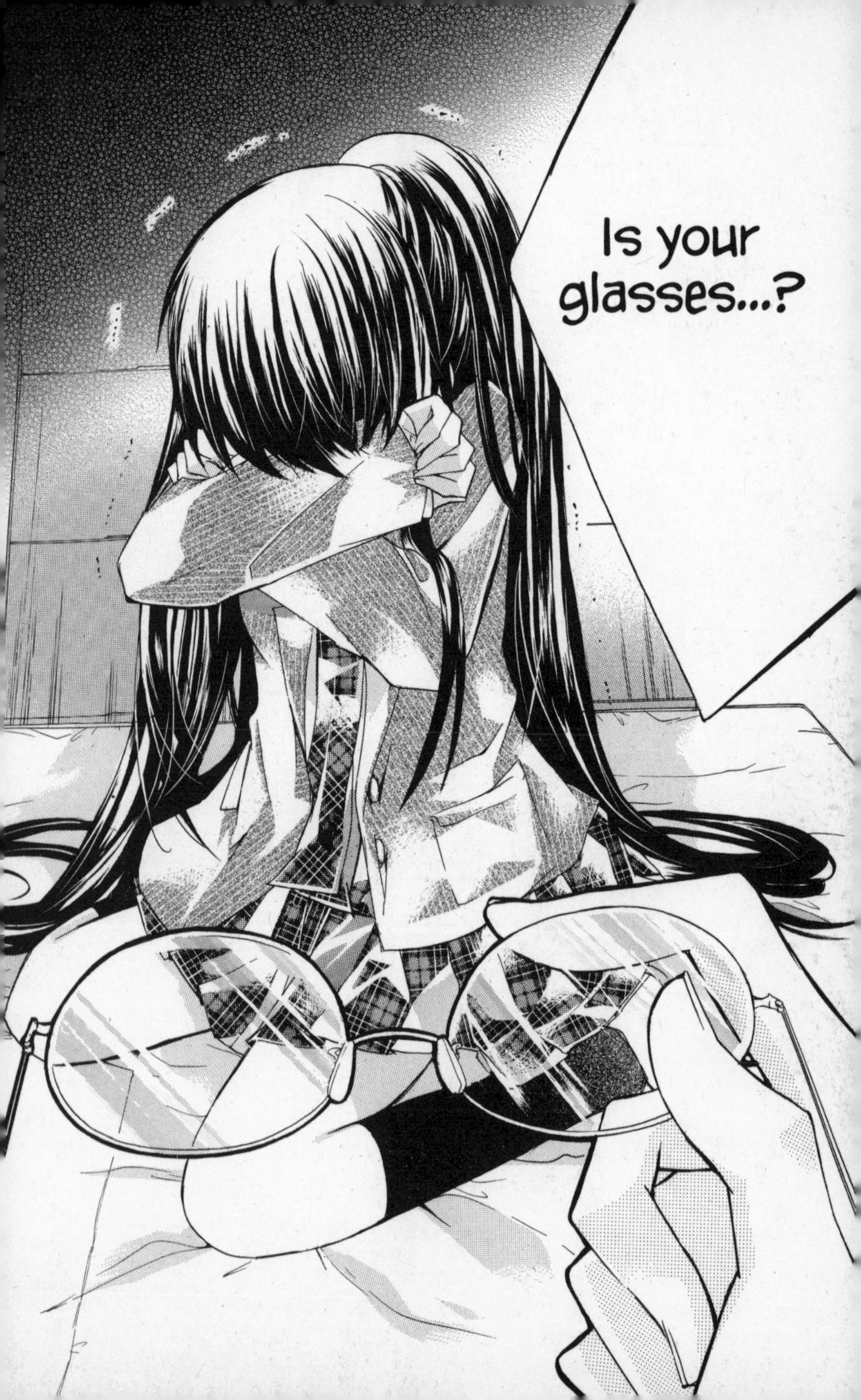
Is your glasses...?

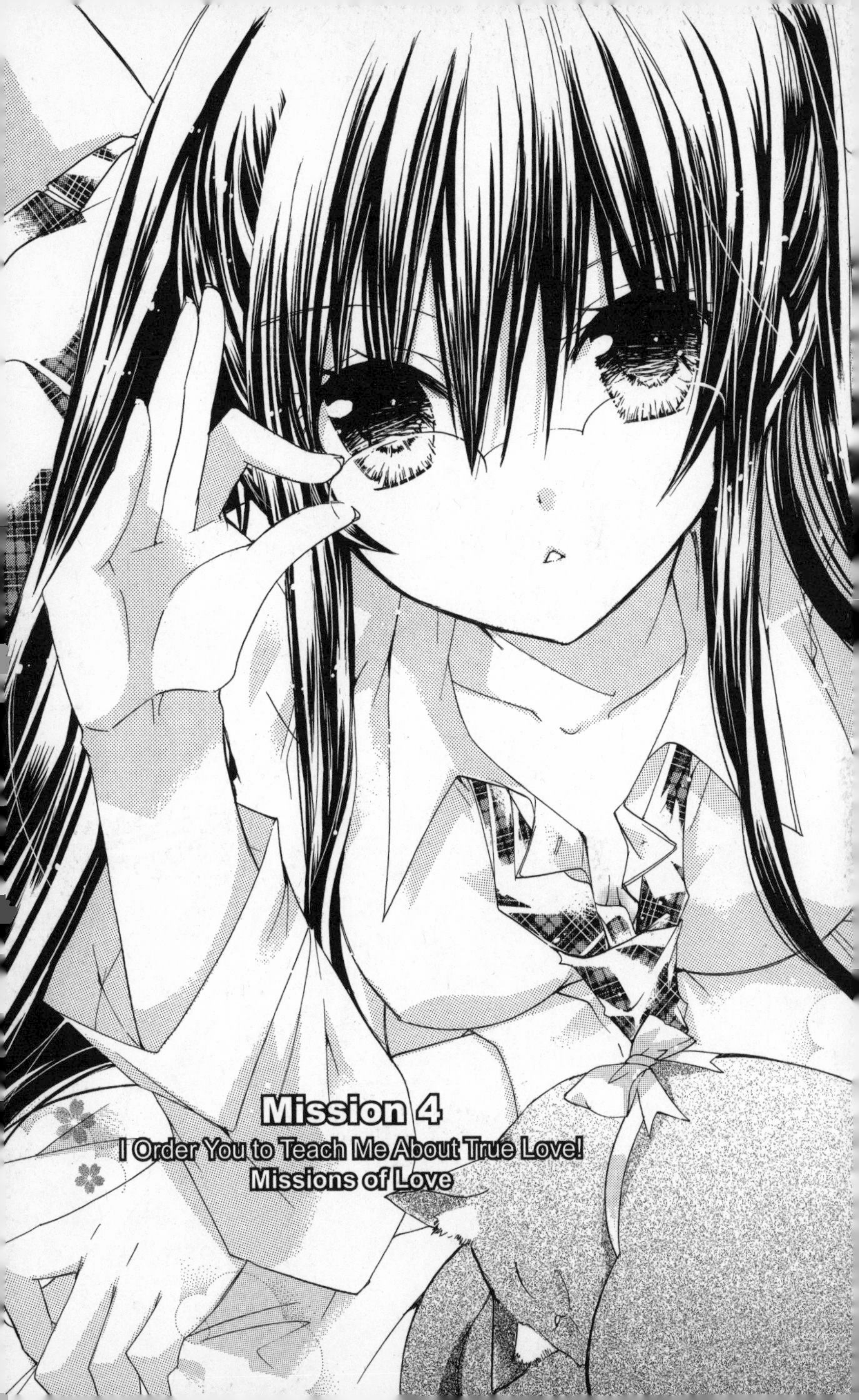
Mission 4
I Order You to Teach Me About True Love!
Missions of Love

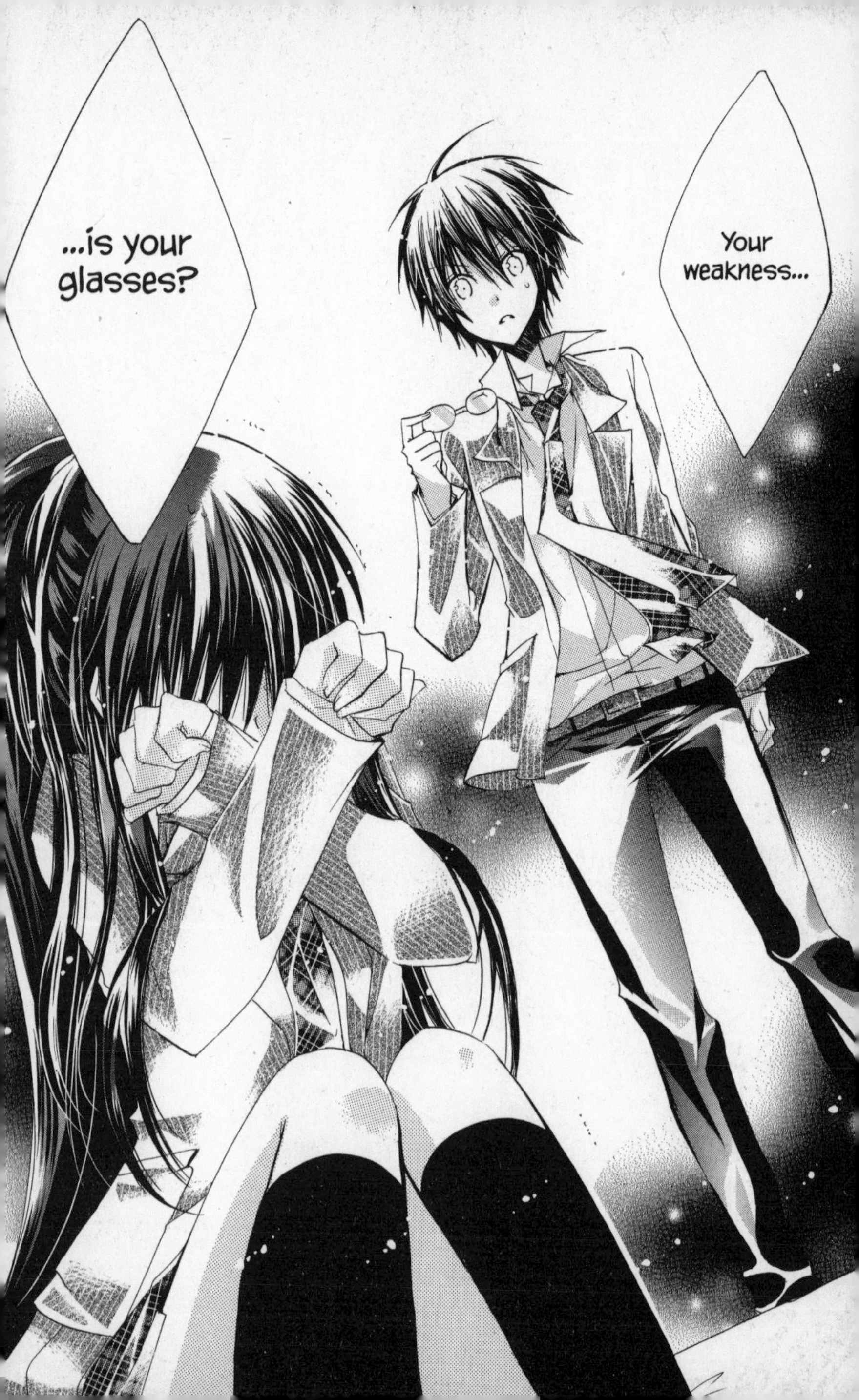
Your weakness...
...is your glasses?

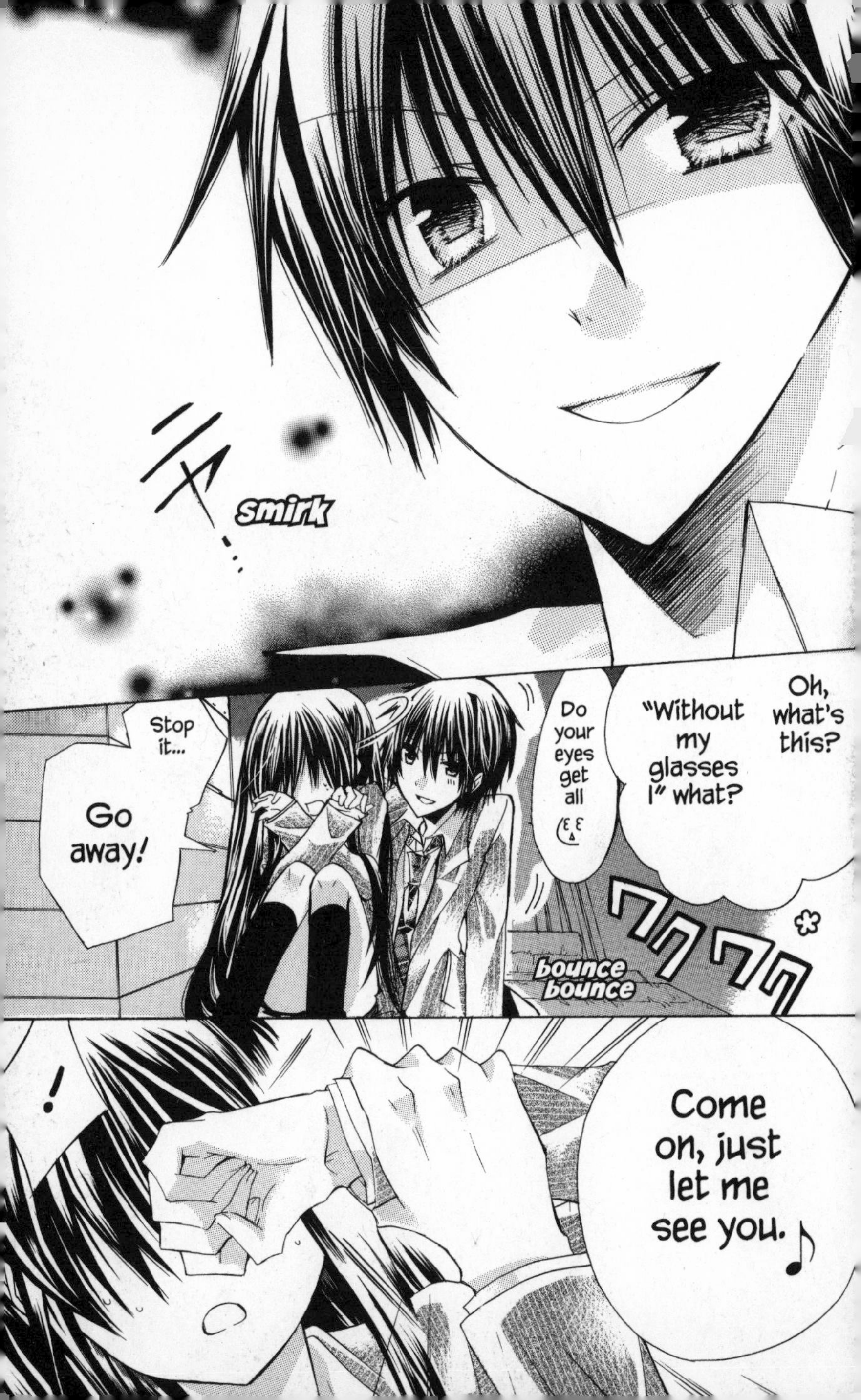
smirk
Oh, what's this?
"Without my glasses I" what?
Do your eyes get all (ε 3)
bounce bounce
Stop it...
Go away!
Come on, just let me see you. ♪
!

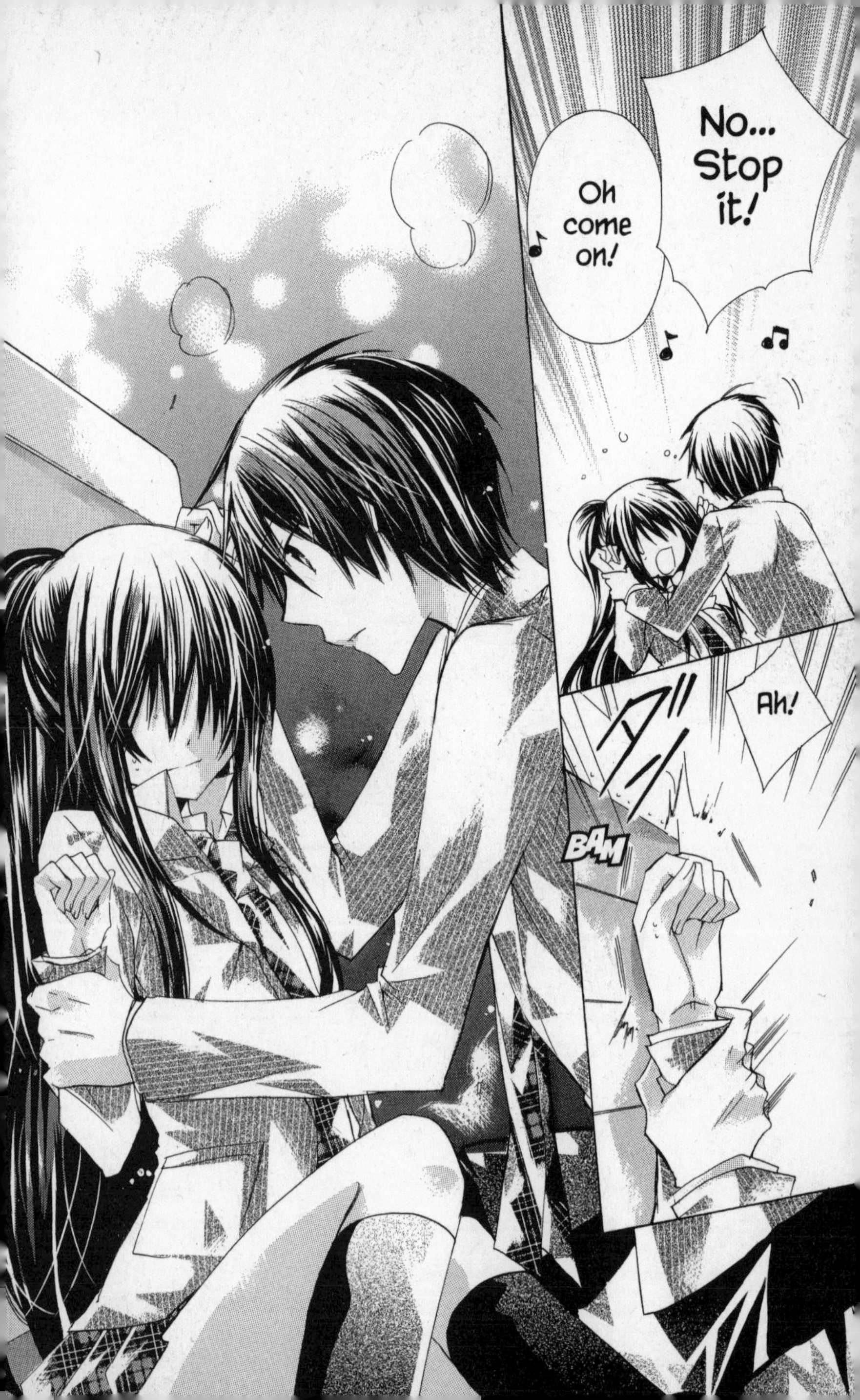
No... Stop it!
Oh come on!
Ah!
ダッ
BAM

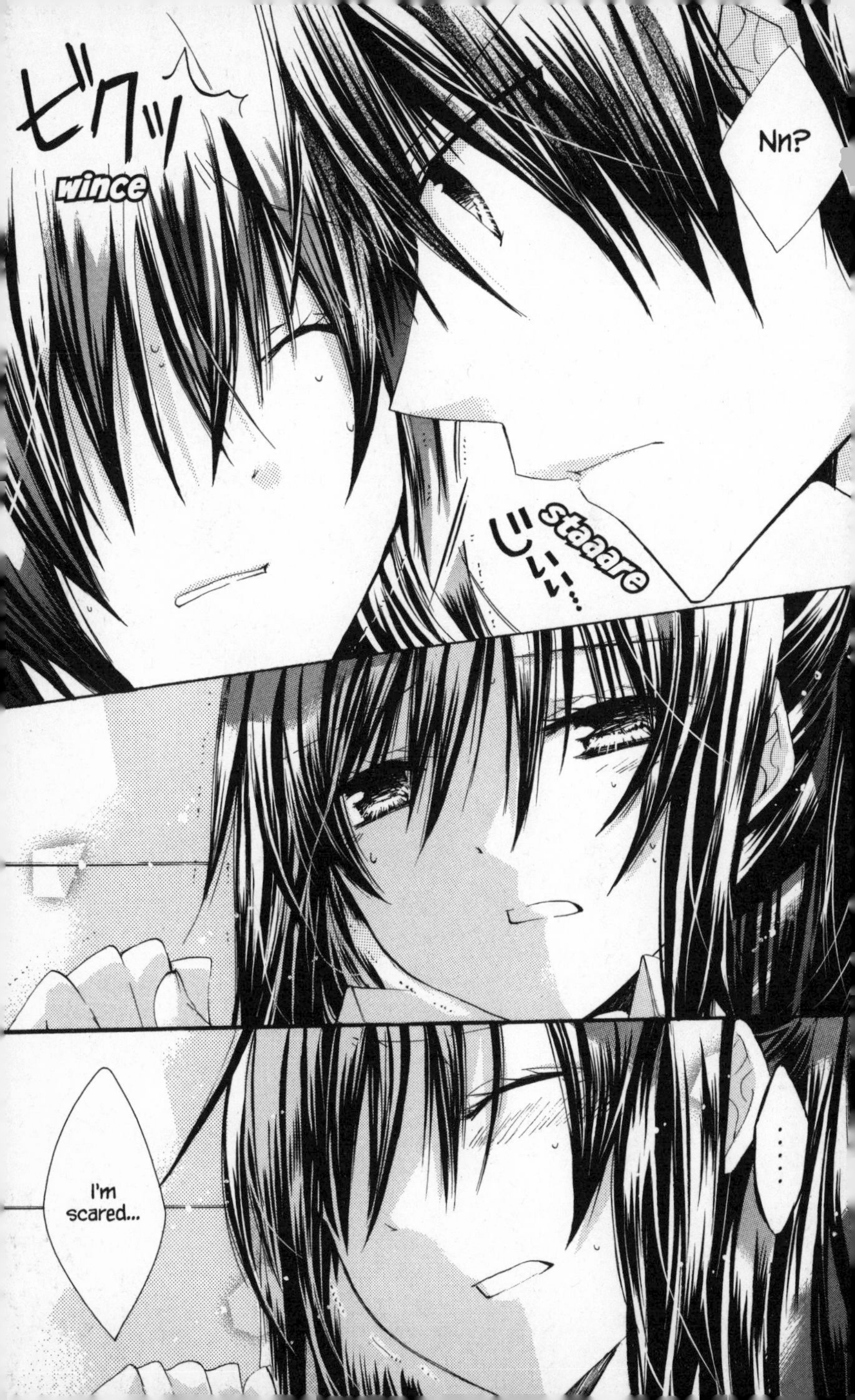

Nn?
ビクッ
wince
Staaare
じぃぃ…
……
I'm scared...

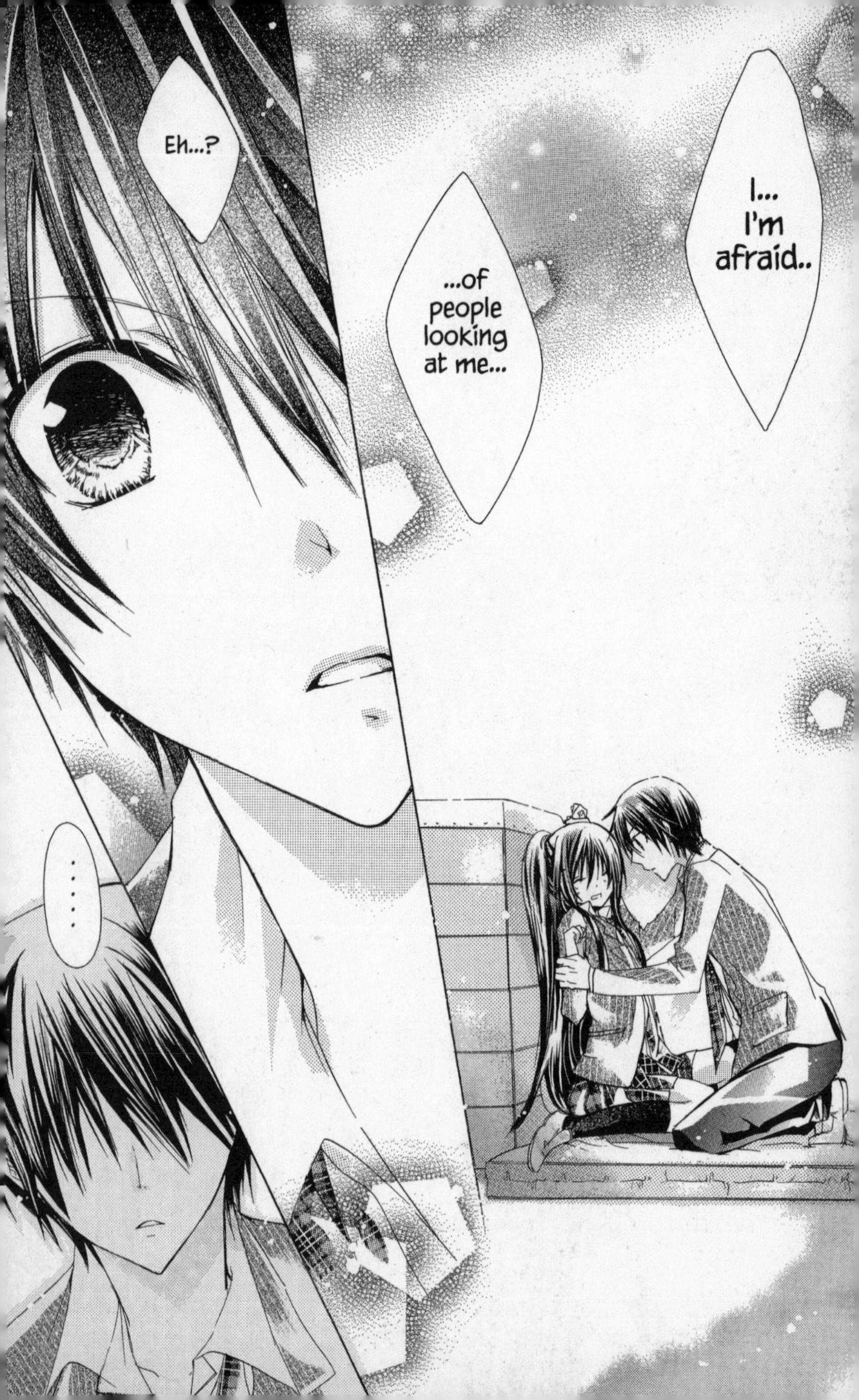
I... I'm afraid..
...of people looking at me...
Eh...?
......

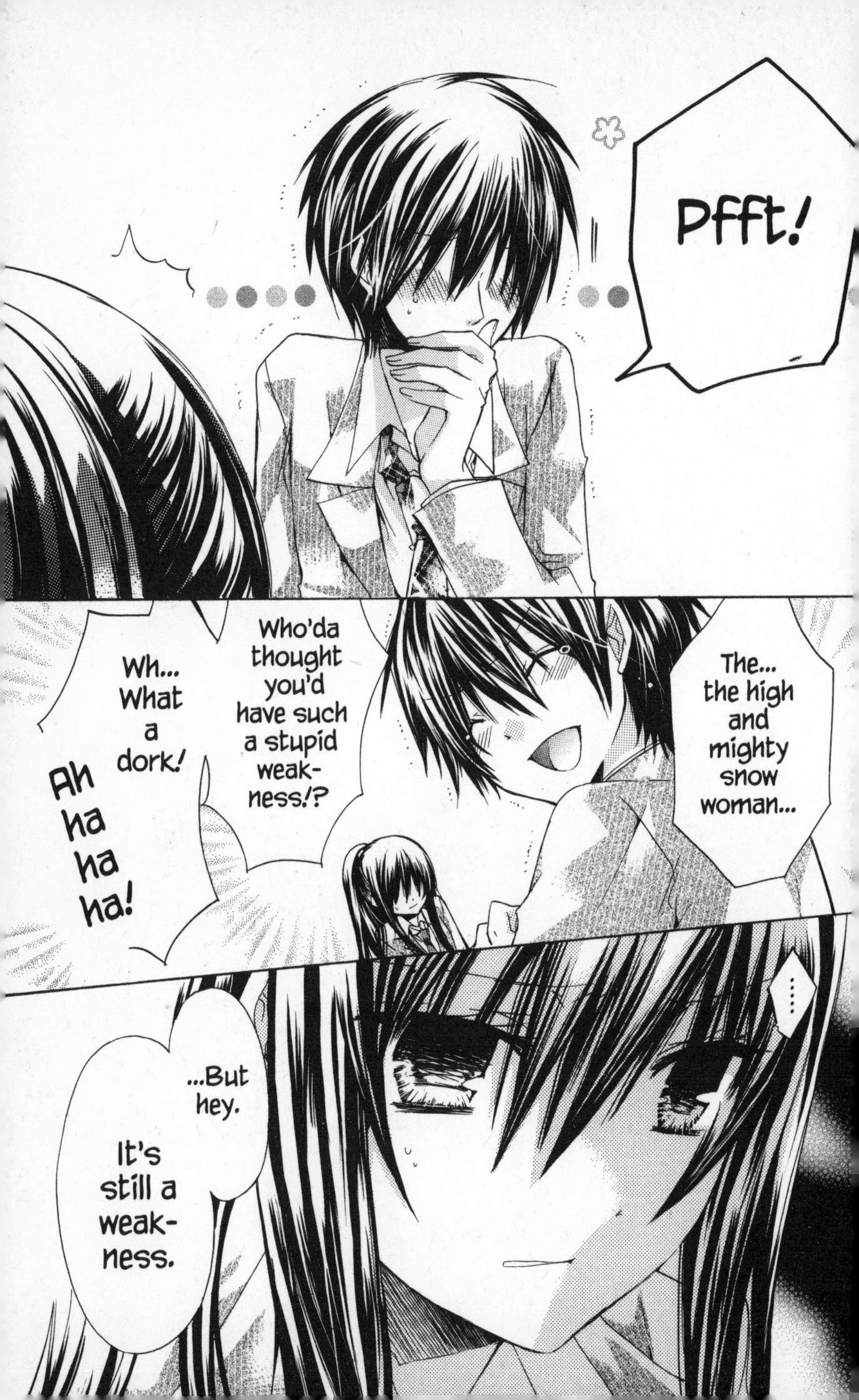
Pfft!
The... the high and mighty snow woman...
Who'da thought you'd have such a stupid weak-ness!?
Wh... What a dork!
Ah ha ha ha!
......
...But hey.
It's still a weak-ness.

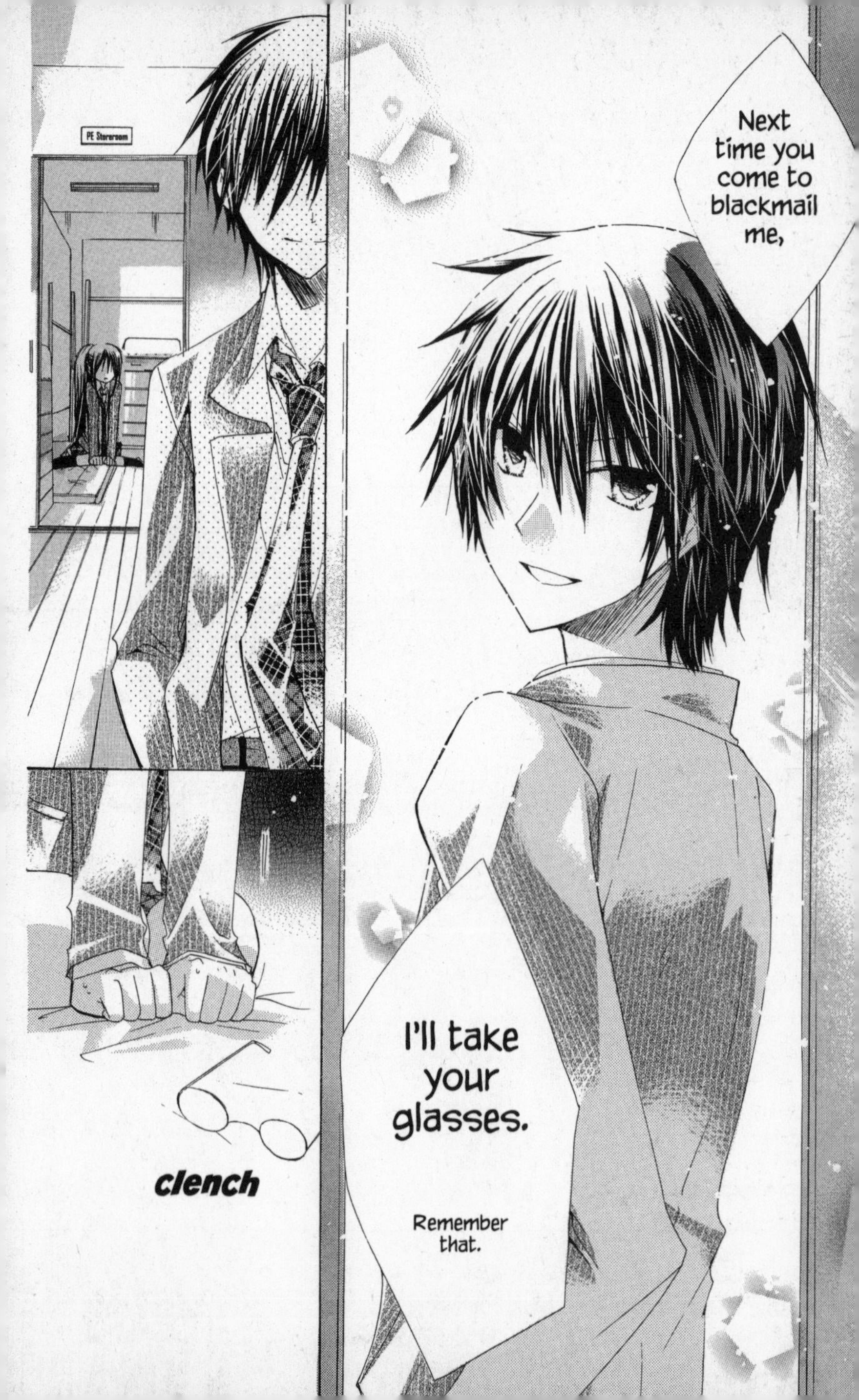
Next time you come to blackmail me,
I'll take your glasses.
Remember that.
PE Storeroom
clench

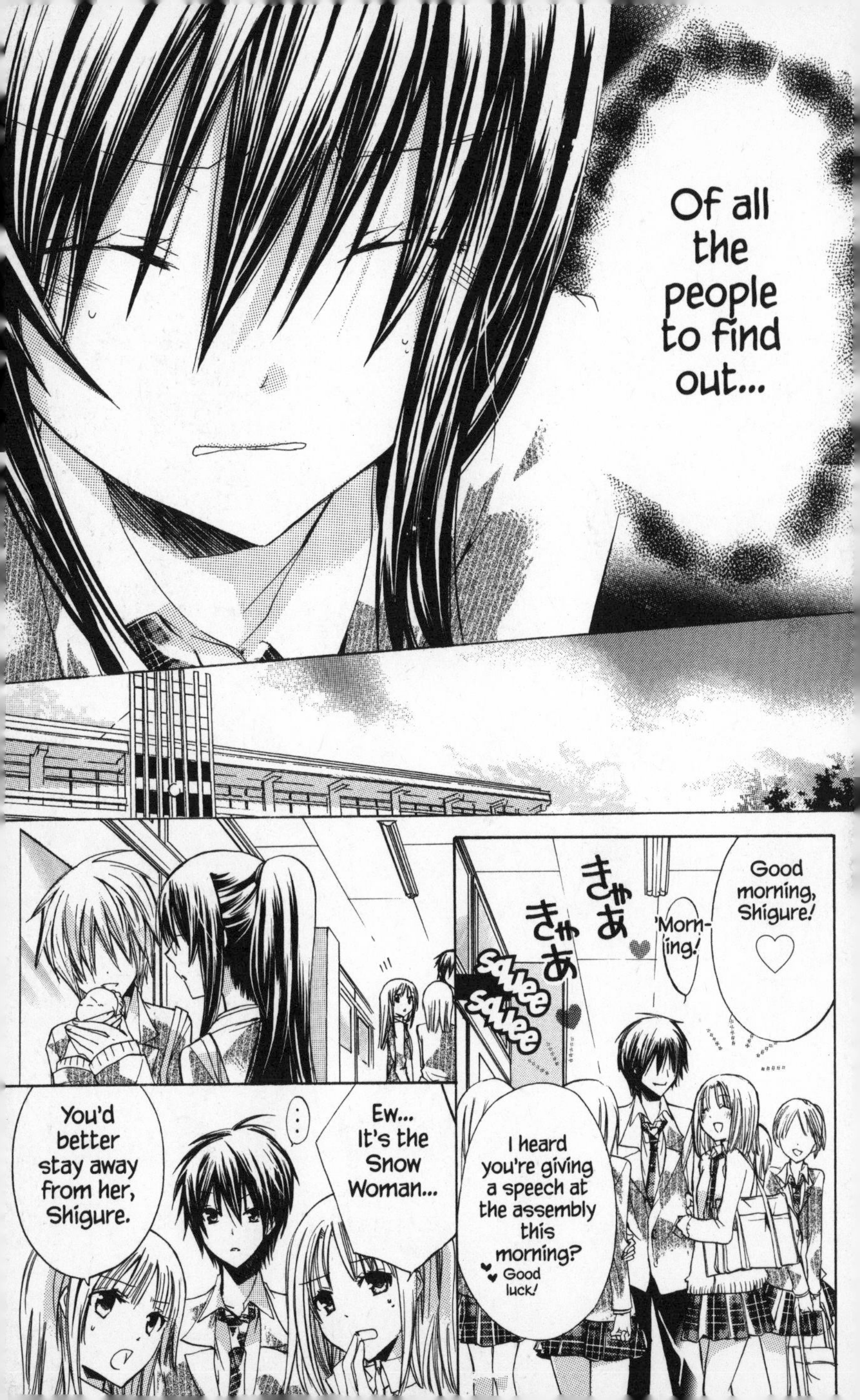
Of all the people to find out...
Good morning, Shigure!
'Morning!
きゃあ
きゃあ
squee
squee
I heard you're giving a speech at the assembly this morning?
Good luck!
Ew... It's the Snow Woman...
...
You'd better stay away from her, Shigure.

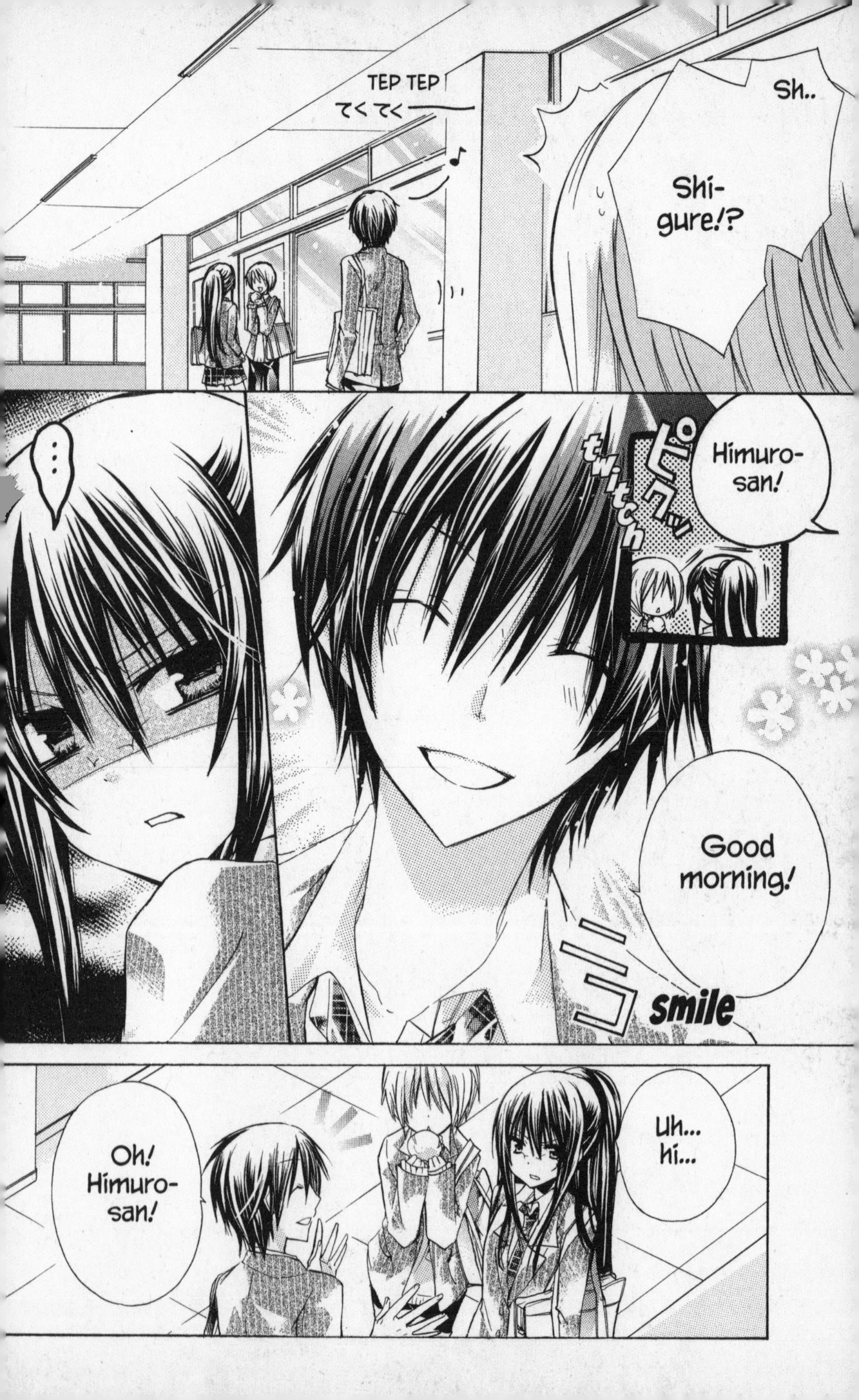

Sh..
Shi-gure!?
TEP TEP
てくてく
Himuro-san!
ピクッ
twitch
Good morning!
smile
...
Uh... hi...
Oh! Himuro-san!

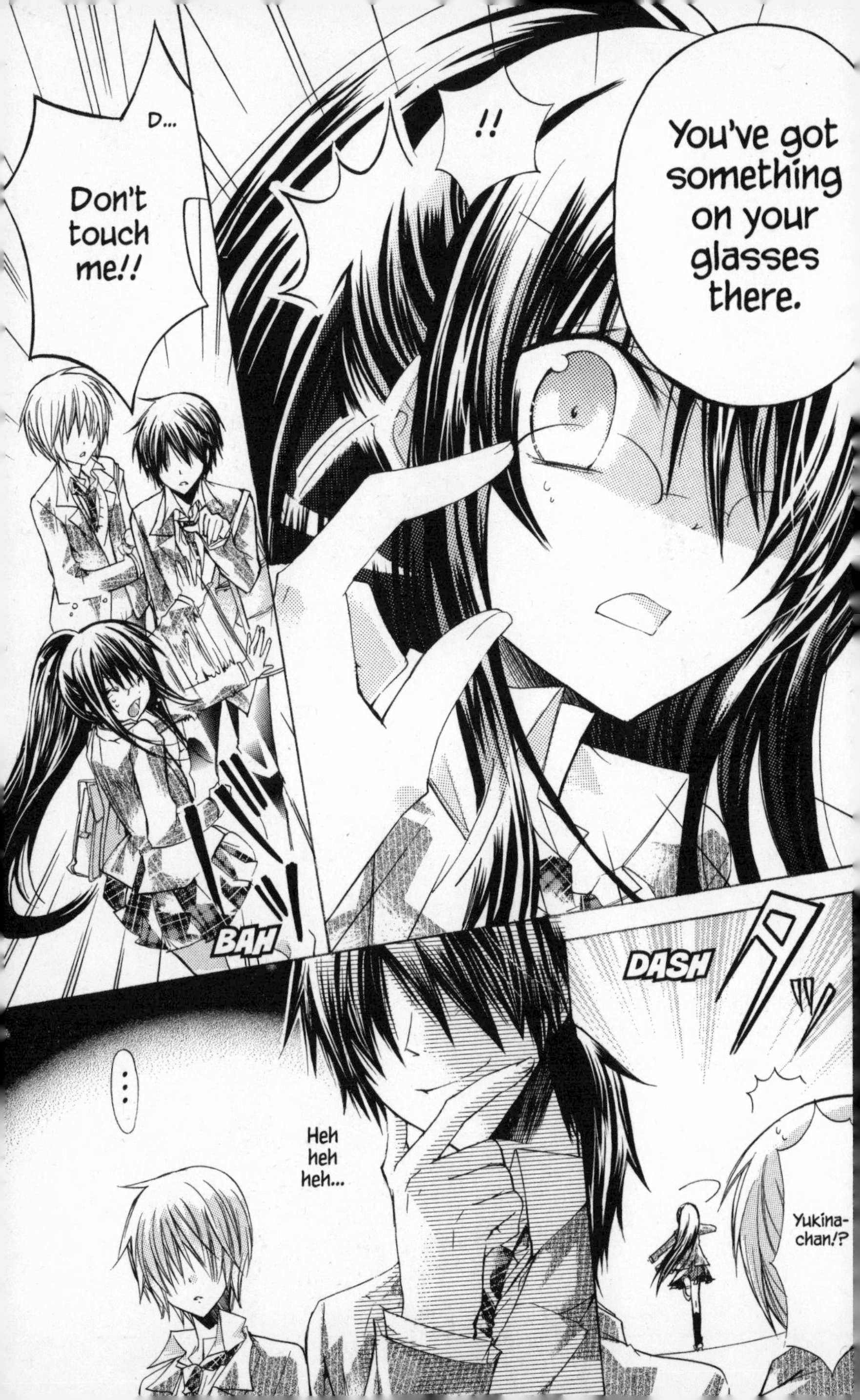
You've got something on your glasses there.
!!
D...
Don't touch me!!
BAH
DASH
Yukina-chan!?
Heh heh heh...
...

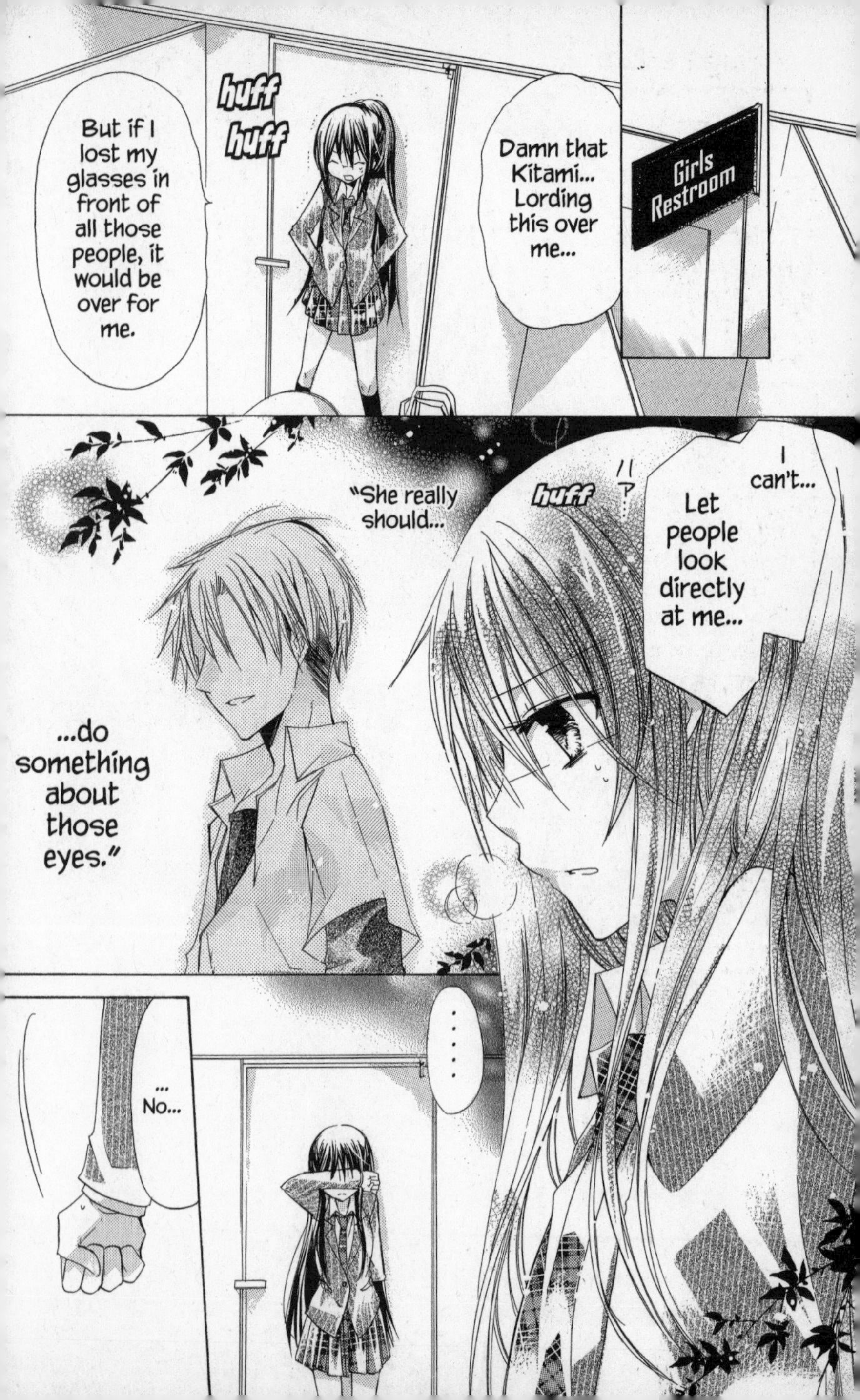
Girls Restroom
Damn that Kitami... Lording this over me...
huff huff
But if I lost my glasses in front of all those people, it would be over for me.
I can't...
Let people look directly at me...
ハァ…
huff
"She really should...
...do something about those eyes."
......
... No...

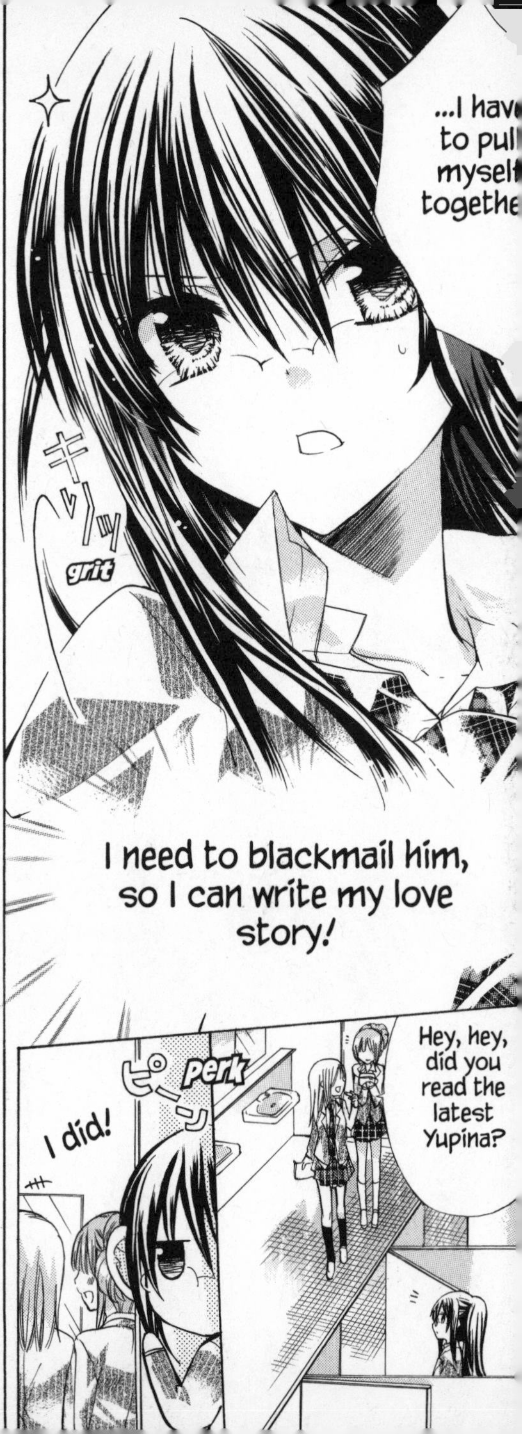
...I hav
to pul
mysel
togethe
grit
I need to blackmail him, so I can write my love story!
Hey, hey, did you read the latest Yupina?
perk
I did!

Shigure-kun

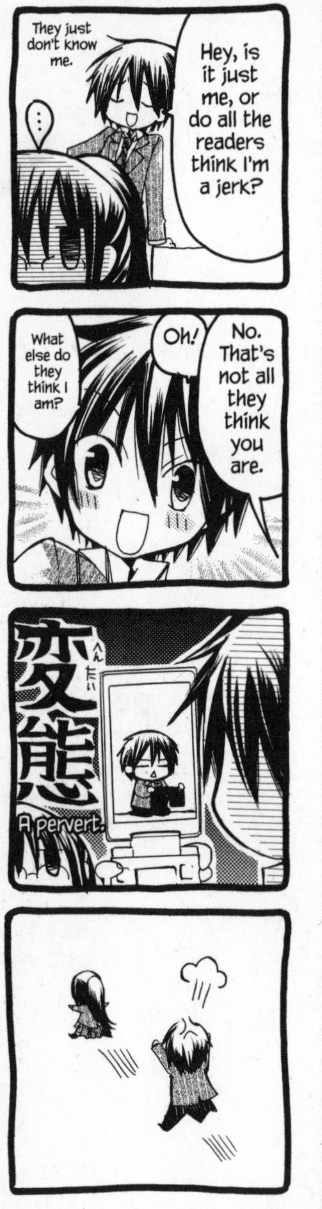
Hey, is it just me, or do all the readers think I'm a jerk?
They just don't know me.
No. That's not all they think you are.
Oh!
What else do they think I am?
変態 へんたい
A pervert.

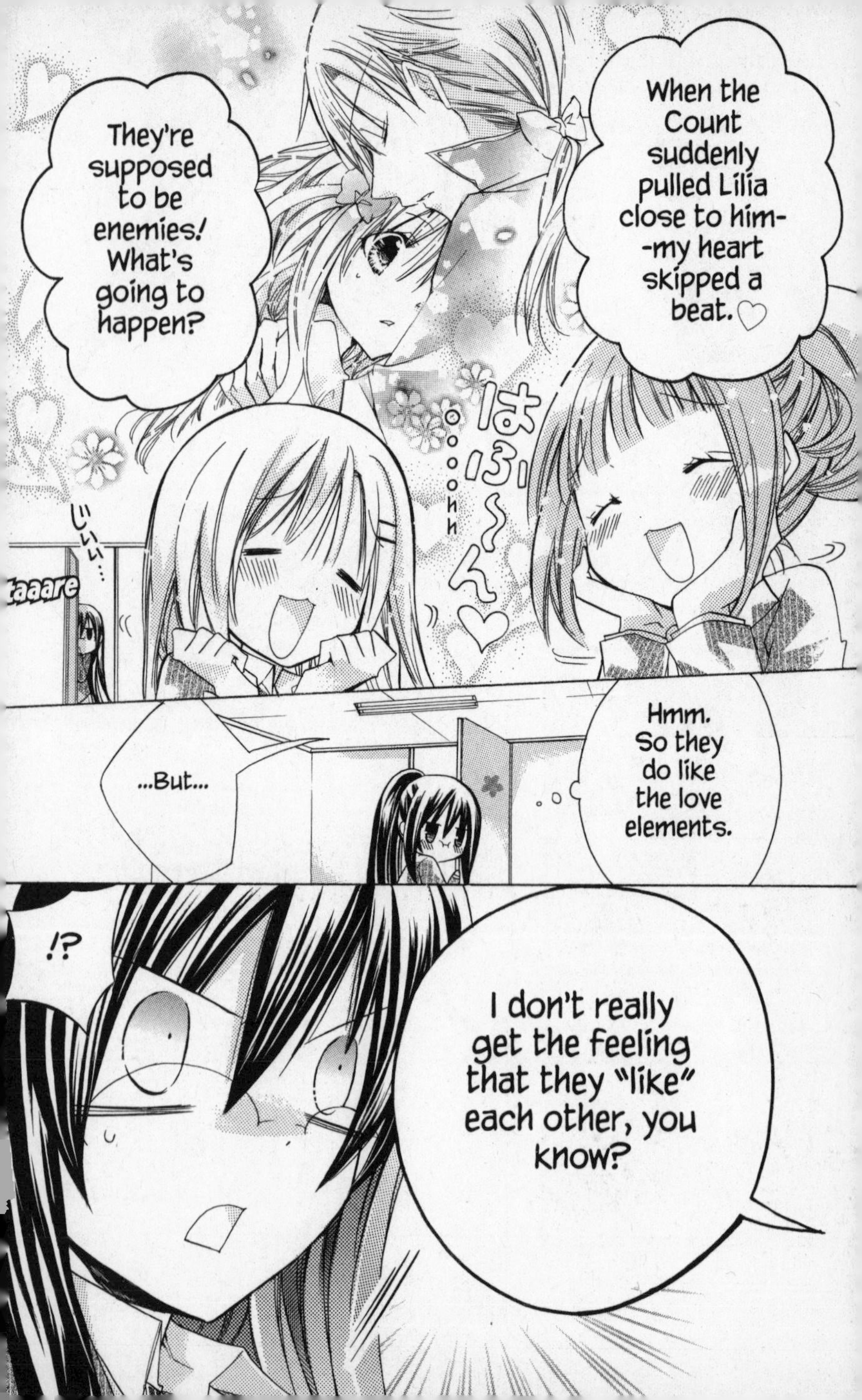
When the Count suddenly pulled Lilia close to him--my heart skipped a beat. ♡
They're supposed to be enemies! What's going to happen?
はふ〜ん♡
Oooohh
じいい…
taaare
Hmm. So they do like the love elements.
...But...
I don't really get the feeling that they "like" each other, you know?
!?

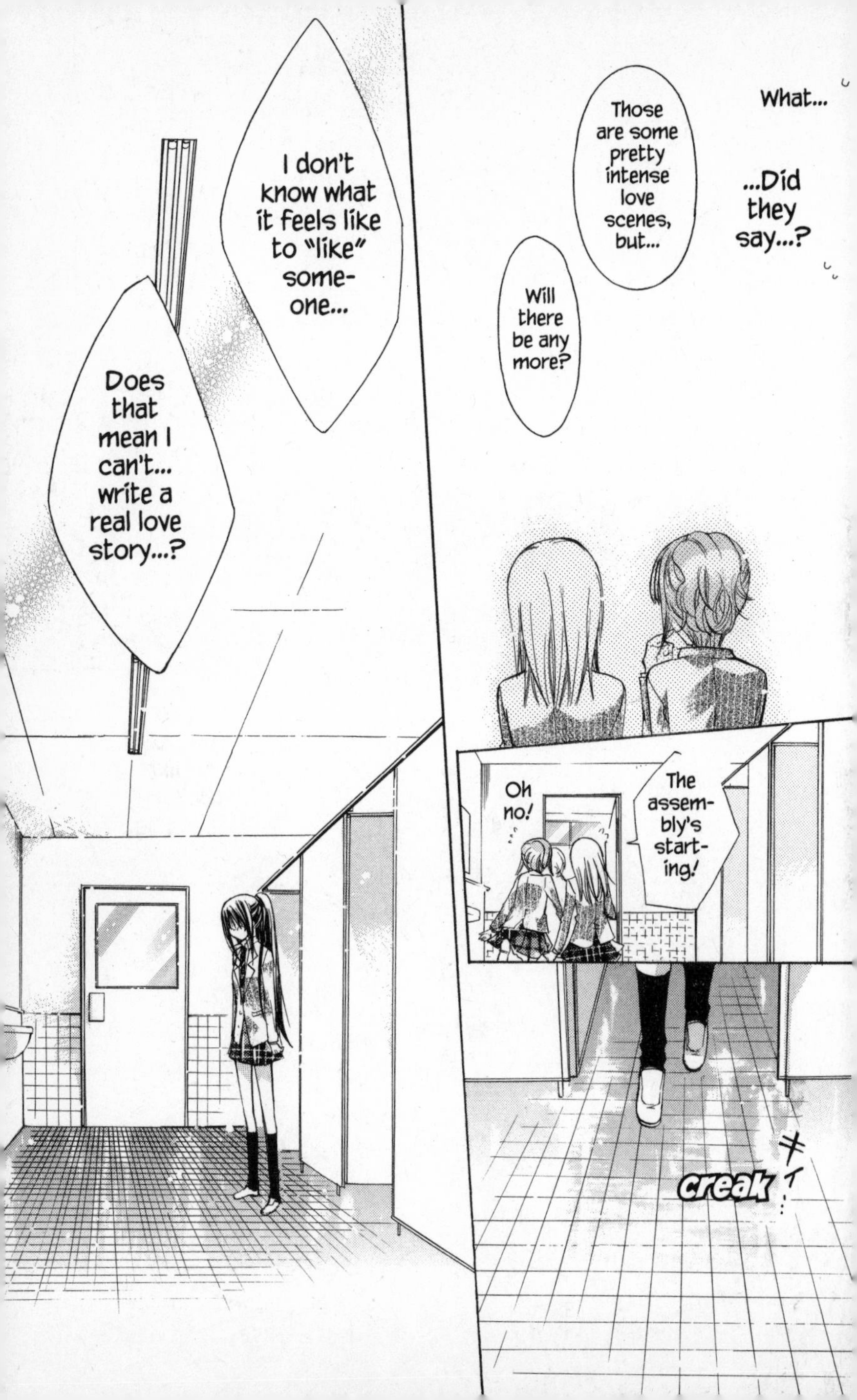
What...
...Did they say...?
Those are some pretty intense love scenes, but...
Will there be any more?
The assembly's starting!
Oh no!
creak
I don't know what it feels like to "like" someone...
Does that mean I can't... write a real love story...?

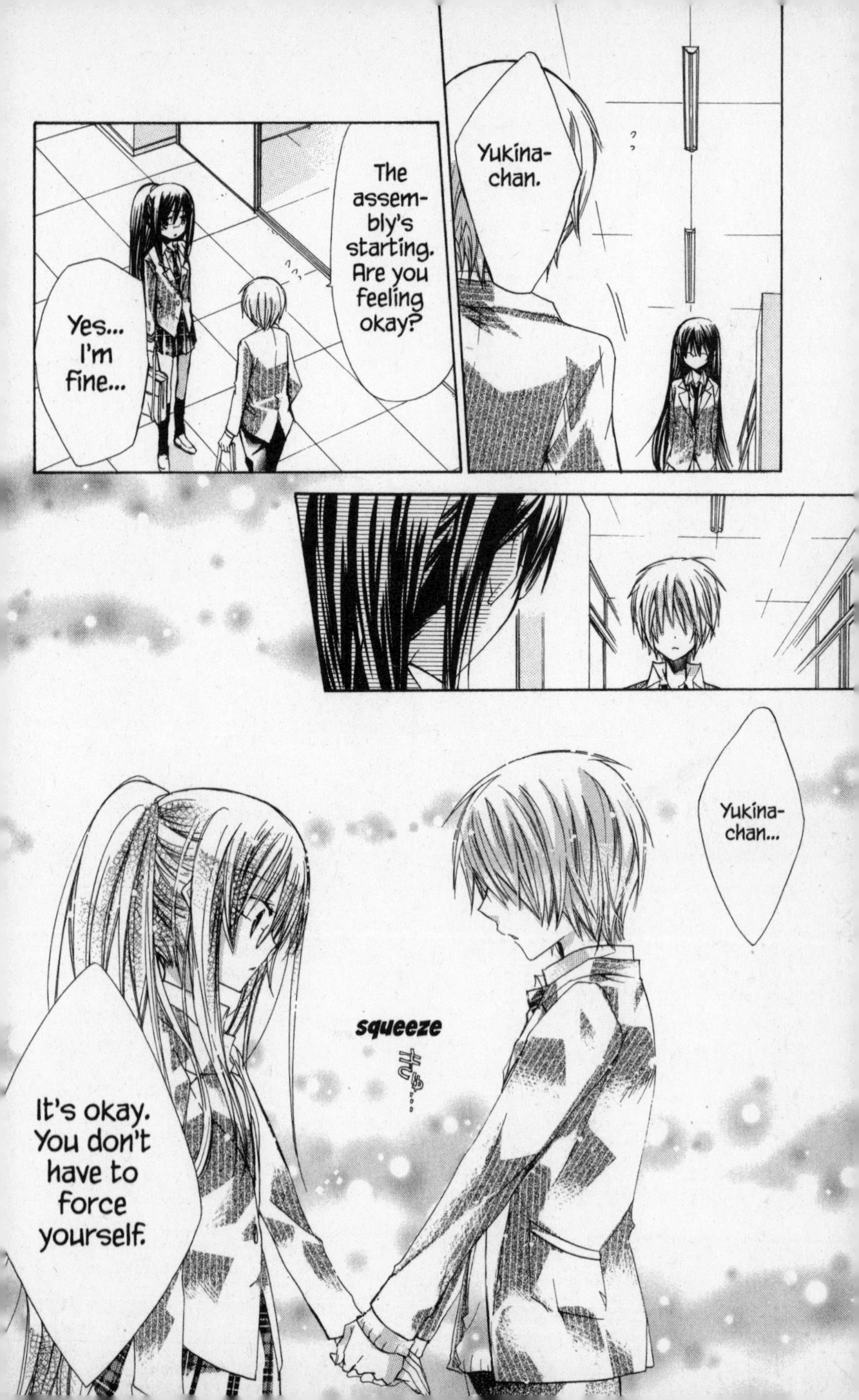
Yukina-chan.
The assembly's starting. Are you feeling okay?
Yes... I'm fine...
Yukina-chan...
squeeze
It's okay. You don't have to force yourself.

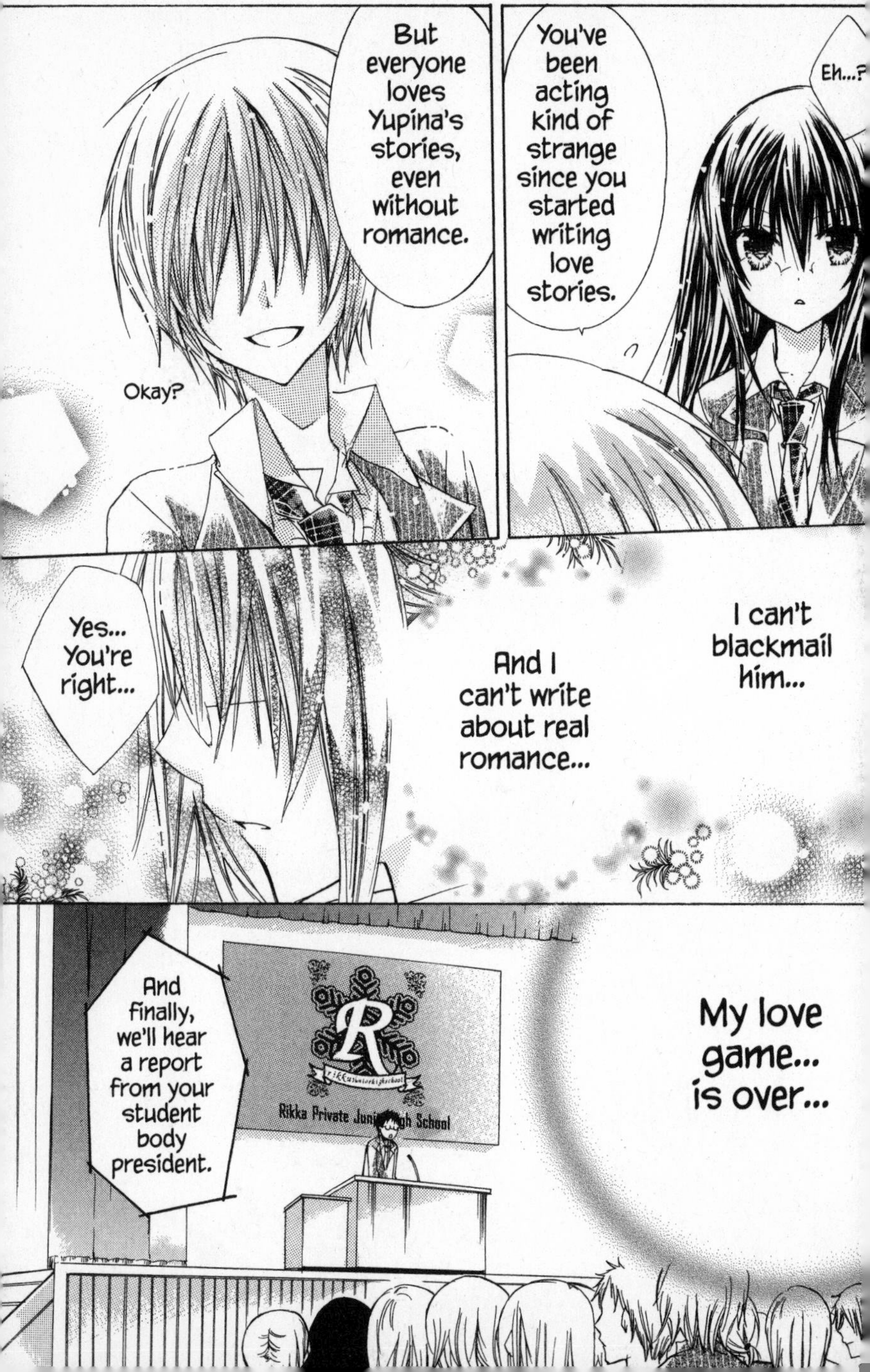

Eh...?
You've been acting kind of strange since you started writing love stories.
But everyone loves Yupina's stories, even without romance.
Okay?
I can't blackmail him...
And I can't write about real romance...
Yes... You're right...
My love game... is over...
And finally, we'll hear a report from your student body president.

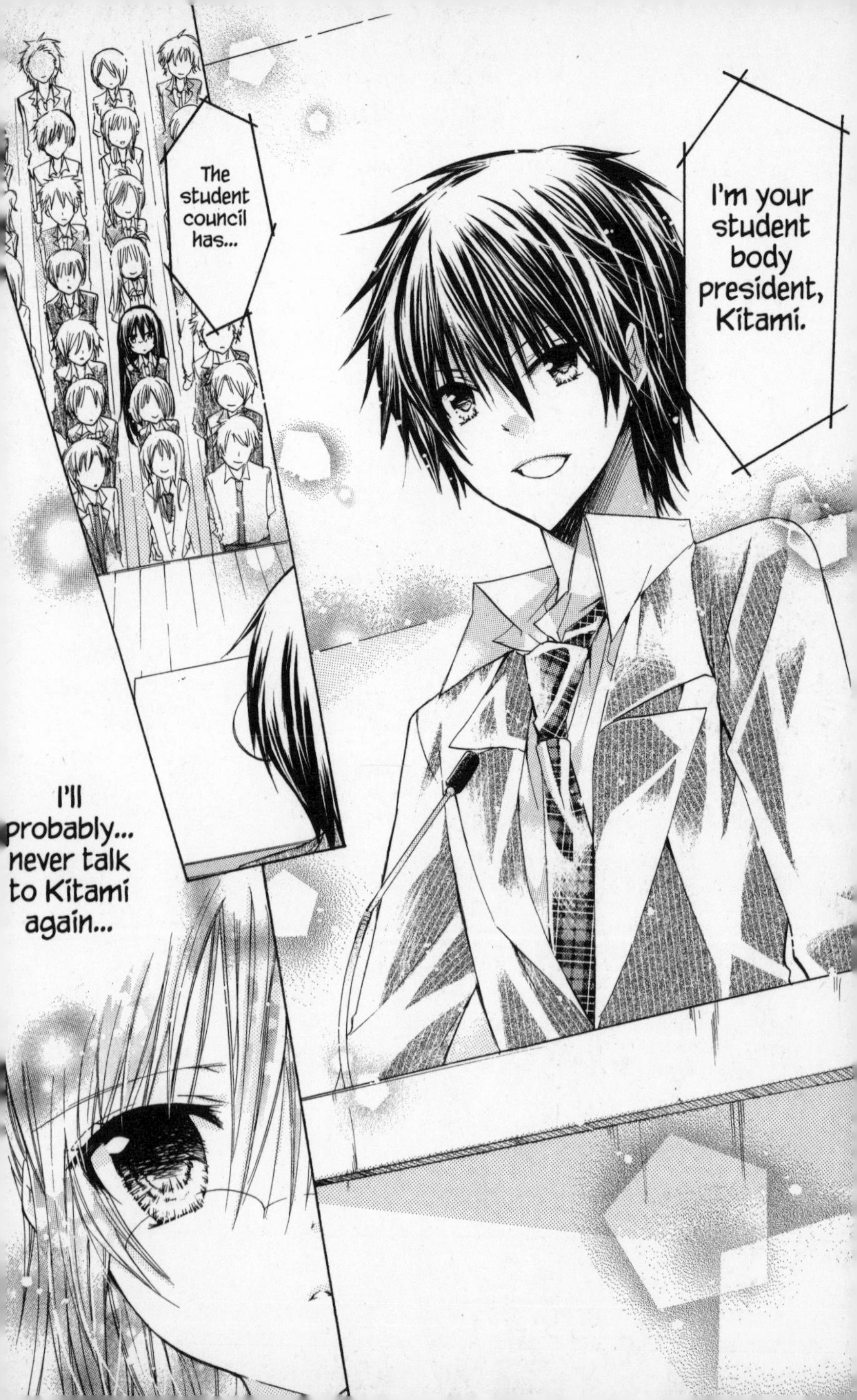
I'm your student body president, Kitami.
The student council has...
I'll probably... never talk to Kitami again...

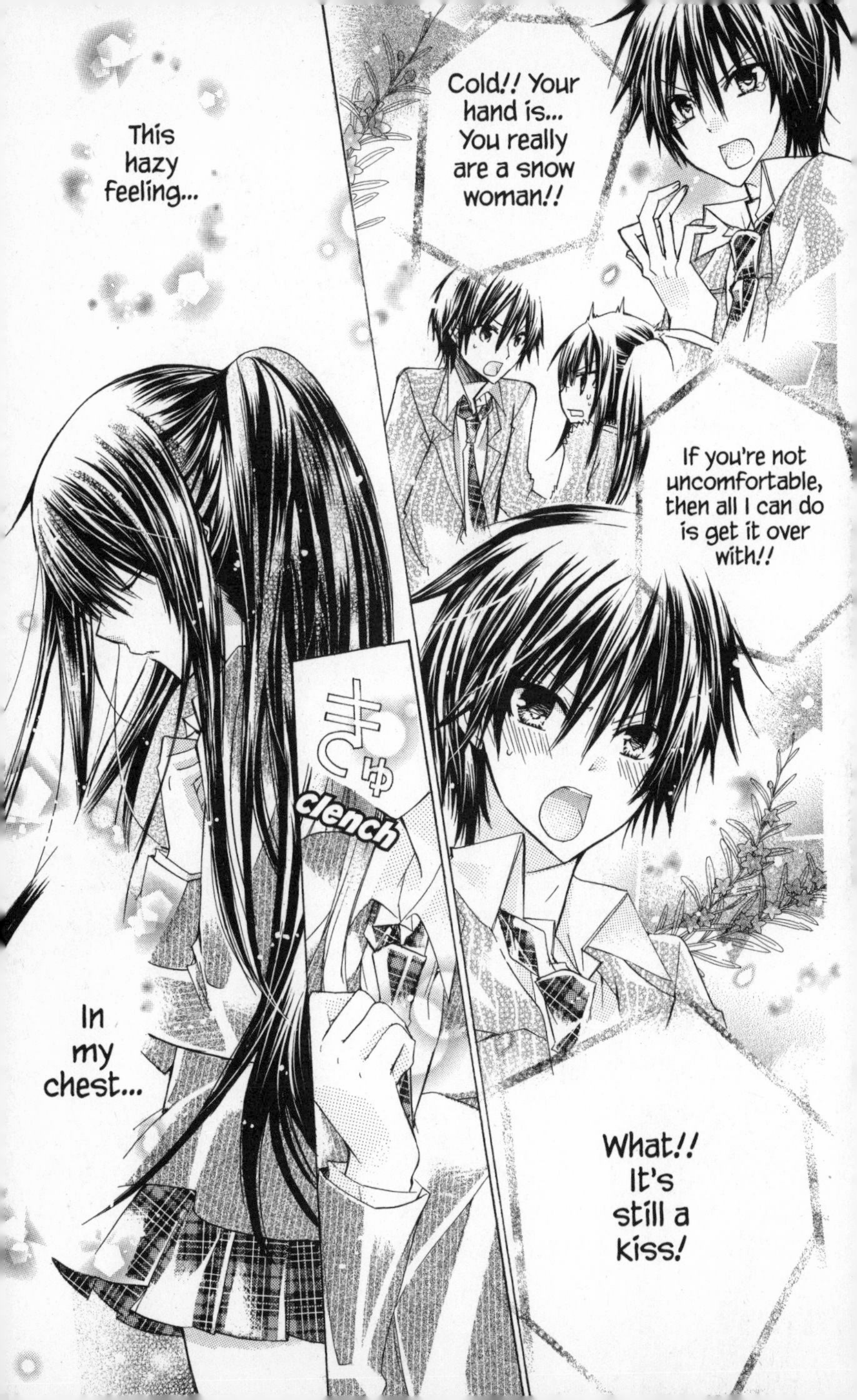
Cold!! Your hand is... You really are a snow woman!!
If you're not uncomfortable, then all I can do is get it over with!!
What!! It's still a kiss!
This hazy feeling...
きゅ
clench
In my chest...

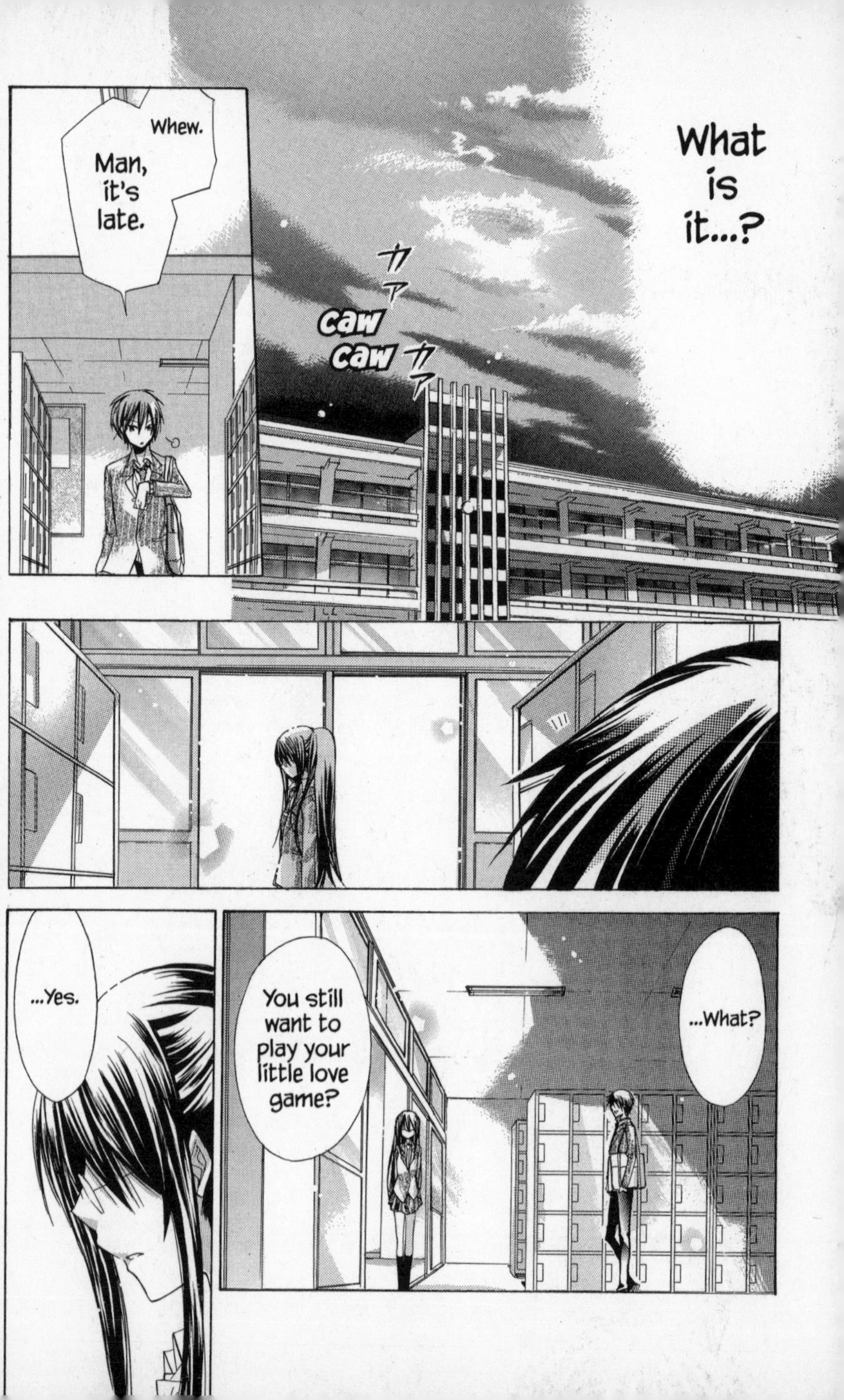
What is it...?
カァ
Caw
caw
カァ
Whew.
Man, it's late.
...What?
You still want to play your little love game?
...Yes.

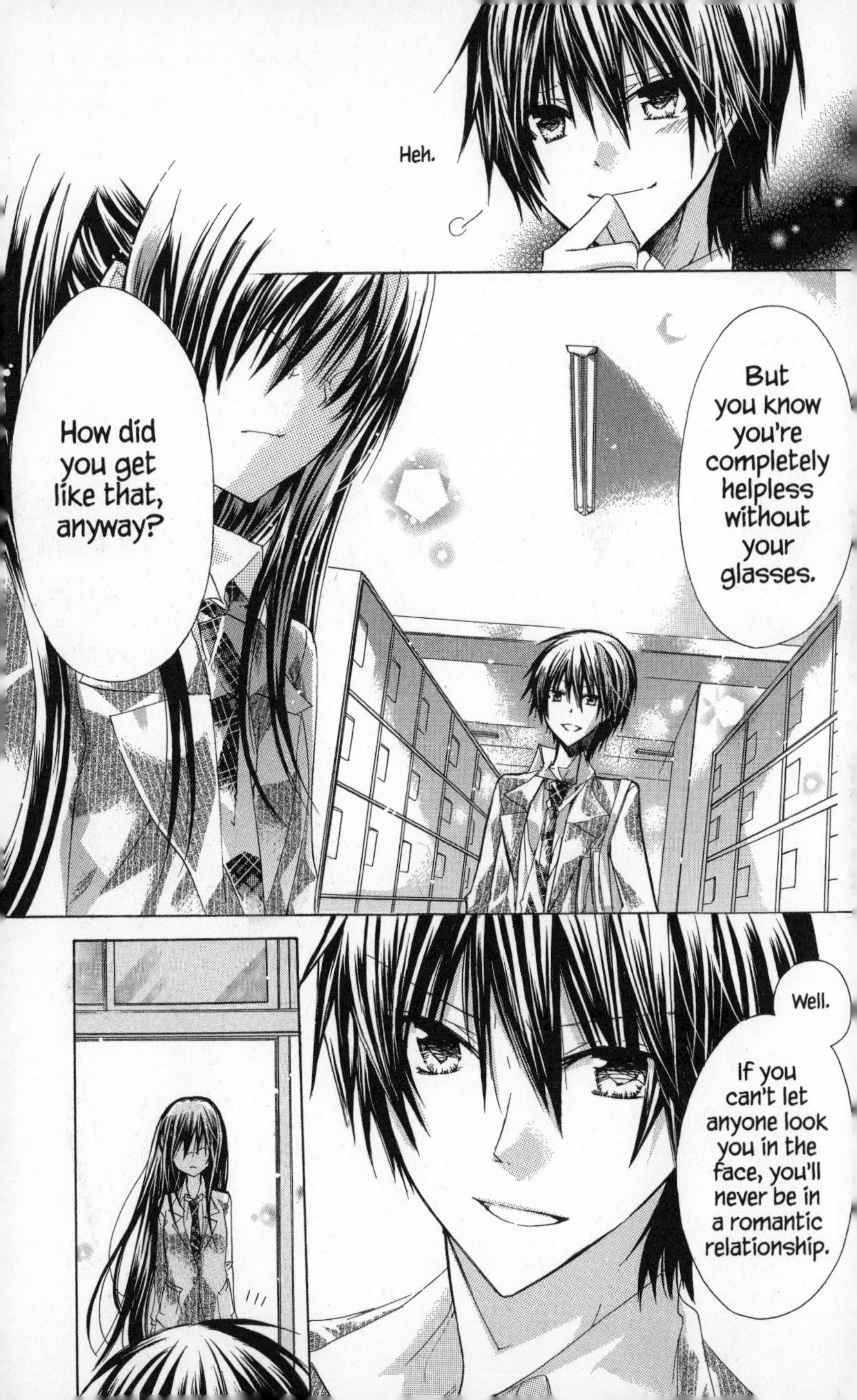
Heh.
But you know you're completely helpless without your glasses.
How did you get like that, anyway?
Well.
If you can't let anyone look you in the face, you'll never be in a romantic relationship.

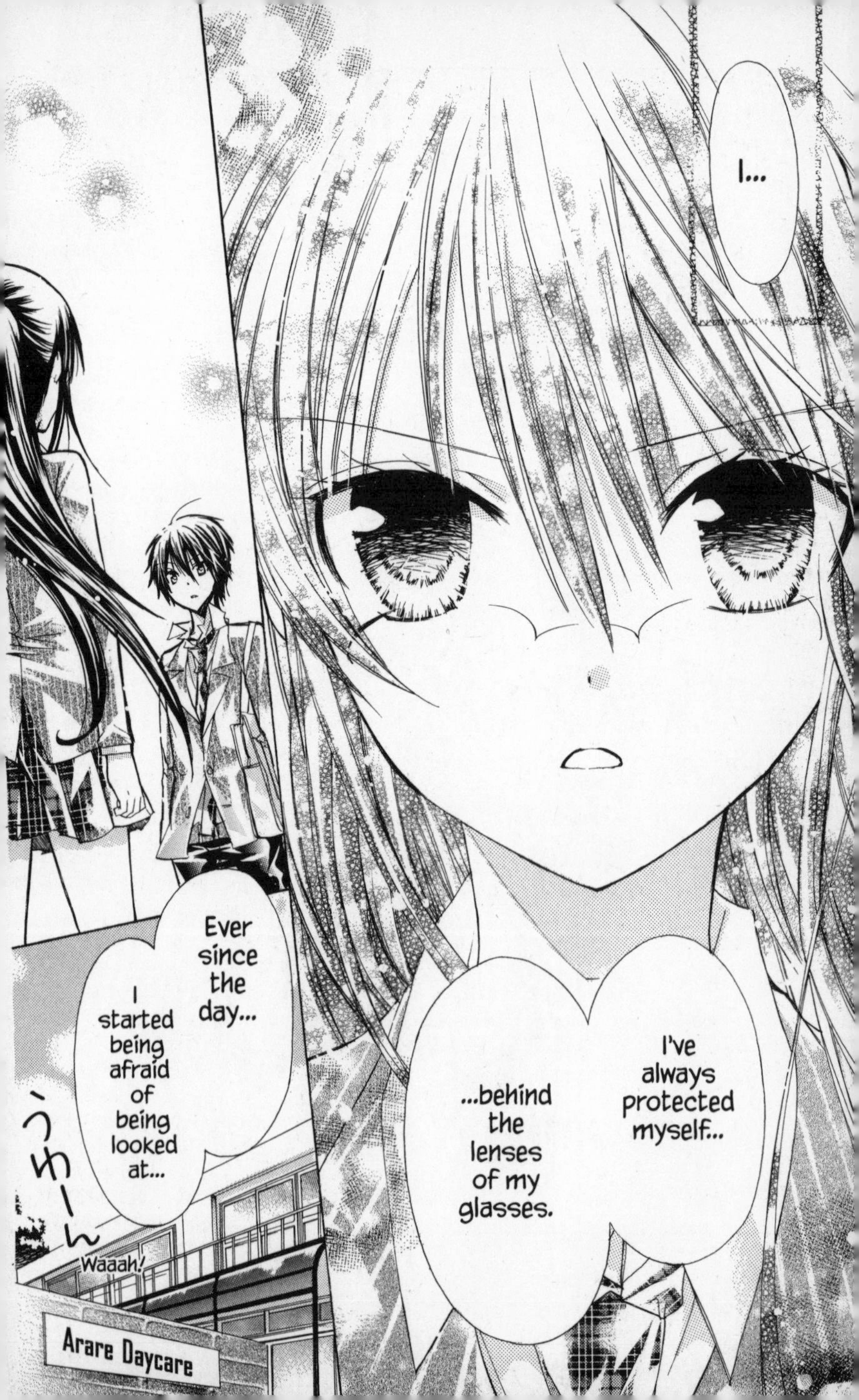
I...
I've always protected myself...
...behind the lenses of my glasses.
Ever since the day...
I started being afraid of being looked at...
うわーん
Waaah!
Arare Daycare

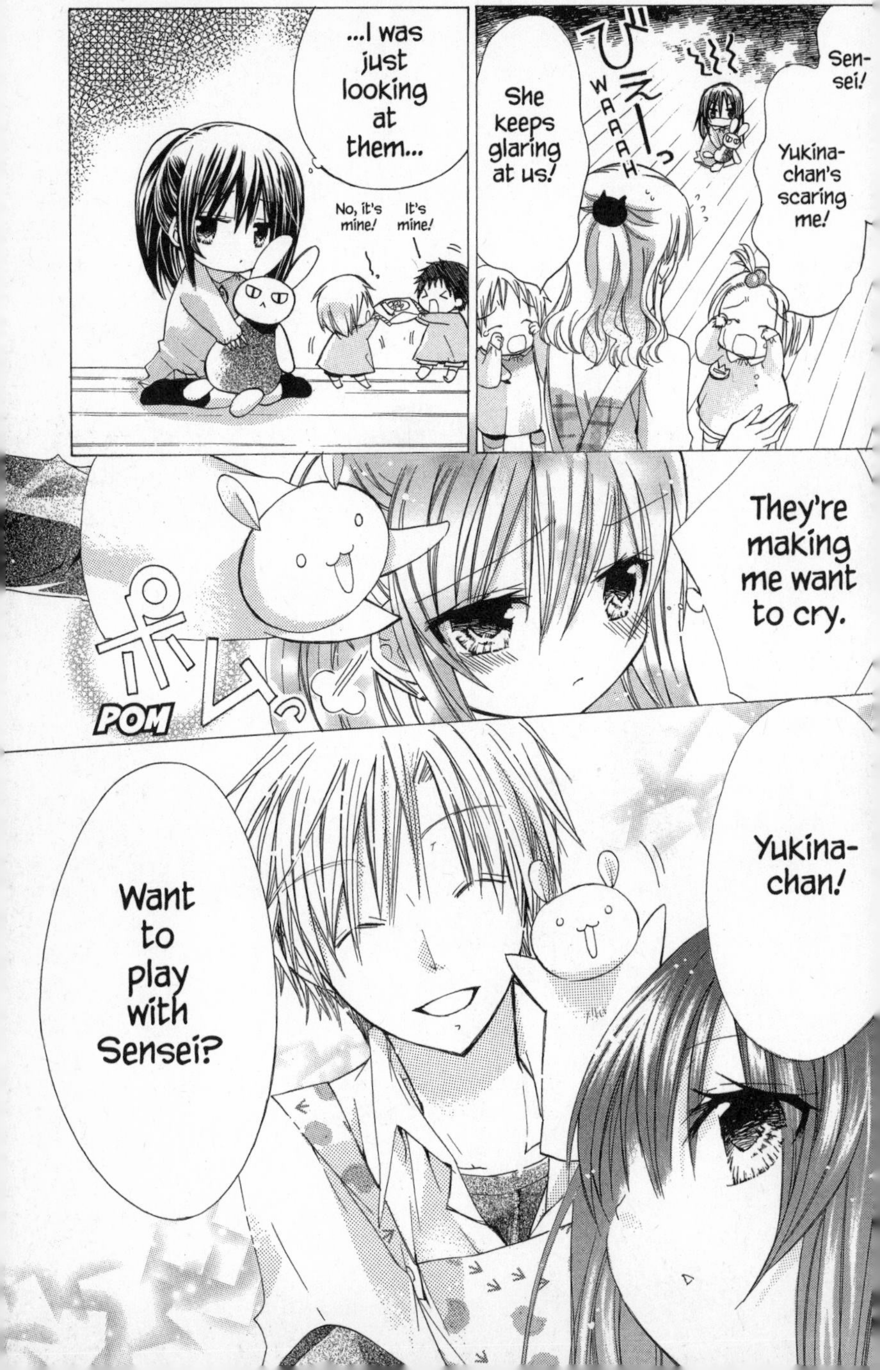

Sen-sei!
Yukina-chan's scaring me!
WAAAAH
She keeps glaring at us!
...I was just looking at them...
It's mine!
No, it's mine!
They're making me want to cry.
POM
Yukina-chan!
Want to play with Sensei?

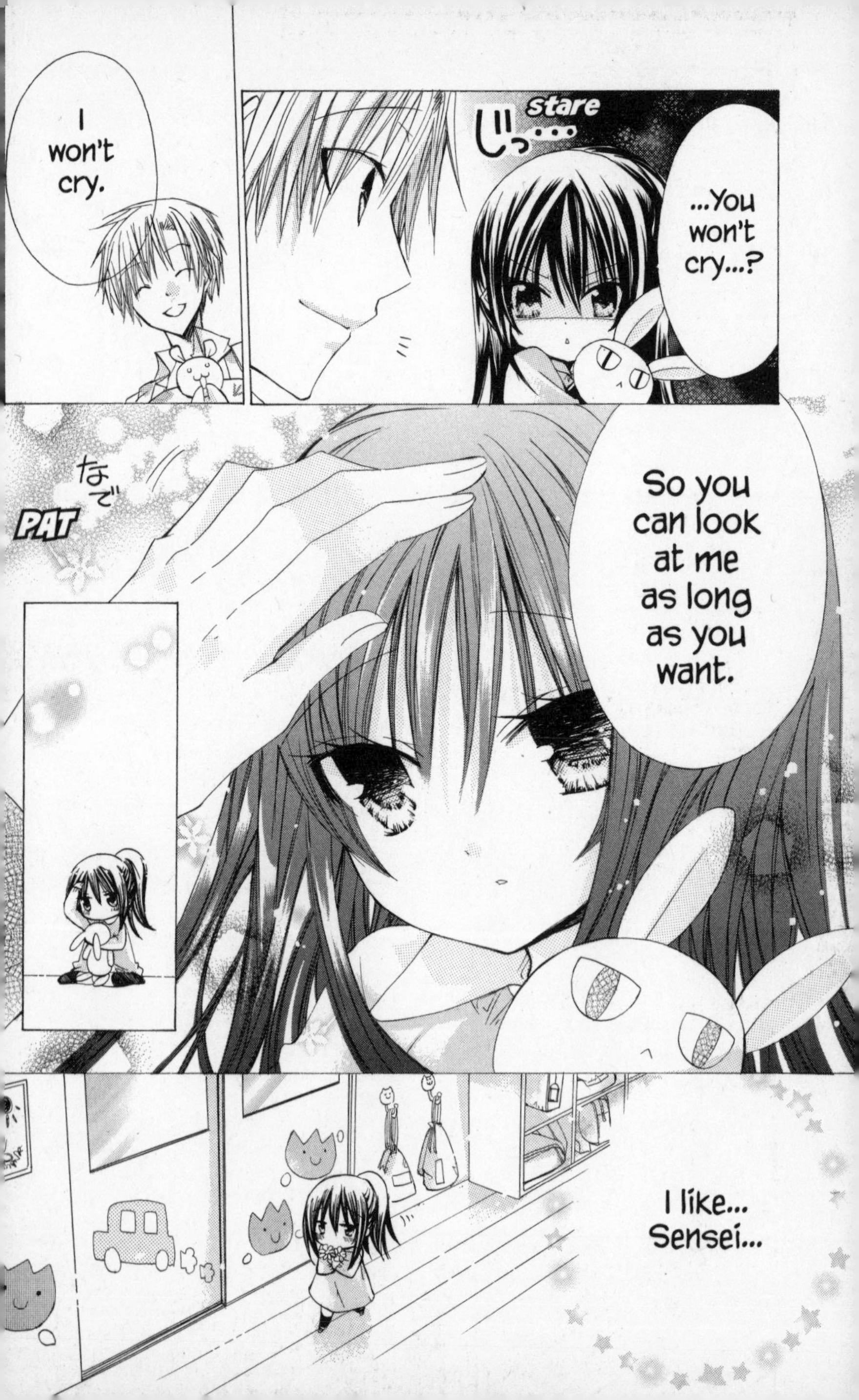
...You won't cry...?
じっ...
stare
I won't cry.
So you can look at me as long as you want.
なで
PAT
I like... Sensei...

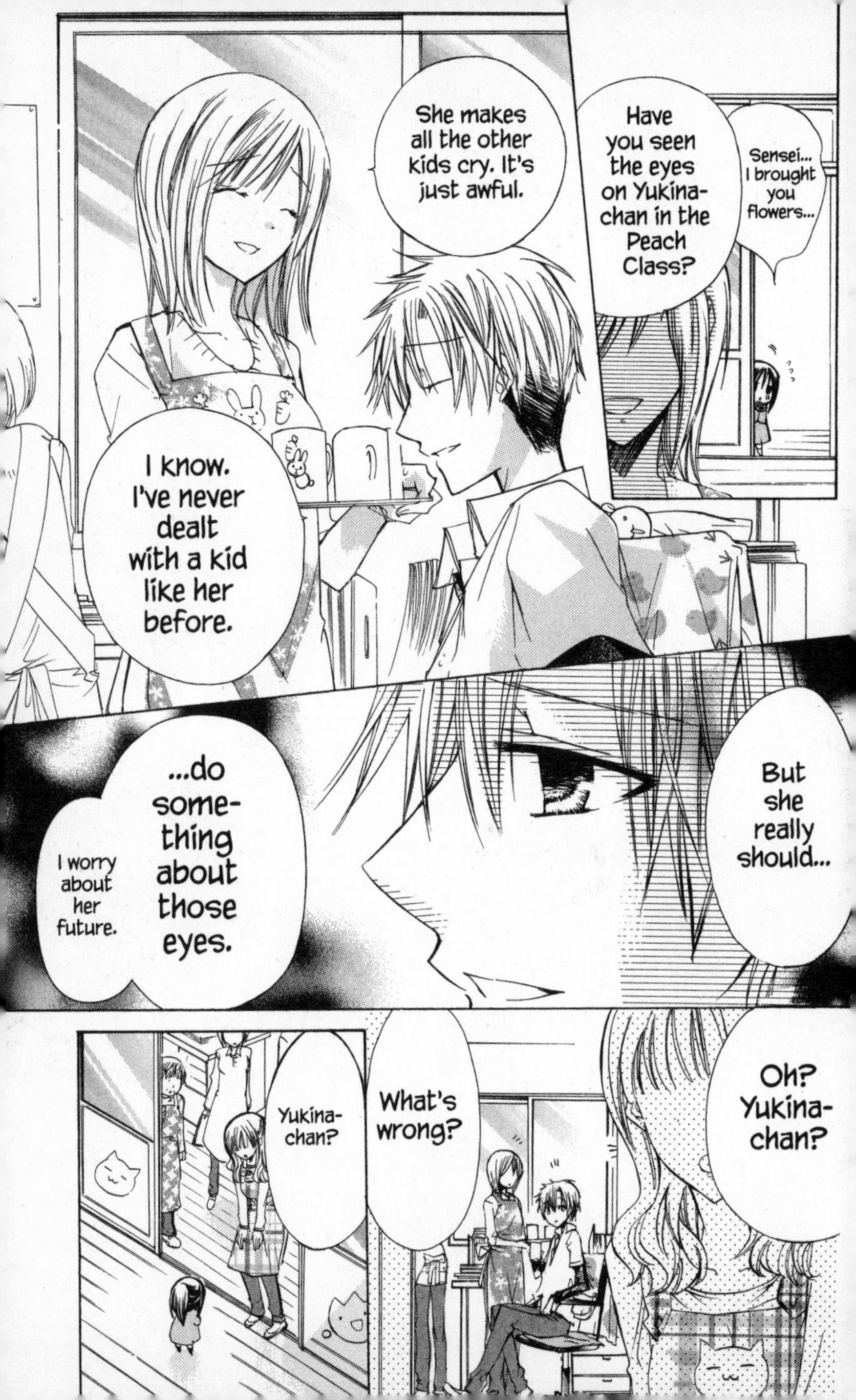
Have you seen the eyes on Yukina-chan in the Peach Class?
Sensei... I brought you flowers...
She makes all the other kids cry. It's just awful.
I know. I've never dealt with a kid like her before.
But she really should...
...do something about those eyes.
I worry about her future.
Oh? Yukina-chan?
What's wrong?
Yukina-chan?

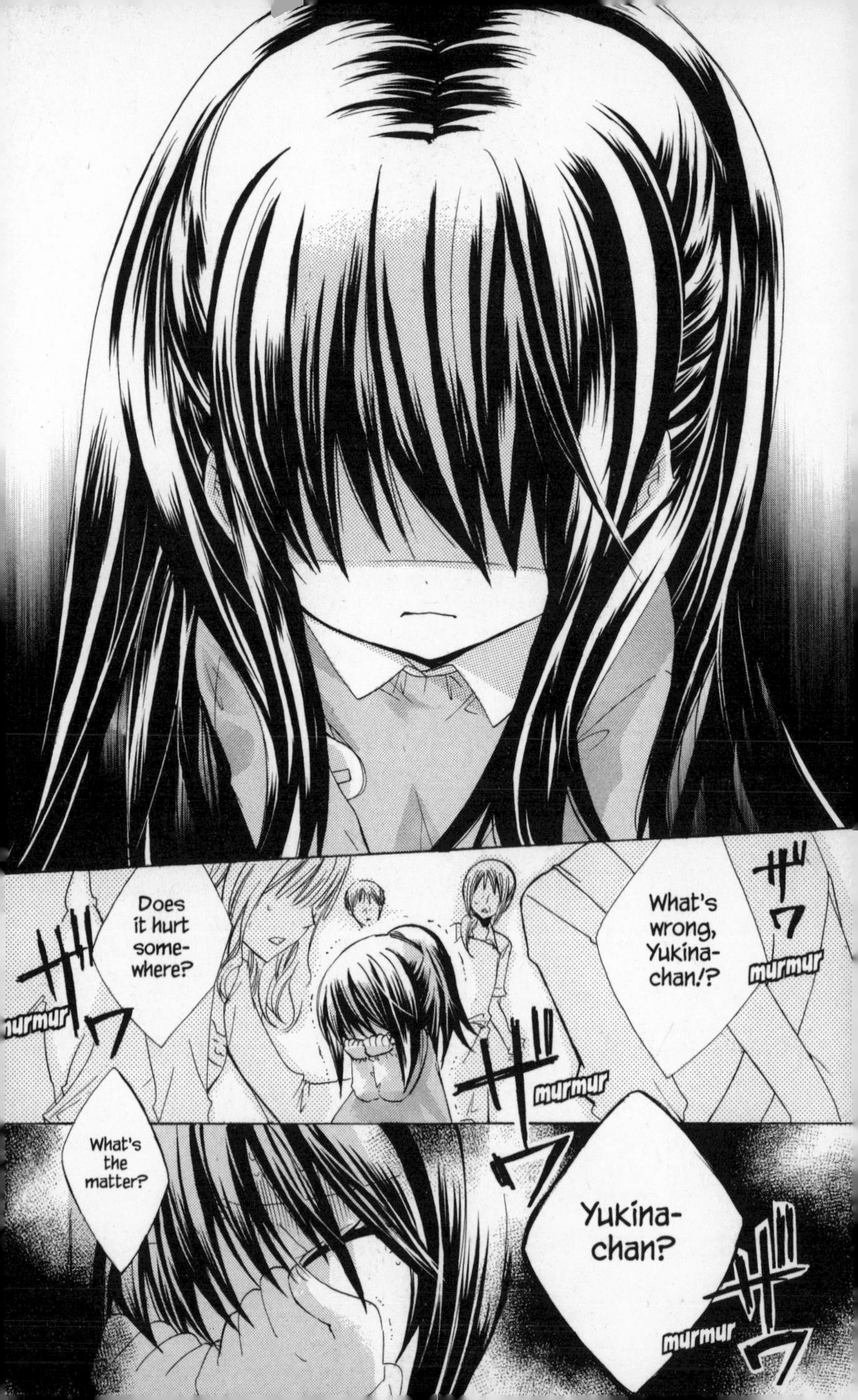
ザワ
murmur
What's wrong, Yukina-chan!?
ザワ
murmur
Does it hurt some-where?
ザワ
murmur
ザワ
murmur
Yukina-chan?
What's the matter?

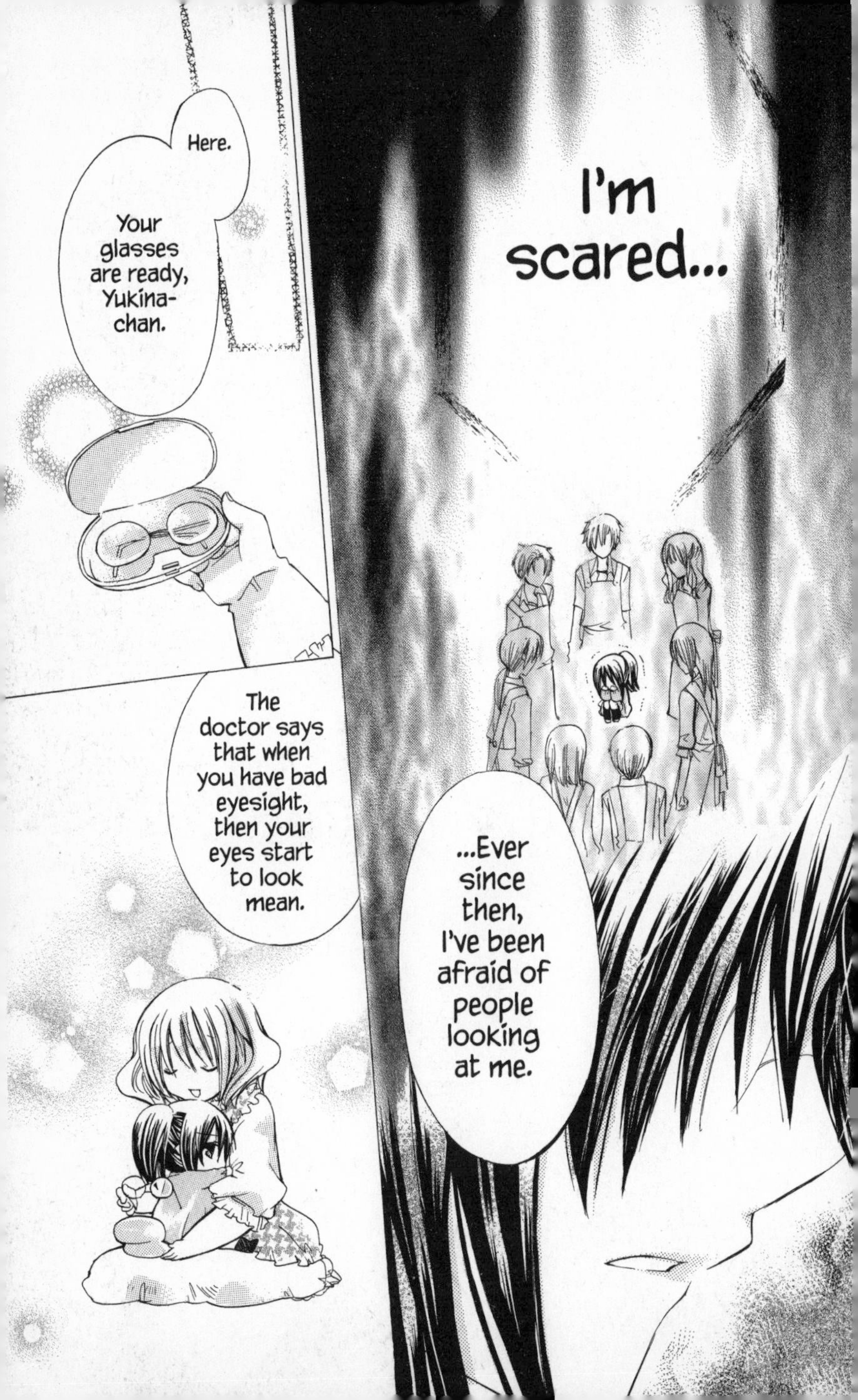
I'm scared...
...Ever since then, I've been afraid of people looking at me.
Here.
Your glasses are ready, Yukina-chan.
The doctor says that when you have bad eyesight, then your eyes start to look mean.

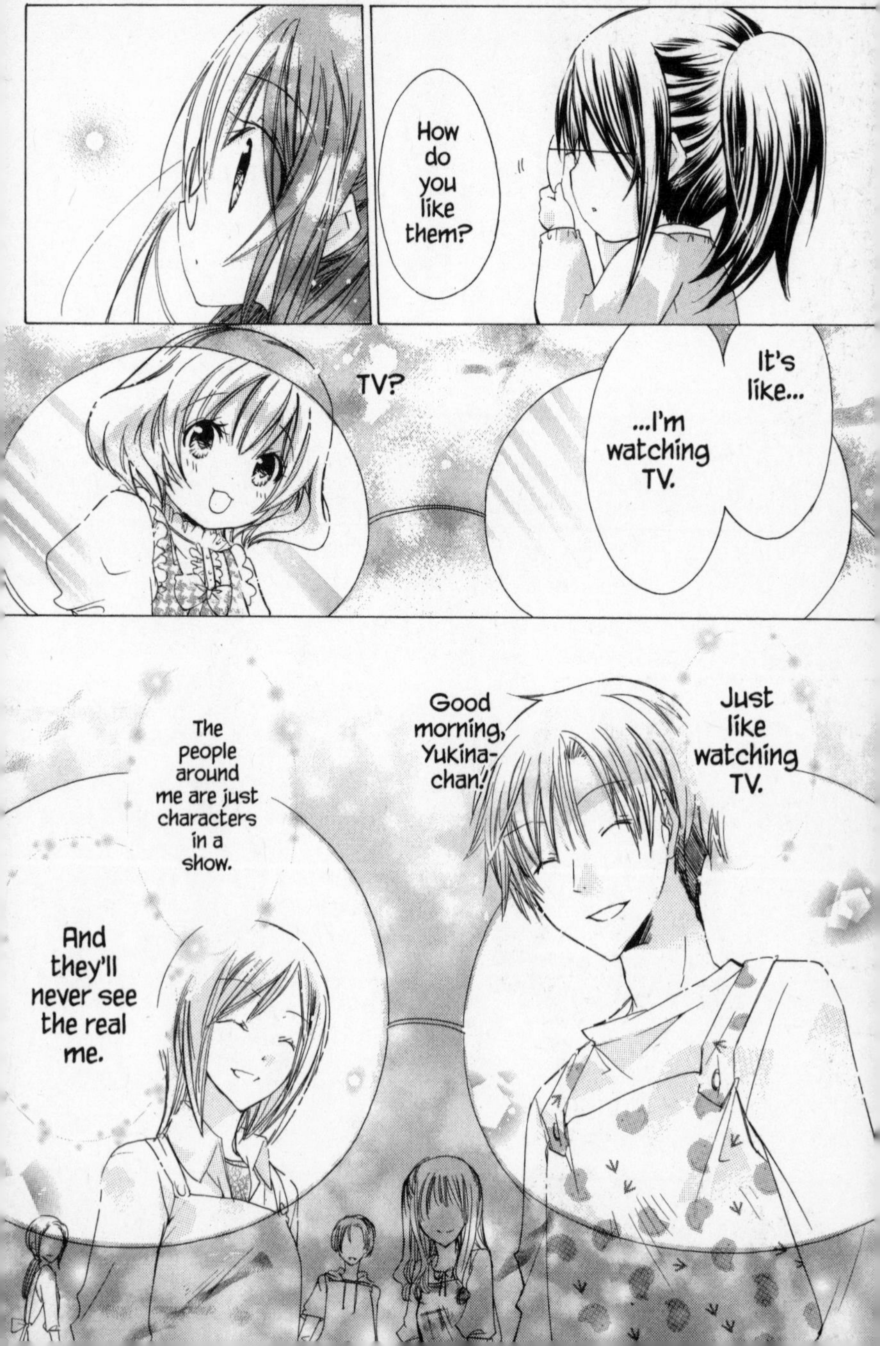
How do you like them?
It's like...
...I'm watching TV.
TV?
Just like watching TV.
Good morning, Yukina-chan!
The people around me are just characters in a show.
And they'll never see the real me.

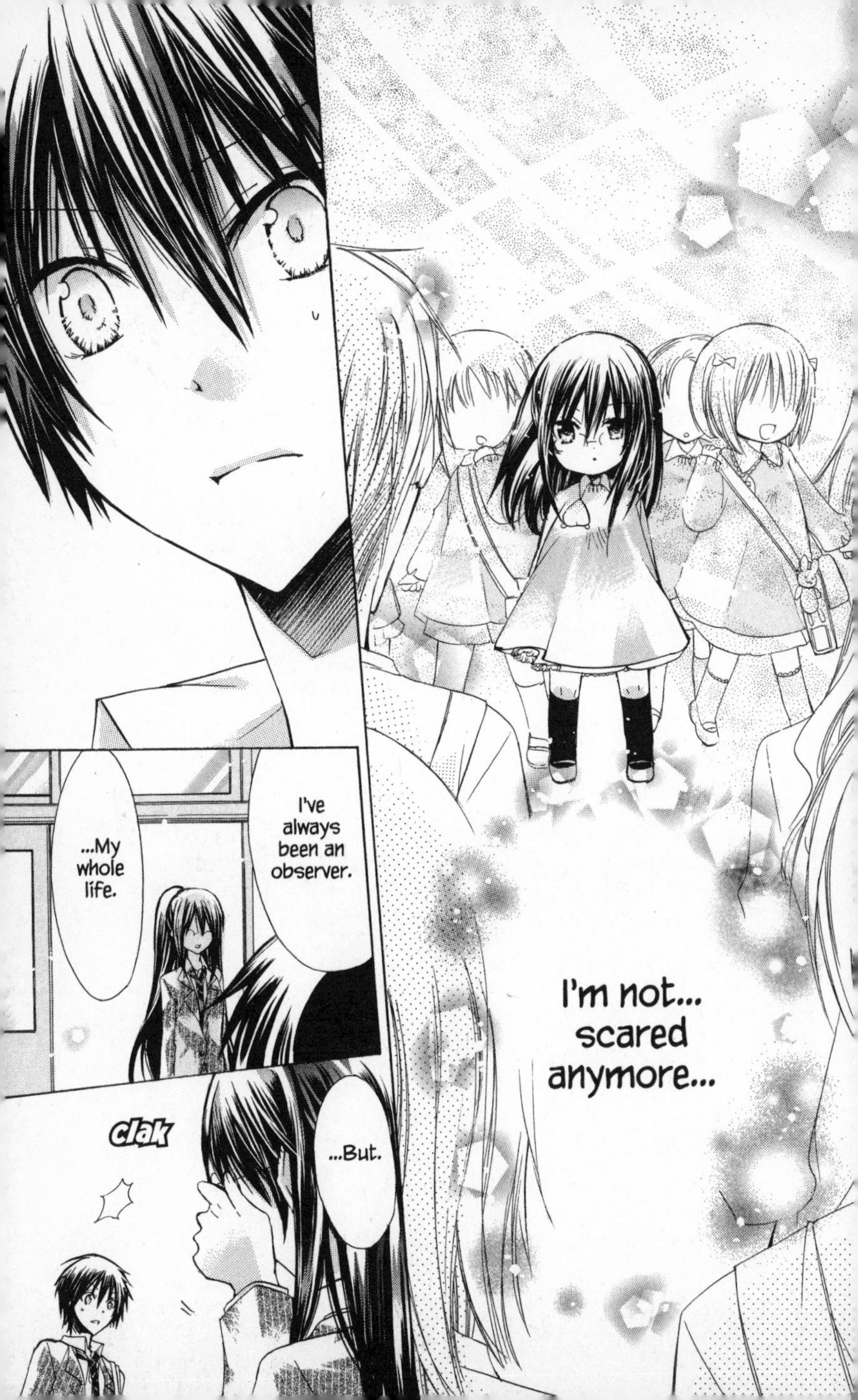
I'm not... scared anymore...
I've always been an observer.
...My whole life.
clak
...But.

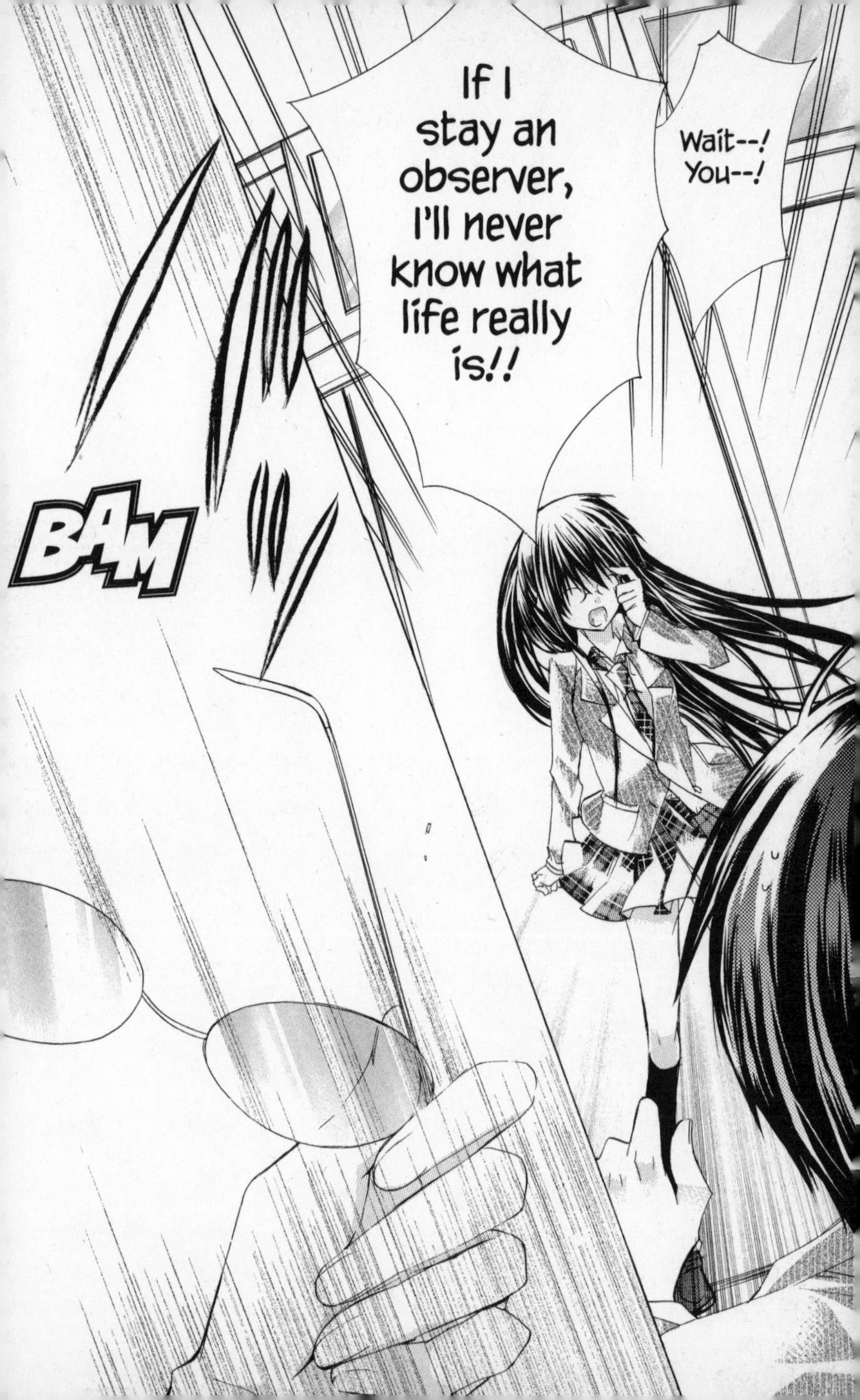
Wait--! You--!
If I stay an observer, I'll never know what life really is!!
BAM

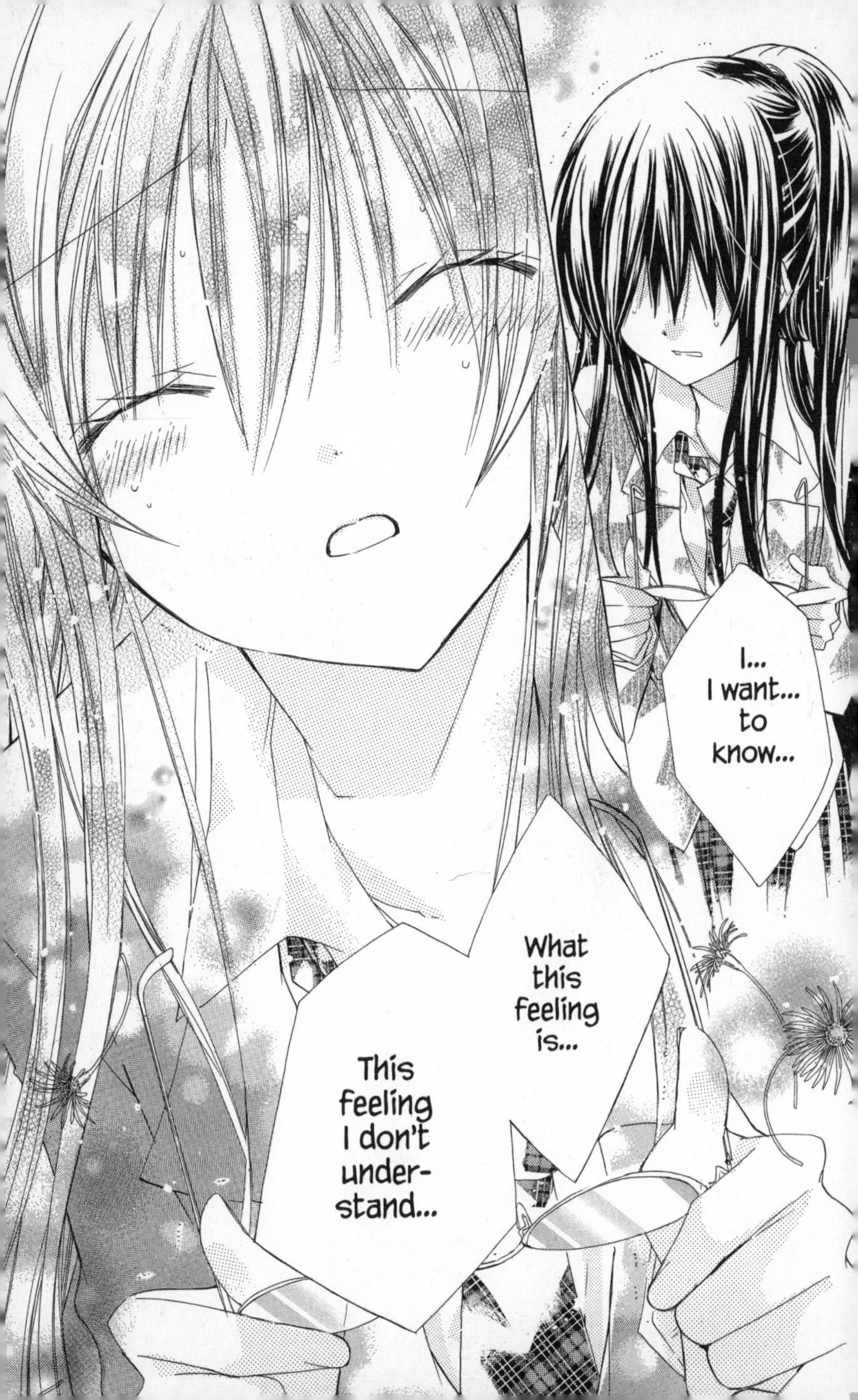
I... I want... to know...
What this feeling is...
This feeling I don't under-stand...

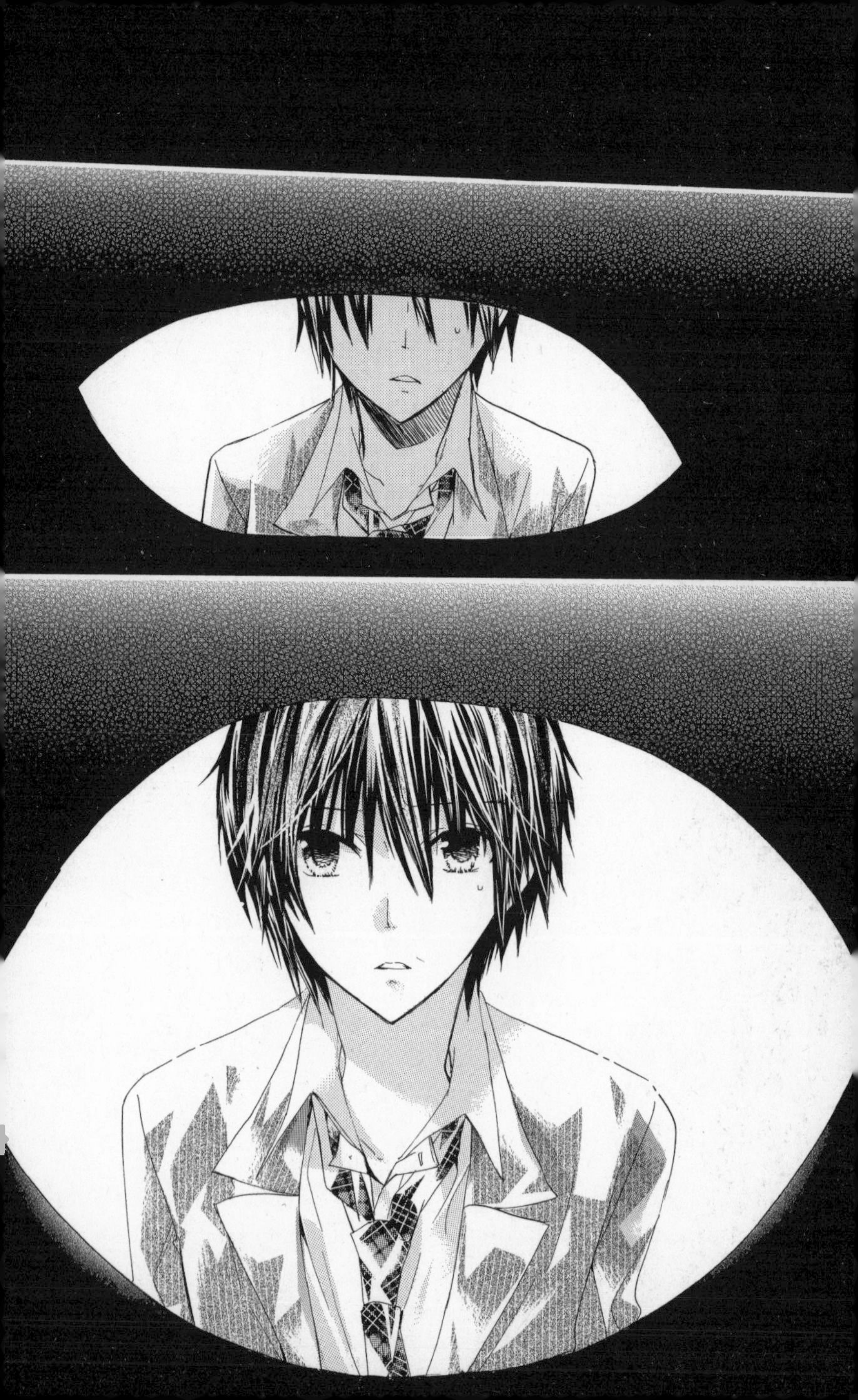

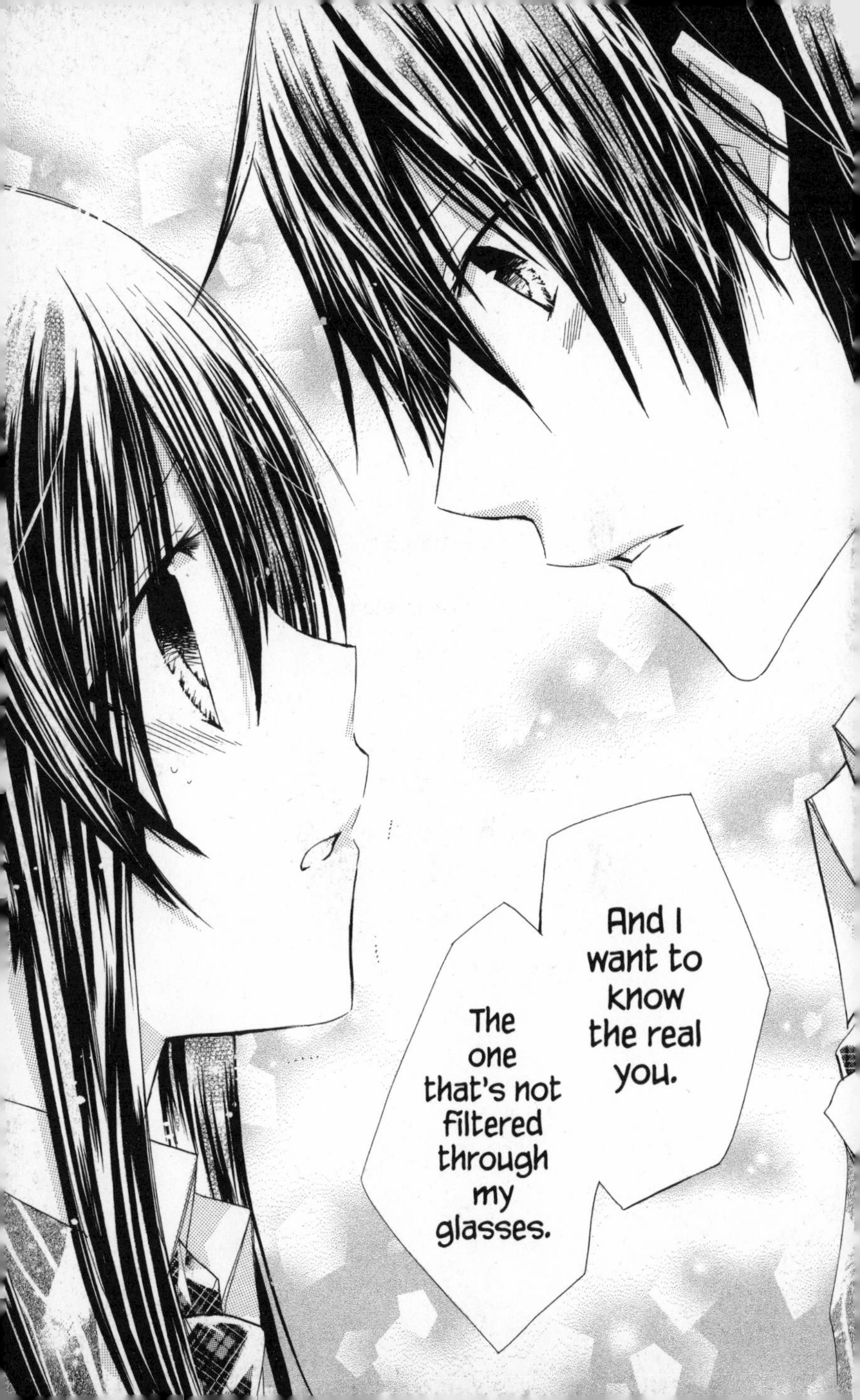
And I want to know the real you.
The one that's not filtered through my glasses.

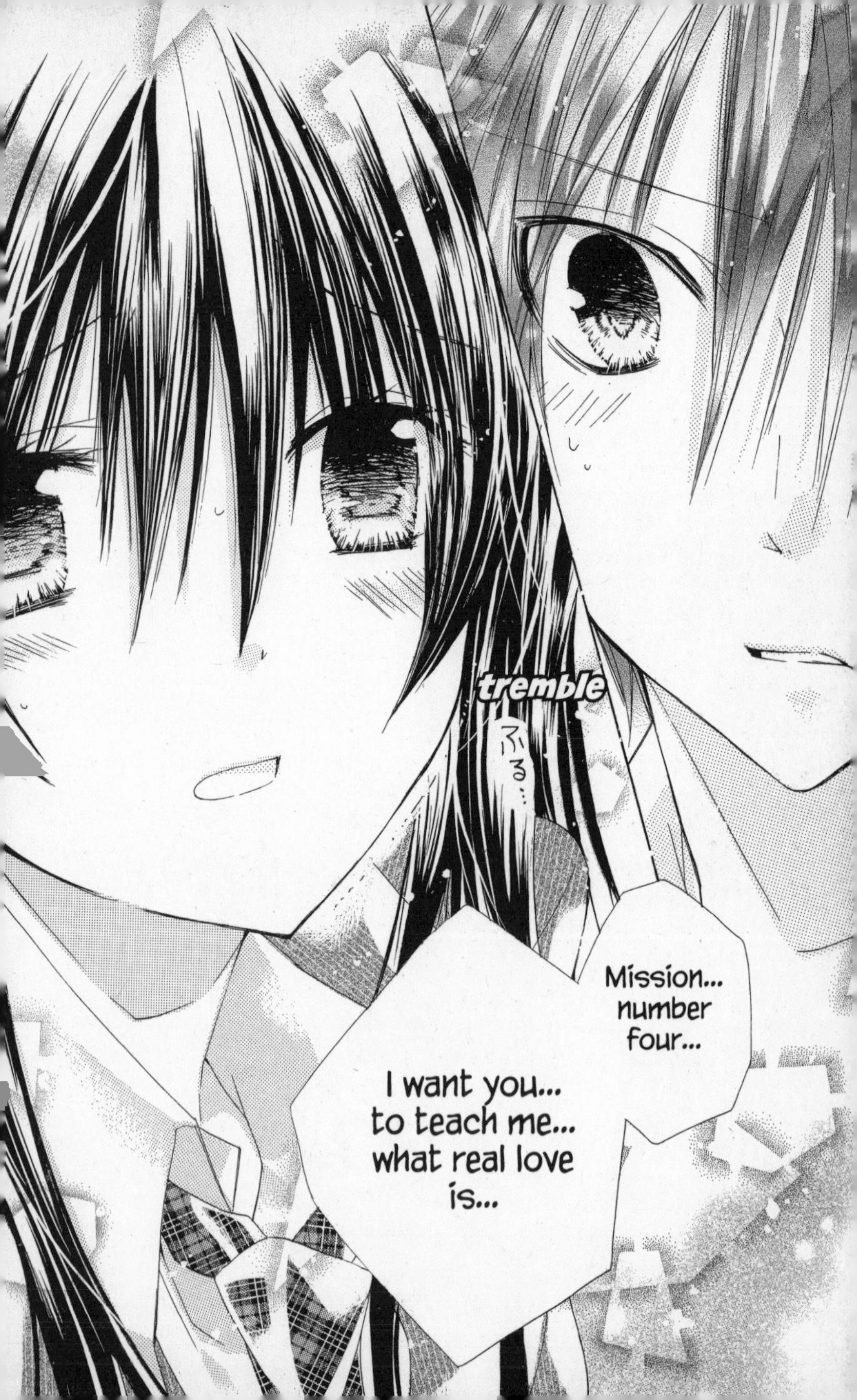
tremble
ふる…
Mission... number four...
I want you... to teach me... what real love is...

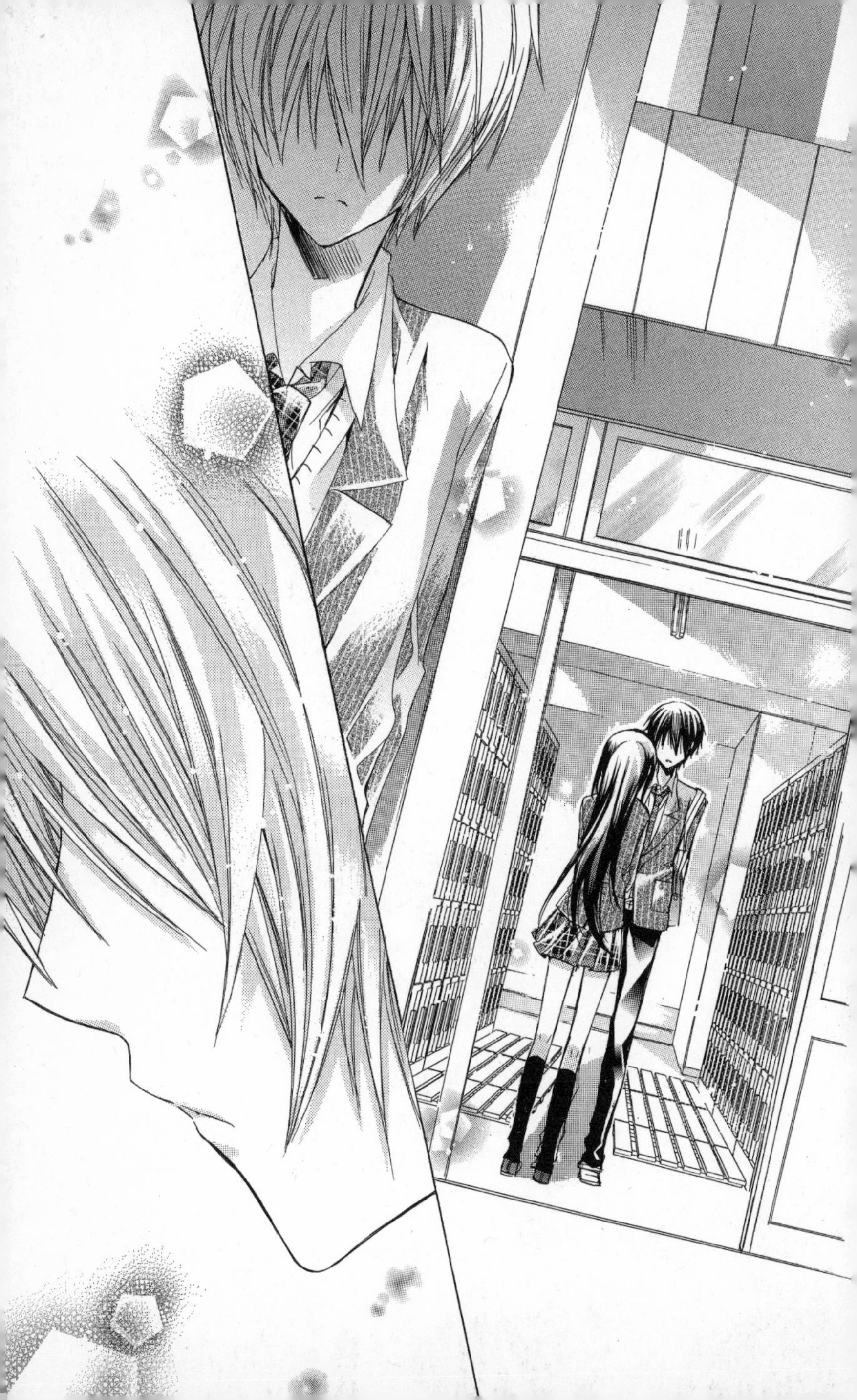

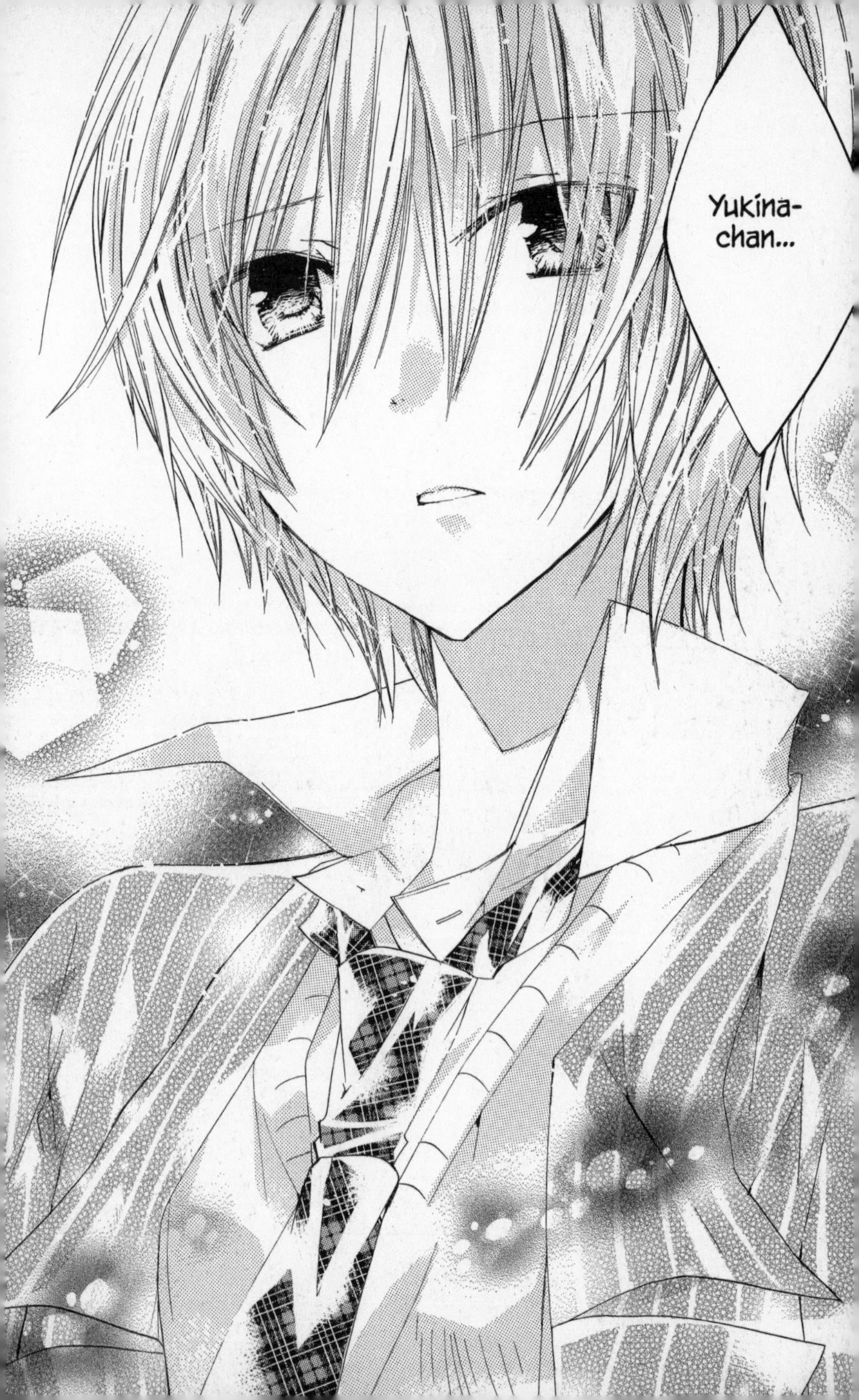
Yukina-chan...

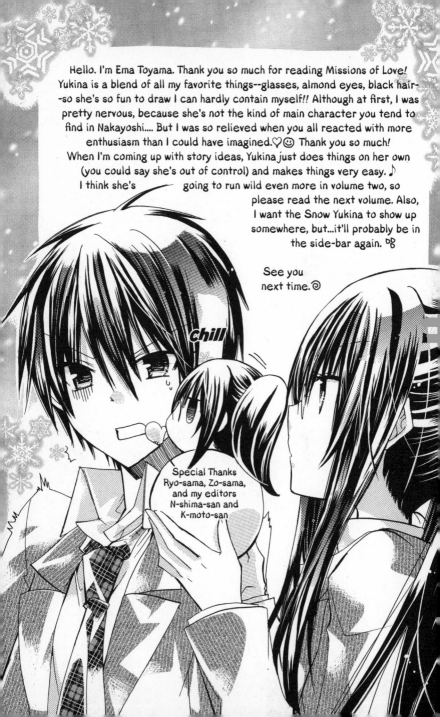

Hello. I'm Ema Toyama. Thank you so much for reading Missions of Love! Yukina is a blend of all my favorite things--glasses, almond eyes, black hair--so she's so fun to draw I can hardly contain myself!! Although at first, I was pretty nervous, because she's not the kind of main character you tend to find in Nakayoshi.... But I was so relieved when you all reacted with more enthusiasm than I could have imagined.♡☺ Thank you so much! When I'm coming up with story ideas, Yukina just does things on her own (you could say she's out of control) and makes things very easy.♪ I think she's going to run wild even more in volume two, so please read the next volume. Also, I want the Snow Yukina to show up somewhere, but...it'll probably be in the side-bar again.

See you next time.◎

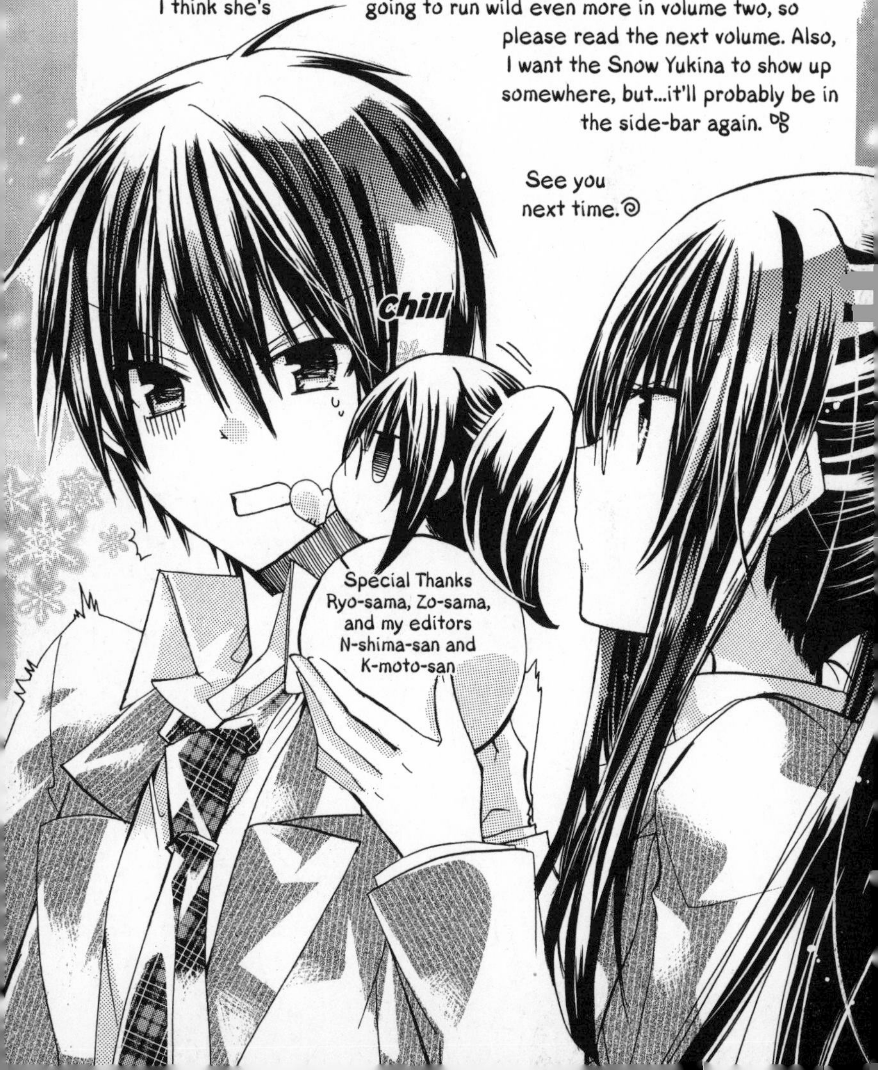
Chill
Special Thanks Ryo-sama, Zo-sama, and my editors N-shima-san and K-moto-san

Next Mission

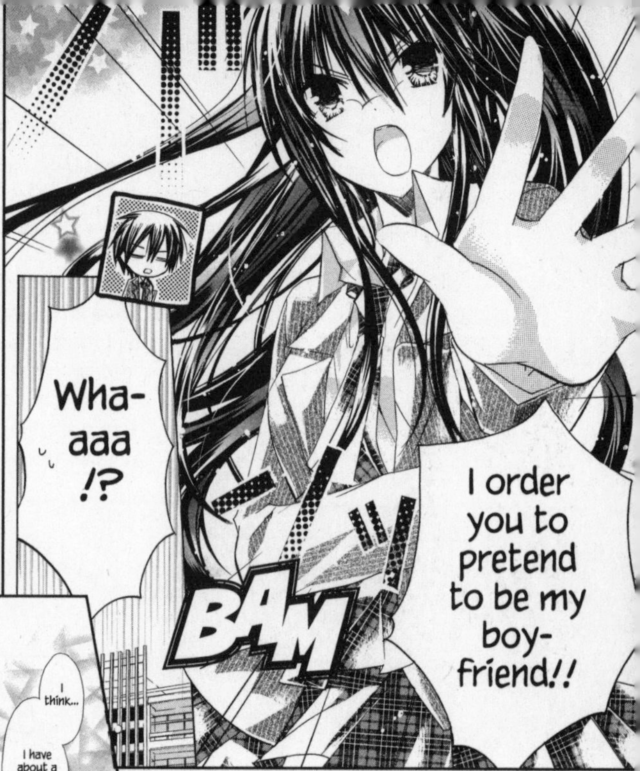
I order you to pretend to be my boy-friend!!
Wha-aaa!?
BAM

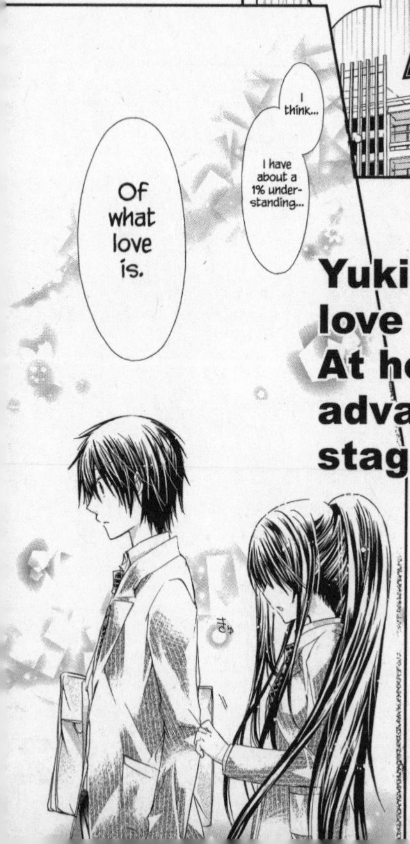
I think...
I have about a 1% under-standing...
Of what love is.

Yukina's curiosity about love is unstoppable!! At her orders, their love advances to the next stage!

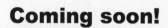

Coming soon!

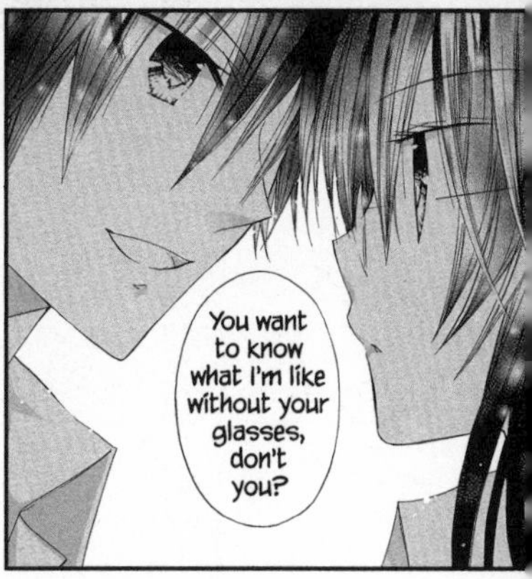
You want to know what I'm like without your glasses, don't you?

But Shigure won't go down without a fight!

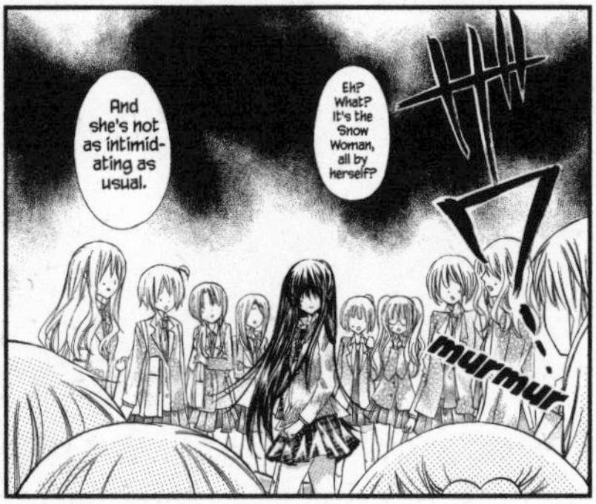
Eh? What? It's the Snow Woman, all by herself?
And she's not as intimidating as usual.
murmur

After falling into Shigure's trap, Yukina is rescued by Akira!

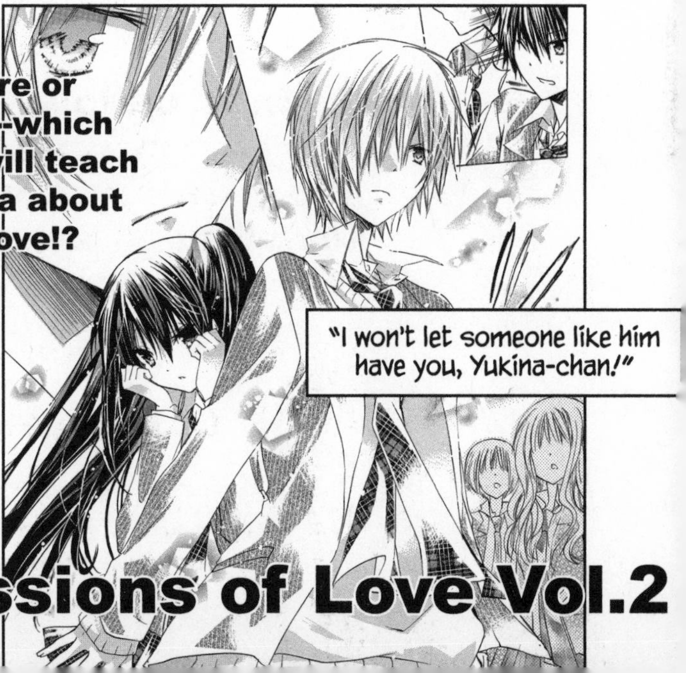
"I won't let someone like him have you, Yukina-chan!"

Shigure or Akira--which one will teach Yukina about true love!?

Missions of Love Vol.2

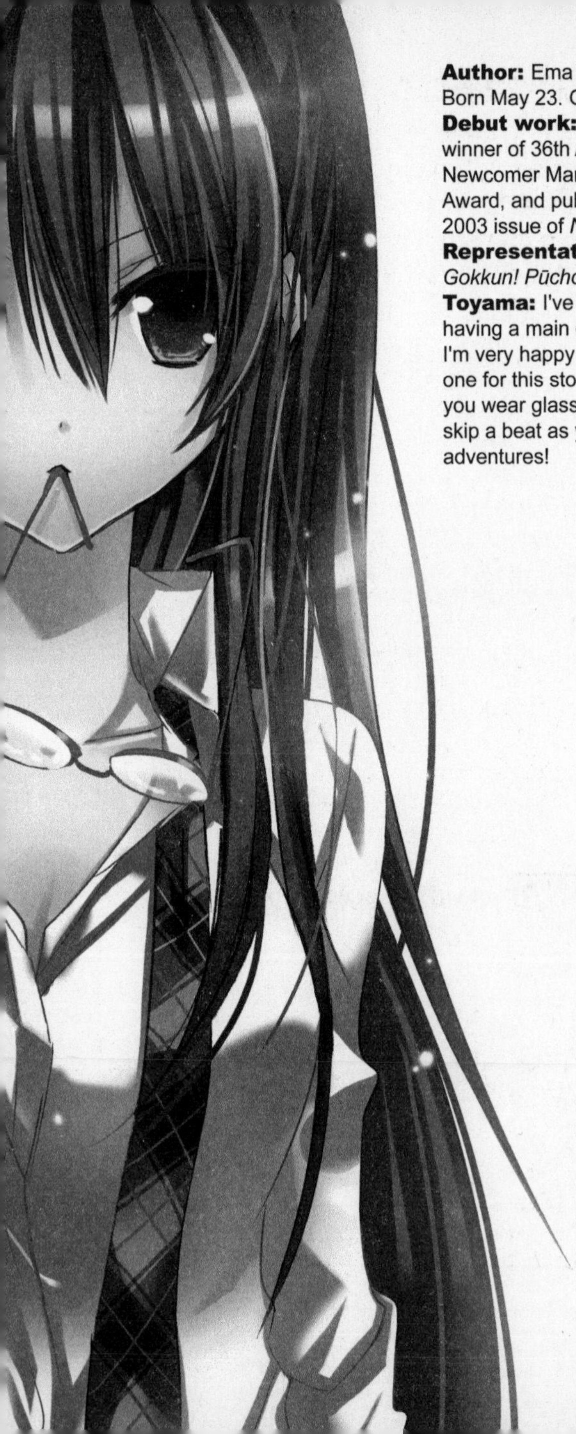

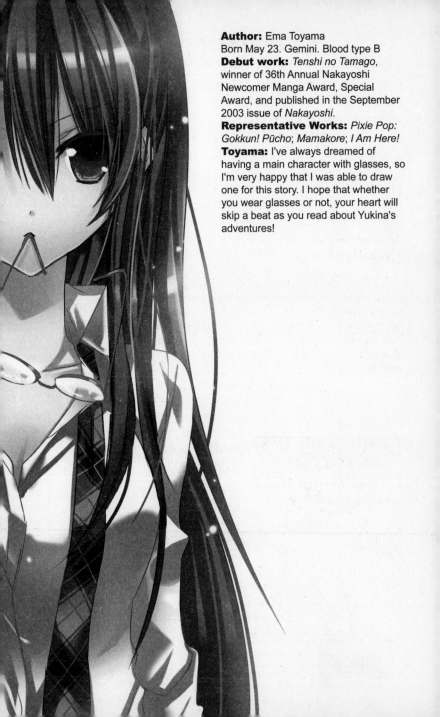

Author: Ema Toyama
Born May 23. Gemini. Blood type B
Debut work: *Tenshi no Tamago*, winner of 36th Annual Nakayoshi Newcomer Manga Award, Special Award, and published in the September 2003 issue of *Nakayoshi*.
Representative Works: *Pixie Pop: Gokkun! Pūcho*; *Mamakore*; *I Am Here!*
Toyama: I've always dreamed of having a main character with glasses, so I'm very happy that I was able to draw one for this story. I hope that whether you wear glasses or not, your heart will skip a beat as you read about Yukina's adventures!

Translation Notes

Japanese is a tricky language for most Westerners, and translation is often more art than science. For your edification and reading pleasure, here are notes on some of the places where we could have gone in a different direction with our translation of the work, or where a Japanese cultural reference is used.

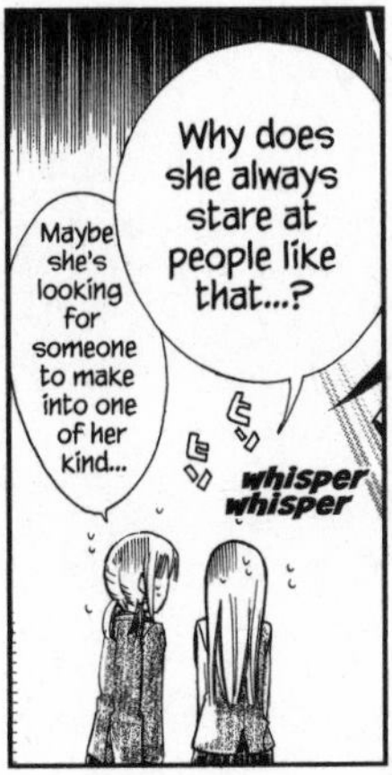
Why does she always stare at people like that...?
Maybe she's looking for someone to make into one of her kind...
whisper whisper

Snow Woman, page 10

The term "snow woman" may sound like a cute girlfriend for Frosty, but in Japanese folklore, a snow woman (*yuki-onna*) is much more sinister. The *yuki-onna* appears in snowy places; she is very beautiful, but her eyes strike terror into the hearts of men. She is also known for ruthlessly killing people with her coldness.

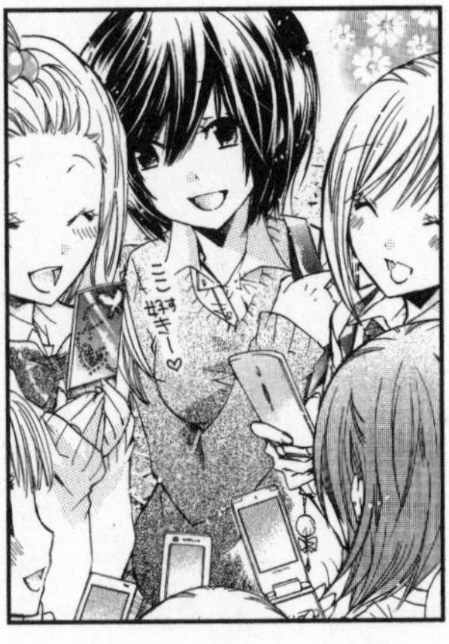

Cell phone novels, page 12

As the name suggests, a cell phone novel is a novel published via cell phone text message. Because of the character limitations of text messaging, each chapter is very short. However, because of the Japanese writing system, a writer can fit a lot more information into one Japanese text message than she can in an English one. Still, that doesn't make the chapters much longer, and the excerpts of Yupina's novel that you see in this manga are probably entire chapters.

The Demon's Reflection, page 14

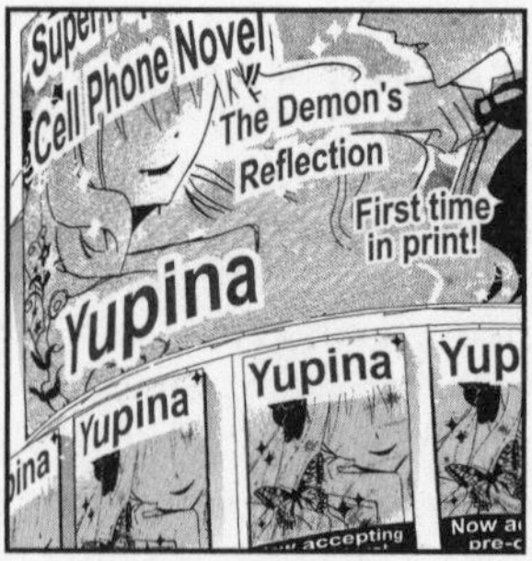
Cell Phone Novel
The Demon's Reflection
First time in print!
Yupina
Yupina
Yupina
accepting

The title of Yupina's cell phone novel is a play on words. Akuma de Reflection means "[it is] a demon and a reflection," but Akumade Reflection means "nothing more than a reflection." This is a subtle reference to the fact that all of Yupina's novels are Yukina's reflections in novel form, but Yukina also takes advantage of the double meaning to apply both to the story in the novels.

A gold notebook or a silver notebook, page 32

This is a reference to one of Aesop's Fables, "The Golden Axe," also known as "The Honest Woodcutter." A woodcutter drops his axe in a river, and cries at the loss of his only means of earning a living. The Greek god Hermes appears and brings a golden axe out of the river, asking the woodcutter if that was what he lost. When the woodcutter says it was not, Hermes brings a silver axe out of the river. The woodcutter still refuses it, and only accepts when Hermes brings his own axe. Impressed by his honesty, Hermes awards the woodcutter with all three axes. Common retellings in Japan replace Hermes with a goddess or nymph.

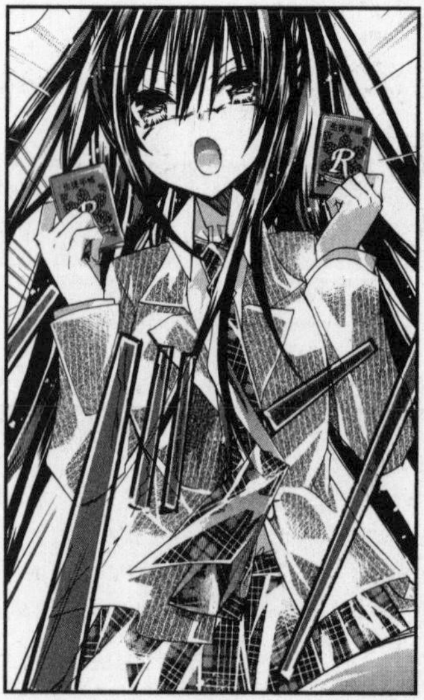

Snow Yukina, page 65

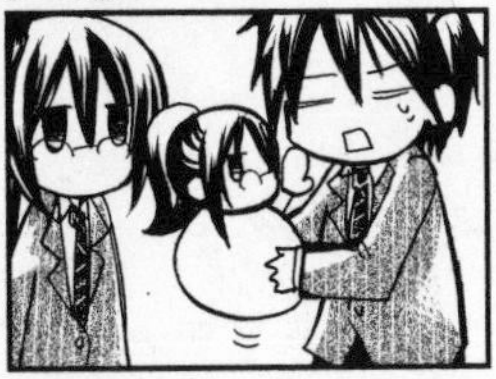

Snow Yukina is actually a little bit redundant, because the yuki in Yukina means "snow." The Japanese name of the character is Yukina Daruma, which is a play on yuki daruma, or snowman. Incidentally, many of the names in this series have something to do with the weather, mainly snow and ice. Yukina Himuro has both ice (Himuro = ice house) and snow (Yukina = snow flower), the school is Rikka Junior High (Rikka = snowflake), and Arare Daycare shares its name with hail (although it was probably named for the Japanese treat that was named for its resemblance to hail). Shigure, on the other hand, is named for the rain (Shigure = rain in late autumn or early winter). Akira's name means "crystal," which might go with snow, but the Chinese character for his name is made up of three suns and can mean "bright" or "radiant," so it may be a reference to sunny weather.

X-Shina!, page 103

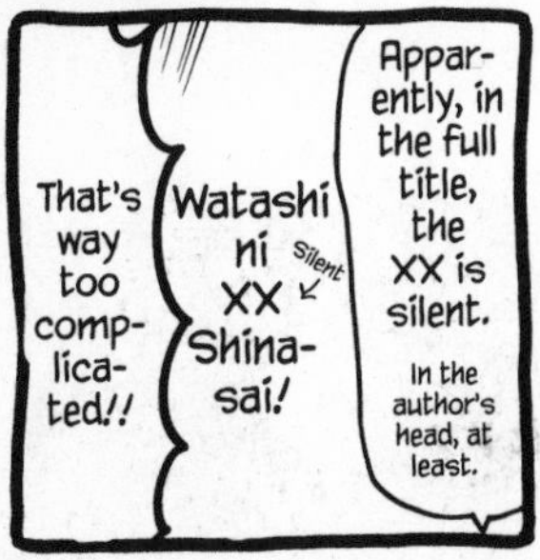
Apparently, in the full title, the XX is silent.
In the author's head, at least.
Watashi ni XX Shinasai!
Silent
That's way too complicated!!

In Japan, the title of this manga is Watashi ni XX Shinasai!, literally "Do [insert here] to/for me!" As Toyama-sensei explains, the XX is silent in the full title, so when said out loud, the title (Watashi ni Shinasai!) can mean "choose me!" The author's favorite abbreviation, X-Shina! is pronounced "batsu-shina!" In this case, the X (batsu) can refer to any of the things that might be inserted into the full title, or, since batsu can mean "penalty," it can refer to Yukina's blackmailing--she got the better of Shigure, so now he has to accept whatever penalty she assigns him.

I can't find my slippers, page 105

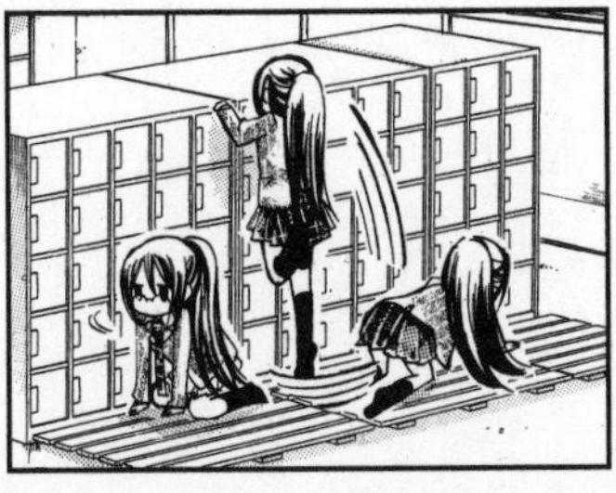

In Japan, it is customary to take off your street shoes when entering buildings such as homes, dojos, and other buildings. Schools are included, and so students have their "indoor shoes," called uwabaki, translated here as "slippers." When they get to school, they take off their street shoes and put on their slippers to wear around the building. The pair of footwear not being worn is stored in lockers like the ones in this panel.

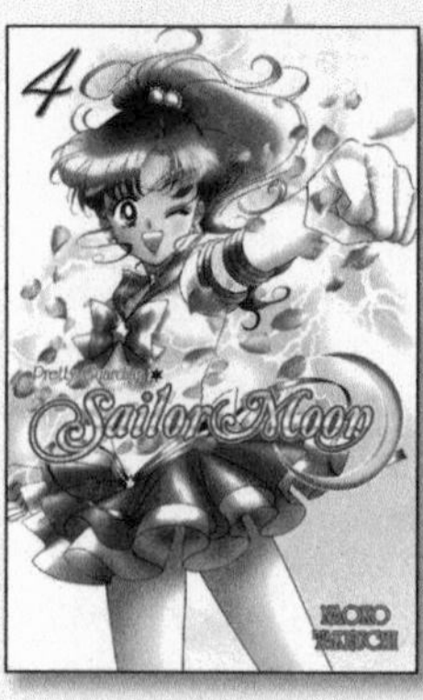
4
Pretty Guardian
Sailor Moon
NAOKO TAKEUCHI

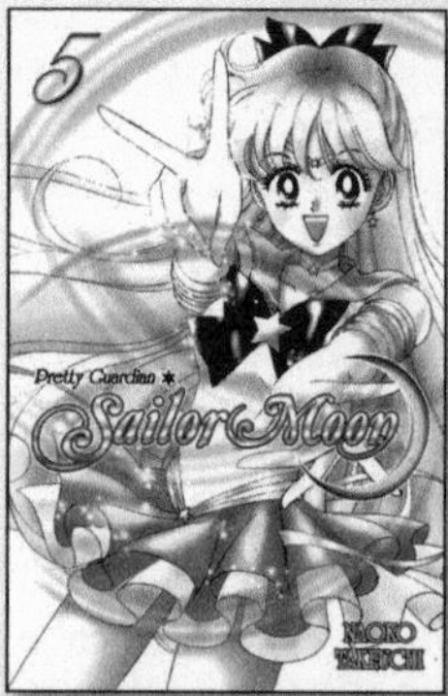
5
Pretty Guardian
Sailor Moon
NAOKO TAKEUCHI

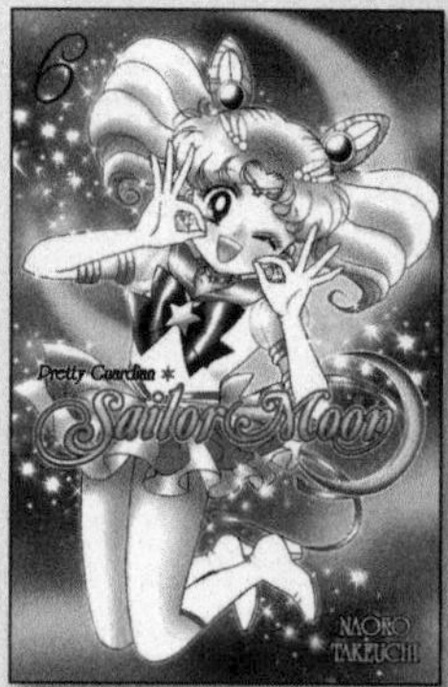
6
Pretty Guardian
Sailor Moon
NAOKO TAKEUCHI

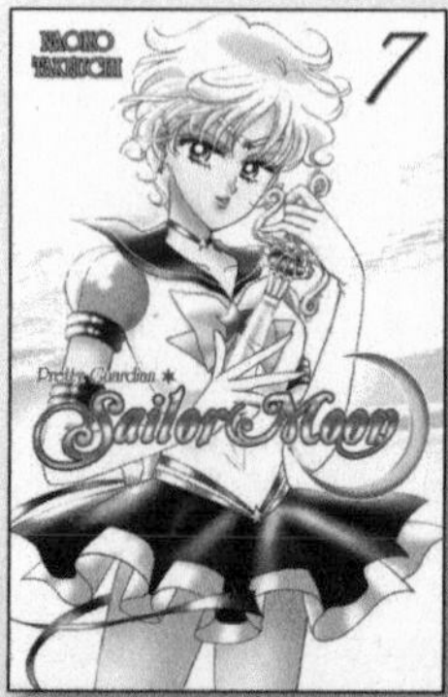
NAOKO TAKEUCHI
7
Pretty Guardian
Sailor Moon

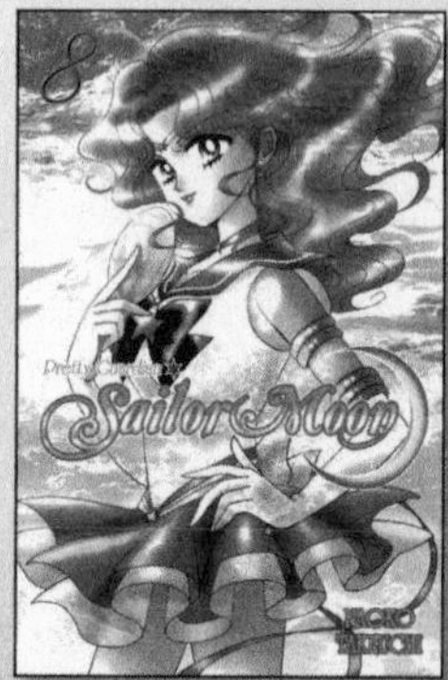
8
Pretty Guardian
Sailor Moon
NAOKO TAKEUCHI

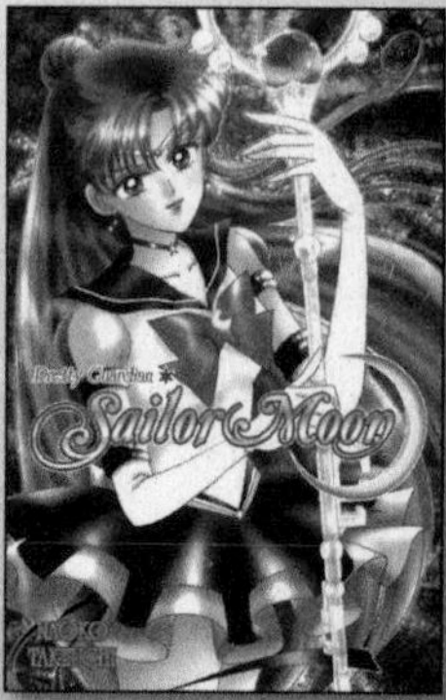
Pretty Guardian
Sailor Moon

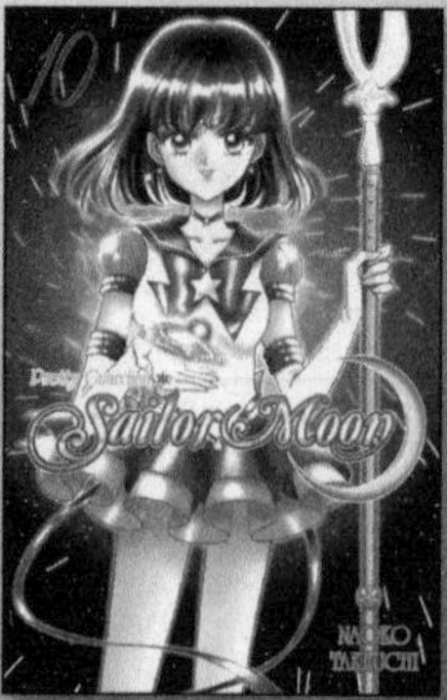
10
Pretty Guardian
Sailor Moon
NAOKO TAKEUCHI

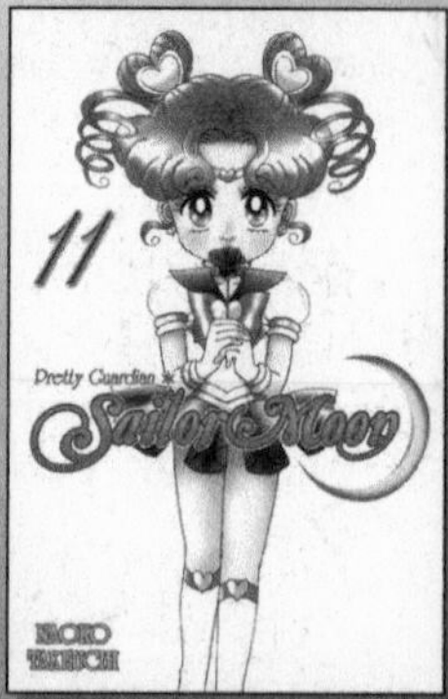
11
Pretty Guardian
Sailor Moon
NAOKO TAKEUCHI

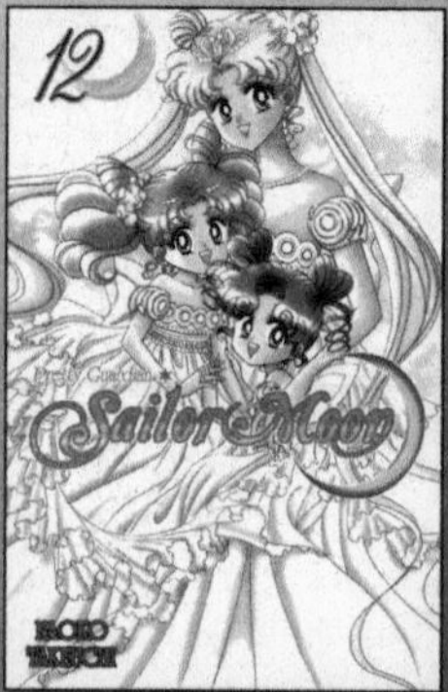
12
Pretty Guardian
Sailor Moon
NAOKO TAKEUCHI

KC
KODANSHA COMICS

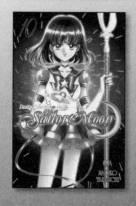

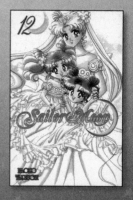

The Pretty Guardians are back!

Kodansha Comics is proud to present ***Sailor Moon*** with all new translations.

1
Pretty Guardian
Sailor Moon
NAOKO
TAKEUCHI

2
Pretty Guardian
Sailor Moon
NAOKO
TAKEUCHI

3
Pretty Guardian
Sailor Moon

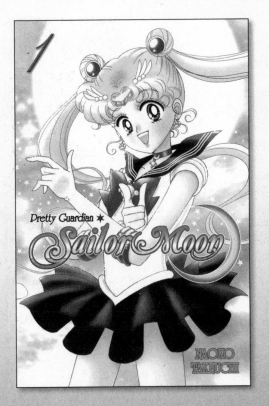

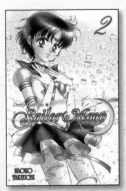

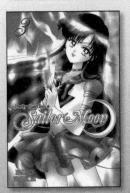

For more information, go to **www.kodanshacomics.com**

THE wallflower

YAMATONADESHIKO SHICHIHENGE

BY TOMOKO HAYAKAWA

It's a beautiful, expansive mansion, and four handsome, fifteen-year-old friends are allowed to live in it for free! But there is one condition—within three years the young men must take the owner's niece and transform her into a proper lady befitting the palace in which they all live! How hard can it be?

Enter Sunako Nakahara, the horror-movie-loving, pock-faced, frizzy-haired, fashion-illiterate hermit who has a tendency to break into explosive nosebleeds whenever she sees anyone attractive. This project is going to take far more than our four heroes ever expected; it needs a miracle!

1
THE wallflower
YAMATONADESHIKO SHICHIHENGE
TOMOKO HAYAKAWA

Ages: 16+

Special extras in each volume! Read them all!

KC KODANSHA COMICS

VISIT WWW.KODANSHACOMICS.COM TO:

- View release date calendars for upcoming volumes
- Find out the latest about new Kodansha Comics series

A Kodansha Comics Trade Paperback Original.

Missions of Love volume 1 copyright © 2009 Ema Toyama
English translation copyright © 2012 Ema Toyama

Published in the United States by Kodansha Comics, an imprint of Kodansha USA Publishing, LLC, New York.

Publication rights for this English edition arranged through Kodansha Ltd., Tokyo.

First published in Japan in 2009 by Kodansha Ltd., Tokyo, as *Watashi ni xx shinasai!*, volume 1.

ISBN 978-1-61262-274-3

Printed in the United States of America.

www.kodanshacomics.com

9 8 7 6 5 4 3 2

Translator: Alethea Nibley & Athena Nibley
Lettering: Paige Pumphrey

Mission 0: Go Right to Left.

Japanese manga is written and drawn from right to left, which is opposite the way American graphic novels are composed. To preserve the original orientation of the art, and maintain the proper storytelling flow, this book has retained the right to left structure. Please go to what would normally be the last page and begin reading, right to left, top to bottom.